THE LEXICAL AND METRICAL PHONOLOGY OF ENGLISH

This is the first full-scale discussion of English phonology since Chomsky and Halle's seminal *The Sound Pattern of English (SPE)*. The book emphasizes the analysis using ordered rules and builds on *SPE* by incorporating lexical, metrical, and prosodic analysis and the insights afforded by Lexical Phonology. It provides clear explanations and logical development throughout, introducing rules individually and then illustrating their interactions. These features make this influential theory accessible to students from a variety of backgrounds in linguistics and phonology. Rule-ordering diagrams summarize the crucial ordering of approximately eighty-five rules. Many of the interactions result in phonological opacity, where the output either does not provide evidence of the effect of the rule or does not contain the necessary conditions for its application. This demonstrates the superiority of a rule-based account over output-oriented approaches such as Optimality Theory or pre-Generative structuralist phonology.

JOHN T. JENSEN is the author of *Morphology: Word Structure in Generative Grammar* (1990), *English Phonology* (1993), and *Principles of Generative Phonology: An Introduction* (2004). He has published articles in *Phonology, Linguistic Inquiry, Language, Linguistic Analysis, Nordic Journal of Linguistics, Papers in Linguistics*, and *Glossa*.

THE LEXICAL AND METRICAL PHONOLOGY OF ENGLISH

The Legacy of *The Sound Pattern of English*

JOHN T. JENSEN

University of Ottawa

CAMBRIDGE
UNIVERSITY PRESS

CAMBRIDGE
UNIVERSITY PRESS

University Printing House, Cambridge CB2 8BS, United Kingdom

One Liberty Plaza, 20th Floor, New York, NY 10006, USA

477 Williamstown Road, Port Melbourne, VIC 3207, Australia

314–321, 3rd Floor, Plot 3, Splendor Forum, Jasola District Centre, New Delhi – 110025, India

103 Penang Road, #05–06/07, Visioncrest Commercial, Singapore 238467

Cambridge University Press is part of the University of Cambridge.

It furthers the University's mission by disseminating knowledge in the pursuit of
education, learning, and research at the highest international levels of excellence.

www.cambridge.org
Information on this title: www.cambridge.org/9781108841504
DOI: 10.1017/9781108889131

© John T. Jensen 2022

First published 2022

A catalogue record for this publication is available from the British Library.

Library of Congress Cataloging-in-Publication Data
NAMES: Jensen, John T. (John Tillotson), author.
TITLE: The lexical and metrical phonology of English : the legacy of The sound pattern of English /
John T. Jensen.
DESCRIPTION: Cambridge, United Kingdom ; New York, NY : Cambridge University Press, 2022. |
Includes bibliographical references and index.
IDENTIFIERS: LCCN 2021057994 (print) | LCCN 2021057995 (ebook) | ISBN 9781108841504
(hardback) | ISBN 9781108794916 (paperback) | ISBN 9781108889131 (epub)
SUBJECTS: LCSH: Chomsky, Noam. Sound pattern of English. | English language–Phonology. |
English language–Grammar, Generative.
CLASSIFICATION: LCC PE1133.C53 J46 2022 (print) | LCC PE1133.C53 (ebook) |
DDC 421/.5–dc23/eng/20220124
LC record available at https://lccn.loc.gov/2021057994
LC ebook record available at https://lccn.loc.gov/2021057995

ISBN 978-1-108-84150-4 Hardback
ISBN 978-1-108-79491-6 Paperback

Contents

Figures

Preface

My goal in this book is to give an internally consistent, coherent, and complete analysis of the phonology (and morphology) of English as developed in *The Sound Pattern of English* (Chomsky & Halle 1968; *SPE*) and subsequent modifications using metrical, prosodic, and lexical approaches. It will be instructive for students in terms of theoretical argumentation and the application of a well-worked-out model for the detailed analysis of a single language, while introducing theoretical issues to explore. The book is intended for students who have had at least one previous introductory course in general phonology, or indeed for anyone interested in this subject. The concept of the prosodic hierarchy lends an overall unity to the work and in addition suggests some revisions to certain assumptions about syllable structure and stress that have been made in the literature. In the main, I follow the major authors on the various proposals, while adding my own interpretation or changes where I find it necessary. For example, I largely follow Hayes (1982) on stress, including his use of metrical trees, rejecting his later (Hayes 1995) use of metrical grids, for reasons which I believe I have amply justified. The use of trees allows the stress system to fit better into the prosodic hierarchy, thus keeping the approach internally consistent. There are empirical arguments also, in that trees give more accurate results for the Rhythm Rule. As another example, I include the onset in the first mora of the syllable, even though most authors attach the onset directly to the syllable node, without explicit justification. This again fits better with the prosodic hierarchy, since it avoids a gratuitous violation of the strict layer hypothesis. It is important for students to understand the nature of linguistic argumentation, and how certain commonly accepted ideas may be wrong or inadequate.

Other Approaches

There are several book-length works dealing with the phonology of English and its relation to theoretical issues, each in its way an important contribution. None seeks to attain the scope of coverage of the present work. Giegerich (1992) focuses on a phonemic study of three 'reference accents': Southern British Received Pronunciation, General American, and Standard Scottish English. He includes some discussion of syllabification, stress, and several theoretical issues that go beyond phonemic theory. John Harris (1994) discusses a number of phenomena within a principles-and-parameters approach, but regards such phenomena as velar softening, vowel shift, and spirantization as outside the scope of this approach. He concentrates on phenomena where there is dialect variation, while I am primarily concerned with things that are common across dialects. Hammond (1999) discusses certain aspects of English phonology from the perspective of Optimality Theory. Due to the limitations of this theory, his discussion is limited to "distributional regularities in mono-morphemic English words" (vii). Thus he has nothing to say about alternations or rules such as Spirantization, Palatalization, Vowel Shift, or Trisyllabic Laxing. Although he discusses stress, he does not discuss stress alternations such as the Rhythm Rule. Burzio (1994) discusses English stress, but with only limited discussion of the interaction of stress with segmental rules. He makes a number of theoretical assumptions that are quite different from most other discussions of this topic. For example, he denies that the final syllable of words like *satire* is stressed, claiming that there is no evidence for stress in this position (1994: 3). But, if we consider the interaction of stress with segmental rules, there is indeed such evidence, since the /t/ of *satire* is aspirated, indicating that it is initial in a foot, and the underlying /i/ in the final syllable undergoes Vowel Shift, indicating that it is stressed. Conversely, Halle and Mohanan (1985) offer a discussion of the major segmental processes of English, but have only a single undifferentiated category of 'stress rules' in their list of ordered rules. This is yet another indication of the need to view the whole picture and not to examine partial subsystems in isolation. In short, due to various limitations, none of these discussions is able to integrate a large variety of data and theory into a unified whole.

Rationale

This work constitutes a significantly updated version of my earlier *English Phonology* (Jensen 1993). The overall organization of the first seven chapters remains as in the earlier book, although each chapter has been entirely rewritten and there has been some reorganization of the material. The major substantive changes have been in the analysis of the stress system.

I have dispensed with Hayes's (1982) rule of Long Vowel Stressing. By not marking word-final syllables containing a long vowel as extrametrical, those syllables are stressed by the normal operation of the English Stress Rule. The English Stress Rule is simplified to be quantity sensitive throughout rather than just at right edges. The examples that appear to require quantity-insensitive retraction are treated by Arab Destressing (as in Kager 1989). Most other changes involve discussing a greater range of rules and expanding the discussion of others.

The argument in favour of trees over grids is entirely new, in general and with respect to Jensen (1993), and something that needs to be expressed in view of the widespread acceptance of the grid framework for stress. I discuss a total of eighty-five rules, nearly twice as many as the forty-eight examined in Jensen (1993), together with their ordering. The clarification of the cyclic operation of stress rules toward the end of Section 4.5 is also a novel contribution. In Section 4.7 I offer an account for the shift in stress in words like *résident* (from *reside*), as opposed to the retention of the stress pattern of *cohérent* (from *cohére*) in terms of a minor (lexically marked) rule to shift the stress. Other cases of stress preservation in derivatives such as *óxygenàte* and *hóspitalìze* are ascribed to the ability of +*ate* or -*ize* to support a foot by itself; this is contrasted with suffixes like +*ic*, +*ity*, and +*ify*, which need material from their bases to become fully metrified, and so consequently tend to shift the stress. I propose that cyclic stress assignment overrides the previously assigned stress only to the extent necessary to incorporate newly added morphological material. This treatment removes some of the criticisms of Lexical Phonology that have assumed too close a correspondence between stress shifting and stratal assignment of affixes.

While adopting aspects of post-*SPE* developments, primarily metrical, lexical, and prosodic phonology, I express many of the rules in the *SPE* rewrite-rule framework. This is in line with my conviction that the purpose of phonology is to express phonological patterns and generalizations, and that it cannot be restricted to processes that appear to be natural in some representational terms, such as autosegmental spreading. As Hale and Reiss (2000: 165) put it, "grammars do contain arbitrary processes."

Chapter 8 is wholly new. It contains three sections. The first is a much-expanded discussion of umlaut and ablaut, arguing for considering these as *morphological* rules that affect the meaning of items, rather than as phonological rules that spell out prespecified categories, as assumed in much of the previous work on Lexical Phonology and Morphology. The second section discusses apparent problems with affix order and subcategorization and offers possible solutions. The third section discusses Optimality

Theory and the problems it faces in describing some of the salient processes of English phonology. Generative phonology was developed in part to deal with opaque interactions, which constituted a major problem for the earlier taxonomic approaches to phonology, with their surface orientation. It is not surprising that Optimality Theory, which is also surface oriented, has difficulty with opaque interactions, which abound in English phonology. I conclude that Optimality Theory has little to offer by way of explanation in English phonology and that the lexical theory including ordered rules is preferable.

Transcriptions

The phonetic symbols used are those of the International Phonetic Alphabet (IPA), with two additions. One is the symbol [ɨ] for the lax [–ATR] high back unround vowel, for which the IPA does not provide a symbol. The distinction between tense [+ATR] and lax [–ATR] vowels is important for an adequate treatment of English vowels, and we need to have symbols for both values of [ATR] for all vowel articulations. For nonlow vowels there is a different symbol for each member of the pair. The IPA does not distinguish this feature systematically, but rather employs symbols that differ in height. For example, IPA classifies [e] as 'close-mid' and [ɛ] as 'open-mid'; we take both to be mid ([–high, –low]) and [e] as tense ([+ATR]) and [ɛ] as lax ([–ATR]). For the low vowels I employ the IPA left-tack diacritic (̟) to indicate the tense variety; thus [ɒ̟] is the [+ATR] counterpart of [–ATR] [ɒ]. Another is [ň] for the postalveolar nasal, which the IPA does not distinguish from [n]. In some cases where I quote other authors, I retain their transcriptions if no confusion can arise; these instances are noted where they occur. My use of the symbol [ə] differs somewhat from what might be expected. *SPE* used [ə] only for a reduced vowel and excluded it from underlying representations. This creates a problem for vowels that are always realized as [ə], as in the final vowel of *sofa* or the initial vowel in *above*. *SPE* would need to make an arbitrary choice of some unreduced vowel to represent these. I use [ə] for the stressed vowel of *but* as well as for the unstressed vowel of *sofa*, for three reasons. First, vowel quality and stress are independent variables; there is no reason to have a special symbol for an unstressed vowel in one case only. Second, [ə] is not the only vowel that appears in unstressed syllables in English – in many dialects [ɪ] and [ʊ] occur is such positions also. Finally, there is need for a symbol for the tense ([+ATR]) counterpart of [ə] for an adequate description of English vowel shift – I employ [ʌ] for this purpose, restricting [ə] to use as a lax ([−ATR]) version of this vowel quality, whether stressed or unstressed.

Since my focus is not on English dialects, I have tried to make transcriptions as dialect neutral as possible, providing both NA (North American) and RP (Standard Southern British) where appropriate, unless the discussion specifically involves a phenomenon peculiar to a particular dialect.

Acknowledgements

I have used versions of this material in courses at the University of Ottawa in both English phonology and phonological theory. Students on those courses have made a number of useful comments that I have made use of in several revisions. I am especially grateful to my editor Helen Barton and the four readers for Cambridge University Press, whose detailed and insightful comments have been of the greatest value in improving the final version. My wife, Margaret Stong-Jensen, has read through numerous drafts and partial drafts and provided both editorial and linguistic insights. I am alone responsible for any remaining errors or inconsistencies.

CHAPTER I

Theories of Phonology

Phonology is primarily concerned with analyzing the sound patterns of language, along with the interaction of these sound patterns with other aspects of grammar, especially syntax and morphology. In the generative tradition the grammar as a whole describes the (largely implicit) knowledge that a native speaker has about his or her language. *The Sound Pattern of English* (Chomsky & Halle 1968; henceforth *SPE*) is a major landmark both in phonological theory and in the phonological description of English, since it signalled a shift in focus to generative phonology, in contrast to the earlier focus on descriptive phonology. Descriptive (or structuralist) phonology seeks to discover the distinctive or contrastive sounds of a language by finding pairs of words that differ minimally, such as *sip* and *zip*. These words differ only in the voicing of the initial segment, thus demonstrating that voicing is distinctive in these two sounds (and also in many other pairs) and so /s/ and /z/ must be considered distinct sounds or *phonemes* in English. In many ways *SPE* has defined phonological issues ever since its appearance. It resolved many of the inadequacies of the earlier structuralist approaches, but left a number of unresolved issues, many of which are still controversial. We will consider a number of these issues as we proceed.

1.1 Generative Phonology and *SPE*

The descriptive approach to phonology emphasized the determination of the distribution of segments in terms of surface contrast (e.g., Hockett 1942). For example, the segments [tʰ] as in *top* and [t] as in *stop* are in complementary distribution in that they cannot appear in the same surface context and thus never serve to distinguish utterances. We can give a rule that governs the appearance of aspirated stops including [tʰ], which we give as rule (27) in Chapter 5. Generative phonology broadened the scope of phonology to include morphophonemics, since many of the variations in

the phonetic shape of morphemes are definable in phonological terms. *SPE*
(pp. 11–12) discusses the example in (1), where the transcription is ours.

(1)   a.   telegraph   [ˈtʰɛlɪˌɡɹæf]
        b.   telegraphy   [tʰɪˈlɛɡɹəfi]
        c.   telegraphic   [ˌtʰɛlɪˈɡɹæfɪk]

The stem *telegraph* appears in three different phonetic shapes depending on
what suffix, if any, is attached to it. This variation is entirely predictable in
terms of the rules of English phonology that we will discuss, in particular
stress assignment (Chapter 4) and vowel reduction (Section 7.2.3 of
Chapter 7). The vowels [ɛ] and [æ] appear in stressed positions and are
replaced by [ɪ] and [ə], respectively, in unstressed positions. The most
economical way to treat this is by assuming an underlying representation
for *telegraph* that contains only the vowels that appear under stress, as in (2).

(2)   /tɛlɛɡɹæf/

This underlying representation is somewhat abstract, in that it does not
appear unchanged in any of the words in which it appears. See further
discussion in Section 2.5 of Chapter 2.

A second example is that of final devoicing in German (3).

(3)   *orthographic*   *phonetic*   *underlying*   *gloss*
        a.   Bund   [ˈbʊnt]   /bʊnd/   'union'
        b.   Bunde   [ˈbʊndə]   /bʊnd + ə/   'union (dative)'
        c.   bunt   [ˈbʊnt]   /bʊnt/   'colourful'
        d.   bunte   [ˈbʊntə]   /bʊnt + ə/   'colourful (inflected)'
        e.   und   [ʊnt]   /ʊnt/   'and'

The uninflected forms of 'union' and 'colourful' are pronounced identi-
cally. With an inflectional suffix the pronunciation differs. In generative
phonology we assign each morpheme a unique underlying representation,
/bʊnd/ for 'union' and /bʊnt/ for 'colourful.' When these are uninflected,
the morpheme-final /d/ or /t/ is also word final. The rule required is Final
Devoicing (4), which operates in these cases, giving both *Bund* and *bunt* an
identical phonetic representation with a voiceless stop. The symbol #
represents the word boundary.

(4)   *Final Devoicing (German)*
        [–son] → [–voice] / ____ #

With an inflectional suffix, the stop is no longer word final and the
underlying voiced or voiceless character of this sound appears phonetically.

The word for 'and' has no alternations and so its underlying representation is the same as its phonetic representation (despite the spelling, which shows *historical* voicing). A theory of phonology that confines itself to describing contrast and distribution of variants is unable to capture final devoicing as a phonological generalization, despite its phonologically exceptionless nature. The sounds [t] and [d] must be distinct phonemes since they contrast in words like *Bunde* and *bunte*, and they contrast also in other positions of the word as in the initial position of *Draht* [drɑːt] 'wire' and *trat* [trɑːt] 'stepped.' Thus the words *Bund* and *bunt* must be analyzed as *phonemically* identical according to structuralist principles, and hence the alternation between [bʊnt] and [bʊnd] for 'union' must be analyzed as a matter of *morphology* rather than phonology. This implies that these two phonemic forms must be set up as distinct *allomorphs* of the morpheme for 'union.'[1] This is a very uneconomical description, since literally hundreds of morphemes would require a similar pair of allomorphs that differ just in the voicing of their final obstruent. It has the further disadvantage that it fails to distinguish these phonologically predictable variants of a morpheme from completely suppletive forms, such as *go* and *went* in English. Generative phonology concedes that *go* and *went* are allomorphs but denies this status to phonologically predictable forms (called *alternants*) like [bʊnt] in *Bund* and [bʊnd] in *Bunde*.

A related problem arises when there are asymmetries in the phonological system. Halle (1959) observes that voicing is generally distinctive (contrastive) in Russian obstruents, as we observed in German. This is shown in (5).

(5)   [pɑˈka]   'while'   [baˈka]   'sides'
      [ˈtom]   'volume'   [ˈdom]   'house'
      [ˈsloj]   'layer'   [ˈzloj]   'bad'
      [ˈʃar]   'sphere'   [ˈʒar]   'heat'
      [ˈklup]   'club'   [ˈglup]   'stupid'

But three Russian voiceless obstruents, /x, ʃ, ts/, have no contrastive voiced counterparts, although the corresponding voiced obstruents, [ɣ, ʤ, ʣ], exist phonetically in Russian. Russian has a rule of voicing assimilation by which an obstruent takes on the voicing of an immediately following obstruent within a phonological phrase. This rule affects all obstruents,

---

[1] In generative practice, the term 'allomorph' is restricted to variation in morpheme shape that is not phonologically predictable and must be lexically listed or stated by allomorphy rules (Aronoff 1976). Phonologically predictable variants are known as *phonological alternants* and are simply the outcome of regular, general phonological rules.

regardless of whether they have contrastive voiced counterparts or not, as shown in (6).

(6)   a.   ['mok lʲi]   'whether he soaked'   ['moɡ bɨ]   'were he to soak'
        b.   ['ʒɛtʃ lʲi]   'whether he burned'   ['ʒɛdʒ bɨ]   'were he to burn'

In the most economical grammar, this assimilation is expressed by a single rule. But in a grammar that insists on a separate level that contains all and only the contrastive segments of the language (e.g., Hockett 1942), the rule would have to be expressed twice: once morphophonemically, to account for (6a), and again phonemically, to account for (6b). This forces a single generalization to be split up into two rules (Halle 1959: 22–23).

In German devoicing and Russian voicing assimilation, the context for the rule is visible in the phonetic output. Sometimes this is not the case, as in the following example discussed by discussed by Malécot (1960) and Chomsky (1964). In many varieties of English, a vowel is nasalized if a nasal consonant immediately follows. In certain cases, a nasal vowel may appear phonetically even if no nasal consonant immediately follows phonetically. Consider the examples in (7).

(7)   a.   pin   ['pʰĩn]   f.   hut   ['hət]
        b.   had   ['hæd]   g.   hunt   ['hə̃t]
        c.   hand   ['hæ̃nd]   h.   hit   ['hɪt]
        d.   cat   ['kʰæt]   i.   hint   ['hɪ̃t]
        e.   can't   ['kʰæ̃t]   j.   lip   ['lɪp]
                                         k.   limp   ['lɪ̃p]

Since (7d) and (7e) constitute a minimal pair, the nasal vowel [æ̃] must be counted as a phoneme of English, by a strict application of the structuralist principles of contrast and distribution. This seems wrong intuitively, but beyond that, we can observe that this contrast appears only before a voiceless stop. In all other positions, a nasal vowel can appear only before an overt nasal consonant, which itself occurs word finally (7a) or before a voiced consonant (7c), as well as in other positions. This situation, in which a contrast occurs in some environments but not in others, is a sure sign that another rule is involved. Chomsky (1964: 82) points out that a completely general and straightforward analysis involves the interaction of two rules that apply in the order given in (8).[2]

---

[2] Nasal Consonant Deletion will be slightly revised in Chapter 5, Section 5.3.3. We assume that Vowel Nasalization affects an entire diphthong when that is the nucleus preceding the nasal consonant. Also, Nasal Consonant Deletion applies only when the nasal consonant is homorganic with the following stop; for example, it does not apply in *Fromkin*.

(8)   a.   *Vowel Nasalization*

$$V \rightarrow [+\text{nasal}] \ / \ \underline{\hspace{1cm}} \ \begin{bmatrix} C \\ +\text{nasal} \end{bmatrix}$$

       b.   *Nasal Consonant Deletion*

$$\begin{bmatrix} C \\ +\text{nasal} \end{bmatrix} \rightarrow \emptyset \ / \ V\underline{\hspace{1cm}} \begin{bmatrix} C \\ -\text{voice} \end{bmatrix}$$

These rules presuppose the underlying representations in (9) for the words of (7). We use the term *underlying representation* rather than *phonemic representation* when the discussion concerns generative phonology. Notice that the underlying representation of *can't* cannot be determined by application of phonemic procedures. In fact, it is determined implicitly by using grammatical information, its relation to *can*, in violation of strict phonemic orthodoxy, as for example Hockett's (1942: 20–21) statement that "[t]here must be no circularity: phonological analysis is assumed for grammatical analysis, and so must not assume any part of the latter. The line of demarcation between the two must be sharp."[3].

(9)   a.   pin   /pɪn/
       b.   had   /hæd/
       c.   hand   /hænd/
       d.   cat   /kæt/
       e.   can't   /kænt/

The derivations in (10) illustrate the operation of the rules in (8) on the underlying representations of (9). Note that the rules must apply in the order given. According to *SPE* (p. 342), "[t]he hypothesis that rules are ordered. . .seems to us to be one of the best-supported assumptions of linguistic theory." The output [kʰæ̃t] from the input /kænt/ is a case of *opacity*, since the nasal vowel in the output is not in the context of nasalization in the output, because this context was destroyed by the application of Nasal Consonant Deletion. We will encounter many examples of opacity in the course of our investigation into the phonology of English.

(10) | Underlying representations | /pɪn/ | /hæd/ | /hænd/ | /kæt/ | /kænt/ |
        |---|---|---|---|---|---|
        | Vowel Nasalization (8a) | ĩ | —— | æ̃ | —— | æ̃ |
        | Nasal Consonant Deletion (8b) | —— | —— | —— | —— | ∅ |
        | Phonetic representations | [ˈpĩn] | [ˈhæd] | [ˈhæ̃nd] | [ˈkʰæt] | [ˈkʰæ̃t] |

---

[3] An important exception to this statement is Pike (1947), who argued that grammatical information is necessary for phonemic analysis.

In this way, generative phonology resolves the contradiction in phonemic theory noted above, by an appeal to *ordered rules*. Rather than assuming that all the rules apply to the phonemic representation, as in phonemic theory, generative phonology provides a series of rules such that the first rule applies to the underlying representation, the next rule applies to the output of the first rule, and so on until the last rule is reached, the output of which is the phonetic representation. This picture is somewhat complicated by the necessity of applying some rules cyclically, that is repeatedly to increasingly larger units (see Chapter 6), but the basic principle remains the same.

Consider a second example of the need for rules to be ordered. In most North American varieties of English, the alveolar stops /t/ and /d/ are realized as a flap [ɾ] in various contexts, one of which is between vowels (including diphthongs) where the second vowel is unstressed.[4] We will call this rule *Flapping*. This is an example of *neutralization*: the distinction between these two sounds is lost, or *neutralized*, in particular contexts. In the same dialects, the diphthong /aɪ/ has two realizations: [ɑɪ] or [əɪ], where the latter appears before a voiceless consonant (Chambers 1973). We will call this rule *Diphthong Shortening*.[5] This rule is responsible for the difference in the diphthong in words like *write* and *ride*, as in (11).

(11)   a.   write   [ˈɹəɪt]
        b.   ride   [ˈɹɑɪd]

Like nasalized vowels, the raised diphthong sometimes appears phonetically in the 'wrong' environment, i.e., before a phonetically voiced consonant, but only when that consonant is a flap. This is shown in (12).

(12)   a.   writer [ˈɹəɪɾəɹ]
        b.   rider   [ˈɹɑɪɾəɹ]

Because the raised diphthong [əɪ] contrasts with [ɑɪ] in this context, phonemic theory would be forced to regard these diphthongs as separate phonemes.[6] However, the only case where the raised diphthong appears

---

[4] For a more complete discussion of this rule see Section 5.3.8 of Chapter 5.

[5] This rule is sometimes called Canadian Raising. Geographically it is much more widespread, appearing at least in much of the Northeastern United States. In Canada it also affects the diphthong /aʊ/, and pronunciations like [həʊs] for 'house' are something of a shibboleth for Canadian English. We abstract away from this variation in the present discussion.

[6] It might be objected that the real difference is between [ə] and [ɑ], which contrast elsewhere as in *sum, psalm*. However, the argument still holds, because there is a context where they do not contrast, namely before [ɪ] plus a consonant, unless that consonant is [ɾ].

before a flap is when the flap is related to an underlying /t/, as in *writer*, not where it is related to an underlying /d/, as in *rider*. This again is a case of opacity, and can be resolved in the same way as the vowel nasalization case, that is with two ordered rules, as in (13).[7]

(13)   a.   *Diphthong Shortening*

$$V \rightarrow \left[\begin{array}{c} -\text{low} \\ -\text{ATR} \end{array} \right] / \underline{\qquad} [-\text{cons}][-\text{voice}]$$

(A low vowel is raised and laxed before a glide and a voiceless consonant.)

        b.   *Flapping*

$$\left[\begin{array}{c} +\text{cor} \\ -\text{strid} \\ -\text{cont} \end{array} \right] \rightarrow \left[\begin{array}{c} +\text{cont} \\ +\text{son} \\ +\text{voice} \end{array} \right] / [-\text{cons}] \underline{\qquad} \left[\begin{array}{c} V \\ -\text{stress} \end{array} \right]$$

(An alveolar stop (/t/ or /d/) becomes a flap [ɾ] if it follows a [–consonantal] segment (vowel or glide) and precedes a stressless vowel.)

The derivations in (14) show how these rules work when applied in this order. Notice that the underlying representations required cannot be inferred by phonemic methods, both because they require disregarding the superficial (phonetic) contrast between the diphthongs, and because they involve reference to grammatical information, namely the fact that *writer* and *rider* are derived morphologically from *write* and *ride*, respectively, by the addition of an agentive suffix /+əɹ/.[8] In derivations we write the change effected by each rule just under the corresponding segment(s) of the preceding line; nonapplication of a rule is indicated by a long dash.

(14)   Underlying representations   /ɹɑɪt + əɹ/   /ɹɑɪd + əɹ/
        Diphthong Shortening   əɪ   —————
        Flapping   ɾ   ɾ
        Phonetic representations   [ˈɹəɪɾəɹ]   [ˈɹɑɪɾəɹ]

---

[7] These rules will be revised in Chapter 5.

[8] The underlying representation of the vowels of the stems is actually more abstract, as will be demonstrated in Chapter 7. We start here with a representation that has already undergone a number of rules. There are also words like *item* in which morphological information plays no role and which follow a derivation just like that of *writer*, showing that these rules are purely phonological in nature.

The situation where the phonetic representation shows the effect of a rule having applied even though its context is no longer apparent (*overapplication:* McCarthy 1999) is one form of phonological opacity and is extremely common in phonological systems. A second type of opacity occurs when a rule fails to apply even when its context is present phonetically (*underapplication*). The rule Velar Softening, (41) in Chapter 7, converts /k/ to /s/ when a nonlow front vowel or glide follows, as in *medi[s]ine* from the root *medic* with final [k]. However, Velar Softening does not affect *medi[k]ate*, where /k/ is followed by the diphthong /eɪ/. Again the explanation lies in another rule, in this case Vowel Shift (Section 1.1.1), which among other effects converts underlying /æ/ to /e/ and which is ordered after Velar Softening. The suffix -*ate* has the underlying representation /æt/ which contains a low vowel which cannot trigger Velar Softening. Both forms of opacity have proved to be major obstacles for theories of phonology that reject rule ordering, both structuralist (Hockett 1942) and more recently Optimality Theory (e.g., McCarthy 1999).

1.1.1   Principles of Generative Phonology

The basic principles governing generative phonology are those in (15).

(15)   a.   *Morphological uniqueness:* Except in cases of suppletion, every morpheme has only one phonological form. Any variation in phonetic shape of a morpheme results from the operation of regular phonological rules. (Cf. the quotation from Bloomfield 1939 on page 9.)

         b.   *Criterion of predictability:* Underlying phonological representations are chosen in such a way as to maximize predictability of phonetic forms on phonological grounds.

         c.   *Criterion of naturalness:* Phonological representations are stated in terms of phonetic features. They differ from phonetic representations only to the extent that there is justification for a more abstract representation. Unless some phonological rule intervenes, underlying representations are preserved phonetically. Underlying representations are chosen in such a way that the rules required to produce phonetic forms are maximally natural. (Cf. Postal 1968.)

         d.   *Criterion of simplicity:* Underlying phonological representations and phonological rules are chosen so that the overall grammar is maximally simple.

e.   *Preference of phonological solutions:* Phonological solutions are
     preferred to morphological solutions (e.g., arbitrary lexical
     markings or suppletion), other things being equal.

Underlying representations can differ from phonetic representations only
to the extent required to express certain generalizations. For example, a
word like *cat* [kʰæt'] has the underlying representation /kæt/, since the
aspiration of the initial /k/ and the glottalization of the final /t/ are
predictable aspects of the pronunciation. By the criterion of simplicity this
is preferable to including the aspiration of [kʰ] in the underlying representation because this aspiration would need to be included in the underlying
representation of hundreds of morphemes beginning with a voiceless stop,
which would be more complex. By the criterion of naturalness the underlying representation is expressed in terms of the same phonetic features as
the output.

Bloomfield (1939: 58), though normally considered to be among the
structuralists, expresses a similar outlook in his discussion of Menomini
morphophonemics.

> The process of description leads us to set up each morphological element in
> a theoretical *basic* form, and then to state the deviations from this basic
> form which appear when the element is combined with other elements. If
> one starts with the basic forms and applies our statements. . .in the order in
> which we give them, one will arrive finally at the forms of words as they are
> actually spoken.

Bloomfield goes on to caution that "[o]ur basic forms are not ancient
forms, say of the Proto-Algonquian parent language, and our statements of
internal sandhi are not historical but descriptive, and appear in a purely
descriptive order." Thus, Bloomfield allows phonological rules to go beyond
stating the distribution of sounds per se and to account for morphological
alternations as well, just as generative phonology does. A phonology that
restricts itself to describing distributions based on phonetic contrasts alone,
such as Hockett (1942), cannot do this.

An example of the principles in (15) concerns certain alternations
related by the rule of Vowel Shift (fully discussed in Section 7.1 of
Chapter 7) together with a number of other rules affecting vowel quality.
The examples in (16) are representative. The abbreviation RP ('received
pronunciation') indicates a standard southern British pronunciation while
NA indicates a North American pronunciation.

(16)

	underlying representation of stem	orthographic	phonetic	orthographic	phonetic
		underived word		**derived word**	
				u.r. of suffix /+ ɪtɪ/	
		orthographic	*phonetic*	*orthographic*	*phonetic*
a.	/sæn/	sane	[ˈseɪ̃n]	sanity	[ˈsænɪtɪ] (RP) [ˈsænɪɾi] (NA)
b.	/sɹɪen/	serene	[sɪˈɹĩĩ̃n]	serenity	[sɪˈɹɛnɪtɪ] (RP) [sɪˈɹɛnɪɾi] (NA)
c.	/səblim/	sublime	[səˈblɑ̃ĩm]	sublimity	[səˈblĩmɪtɪ] (RP) [səˈblĩmɪɾi] (NA)

In order to account for these alternations and similar alternations in many other words, we can set up the underlying representations for the stems given in the first column along with underlying representations of a number of affixes, of which -*ity* is a typical example. If no affix is added, the vowel undergoes a sequence of rules, one of which, Vowel Shift, affects the height of stressed, tense vowels, and which together produce the diphthongs in (16) in the *phonetic* column shown under *underived word*. If the suffix -*ity* is added, the form meets the structural description of a rule that laxes vowels when followed by two additional syllables the first of which is unstressed. This rule is called Trisyllabic Laxing (fully discussed in Section 6.2 of Chapter 6). The lax vowel is not subject to Vowel Shift, and the result is shown under the *phonetic* column under *derived word*. The underlying tense vowel never emerges unchanged in phonetic representations: it is either laxed or vowel shifted. But it is not unreasonable to assume that English speakers relate such pairs as [æ] and [eɪ] on the basis of such alternations despite their phonetic distance. It is not likely that sheer conservatism is responsible for the persistence of conventional spelling such as <a> for both these sounds and the practice of some dictionaries to write [ā] for [eɪ] 'long a' and [ǎ] for [æ] 'short a' in their transcriptions. In fact, it takes some phonetic training to realize that these sounds are *not* that close phonetically. This very fact provides an argument for vowel shift as a synchronic process, since a phonological rule relating the phonetic values of the three pairs illustrated in (16) *directly* would be quite complex to state, compared with the rules of laxing and vowel shift. Indeed, there are alternations that show the need for a rule operating in the reverse direction, as shown in (17), where the alternating vowels are shown in boldface.

(17)   *no vowel shift   vowel shift*

various   variety
hysterical   hysteria
mystery   mysterious
germanic   germanium

We assume that the underlying representations of the alternating vowels in
(17) are lax. One reason is that the boldfaced vowel of *various, mystery* would
be stressed if it were tense in its underlying form. There are several contexts
in which vowels in English undergo tensing, one of which is before another
vowel (*variety*), and another is before C*i*V (*hysteria, mysterious, germanium*;
fully discussed in Section 6.3.1 of Chapter 6). The vowels tensed in these
contexts undergo Vowel Shift if stressed. By separating the tensing and
laxing processes from Vowel Shift, we can achieve a maximally simple
analysis of the alternations in both (16) and (17).

1.1.2.   Rule-Writing Conventions

We will employ two complementary formats for phonological rules. The
first and most common is the linear format, which can be given schematically as in (18).

(18)   P → Q / Y____Z

In (18), terms P, Q, Y, and Z are feature matrices. Rule (18) could also be
written (equivalently) as in (19).

(19)   Y   P   Z
            ↓
            Q

In either arrangement, the combination YPZ is the *structural description* of
the rule, P is the *input*, Q is the *structural change*, and Y____Z is the *context*.

   Term Q should include *all* and *only* the features that are changed by the
operation of the rule. In German Final Devoicing (4), the change is
specified as [–voice]. It is neither necessary nor desirable to include features
that change in term P. In German Final Devoicing (4), the input is
specified simply as [–son] (i.e., [–sonorant]), which specifies the class of
all obstruents. We could specify the input as $\begin{bmatrix} -\text{son} \\ +\text{voice} \end{bmatrix}$ which would
specify the class of voiced obstruents. This rule would have the same effect

as the rule as given, but it does no harm to simplify the rule by specifying the input simply as [–son] and letting the rule apply to all obstruents, in accordance with the criterion of simplicity (15d). If the input happens to be voiceless to begin with, it undergoes no change, a situation referred to as *vacuous application.*

Term P could also be null (written Ø), in which case we have a rule of *insertion.* An example is *j*-Insertion, (12) in Chapter 7. If Q is null, we have a *deletion* rule, as in Nasal Consonant Deletion (8b). The terms Y and Z provide the left and right contexts for the rule. As an example, Spirantization, (56) in Chapter 7, states that a coronal obstruent becomes a strident continuant when preceded by either a sonorant or a noncontinuant and followed by the glide /j/. The context may include boundaries, as in German Final Devoicing (4). If either Y or Z or both are unspecified, the rule operates in any (left, right, or both) context.

The second of the two rule formats that we will employ is based on autosegmental phonology (Section 1.5.1), and involves adding and deleting association lines. This can be used for complete assimilation, as in *n*-Assimilation, (42a) in Chapter 6, where /n/ takes on all the features of the immediately following sonorant. In this notation, a line with two cross bars (╪) signifies an association to be deleted, while the dotted line (⁝) signifies an association to be added.

In either format we use C as an abbreviation for any consonant and V for any vowel. Some other notations we will use in conjunction with both formats include curly braces, {}, to enclose alternatives that are not easily expressed as feature matrices. This is illustrated by Spirantization, (56) in Chapter 7, where the left context is either a sonorant or a noncontinuant. The early lower-case letters of the Greek alphabet, α, β, etc., indicate feature values that can be either + or –, but have the same value in every occurrence in a given application of the rule. Examples are Diphthongization, (4) in Chapter 7, and Stem-Final Tensing, (20) in Chapter 7. This format is often used for partial assimilations, as in *n*-Assimilation, (42b) in Chapter 6, where /n/ assimilates to a following obstruent in point of articulation, but retains its nasality.

Parentheses enclose items that may be present or absent in a given application of a rule. Parentheses are interpreted disjunctively, so that the rule with the parenthetical material is tried first, and, if it applies, the rule without that material is skipped. An example is Dialectal *j*-Deletion, (13) in Chapter 7. This notation figures prominently in the *SPE* treatment of English stress, as discussed in Section 3.2 of Chapter 3. Parentheses can even be nested, as in (7) in Chapter 3. This is interpreted as trying the rule with all the parenthesized material first, then the rule with the innermost parentheses omitted, and so on, until the last version is reached with all the parenthetical material omitted. This nesting is also disjunctive, so that, if any expansion of the rule applies, all others are skipped. As argued in Chapter 4, it is better to treat stress in a metrical and parametric approach, as developed there.

A variant of parenthesis notation is angled brackets, < >, occurring in pairs (or more), such that all such pairs are either present or absent in a given application of the rule. An example is Velar Softening, (41b) in Chapter 7.

Some rules state a given change both before and after a particular context using the mirror-image notation, where the percent sign (%) appears in place of the usual slash (/). An example is Voicing Assimilation, (77) in Chapter 7.

Some other notational conventions can be enumerated. One is the use of subscripts and superscripts to indicate variables. For example, C_0 represents zero or more consonants. More generally, any feature matrix can be provided with both a subscript and a superscript to indicate the minimum and maximum number of that unit in a given rule, as in (20), which indicates at least n and at most m units X.

(20) X_n^m

1.1.3   Abstractness in SPE

This analysis of vowel alternations is somewhat abstract, in the sense that the underlying representations differ from their various phonetic manifestations. However, this abstractness is limited by the criteria of naturalness and simplicity. A form like [dɒg] 'dog' can have the underlying representation /dɒg/ and no rules need to apply to it. The proposal of Fudge (1967) that underlying representations should be wholly abstract with no phonetic content would entail that 'dog' might be underlying /☼¼♀/, necessitating otherwise wholly unnecessary rules to convert, e.g., /☼/ to [d].

There is no principled limit to the degree of abstractness of *SPE*'s underlying representations. In a few cases *SPE* proposed underlying representations that appear to be too abstract. The word *nightingale* is a case in point. The first syllable of this word contains the phonetic diphthong [ɑɪ] (or [əɪ] by Diphthong Shortening), although it is in the context that would be expected to undergo Trisyllabic Laxing, just as occurs in *sublimity*. To avoid this result, *SPE* proposed an underlying representation /nɪxtɪngæl/

(our symbols), with a velar fricative closing the first syllable, which contains a lax rather than a tense vowel. After Trisyllabic Laxing, but before Vowel Shift in the order of rules, *SPE* proposed rules that convert the sequence /ɪx/ to /i/, which would give the correct phonetic output. Phonetically, modern English has no velar fricative [x] although historically, Old and Middle English did have this segment, and it still occurs in the German cognate *Nachtigall*. Nevertheless, it seems to overstep the permissible bounds of abstractness to include underlying segments that never appear phonetically. In a later development, Lexical Phonology, it became possible to avoid such underlying representations by restricting rules like Trisyllabic Laxing to derived environments, that is, where its context is created by the addition of a morpheme, as occurs in *sublimity* but not in *nightingale*. The same underlying /x/ appears in the word *right*, *SPE* /ɹɪxt/, in order to prevent it from laxing in the derivative *righteous*, which has a trisyllabic underlying representation in *SPE*. Their rather ingenious argument for this move, along with a less abstract alternative, is discussed in Chapter 7, Section 7.4.4

Another abstract element in *SPE* is their proposal that a number of words have an underlying final /ɛ/ which is always deleted. One argument for this is that other short lax vowels appear underlyingly in that position, so the lack of /ɛ/ there is an unexplained gap, unless we assume that it does appear sometimes underlyingly but is deleted. *SPE* analyzes words like *ellipse* as having an underlying final /ɛ/ in order to get it stressed properly on the final syllable, since otherwise stress would fall on the first syllable. In Chapter 4 we will find that the stress of *ellipse* can be correctly predicted in another way, but an abstract final /ɛ/ will be invoked to account for the alternation of *reduce* and *reduction*, and some other phenomena, in Chapters 6 and 7.

1.1.4 English Stress in SPE

A major portion of *SPE* is devoted to an analysis of English stress. Because there are situations in English where stress in contrastive, taxonomic theory was forced to include phonemes of stress (e.g., Trager & Smith 1951). Nevertheless there are significant regularities to stress in English, especially in phrases and compound words, while stress in simple words is more idiosyncratic. Some of the flavour of the *SPE* stress system can be seen by having a look at the stress of phrases and compounds, assuming that word stress has already been assigned. We will return to stress in simple words in Chapter 4, where we will develop a metrical analysis.

In *SPE* stress is a multivalued feature, in fact the only feature in *SPE* which is not binary. The feature [1 stress] indicates primary, or strongest, stress, within a given domain, while successively weaker degrees of stress are indicated with increasing numbers, so that [2 stress] is secondary stress, [3 stress] is tertiary stress, and so on. There is no limit in principle to the available number of stress degrees. Somewhat anomalously the feature [0 stress] is used as the equivalent of [–stress], while all other stress numbers are instantiations of [+stress]. Since *SPE* is a linear theory, in which phonological representations consist of a single sequence of segments and boundaries, stress is necessarily assigned to individual segments, basically vowels. Most stress rules in *SPE* assign primary stress. In the case of phrases and compounds, primary stress assignment will be to a vowel which already has primary stress, which would seem to be vacuous, i.e., to have no effect. However, it has the effect of reducing other stresses in the domain by one degree, by the *Stress Subordination Convention* (21).

(21)   When primary stress is placed in a certain position, then all other stresses
        in the string under consideration at that point are automatically weak-
        ened by one (*SPE*: 16–17).

The phrase "weakened by one" means that one is added to the stress number already present in a given position. *SPE* proposes the Compound Stress Rule (22) to determine the stress of compound words (this formulation is taken from Liberman & Prince 1977: 253, which is slightly more accurate). The letters P and Q are variables ranging over strings subject to the conditions stated and ## is a boundary between two lexical categories, including compounded elements.

(22)   *Compound Stress Rule (SPE)*

$$\begin{bmatrix} V \\ 1\ stress \end{bmatrix} \rightarrow [1\ stress]\ /\ \underline{\quad} Q(\#\#P)\ ]_{NAV}$$

        where Q contains no [1 stress] and P contains no ##.

Basically, rule (22) assigns primary stress to the penultimate primary stress in lexical categories (NAV, that is nouns, adjectives, and verbs).

SPE also introduced the important notion of the *phonological cycle*. When rules apply cyclically,[9] they apply first to the smallest relevant unit, then they apply to the next larger unit, and so on, until the highest unit (usually a sentence) is reached. Nearly all the rules designated as cyclic in

---

[9] We will discuss the specifics of cyclic application, and which rules fall into this category, in
  Chapter 6.

SPE are stress rules; the others are called word-level rules. In addition to the Compound Stress Rule, *SPE* proposed the Nuclear Stress Rule (23), which assigns primary stress in phrases (again in Liberman & Prince's 1977: 252 formulation), where phrases are NP, VP, AP, S.

(23)   *Nuclear Stress Rule (SPE)*

$$\left[\begin{matrix} V \\ \text{1 stress} \end{matrix} \right] \rightarrow [\text{1 stress}] / \underline{\quad} Q]_{\text{phrases}}$$

where Q contains no [1 stress]

We can illustrate these rules with a few examples in (24). In (24a) we have a compound; in (24b) we have the same two words but as a phrase. In (24c) we have a more complex compound and in (24d) a compound of two compounds. In the last two cases the underlines indicate the cyclic domains under consideration on the particular application of the rule.[10]

(24)   a.   [[black]$_A$ [board]$_N$]$_N$ 'blackboard (for writing on, e.g., in class)'
            1   1   stress assigned by other rules to individual words
            1   2   CSR, Stress Subordination Convention

       b.   [[black]$_A$ [board]$_N$]$_{NP}$ 'a board which is black'
            1   1   stress assigned by other rules to individual words
            2   1   NSR, Stress Subordination Convention

       c.   [[[black]$_A$ [board]$_N$]$_N$ [eraser]$_N$]$_N$ 'eraser for a black board'
            1   1   1   stress assigned to individual words
            1   2   CSR, first cycle
            1   3   2   CSR, second cycle

       d.   [[[law]$_N$ [degree]$_N$]$_N$ [[language]$_N$[requirement]$_N$]$_N$]$_N$
            1   1   1   1   stress assigned to individual words
            1   2   1   2   CSR, first cycle (twice), SSC
            2   3   1   3   CSR, second cycle, SSC

Because of cyclic application of stress rules and the Stress Subordination Convention, longer phrases will have nonprimary stresses repeatedly reduced. *SPE* illustrates this with the phrase *sad plight*, which in isolation has the stress contour 21. When embedded in the sentence *my friend can't help being shocked at anyone who would fail to consider his sad plight*, the stress contour of *sad plight* is 81 because "the surface structure might indicate that the word *plight* terminates no less than seven phrases to which the Nuclear Stress Rule applies" (*SPE*: 23), so that primary stress is assigned to *plight* on seven successive cycles, with seven concomitant

---

[10] We adopt Halle and Mohanan's (1985) notation of double square brackets [[ ]] to indicate morphological constituent boundaries in order to distinguish these from regular square brackets [ ], used to indicate distinctive feature complexes or phonetic transcriptions.

reductions of the stress on *sad.* SPE acknowledges, however, that "the actual internal relations of stress in *sad plight* are the same" in the full sentence or in shorter phrases or in isolation. In Chapter 4 we will show how the metrical approach to stress resolves this apparent paradox.

The phonological cycle applies within words in the SPE system as well. They illustrate this with the word *theatricality*. We will not cite the SPE rules, since they are rather complex and we will develop a different system in Chapter 4. Within words in SPE, primary stress is assigned not to existing primary stresses but to positions in the word determined by counting syllables from the end of the word. This is in accordance with a procedure to be explicated in Chapter 4 in a metrical framework. The derivation is given in (25).

(25)   ⟦ ⟦ ⟦ theatr ⟧ N ic + al ⟧ A ity ⟧ N

$\underline{\quad1\quad}$	rule for noun stress
$\underline{\quad21\qquad\qquad}$	rule for adjectives
$\underline{\quad32\qquad\quad1\quad}$	rule for nouns

Thus the cyclic assignment of stress and the Stress Subordination Convention work the same way in words as they do in phrases and compounds.

While the Stress Subordination Convention is necessary for the SPE stress numbers to work out right, it should be observed that this convention is actually an artefact of the way that the SPE stress numbers work, that is, the convention that higher numbers indicate lower rather than higher degrees of stress. Suppose we consider for a moment what would happen if SPE stress numbers ran in the opposite direction, that is, with higher numbers indicating successively higher degrees of stress, and if we adopted the convention that the highest number in any domain indicates primary stress, as briefly explored by Halle and Vergnaud (1987: 36ff). The stress rules would then be rewritten so as to *raise* the designated highest stress number in a given domain by one degree. In certain details this system would not make exactly the same predictions as the SPE system; for example, *blackboard eraser* would come out with 311 (3 here designating highest stress) rather than the desired 312, whereas *law degree language requirement* would emerge with 2131 (3 highest stress), exactly parallel to the SPE 2312 derived in 21d). Possibly discrepancies of this sort led Chomsky and Halle to the system that they in fact proposed. Nevertheless, it is worth keeping this alternative in mind, since something very much like it was proposed under the rubric of the metrical grid in metrical phonology (Section 1.2).

1.1.5   Other Issues for SPE

The *SPE* system did not allow for a specific morphological component.[11] For *SPE*, the lexicon is simply a list of morphemes and information regarding how they can be used in syntactic structures. The syntax is responsible for much of the morphology in forming the surface structure of a sentence, but there are some mismatches between the output of the syntax (the surface structure) and the appropriate input for the phonological component. The syntax produces a hierarchical constituent structure including both lexical categories (nouns, verbs, adjectives, and adverbs) and grammatical morphemes. *SPE* (pp. 12–13) assumes that each lexical category and each phrasal category that dominates a lexical category in the syntactic surface structure is provided with a boundary symbol # on each side. They give the sentence in (26) as an example.

(26)

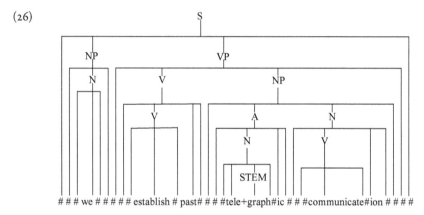

we # # # # # establish # past# # # #tele+graph#ic # # #communicate#ion # # #

The category STEM dominating *graph* is not a lexical category, so it does not receive the # boundary before and after it; however, the noun *telegraph* does. Likewise 'past' is a grammatical morpheme and so does not receive the # boundary before and after it, but the verb *establish* does, as does the concatenation of *establish* plus 'past'. The noun *communication* is derived from the verb *communicate* by the addition of the suffix *-ion*. The noun and the verb both receive the # boundary before and after, so that there is a # boundary between the verb and the suffix. However, for the purpose of

---

[11] A specific proposal for a morphological component within the *SPE* tradition is made in Aronoff (1976). Morphology plays a major role in Lexical Phonology, a major post-*SPE* development discussed in more detail in Chapter 6.

certain phonological rules, among them stress assignment, the # boundary is not appropriate here, so it must be replaced by a + boundary (formative boundary for *SPE*). This is also the case of the # boundary between *graph* and the suffix *-ic* in *telegraphic*. Thus these two words appear as in (27) for the operation of phonological rules. The replacement of the # boundary by the + boundary between *graph* and *-ic* is effected by a readjustment rule.

(27)   communicate+ion
         tele+graph+ic

Another example of a readjustment rule in *SPE* concerns the grammatical morpheme 'past.' Syntactically and semantically a past tense is the same regardless of what verb is involved, but morphologically and phonologically it is quite different for irregular verbs than for regular ones. *SPE* gives the example of two verbs for which the surface syntactic structures are shown in (28a). These are converted to an appropriate input for phonology by readjustment rules, shown in (28b).

(28)   a.   [[mɛnd] past]   [[sɪng] past]
         b.   [[mɛnd] d]   [sæng]

Following Halle (1959), *SPE* employs a category of lexical redundancy rules (referred to as morpheme structure rules in Halle 1959) that express regularities within morphemes. For example, they state a rule (*SPE*: 171) that specifies a consonant as /s/ at the beginning of a morpheme if the following segment is a true consonant, i.e., not a liquid or glide. They remark that it is not always possible to determine whether a given rule is a lexical redundancy rule or a rule of the phonology. An example of the latter is the rule that allows only lax vowels before the clusters [kt] and [pt] in words like *evict, apt, crypt*. This restriction also applies when these clusters occur across a morpheme boundary, as in *descrip+tion, satisfac+tion*. Thus, this restriction must be stated as a phonological rule. However, the past tense [t] as in *aped, liked* must be exempt from the rule, which in their terms results from this past tense morpheme being preceded by the # boundary. This question is resolved in the theory of Lexical Phonology, where it is possible for a single rule to function both as a lexical redundancy rule and as a phonological rule. (See further discussion in Section 1.4.3.)

Chomsky and Halle characterized *SPE* as "an interim report on work in progress rather than an attempt to present a definitive and exhaustive study of phonological processes in English" (p. vii). Subsequent work has suggested a number of improvements, changes, and complete reanalyses of various aspects of English phonology, and of phonological theory in general. In the following sections we will highlight two of the most important of these developments. First, in Section 1.2, we will discuss the metrical theory of stress and how it improves on the numerical theory of *SPE*. This will also serve to introduce the prosodic hierarchy, Section 1.3, which plays an important role in subsequent chapters. Then, in Section 1.4 we will discuss the expanded role of the lexicon in accounting for word bounded morphology and phonology in the theory of Lexical Morphology and Phonology.

1.2   Metrical Phonology

As we saw in Section 1.1.4, the feature [stress] in *SPE* is multivalued, the only feature with this property in their theory. The feature [stress] differs from other features in another way: all other features in *SPE* have a locally defined value; that is, the plus or minus value of a feature like [high] is determined for each individual segment by reference to that segment alone. By contrast, stress is inherently a *relational* notion: an element is perceived as stressed by virtue of comparison to another element rather than by a local value of the element in question. Liberman and Prince (1977, henceforth L&P) proposed to capture the relational aspects of stress by constructing *metrical trees* to organize the elements of an utterance. These metrical trees allow only binary branching, where one branch is labelled *s* (for *strong*) and the other is labelled *w* (*weak*). L&P retained the feature [stress], however, but reduced it to a binary feature like the other features in *SPE*. This is because there is not a one-to-one correspondence between *strong* and stress and between *weak* and nonstress: although a strong node may not be unstressed, a weak node may be stressed, but less strongly stressed than its corresponding strong node. To illustrate this, consider the words *annexe* and *Phoenix* in (29), where the first word has two stresses and the second has one.

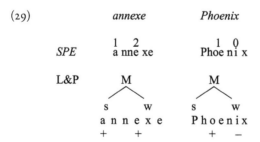

(29)   *annexe*   *Phoenix*

              SPE   1 2   1 0
                        a nne xe   Phoe ni x

              L&P   M   M
                         ⌒   ⌒
                        s   w   s   w
                        a n n e x e   P h o e n i x
                        +   +   +   −

The node label *M* at the top of each tree is for French *mot* 'word.' The strong-weak labelling beneath the node M signifies that, in each word, the first syllable is stronger than the second. In due course we will examine other cases where the left node is labelled weak and the right strong. The plus and minus signs below each word signify stress as a binary feature. L&P impose an absolute requirement on trees that a strong node may not immediately dominate [−stress]. In constructing more complex trees for longer words, this procedure results in sequences of a stressed syllable followed by any number of unstressed syllables, + −, + − −, + − − −, and so on, forming a left-branching metrical subtree, which they call a *left foot*. Such units are joined into a right-branching tree, labelled according to the principle that the right node is strong if and only if it is branching. Whenever any node is labelled strong, its sister branch is of necessity labelled weak. According to these procedures, the word *teleological* is given the word tree in (30).

(30)

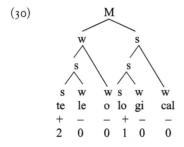

In order to show that no information is lost by treating stress in trees as opposed to *SPE* stress numbers, L&P (p. 259) propose an algorithm (31) to recover *SPE* stress numbers from the tree.

(31)   If a terminal node *t* is labelled *w*, its stress number is equal to the number of nodes that dominate it, plus one. If a terminal node *t* is labelled *s*, its stress number is equal to the number of nodes that dominate the lowest *w* dominating *t*, plus one.

Although they state this algorithm in terms of terminal nodes, it clearly gives the correct results only for *stressed* terminals, as shown in its application to *teleological* in (30). L&P illustrate its application to phrases with the example in (32), where R stands for the root of the tree.

(32)

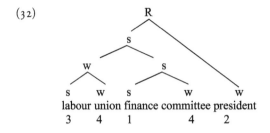

labour union finance committee president
3   4   1   4   2

In addition to metrical trees, L&P introduce a second notation for stress: the *metrical grid*. The grid is constructed from the tree by assigning place holders to each syllable such that a greater number of place holders is assigned to any node marked strong (or the strongest node embedded under a node marked strong) than to the node's weak sister. This is called the *Relative Prominence Projection Rule*, or *RPPR*. For example, metrical grids for *teleological* (30) and *labour union finance committee president* (32) would be as in (33).

(33)   a.   x
                  x   x
                  x   x x   x   x   x
                  t e l e o l o g i c a l

        b.   x
                  x   x
                  x   x   x   x   x
                  labour union finance committee president

It would seem redundant to have two representations for stress: one or the other should be sufficient. L&P attempt to motivate the addition of the grid to metrical structure by way of the English Rhythm Rule, which reverses the relative prominence of two stresses in the context of a *stress clash*, a situation where two prominent stresses occur too close together. When a word or phrase with main stress at the end is embedded within a larger phrase and followed by a more strongly stressed item (as is usual in phrases), the original main stress of the first item is reduced and a previous stress is increased. This is illustrated by the phrases in (34a, b), where stresses are indicated in terms of *SPE* numbers. The failure of the Rhythm Rule in (34c), which seems to meet its requirements, will be discussed in terms of various approaches to the Rhythm Rule.

(34)   2 1   2 3   1
        a.   thirteen   thirteen men
             2   1   2   3   1
        b.   achromatic   achromatic lens
             2 1   3 2   1   3   2 3   1   3
        c.   Alberta   Alberta cow boy   *Alberta cow boy

Whereas *thirteen*, in isolation, has its primary stress on the second syllable, in the phrase *thirteen men* the first syllable of *thirteen* has a greater degree of stress than the second syllable. The Rhythm Rule can be formulated in terms of *SPE* stress numbers, metrical trees, or metrical grids. Kiparsky (1966: 95) gives a rule for German in the *SPE* framework, which we have adapted for English in (35).[12]

(35) $[<1\text{stress}] \rightarrow [2 \text{ stress}] / \underline{\quad} X [1 \text{ stress}]$
        where X contains $[-\text{stress}]_0^n [+\text{stress}] [-\text{stress}]_0^n$
        with concomitant application of the Stress Subordination Convention (18), except that primary stress is not reduced.

A version of the Rhythm Rule for English in terms of the metrical tree is proposed by Kiparsky (1979: 424). We give this formulation in (36).

(36)

L&P propose a formalism similar to (36) for the structural change of the Rhythm Rule but determine the rule's applicability by appealing to the notion of stress clash on the grid. This is defined as two adjacent grid marks whose corresponding grid marks on the next level down are also adjacent (Liberman & Prince 1977: 312; Prince 1983: 32). Let us consider the applicability of each of the three formulations with respect to *thirteen men*. The diagram in (37) shows the metrical tree, the *SPE* stress numbers, and the metrical grid (with asterisks indicating the stress clash), all before the Rhythm Rule applies.

(37)

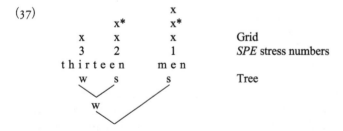

	x		
	x*	x*	
x	x	x	Grid
3	2	1	*SPE* stress numbers
thirteen		men	
w	s	s	Tree
	w		

---

[12] Note that [–stress] can include consonants as well as unstressed vowels, given *SPE* conventions. The notation [<1 stress] should be understood in terms of the *SPE* stress number convention, i.e., as a numerical value *greater* than 1, indicating a degree of stress weaker than primary stress.

In (37), there is a stressed element with less than primary stress (the first syllable, with [3 stress]) followed by a stressed element (the second syllable, with [2 stress]), followed by a [1 stress], and so (35) is applicable. Assigning [2 stress] to the first syllable in accordance with the structural change of (35), and reducing the [2 stress] on the second syllable in accordance with the Stress Subordination Convention (21) (but not reducing the primary stress) produces the 231 stress pattern, as required. Likewise, the metrical tree in (37) has the form of the input to rule (36), which consequently says that the weak and strong labelling of the first two syllables is reversed. Finally, the second and third grid columns in (37) contain a clash, as defined by L&P, indicated by asterisks (*) on the corresponding grid marks, since the marks on the second row of these two columns are adjacent, as are the corresponding marks one level down. So all three formulations of the rule predict that the Rhythm Rule will apply.

The situation is similar in *achromatic lens*, whose various stress configurations are given in (38). Even though there is an unstressed syllable between the last stressed syllable of *achromatic* and the word *lens*, these two syllables clash in terms of rules (35) and (36) and the grid definition of clash, and so the Rhythm Rule again applies in this case.

(38)

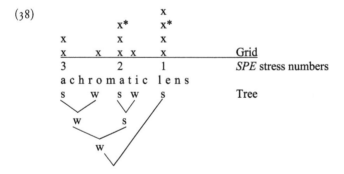

In the phrase *Alberta cowboy*, we also have a clash according to rules (35) and (36), as shown in the structure of (39). L&P note that the Rhythm Rule does not apply in this case, and that the clash required does not appear in the grid for this phrase, predicting nonapplication. They claim that this shows that the grid is necessary to define the clash conditions for the application of the Rhythm Rule, and that these conditions cannot be defined in terms of the tree alone.

(39)

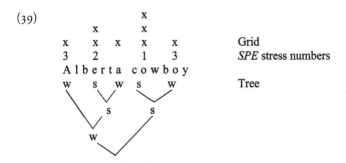

			x		
	x		x		
x	x	x	x	x	Grid
3	2		1	3	*SPE* stress numbers
A l b e r t a	c o w b o y				
w	s w	s	w		Tree

However, this claim for the superiority of the grid for defining the conditions of clash for the Rhythm Rule is illusory. Although in conformity with the RPPR, the grid in (39) does not adequately represent the rhythmic structure of the phrase *Alberta cowboy*, because it gives the first and third syllables each a grid height of one element, despite the fact that the first syllable is stressed and the third syllable is unstressed. If the grid in (39) is adjusted to correct this anomaly, as shown in (40), the first two syllables do present a clash on the grid, and so the Rhythm Rule is predicted to apply, just as in (37) and (38).

(40)

		x		
	x*	x*		
x	x	x	x	
x	x	x	x	x
A l b e r t a	c o w b o y			

Kiparsky (1979: 425) proposes that the Rhythm Rule is subject to the restriction in (41).

(41)   The Rhythm Rule does not apply when it would create a word internal metrical structure of the form (i), where the first *s* is nonbranching.

(i)

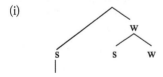

Switching the *w-s* labelling of [Al]$_w$[berta]$_s$ would result in a word-internal *s-w* where the first *s* is nonbranching (dominating *Al*). Thus the Rhythm Rule is blocked in the tree in (39). Since a restriction of this type is required even in the grid theory, once grid representations are adjusted to reflect the distinction between stressed and unstressed syllables, the motivation for the grid as a way of predicting the applicability of the Rhythm Rule vanishes. The metrical tree is thus adequate for all required purposes.

In addition to cases like *Alberta Cowboy* where the metrical grid wrongly predicts application of the Rhythm Rule, there is another class of cases where the metrical grid wrongly predicts nonapplication of the Rhythm Rule. In the phrase *Japanese bamboo* (Prince 1983: 35), the Rhythm Rule can apply, even though no clash appears in the grid, given for this phrase in (42).[13] The tree representation, however, contains the input to (36) and no violation of (41) occurs following Rhythm Rule application. In the tree representation below the phrase, we assume the metrical foot as discussed following the example. Such examples further undermine the motivation for the grid, especially considering that its development was originally intended to provide an input to the Rhythm Rule.

(42)

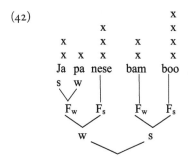

Further development of the metrical tree, especially Selkirk (1980b), eliminated the feature [stress] from the theory altogether by generalizing L&P's notion of left foot, henceforth just *foot*, which we designate by F. In Chapter 4 we will develop a version of this theory, defining the foot as a unit containing one, and only one, stressed syllable. Under this conception, the contrast between *annexe* and *Phoenix* is represented as in (43) rather than as in (29), where ω = phonological word, replacing L&P's M.

---

[13] A reader points out that the clashing configuration does appear in this grid on the syllables *nese* and *bam* (and also on the syllables *bam* and *boo*), but the Rhythm Rule would require a clash on the syllables *nese* and *boo*, which is not present in this grid.

(43)   *annexe*   *Phoenix*

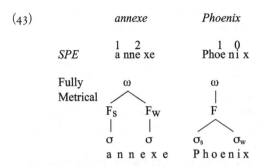

We can refer to this as the *fully metrical theory*, providing metrical units at different levels and labelling every branching pair of sister nodes strong and weak. Thus *annexe* consists of two feet, the left of which is labelled strong because it is the main stress, and the right weak since it is a weaker stress, but still a stress because it is a foot. By contrast, *Phoenix* has only one foot because it has only one stress. This foot cannot be labelled, since it has no sister, but it contains two syllables, where the left syllable is labelled strong because it is the stressed syllable of the foot. We shall discuss later how a fully metrical system extends downward as an account of syllable structure (Chapter 3) and upward as an account of higher prosodic categories (Chapter 5).

Subsequent developments involved a retreat from a fully metrical position to something more like the *SPE* system. Recognizing that the L&P formalism is somewhat redundant in its use of both trees and grids, Prince (1983) proposed a grid-only theory. He proposed rules that construct a grid directly, rather than as a structure that depends on the prior construction of a tree. This is a considerably restricted theory, and in fact remedies a slight anomaly in the fully metrical theory that had developed up to that point, specifically Hayes (1980; 1982). Hayes proposed rules that make certain elements *extrametrical* prior to the application of stress rules and also rules of *destressing* that remove metrical feet under specific conditions. These procedures resulted in certain syllables being left stray – unattached to any foot. For example, in *abracadabra*, the result of stress assignment, that is foot construction, is (a)(braca)(dabra), where parentheses delimit the feet. A destressing rule removes the second foot (braca), leaving two stray syllables. One option would be to leave such syllables unattached. Hayes takes a second option, providing *rules of adjunction* that attach stray syllables to an adjacent foot, in his interpretation, always to the left (unless the only available foot is on the right). This results in some intuitively incorrect foot divisions. In this example, adjoining both stray syllables (braca) to the left, gives (abraca)(dabra). Prince points out that this foot structure, which he calls the 'distributional' foot (1983: 88, fn. 3), differs from the 'felt' foot, the intuitively correct (abra)(cadabra). For Prince, this situation raises the question of the viability of the foot as a unit of metrical structure. However, the possibility exists that Hayes's adjunction procedure is incorrect, and indeed Withgott (1982) proposed an adjunction procedure that produces the intuitively correct footing of this and similar words. We will develop a more complete analysis of footing, defooting, and adjunction in Chapter 4.

The grid-only theory is actually not a metrical theory, in the sense that a metrical theory represents relations between units, as in the strong-weak labelled trees of L&P. The grid alone is essentially linear: each vowel has a grid column constructed on it just as in *SPE* each vowel is associated with a stress number. The grid and the *SPE* system are essentially congruent if the stress numbers are reversed, so that higher numbers express higher degrees of stress, (cf. Halle & Vergnaud 1987: 36ff.). The difference lies in the possibility of manipulating grid marks individually, as in Prince's (1983) version of the Rhythm Rule. Prince's rule is stated as Move-x, and operates on a grid as in (44). The grid mark over the syllable *teen* moves leftward to the adjacent column over *thir*, resolving the clash.

(44)

		x				x
	x*	x*		x		x
x	x	x	→	x	x	x
thirteen	men		thirteen	men		

As Halle and Vergnaud note, the movement of a grid mark provides a more explanatory expression of the Rhythm Rule than a version that adjusts numerical values in a way analogous to Kiparsky's rule for German, adapted for English in (35).

If this approach, with grid construction followed by movement of grid marks under clash, could be maintained, it would be a more constrained, hence more explanatory, theory than the elaborate trees of L&P. However, considerable evidence emerged that constituency is required in metrical structure (Hayes 1995: 41–48; see also Kenstowicz 1994). For example, when a stressed vowel is deleted, stress typically migrates to an adjacent syllable within the foot, specifically, rightward if the language has left-dominant feet (the stressed syllable is at the left of the foot), leftward if the language has right-dominant feet. Second, Hayes (1995: 43–45) notes that the Rhythm Rule cannot be defined entirely in terms of the grid, but requires constituency. Prosodic morphology provides another source of evidence for prosodic constituency, in that the foot is among the units that are relevant for morphological phenomena such as reduplication, truncation, etc. (McCarthy & Prince 1986; 1990). Related to that is the fact that some languages have a restriction on the minimal size of words, and this is often one foot. Thus some constituency is needed—the question is how much. A return to a fully metrical theory would be the obvious approach, but surprisingly, few researchers have taken this tack. Most researchers have adopted a hybrid notation called the *bracketed grid*, in which certain grid elements are grouped into constituents. The extent of this constituency varies. Halle and Vergnaud (1987) is a typical example of this trend. Representing constituency by bracketing asterisks on various levels of the grid, their system has the effect of reproducing tree structure. In (45) we give their representation of *Apalachicola* (1987: 233).

(45)
```
                            *
(*           *              *)
(*    *)    (*    *)    (*    *)
A     pa    la    chi    co    la
```

Hayes (1995) also works within a bracketed grid theory. In contrast to his earlier studies, here he avoids adjunction, thereby achieving somewhat simpler structures than appear in tree theory. However, not using adjunction makes it difficult to account for segmental processes that are stated in terms of the foot, which we will explore in detail in Section 5.3.3 of Chapter 5. Our position is that metrical and prosodic structure is not just a means of representing stress but has to be integrated into an overall grammar. The theory of prosodic phonology shows that prosodic structure is a conditioning factor for many rules of segmental phonology. For example, we will show that Aspiration in English is conditioned by foot structure: voiceless stops and affricates are aspirated when they stand at the beginning of a foot. For this to work properly, all syllables need to be footed. Aspiration would be much more difficult to account for with metrical structures that exclude adjunction. There are at least four other segmental rules that require foot structure for their operation, and which will only work if all syllables are footed.[14] Therefore, in a more complete grammar, a fully metrical arboreal approach is required, such as we will develop in Chapter 4. Hayes claims (1995: 109) that "the same phenomena have also been plausibly analyzed with syllable structure rather than

---

[14] These include Palatalization (Section 7.4.2), Dialectal *j*-Deletion (Section 7.1.2), *h*-Deletion (Section 7.4.8), Nasal Consonant Deletion (Section 5.3.3), and Compensatory Syllabification (Section 5.3.3).

foot structure, as in Kahn 1976." However, Kahn's syllable structures, including the dubious concept of ambisyllabicity, do not always make the correct predictions, as argued in Jensen (2000). To get the correct segmental results, we need foot structure that includes adjunction. An extension of bracketed grid theory to include adjunction would be essentially equivalent to tree structure.

While Halle and Vergnaud (1987) argue against the numerical representation of stress, they do not argue against the arboreal representation. I am not aware of any arguments against arboreal theory; most recent discussions of metrical theory simply assume bracketed grid notation without argument. A number of arguments can be brought to bear that favour arboreal representations over bracketed grids. Indeed, some of these are due to advocates of bracketed grids, such as Hayes. Hayes (1995: 376ff.) notes a number of problems that arise in bracketed grid theory, and proposes ad hoc solutions. To the extent that arboreal theory treats the same phenomena without ad hoc additions, it is to be preferred over bracketed grids.

One problem arises in phrasal stress, In *SPE*, the Nuclear Stress Rule (23) assigns main stress to the final element of a phrase, with reduction of the remaining stresses in the phrase by one degree by the Stress Subordination Convention (21). The metrical (or prosodic) equivalent is to construct a tree with right nodes labelled strong, discussed in detail in Section 5.3.6 of Chapter 5. In grid theory (with or without brackets), this is expressed by adding a grid mark to the rightmost member of the phrase, a procedure which Prince (1983) refers to as End Rule Right. This works fine for simple phrases like (46).[15]

(46)   (x)
     (x .)   (x)   (x .)   (x)
     Joseph + left   →   Joseph left

With more complex phrases, difficulties are encountered. Hayes gives the example in (47).

(47)   (x)
     (x)   (x)
     (x   .) (x)   (x)   (x   .) (x) (x)
     mighty oaks + fell   →   *mighty oaks fell

---

[15] In Hayes's grid notation, the lowest line of x-marks is eliminated, so that all x-marks represent stress. A period within a constituent marks a completely stressless syllable. Hayes (1995: 39) makes it clear that this modification is for brevity only; hence, it does not affect arguments relating to the viability of the grid notation.

Here it is impossible to promote the stress on *fell* without violating the Continuous Column Constraint, which requires that a grid column not contain any gaps. Since, as Hayes puts it, "constituents being concatenated can differ in their internal complexity, they can differ in the height of their tallest grid column" (1995: 376) and "there are apparently no languages in which phrasal stress rules refer to how many grid marks appear in their inputs" (1995: 377). Hayes seeks to remedy this situation by proposing a convention that equalizes the height of the tallest grid columns in concatenated constituents. This would interpose an additional grid mark over the x on *fell* in (47), so that the rule that promotes stress in the output of the rule would give a continuous column of three grid marks. The need for this convention is clearly an artefact of the grid notation, since no such problem arises in arboreal theory, as shown by the tree structures for these two phrases in (48).[16] Clearly, the internal complexity of the phrases has no effect on their labelling, and no adjustments are required to achieve this result. As Hayes puts it (1995: 378) "phrasal stress rules in bracketed grid theory are much like phrasal stress rules in pure tree theory, in that they make the right- or leftmost element strongest, irrespective of its internal structure. The only difference is that within bracketed grid theory, extra structure must sometimes be added to preserve well-formedness."

(48)　　a.　　　　　　　　b.

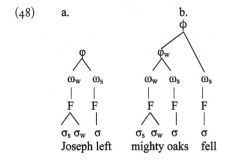

Joseph left　　mighty oaks　fell

The opposite sort of problem arises with phrases like *John saw Mary*, where the rightmost element is already the strongest in its own phrase. From the concatenation in (49a), Hayes proposes to add an additional layer of the grid with a mark over *Mary*, giving (49b).

---

[16] We omit the clitic group here for simplicity: see Section 5.3.5 of Chapter 5 for some discussion of this category. We assume that phrases (designated by φ) can be nested, giving prosodic structures that parallel the syntax. Such nesting is syntactically motivated, unlike the Continuous Column Constraint and the Stress Equalization Convention of grid theory.

(49)   a.   b.

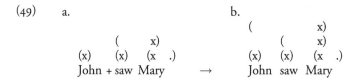

In addition, Hayes needs to have a rule of Beat Addition to amplify the stress on *John* here, since *John* has a greater degree of stress than *saw* in this phrase. This is accomplished by creating a new domain with an associated grid mark over *John* in (49). This is shown in (50a), No such adjustment is needed in arboreal theory, since the correct relative relations are derived from the depth of embedding, shown in (50b), where the *SPE* stress numbers, derived by (31), are shown below the tree.

(50)   a.   b.

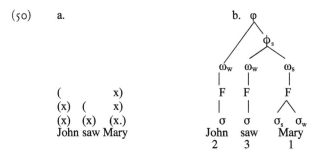

Hayes's theory encounters other difficulties in accounting for the Rhythm Rule. He considers (1995: 383) two phrases that seem to have the same rhythmic pattern, even though their constituent structure is different. In (51), the Rhythm Rule operates as expected in both grid theory and tree theory.

(51)

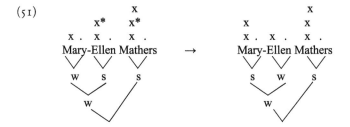

But in (52), while the tree structure gives the appropriate rhythm directly, with no application of the Rhythm Rule, the grid fails to provide the necessary higher degree of stress to the first constituent relative to the second. The tree representation, on the other hand, correctly gives the stress contour 231 according to algorithm (31).

(52)

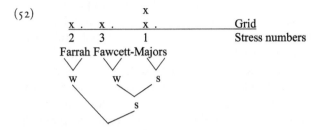

Hayes proposes to remedy this in bracketed grid theory by employing the rule of Beat Addition to add a grid mark over the first syllable of *Farrah*. In addition, another grid mark must be added over the first syllable of *Majors* to maintain this as the strongest syllable in the phrase as a whole. This same rule applies in phrases like *John saw Mary* (50), which has a similar grid and tree structure. Like the convention that adds an extra grid mark over *fell* in (47), the need for Beat Addition is an artefact of the bracketed grid notation, and is entirely unnecessary in an arboreal approach to stress.

Kager (1989) represents a more restricted version of bracketed grid theory which allows only binary constituents. In his system, a syllable is stressed if it is heavy, that is if it has a long vowel or is closed by a consonant in the coda. However, some short-vowel closed syllables can be destressed. Stress on light syllables comes about by construction of binary left-headed feet. A few examples are given in (53).

(53)

```
      x                    x
  x   x      x      x      x    x
  x   x     (x  x) (x  x)  x    x
  annexe   Phoenix  A d i r o n d a c k
```

In *Phoenix*, the two syllables constitute a foot, with a single stress on the left, indicated by a grid mark on the second level above the first syllable. In *annexe*, however, no binary constituent can be constructed since both syllables are stressed. This is shown by a grid mark on the second level for both syllables, with the primary stress indicated by a grid mark on the third level over the first syllable. In *Adirondack* the first two syllables form a constituent, but no binary constituent can be constructed on the last two syllables, since these are both stressed, by virtue of being heavy. Kager refers to this as the 'compositional property of stress,' in that stress compositionally reflects syllable weight and binary constituents, themselves essentially autonomous.[17] Kager's approach does indeed capture many interesting properties of stress in both English and Dutch, but, like Hayes, his metrical structures do not provide the appropriate input to segmental rules, such as Aspiration (see the full discussion in Chapter 5).

Idsardi (1992; 2009) proposes the simplified bracketed grid theory (SBG) in which parentheses need not be paired, but left and right brackets can be inserted into grids independently. For word stress there are three lines to the metrical grid. The lowest line, line o, has a grid mark for each stressable element, typically vowels. On this line left and/or right brackets can be inserted by various rules, or they may be present in underlying representations in the case of lexically specified stress. A right bracket groups everything to its left into a constituent up to the next bracket or the beginning of the word; a left bracket similarly groups everything to its right up to the next bracket or word edge. A grid mark adjacent to a bracket (left or right as a parameter setting) is the head of its constituent and projects a grid mark on the next line up, line 1. These marks are interpreted as potential stresses. A bracket inserted into line 1 yields a constituent (right or left headed according to a parameter) that projects a grid mark on line 2. This grid mark is interpreted as main stress.

This system may leave some elements of a word outside of any constituent. In common with other versions of grid theory, it does not provide appropriate input to segmental rules, nor does it fare any better than Hayes's theory in accounting for the Rhythm Rule.

Halle (1997) discusses the stress and accent systems of a number of Indo-European languages in terms of this theory, principally Russian, Serbo-Croatian, Sanskrit, and Lithuanian. In these languages some morphemes have inherent accents which can be notated with a left parenthesis to the left of the stressed vowel in underlying representations. Some stems are postaccenting, represented with a left parenthesis after their rightmost vowel; other stems are unaccented. A set of rules operating on these representations produces the correct phonetic stresses in these languages. However, English differs from these languages in a number of respects. In particular, English does not have lexically specified accents; in fact, Halle attributes the rise of initial stress in Germanic precisely to the loss of lexically specified accents there and in several other Indo-European families. Thus, SBG theory may not contribute much to our understanding of

---

[17] In a case like *annexe*, Kager assigns primary stress to an element which does not get stress either by virtue of being heavy or by heading a binary constituent.

English stress. See Section 4.8 in Chapter 4 for a discussion of the application of SBG to the stress of regular nouns in English.

There is abundant evidence for constituency in metrical structures. However, since the relative prominence of metrical elements is fully represented by the strong-weak labelling of the metrical tree, there is no evidence for a grid representation in addition to the constituency as represented in the tree. We summarize in (54) the reasons for adopting arboreal representations for stress in English rather than the (simplified) bracketed grids.

(54) a. Trees provide the appropriate structures for segmental rules; grids do not.
      b. Trees form a natural part of the prosodic hierarchy, whereas grids stand apart from other prosodic categories.
      c. Trees provide a superior account of the Rhythm Rule. In particular, trees allow for the Rhythm Rule to operate in phrases like *Japanese bamboo*, while grids incorrectly predict nonapplication in such phrases; trees correctly block the Rhythm Rule in phrases like *Alberta cowboy*, while grids incorrectly predict application in such phrases.
      d. Ad hoc adjustments are required in the grid approach; no such adjustments are needed with trees.

1.3 The Prosodic Hierarchy

The prosodic hierarchy provides the organization of the sounds of an utterance. This is a sequence of increasingly inclusive units, of which the lowest is the mora and the highest is the utterance. The lowest units are formed in the lexicon: the mora, which groups segments, and the syllable, which groups moras, are formed by rules of syllabification, discussed in detail in Chapter 3. The foot and the phonological word are formed by rules of stress assignment, discussed in Chapter 4. The higher units are formed postlexically after words have been inserted into syntactic structures. These units are formed with reference to syntactic structure but may not be isomorphic to syntactic units. The highest unit, the utterance, frequently comprises a sentence, but may in some cases include more than a single sentence. All the prosodic units are governed by the strict layer hypothesis, which maintains that each unit contains only units of the next lower type. We will find some systematic exceptions to this hypothesis in the stress system of English, where a syllable can be adjoined to a foot in such a way that a new foot dominates the adjoined syllable along with the original foot. Similarly, a compound word can be a phonological word that dominates two other phonological words. The units of the hierarchy exhibit binary branching, where one of the branches is labelled *s* (for *strong*) and the other *w* (for *weak*). It may be the case that the intonation phrase exhibits n-ary (flat) branching where one of the branches is labelled strong and the others weak. In addition, the three highest units may undergo restructuring under certain circumstances. We discuss all these issues in detail in Chapter 5.

1.4 Lexical Morphology and Phonology

1.4.1   The Structure of the Lexicon

The theory of Lexical Morphology and Phonology provides an approach to the relationship of syntax, morphology, and phonology very different from that of *SPE*. In this model the lexicon is more than a list of items; it is an active, generative component of the grammar. The lexicon still contains a list of morphemes, to be sure, but it also includes morphological operations and certain phonological operations. The lexicon provides fully specified words prior to syntactic operations. There is no need for an abstract morpheme 'past' such as is required in *SPE* (cf. 26, 28); rather the past tense forms of verbs are created in the lexicon. The lexicon may be divided into a number of strata (or levels), of which two are needed for English.[18] The verbs *mend* and *establish* form their past tense forms on stratum 2 by suffixing /-d/, which is subject to certain phonological rules. In the case of *mended*, Epenthesis (rule 75 in Chapter 7) inserts /ɪ/ between the stem and suffix giving the phonetic form ['mɛndɪd]. In the case of *established*, the /d/ is devoiced in assimilation (Voicing Assimilation, rule 77 in Chapter 7) to the preceding voiceless obstruent, giving [ɪ'stæblɪʃt]. These phonological rules are likewise on stratum 2. In the case of *sang*, a morphological rule of ablaut (Lowering Ablaut, rule 6 in Chapter 8) on stratum 1 replaces the vowel /ɪ/ with the low vowel /æ/ in generating the past tense form.

The overall model of the grammar in this theory can be diagrammed as in Figure 1.1. It shows two lexical strata for English, each of which includes both a morphological and a phonological component. The first stratum is cyclic, while the second is noncyclic, or postcyclic, since its operations follow the cyclic stratum. The model allows for the application of stratum 1 phonological rules before the morphological operations of that stratum, and

[18] Kiparsky (1982) originally proposed three lexical levels for English, while Halle and Mohanan (1985) propose four, but there is no clear evidence for more than two lexical strata in English.

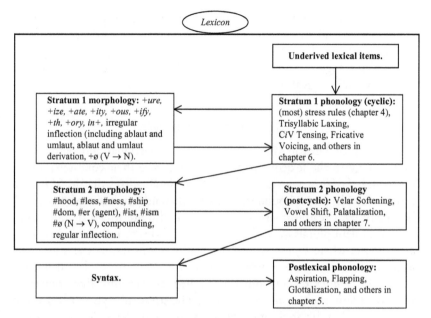

Figure 1.1   The model of Lexical Phonology

then the reapplication of cyclic phonology after each morphological operation. The cyclic rules are subject to the Strict Cycle Condition, according to which cyclic rules can change structure only in derived environments (discussed in Section 4.6 of Chapter 4 and refined in Section 6.2.1 of Chapter 6). On stratum 2, all affixes are added before any phonological operations, and all phonological rules follow the addition of affixes at this stratum. In addition, there is a component of postlexical phonology, which applies after lexical items have been processed by the syntax.

There are a number of indications that this organization is the correct one. Syllabification and stress assignment apply on stratum 1 to underived items. After each addition of an affix on this stratum stress assignment reapplies, which may result in a different stress pattern. Thus we have the forms *sólid, solídify; tótal, totálity; órigin, oríginal, originálity*. The form *originálity* shows the retention of the stress in *original* but reduced to a secondary stress with the assignment of a new main stress further to the right. Addition of stratum 1 affixes does not always result in stress shift, as in examples like *desíre, desírous; óxygen, óxygenàte*. In Chapter 4 we will show how all of these examples fall under the stress rules formulated there, along with some real and apparent exceptional cases.

Although some early presentations of Lexical Phonology assumed cyclic application on all strata (Kiparsky 1982), convincing evidence for cyclic application beyond the first stratum in English is lacking. Accordingly, in the model of Figure 1.1, the phonology of the second stratum applies once after all morphological operations on that stratum.

1.4.2 Lexical Morphology

The theory of Lexical Morphology assigns inflectional and derivational morphology to the lexicon, creating words before their concatenation in the syntax. Stratum 1 includes those derivational affixes that in *SPE* were provided with the + boundary, either inherently or reduced from a # boundary by a readjustment rule. Here are also are irregular inflections, such as umlaut plurals *(foot, feet; goose, geese)* and verb inflections like *keep, kept; sit, sat*, where *kept* is formed by a suffix *-t* on stratum 1 and *sat* is the result of an ablaut rule converting /ɪ/ to /æ/. Stratum 1 also includes a process of *zero derivation* (sometimes called 'conversion') that converts a verb to a noun, such as *survéy$_V$, súrvèy$_N$*. The stress rules give final stress in the verb, and cyclic application of stress after zero derivation gives initial stress on the noun with the final stress retained as secondary. Stratum 2 includes those derivational affixes with the # boundary in *SPE*, regular inflection *(walk, walked; cat, cats)*, and compounding. There is also a zero derivation process on stratum 2 that converts nouns to verbs *(cómfort$_N$, cómfort$_V$)*, where the stress assigned to the noun on stratum 1 is retained in the verb. This follows from the stratal organization since most stress assignment occurs on stratum 1 and stratum 2 is noncyclic.

Some affixes are sensitive to stress, in that their attachment is restricted by the stress pattern of the base. For example, the stratum 2 suffix *#al*, which forms nouns from verbs, can attach only to verbs with final stress, as *retriéve, retriéval* but not *develop, *devélopal*. This implies that rules of stress assignment apply before affixation in such cases. This type of interaction is obviously excluded in the *SPE* system, where all phonology follows all morphology.

1.4.3 Structure Preservation

The rules of the Lexical Phonology are structure preserving in the sense that they operate in terms of the segments and feature specifications that are contrastive in underlying lexical entries. For example, the Trisyllabic Laxing rule introduced in Section 1.1.1 is structure preserving since tense and lax vowels contrast in English underlying representations, as in *mate*, *mat*, with the underlying representations /mæt/, /mæt/. On the other hand, Vowel Nasalization (8a) is not structure preserving, since nasal and oral vowels do not contrast in English underlying representations. This means that Vowel Nasalization must be postlexical.

Lexical phonological rules may both account for alternations and be responsible for the distribution of sounds within morphemes. As we noted in Section 1.1.4, a vowel must be lax before the clusters [kt] and [pt], both within morphemes (*evict, apt, crypt*) and in derivations like *descrip+tion, satisfac+tion*. In lexical terms this means that the rule, our Cluster Laxing, (39) in Chapter 6, is a lexical rule, in fact a stratum 1 rule in view of its inapplicability to stratum 2 inflections like *ape#d, like#d*. Kiparsky (1982: 66) points out that the apparent duplication of lexical redundancy rules and lexical phonological rules is actually the normal case in the theory of Lexical Phonology, whereas it was problematic for the *SPE* framework, where it is referred to as the duplication problem (Kenstowicz & Kisseberth 1979: 427ff.). In Lexical Phonology there is no duplication problem because the rules of the Lexical Phonology function both to fill in redundant values in underlying representations and as rules governing alternations in the active phonology.

English has a rule of Voicing Assimilation (77 in Chapter 7) that accounts for the voicing alternation in verbs like *leave, left; lose, lost*. This rule also predicts that obstruent clusters within morphemes will agree in voicing, as in *adze (*a[tz])*, *huckster (*hu[gzt]er)* (Kiparsky 1982: 67).

One exception to the claim that lexical rules are structure preserving is that rules of stress assignment on stratum 1 build metrical structure although metrical structure is not present in underlying representations. The possibility of underlying stress was suggested by Kiparsky (1982: 50) as a way of accounting for the exceptional stress of words like *vanílla*, but we provide an alternative analysis in Section 4.7. There is also the possibility that some stratum 2 suffixes, like *-ee* in *trainee* are stressed in underlying representation, though they may equally be stressed by rule.

Sometimes a rule applies in the lexical component and exhibits the effects of structure preservation and also applies postlexically, where it may introduce noncontrastive elements. An example is Nasal Assimilation in English. In stratum 1 phonology /n/ of the prefix *in-* assimilates completely to a following sonorant, as in *irrational, illegal*, and it assimilates in point of articulation to a following (anterior) stop, as in *impossible, intolerable*. In these cases the assimilation produces consonants that are lexically contrastive in English: /r, l, m, n/. This assimilation does not occur before fricatives (*infinite*, not *i[m]finite*). Before velar stops the situation is a little unclear: *incongruous* may be *i[n]congruous* or *i[ŋ]congruous*, though within a stress foot we get *co[ŋ]gress*. We argue in Chapter 2 that [ŋ] is not an underlying segment in English, so where [ŋ] is derived on stratum 1 it may not be strictly structure preserving, although [ŋ] is not a new type of segment in that there are nasals at other points of articulation and other velar segments, /g/ and /k/. This is in contrast to the nasal vowels, which constitute a new type of segment. Postlexically nasal assimilation also applies, and here we get nasals at many points of articulation. These are illustrated by phrases (which are formed postlexically by the syntax) such as *i[n̪] Thrace*, *i[ñ] Germany*, *i[ŋ] Canada*, *i[ɱ] France*. The nasals [n̪], [ñ], and [ɱ] do not exist in underlying representations, so Nasal Assimilation here is not structure preserving.

1.4.4   Cyclicity

In *SPE* it is primarily rules assigning stress that are cyclic. These are the rules for which cyclic application is required, since stress assignment must reapply after each morphological operation on stratum 1. But other rules are given cyclic status in Lexical Phonology. Kiparsky (1982: 42) argues that Trisyllabic Laxing applies cyclically in *hypócrisy*. Trisyllabic Laxing is blocked in the first syllable of *hypóthesis* because it is inapplicable when the following syllable is stressed. Its effect in *hypócrisy* is due to Trisyllabic Laxing applying on an earlier cycle to *hypocrite*, where the following syllable is not stressed, followed by derivation with the suffix -*y* and reapplication of stress rules. This is another example of opacity (recall Section 1.1) where Trisyllabic Laxing has applied to a form which lacks the appropriate context in the phonetic form. It is further characteristic of cyclic rules that they conform to strict cyclicity, which blocks their feature-changing function in nonderived environments.

Kiparsky (1982: 31) points out that, unlike *SPE*, in Lexical Phonology there is no need for cyclic assignment of phrasal and sentence stress. The theory of Lexical Phonology predicts this. The rules building phrasal categories and labelling them strong and weak according to the procedures of Chapter 5 give the correct results in the postlexical component without the cycle, since the cycle is confined to stratum 1 of the lexicon.

1.4.5   Strict Cyclicity

In Section 1.1.2 we discussed *SPE*'s derivation of *nightingale*, with an underlying /x/ in the first syllable to prevent the vowel of that syllable from undergoing Trisyllabic Laxing. The alternative is to derive the vowel of the first syllable straightforwardly from /i/, via Vowel Shift, and block Trisyllabic Laxing there by a principle, *strict cyclicity*, that restricts the structure-changing application of cyclic rules to derived environments, where the term *derived environment* refers to an environment created by the addition of a morpheme or by the application of a prior phonological rule. Thus Trisyllabic Laxing can apply in structure-changing fashion in *sublimity*, where the trisyllabic context is created by the addition of the suffix *-ity* to *sublime*. It can also apply in structure-filling fashion in words like *camera*, thus capturing a lexical regularity, in that words that conform to this rule, such as *alibi, pelican, calendar*, are much more common than words that violate it, for example *ivory, stevedore* (Kiparsky 1982: 35). The underlying representation of words like *camera* can be simplified by not specifying the feature [ATR] in the vowels of their antepenultimate syllables; they are specified [–ATR] by Trisyllabic Laxing in feature-filling mode. The first vowel of *nightingale, stevedore* is specified [+ATR] under-lyingly, and Trisyllabic Laxing is blocked in these forms by strict cyclicity.

Kiparsky (1993) discusses this phenomenon under the term *blocking in nonderived environments*. He provides examples in various languages of such blocking in postcyclic (word-level) rules and even in postlexical rules, and conversely examples of cyclic lexical rules that are not subject to such blocking. In his new proposal, such blocking is characteristic only of obligatory neutralization rules, and not restricted to cyclic rules.

McMahon (2000: 88ff.) seeks to restrict English Vowel Shift, a non-neutralization rule, to derived environments only and to locate vowel shift on stratum 1. This entails a significant increase in the complexity of the grammar, since the vowel shift rule has to be split into two rules. The first is Tense Vowel Shift, equivalent to the rule of Vowel Shift illustrated in (16) and (17) of Section 1.1.1 but restricted to derived contexts and so applying to the right column of (17) but not to the underived words *sane, serene, sublime* of (16). For these she proposes underlying representations with the vowels /e/, /i/, and /aɪ/, respectively. These get laxed in the derivatives *sanity, serenity, sublimity* (with the diphthong /æɪ/ also shedding its glide element), giving /ɛ/, /ɪ/, and /æ/, and these undergo a second Vowel Shift rule, Lax Vowel Shift, that operates in the reverse direction of Tense Vowel Shift giving /æ/, /ɛ/, /ɪ/. This is obviously in violation of the simplicity criterion (15d). McMahon's claim is evidently motivated by a desire to restrict abstractness, although most of the discussion around restricting abstractness has involved neutralization rules, especially absolute neutralization (Kiparsky 1968). A second motivation is to seek underlying representations in underived rather than derived forms, but this cannot be

42   Theories of Phonology

maintained in general, as shown by the example of German devoicing (3), where the underlying form of the stem-final stop is found in the inflected form rather than in the uninflected form. We will therefore retain the more general Vowel Shift rule illustrated in (16) and (17) that operates in both underived and derived environments and is situated on stratum 2. We give the complete analysis of Vowel Shift in Section 7.1 of Chapter 7.

Another stratum 2 rule that operates in both underived and derived environments is Velar Softening. In derived environments it accounts for alternations like that of *electri[k]~electri[s]ity*. Velar Softening converts /k/ to [s] and /g/ to /ʤ/ when preceding a nonlow front vowel or glide. Velar Softening must be ordered before Vowel Shift (as already mentioned in Section 1.1), since this simple formulation is possible with this ordering. After Vowel Shift underlying /i/ (which conditions Velar Softening in *criticize*) has become [ɑɪ] whose first element is low and back and not an appropriate context for Velar Softening. Similarly underlying low /æ/ (which does not trigger Velar Softening in *medicate*) would trigger Velar Softening if it were applicable after shifting to [eɪ]. This ordering relation provides an additional argument against McMahon's revised version of Vowel Shift, since her version has the two vowel shift rules on stratum 1 where they are necessarily ordered before Velar Softening.

In nonderived environments Velar Softening accounts for interesting distributional regularities of English (Kiparsky 1982: 34). The /s/ at the beginning of a stem is regularly voiced after a vowel, as in *resign, resist, resume* (Fricative Voicing, Section 6.3.1 of Chapter 6), but not after a consonant, as in *consign, consist*. There is also no voicing in *dissonant*, explained as deriving from a geminate /s+s/ on the basis of the component morphemes *dis-* (as in *disreputable, discourteous*) and *son+ant* (as in *conso-nant*). There is also no voicing of [s] in *criticize*, on the assumption that this [s] derives from /k/ by Velar Softening, which also accounts for the alternation observed in *critic, critical* versus *criticize, criticism*. This requires that Fricative Voicing be ordered before Velar Softening. Indeed, Fricative Voicing is on stratum 1 and applies only in derived environments.

1.5   Other Post-*SPE* Developments

1.5.1   Autosegmental Phonology

Autosegmental phonology (Goldsmith 1976) provides for representations in which certain features are removed from the matrix and assigned to a separate parallel tier, which can be associated to the matrix in various ways. Most commonly tonal features are treated in this fashion. Tone acts somewhat differently from segmental features, in that a single segment may have a tonal contour, or a particular tonal pattern may characterize a number of segmental sequences of different lengths. *SPE* did not treat tone, but referred to Wang (1967), who proposed the set of tone features in (55) to account for level and contour tones, as discussed by Chao (1920).

(55) a. [+contour] the pitch changes in the course of the tone
      b. [+high] the overall pitch is relatively high
      c. [+central] the overall pitch is in the mid range (used only for level tones)
      d. [+mid] the pitch is level 3 (used for one mid level tone only)
      e. [+rising] the pitch rises in the course of the tone
      f. [+falling] the pitch falls in the course of the tone
      g. [+convex] the pitch rises then falls

One problem with this system concerns contour tones and melody levels. In Mende (Leben 1973) nouns may be one, two, or three syllables long. These nouns can appear with one of five tone patterns: *high, low, falling, rising,* and *rising–falling.* These five patterns are the same regardless of the length of the noun. Leben provides the examples in (56) (a few are from Rialland & Badjimé 1989).

(56)

syllables	*one*		*two*		*three*	
high tone (H)	kɔ́	'war'	pélé	'house'	háwámá	'size'
low tone (L)	kpà	'debt'	bèlè	'trousers'	kpàkàlì	'three-legged stool'
falling tone (HL)	mbû	'owl'	kényà	'uncle'	félàmà	'junction'
rising tone (LH)	mbǎ	'rice'	nìká	'cow'	ndàvúlá	'sling'
rising–falling tone (LHL)	mbǎ	'companion'	nyàhà	'woman'	nìkílì	'groundnut'

A word with high tone has high tone on each syllable, whether the word has one, two or three syllables (Leben does not provide examples with three syllables except for rising–falling tone; other three-syllable examples are from Rialland & Badjimé 1989). A low-tone pattern works the same way. With contour tones, the entire contour is realized on a single vowel in a word of one syllable, but spread out over two or three syllables when words are that size. There is no way in Wang's feature system to express the equivalence of the falling tone on *mbû* 'owl' with the high–low sequence on *kényà* 'uncle,' for example. In autosegmental phonology, both are an instance of the tone sequence HL (high–low). Tones are arranged on an autosegmental tier separate from the segmental features, and the two tiers are linked by means of association lines in accordance with the conventions in (57) (Goldsmith 1976: 27).[19]

(57)   a. Associate free autosegments to appropriate segments one to one, left to right.
         b. All appropriate segments must be linked to an autosegment.
         c. All autosegments must be linked to an appropriate segment.
         d. Association lines may not cross.

The conventions in (57) ensure the correct association of tones to the nouns in (56) as long as each noun is associated with one of the five possible tone patterns. In the case of a high tone associated with a two-syllable word, such as *pélé* 'house,' there is a one-to-many association between the tone and the vowels of the word. Conversely, when a contour tone is associated with a one-syllable word, such as *mbû* 'owl' or *mbǎ* 'companion,' there is a many-to-one association between the tones and the vowel. Such associations are not possible in the linear framework of *SPE*.

Tonal stability occurs when a tone remains after the deletion of the segment with which it is associated. The tone may then reassociate to a nearby segment. In KiRundi (Goldsmith 1990: 28–29) only high tones are marked in underlying representations; for example, the word *goré* 'woman' has a high tone on its final syllable. Other vowels receive low tone by default. KiRundi has a rule that deletes a word-final vowel when the next word begins with a vowel. When the word *goré* is followed by a vowel-initial word, its final vowel is deleted but the tone remains, to be associated with the initial vowel of the following word, which otherwise would receive low tone by default (unless it was underlyingly marked for high tone).

Some morphemes may consist solely of a tone. In the Tiv verb system (Pulleyblank 1986), General Past is signalled by a low-tone prefix. Verb stems are also associated with a *floating tone*, i.e., associated with the morpheme as a whole, either high or low. If the General Past low-tone prefix is attached to a low-toned verb stem, the prefix has no effect and the whole word is realized with low tone. Pulleyblank shows that the tone associated with a stem is associated with its first vowel only, and that left-over vowels are associated to low tones by default. Thus, with a high-toned verb stem, the high tone associates to the first stem vowel, and the remaining tones (if the stem is polysyllabic) are realized with low tone.

---

[19] Compare the statement in Pulleyblank (1986: 11), who accepts (57a, d) but claims that further association must be done by language-specific rules.

When a high-toned stem takes a low-tone prefix, the low tone of the prefix has nowhere to attach to the verb stem itself, but stays floating, inducing *downstep* on the high tone on the first vowel of the verb stem. Downstep is the process whereby a high tone, though it remains high phonologically, is phonetically realized on a lower pitch than a preceding high tone, due to the intervening low tone, whether this low tone is itself attached or floating.

Another tense in Tiv, the Recent Past, consists of a high-tone suffix. With a polysyllabic verb stem associated with a floating low tone, the low tone associates with the first vowel of the stem and the high tone of the suffix associates with the second vowel of the stem.

Autosegmental theory finds numerous applications beyond its original domain of tone. Vowel harmony is a feature of a number of languages. Within a particular domain, generally the phonological word, the vowels share the same value of some feature; in Hungarian, Finnish, and Turkish it is [back] (and to a more limited extent [round] in Hungarian and Turkish). This can be expressed autosegmentally by setting [back] on a separate tier and linking it to each vowel of the word. There are numerous complications surrounding this phenomenon in the various languages, such as the existence of neutral vowels that can co-occur with vowels of both values of the harmonic feature. As with the analysis of tone, with vowel harmony the features not involved in the harmonic relation are retained in the standard feature matrices of *SPE*.

A further extension of autosegmental analysis is to consider all features autosegmental, a position that is referred to as *feature geometry*. Versions of this have been proposed by Clements (1985), Sagey (1986), and Clements and Hume (1995). For any segment there is a *root node*, defined by the features [sonorant, consonantal], which dominates two nodes, [laryngeal] and [supralaryngeal]. The [laryngeal] node dominates the features that determine the state of the glottis, such as those discussed in Section 2.3 of Chapter 2 (see the chart in (8) of Chapter 2). The supralaryngeal node dominates the features [nasal], [continuant], and [place]; and the [place] node dominates major articulators [labial], [coronal], and [dorsal]. The [coronal] node dominates [anterior] and [distributed], and the dorsal node dominates [high], [low], and [back]. This scheme permits the expression of place assimilation in consonants by the spreading of the [place] node from one consonant to the next, bringing with it all the place features dominated by [place]. However, this model also reduces the ability of phonological features to cross-classify. *SPE* defines four basic points of articulation as the four logically possible combinations of the features [anterior] and [coronal], which permits the expression of various natural classes, for example [+anterior] comprises labials and anterior coronals, while [–coronal] groups together labials and velars. Neither of these two classes can be expressed as a natural class in the feature geometric model, but each has been observed to behave as a class in some languages, e.g., [+anterior] in English (Section 6.1.2 in Chapter 6).

Autosegmental representations are generally considered to be governed by the *Obligatory Contour Principle* (OCP), which requires that a succession of identical autosegmental units be represented as multiply linked to a single autosegment, at least within morphemes, rather than having a sequence of identical auosegments individually linked to the segmental tier.

1.5.2   Underspecification Theory

Underspecification theory pursues the goal of simplicity (15d) by removing as much redundant information from underlying representations as possible. A problem could arise in that the unspecified value [oF] could function as a value distinct from both [+F] and [–F], where two segments X, Y, are *distinct* if there is a feature F such that one of X, Y is specified [+F] and the other is specified [–F] (paraphrasing *SPE*: 336). Stanley (1967) showed that, if a redundancy rule specifying a value for [oF] could apply after rules that refer to [F], then some segments initially not distinct could become distinct, with [oF] effectively functioning as a third value. For this reason *SPE* did not assume underspecification. Later work showed that this problem can be circumvented in a variety of ways. Archangeli (1984: 85) proposed the *Redundancy Rule Ordering Constraint*, which requires that "[a] redundancy rule assigning 'α' to F, where 'α' is '+' or '–', is automatically ordered prior to the first rule referring to [αF] in [its] structural description." Kiparsky (1982: 54) does this "by stipulating that no feature can appear marked both + and – in the same environment in the lexicon." That is, for any feature [F] in a particular context, only one of [+F] or [–F] can be specified. Pulleyblank (1986) allows both H and L tone to be specified as floating tone features on Tiv verb stems, but they are represented as two different features. A default L tone is assigned to vowels that do not receive a tone from a lexical specification or from a tone as a prefix or a suffix. In this way he incorporates underspecification into his autosegmental analysis.

Underspecification can allow the simplification of rules of epenthesis, since in many languages an epenthetic vowel is the default vowel of the language. For a given feature, languages may differ as to whether it is the + or − value that is present in lexical representations. Archangeli (1984) suggests that Japanese, Telegu, and Spanish, with similar vowel systems, differ in terms of the underlying feature specifications, all using the features [high], [low], and [back] for those vowels.

(58) a. Japanese b. Telegu c. Spanish

a. Japanese

	i	e	a	o	ɨ
[high]	−	−			
[low]			+		
[back]				+	+

b. Telegu

	i	e	a	o	u
[high]	−	−			
[low]			+		
[back]	−	−			

c. Spanish

	i	e	a	o	u
[high]	+				+
[low]			+		
[back]				+	+

In each language epenthesis inserts a vowel: [ɨ] in Japanese, [u] in Telegu, and [e] in Spanish. In each case the vowel inserted is the one with no underlying features, so the rule can simply say to insert a vowel, whose values are then assigned by default. Harris (1983) shows that Spanish has four rules of epenthesis, each of which inserts the vowel [e]. Obviously the grammar is greatly simplified by omitting the feature specifications for [e] from all four of these rules.

Kiparsky (1982: 66ff.) uses underspecification in his discussion of the Strict Cycle Condition (Section 1.4.5). In English the cyclic rule Trisyllabic Laxing applies in a feature-filling function in words like *camera*, whose first vowel can be left unspecified for [ATR] in the lexical representation, and in a feature-changing function in words like *sublim+ity* in a context derived by the addition of the suffix *+ity*. Borowsky (1986) suggests an underspecification account of *right* and *righteous* which avoids the abstract underlying velar fricative that *SPE* used to account for these words. See Chapter 7, Section 7.4.4.

1.5.3   Optimality Theory

Our discussion of English is set within the framework of ordered rules and derivations, according to the lexical model, following *SPE*. Optimality Theory (OT; Prince & Smolensky 1993) rejects this framework and substitutes a system of ranked output constraints. We will not employ this theory in our analysis, but rather offer a detailed critique of it in Section 8.3 of Chapter 8 by considering how the theory fares with respect to the rules discussed throughout the book. In this section we will consider some general theoretical issues that arise with this theory.

According to OT, the actual output of a given underlying representation is the optimal one in terms of the constraint hierarchy of the language. OT rejects *SPE*'s morpheme structure rules (or conditions) that state restrictions on underlying representations, a position known as *richness of the base* (Prince & Smolensky 1993, Kager 1999: 19). The constraints themselves are considered to be universal; the ranking in a particular language constitutes the grammar of that language. The optimal candidate is chosen from a set of candidate outputs, by evaluating each candidate against the ranking of the constraints such that the optimal candidate best satisfies the higher ranked constraints even though it may violate lower ranked ones. This candidate set must be large enough to ensure that the correct candidate is not 'missed' simply by virtue of not being included in the candidate set. In fact, the candidate set must be infinite. For each input, a function GEN generates the set of candidate outputs for that input. In the earliest version of OT, GEN operates on the input by variously marking some elements as unparsed (which violate a constraint Parse) or inserting blank elements to be interpreted as default epenthetic elements (violating a constraint Fill). In later versions, known as Correspondence Theory (McCarthy & Prince 1995), GEN is not so limited; it is allowed to add or delete items, permute items, and change elements freely, as well as to include indices on the elements of each candidate to allow for the evaluation of correspondence. Kager (1999: 21) notes that "the *Generator* component is free to submit any kind of analysis of (English) /bɛd/ that is couched within the universal alphabet of representational options, including excessively unfaithful candidates such as [pɪlow] and [mætrəs]." This is known as *freedom of analysis* (McCarthy & Prince 1993, Kager 1999: 20). In effect the same infinite candidate set will be associated with every input, and this set must apparently contain all possible linguistic expressions in all possible human languages.

   This infinity of possible candidates poses a problem for OT that tends to be dismissed too lightly by advocates of the theory. For example, Kager (1999: 26) notes that linguistic theories are models of linguistic *competence*, that is, the intrinsic knowledge of the native speaker, rather than of *performance*, which is how this knowledge is employed in actual language use. While this is true, it is also true that one can imagine a language user employing a set of ordered rules, such as the rules presented in this book, in actual language use, even if this is not the way in which language competence is actually put into practice. On the other hand, one cannot imagine a speaker actually evaluating an infinite set of candidates with respect to a given constraint hierarchy.

Kager (1999: 26) gives an arithmetic analogy, which a moment's reflection shows to be entirely inappropriate. He notes that "there is a unique solution to the equation" in (59).[20]

(59) $3n^2 - 3 = 45$

He claims that "you will be able to find [the solution] after a moment's thought, even though the candidate set (let us say all integers) is infinite." But this analogy is incorrect. First of all, the candidate set is not the set of integers, but the much larger infinite set of all complex numbers. However, the main objection is that there is a definite *procedure* by which one can determine the correct solutions to any such equation, based on the principle that applying the same mathematical operation on equal expressions yields expressions which are also equal, as long as no division by zero is involved. This procedure applied to (59) yields the steps in (60).

(60) $3n^2 - 3 = 45$
        $3n^2 = 48$ (add 3 to each side)
        $n^2 = 16$ (divide each side by 3)
        $n = \pm 4$ (take the square root of each side)

Since OT explicitly denies that any procedure is involved in deriving the correct output from a given input, the language user is faced with the necessity of examining an infinite set of possible outputs for any given input.

Opaque rule interactions cause serious problems for OT. As we saw in Section 1.1, vowels are nasalized before a nasal consonant in English. In some words like *hint, can't*, this nasal consonant is deleted by a later rule. Hammond (1999) discusses English phonology extensively in terms of OT, and proposes (pp. 21ff.) constraints to account for vowel nasalization as in (61).

(61)   a.   Nasal:
          A vowel before a nasal consonant must be nasalized

       b.   NoNasal
          Nothing is nasalized

As long as Nasal outranks NoNasal, these constraints ensure that *ran* is phonetically [ɹæ̃n] and that *rat* is [ɹæt]. From an input /kænt/ these constraints predict the outcome [kæ̃nt]. To get an output [kæ̃t] we might

[20] In fact there are two solutions, as is generally the case with a quadratic equation, in this case, 4 and −4.

add a constraint (62) that disallows a sequence of a vowel followed by a nasal consonant and a voiceless consonant, where N = any nasal consonant.

(62)   NoVNVoiceless

$$*VN \begin{bmatrix} C \\ -\text{voice} \end{bmatrix}$$

Constraint (62), if ranked above NoNasal, favours the output [kǣt] over [kǣnt] from the input /kænt/. But a further candidate [kæt] satisfies all three constraints, so there is no way for the output [kǣt] to emerge as optimal, regardless of how the constraints are ranked. Hammond discusses a number of other constraints in connection with this example, such as faithfulness constraints that require underlying representations not to change, but none that would overcome the opacity of this example.

The inability to account for opaque interactions is a general problem for OT. Proponents of optimality theory have made a number of proposals to deal with this situation (e.g., McCarthy 1999), but these proposals have the flavour of being patches to the theory rather than offering any real insight into language structure. McCarthy proposes that a specific failed candidate can influence the choice of the actual output, where this failed candidate would be (similar to) an intermediate representation in a standard derivational account. Since English phonology is replete with opaque rule interactions when a considerable number of rules are taken into account, it would seem unfruitful to pursue an account based on optimality theory.

Hammond offers a fairly detailed account of distributional regularities in English in terms of optimality theory, but he specifically avoids trying to account for alternations. As he puts it, "[t]he theory lends itself to this because of its focus on surface regularities. . .[o]ther domains of phonology are not so readily treated or so obviously best treated in terms of such a theory" (1999: vii). In this sense, optimality theory seems to return to the structuralist concern with surface regularities. We contend that the task of phonology includes that of accounting for alternations as well as surface distributional regularities. Therefore, this work is couched in terms of a theory of rules, as in *SPE*, with the enrichments offered by metrical, prosodic, and lexical theories.[21] In Section 8.3 of Chapter 8 we will discuss

---

[21] This does not imply that optimality theory is unable to account for alternations. The alternations involving final devoicing in German in (3) would be accounted for in this theory by a constraint against word-final voiced obstruents. The contention is simply that alternations involving complex rule ordering, where many of the interactions are opaque, become much more difficult to account for in constraint-based theories than in the theory using ordered rules, and correspondingly less insightful.

a number of specific processes in English for which we will give a rule treatment in the course of the book, and show that OT is unable to offer an insightful treatment of these phenomena. While thus rather traditional, the present work is innovative in the sense of trying to integrate these issues into a single system rather than dealing with some aspects of the grammar, such as stress, in isolation from the others.

CHAPTER 2

Segmental Phonology

This chapter investigates the segmental system of English. A traditional concern of phonology is to catalogue the sounds found in a given language, and foreign language textbooks frequently begin with such a catalogue. But this is not as straightforward a task as one might think. The sounds that appear on the taxonomic phonemic level have often served this purpose, but, as we saw in Chapter 1, this level is not so easy to define either. We gave two examples, one involving vowel nasalization and the other involving diphthong shortening, in which taxonomic phonemic analysis introduces pseudodifferentiation; that is apparent phonemes that are not genuinely distinctive in the language. It is clear that we need to investigate the levels of representation in phonology and determine which levels are suited to the determination of the sound inventory of a language.

2.1 Levels of Representation

Since our model of grammar includes phonological rules, we must assume that there are distinct *levels of representation* for phonological forms. Phonological rules can have a variety of effects, as we have seen. For example, a rule may neutralize two originally distinct elements, as final devoicing in German converts underlying /t/ and /d/ into the same phonetic realization [t] in word-final position, as seen in (3) of Chapter 1.[1] Phonological rules may also introduce segment types that

---

[1] It is customary to use square brackets [ ] to enclose (systematic) phonetic representations. In taxonomic phonemic theory slashes (also called solidi) / / were introduced to enclose phonemic representations. In generative phonology slashes usually enclose systematic phonemic (underlying) representations. We will also use slashes to enclose lexical representations in our discussion below. The context usually makes it clear whether underlying or lexical transcriptions are meant in a given case. Sometimes double slashes // // are used to enclose systematic phonemic representations to emphasize the distinction from lexical representations. In addition, we will sometimes use angle brackets < > to indicate orthographic representations.

were not previously present; for example, the English Flapping rule not only neutralizes underlying /t/ and /d/ to the same realization in a particular context but also produces a phonetic segment [ɾ] which was not present prior to the application of this rule. Another example in English is Aspiration, which does not neutralize segments but produces segments that were not present before: [pʰ], [tʰ], [ʧʰ], [kʰ]. So the inventory of segments may be different at different levels. So far we have been assuming two levels of representation, one which forms the input to the phonological rules and the other which forms the output of these rules. We will now consider the characteristics of these levels and whether there may be other levels that are of importance in phonology.

The level of the output of the phonological rules should not be identified with the *physical phonetic level*, characterized by Bloomfield (1933: 85) as a "mechanical record of the gross acoustic features, such as is produced in the phonetics laboratory." This level may contain a host of linguistically irrelevant aspects, such as result from the speaker's mental state, degree of fatigue or intoxication, the possible presence of chewing gum in the mouth, and so on. What is needed is a slightly more abstract level that disregards such factors and concentrates on the linguistically relevant aspects only. Such a level is the *systematic phonetic level*, defined by McCawley (1968: 14) as

> a representation in which all phonetic characteristics are represented which are governed by linguistic regularity in the language. Those characteristics of pronunciation which are caused not by language but by extra-linguistic factors (such as the size and shape of the speaker's vocal organs, his state of mental alertness, the possible presence of chewing gum in his mouth, etc.) are excluded from a phonetic representation. The characteristics recorded in a phonetic representation are thus, roughly speaking, those which, if deviated from, would yield a "foreign accent."

The physical phonetic level can be derived from the systematic phonetic level by rules of *phonetic implementation* (Mohanan 1986: 153). At this level, the division between segments may be blurred, and features may assume multiple values rather than just the two values of binary features. The first effect can be seen in the word *can't*, which we have characterized as having a nasalized vowel at the systematic phonetic level in (7e) of Chapter 1. But the nasalization may start not with the beginning of the vowel but start somewhat later. We can show this in the diagram (1).

(1)   *can't*

systematic phonetic
[kʰæ̃t]

physical phonetic

voice	−	+	−
cont	−	+	−
nas	−	+	−
	[kʰ	æ̃	t]

In a similar way, the English segment /b/ is characterized by the feature
[+voice]. But in English, /b/ and other systematically voiced obstruents,
are fully voiced only when they occur between voiced segments. Mohanan
(1986: 157) illustrates this with the words *bib* and *abbey*. The diagrams in
(2) illustrate the physical distribution of [voice] in these two words. The
initial /b/ of *bib* starts voiceless, with voicing starting somewhat before the
release of the stop at the beginning of the vowel, while voicing stops
shortly after the closure made for the final /b/. In *abbey*, the /b/ remains
voiced throughout, being between vowels. Systematically, all the /b/s in
this example are characterized as [+voice].

(2)   a.   bib   b.   abbey

systematic phonetic
          [bɪb]   [æbi]

physical phonetic

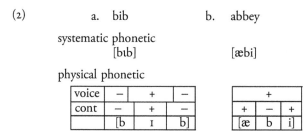

The second effect at the physical phonetic level is that features may
assume multiple values. This can be shown by various pronunciations of
the stop [k] in different contexts. The articulation of [k] is further front in
keel than in *cool*, for example, although in both cases it is systematically
[+back]. The point of contact of the tongue on the palate does not get as
far front in *keel* as the palatal stop [c]. We can say that, at the physical
phonetic level, the feature [back] has many values, several of which are
related to [+back] at the systematic phonetic level.

The second of the two levels we have been assuming to this point is the
underlying level or *systematic phonemic level*, as discussed in Section 1.1.1 of
Chapter 1. This level is fairly abstract, in the sense of its distance from
observed phonetic forms, because it accounts for alternations of the type
we saw in Section 1.1.1 of Chapter 1. For example the underlying vowel /i/

is related to the phonetic diphthong [qɪ] in *sublime* and to the phonetic lax vowel [ɪ] in *sublimity*. In *SPE* and in the approach adopted here, all instances of the diphthong [qɪ] are derived from /i/. Intuitively this diphthong would seem to be something to be included in a catalogue of English sounds, yet it is not included in the list of underlying sounds in English. *SPE* theory specifically denies the existence of any significant level between the systematic phonemic and the systematic phonetic, as in our discussion of Halle's (1959) Russian example in (6) of Chapter 1 and also Chomsky (1964: 72). The theory of Lexical Phonology provides a solution to this problem by providing a lexical level that is the output of the lexical rules and the input to the postlexical rules. This level is not subject to the difficulties that we observed with the taxonomic phonemic level of structuralist phonology. The table in (3) shows the basic characteristics of the four levels we have been discussing. We will introduce some refinements to this scheme in Chapter 6.

(3)

	level	source	characteristics (in English)
a.	underlying (systematic phonemic)	listed underlying representations	no flapping, no glottalization, no diphthongs, no velar nasal, no nasal vowels
b.	lexical	derived from (a) by lexical rules	diphthongs, velar nasal introduced
c.	systematic phonetic	derived from (b) by syntactic concatenation and postlexical rules	glottalization, aspiration, flapping, and vowel nasalization introduced
d.	physical phonetic	derived from (c) by nonlinguistic factors and phonetic implementation	segments no longer discrete, optional deletion of unstressed vowels, etc.

To illustrate this further we show the first three levels of representation for some of the words we have been discussing in (4).

(4)

systematic phonemic	/kæt/	/kænt/	/ɹit + əɹ/	/ɹid + əɹ/	/pɪn/	/sɪng/
lexical	/ˈkæt/	/ˈkænt/	/ˈɹɪɪtəɹ/	/ˈɹɪɪdəɹ/	/ˈpɪn/	/ˈsɪŋ/
systematic phonetic	[ˈkʰæt̚]	[ˈkʰæ̃t̚]	[ˈɹəɪɾəɹ]	[ˈɹɪɪɾəɹ]	[ˈpʰĩn]	[ˈsĩŋ]
	'cat'	'can't'	'writer'	'rider'	'pin'	'sing'

It would be difficult or impossible to catalogue the segments that appear on the physical phonetic level. Actual speech is infinitely varied, and no two utterances are ever exactly alike. It is not difficult to catalogue the segments that appear at the systematic phonetic level. Such a catalogue would be quite detailed and somewhat redundant, and perhaps would not correspond to the native speaker's intuitions as to the sounds of the language. A catalogue of systematic phonemic segments is also useful, but its content depends on fairly complex arguments, which we have deferred until Chapters 6 and 7. With these considerations in mind, it seems best to start with the lexical level. The sounds at this level correspond to native speakers' intuitions as to what are the sounds of the language, which are neither too abstract nor too detailed. This choice also allows us to disregard a certain amount of dialect variation. For example, the segment /t/ is subject to glottalization, aspiration, or flapping in certain contexts, depending on environment and dialect, but we can regard these all as manifestations of the lexical segment /t/. In the next section we present such a catalogue of the consonant segments of English.

2.2   English Consonants

The table in (5) shows the consonants that appear at the lexical level in English, classified in terms of point and manner of articulation.

(5)

	bl		ld		dn		al		pa		pl	ve		gl
	vl	vd	vl	vd	vl	vd	vl	vd	vl	vd	vd	vl	vd	vl
stops	p	b					t	d				k	g	
affricates									ʧ	ʤ				
fricatives			f	v	θ	ð	s	z	ʃ	ʒ				h
nasals		m						n					ŋ	
laterals								l						
approximants		w						ɹ			j			

Key to abbreviations: bl = bilabial, ld = labiodental, dn = dental, al = alveolar, pa = palatoalveolar, pl = palatal, ve = velar. gl = glottal, vl = voiceless, vd = voiced

The symbols are those of the International Phonetic Alphabet. All the consonants in (5) are regarded as 'phonemic' by structuralist analyses of English. Except for [ŋ], they are all also underlying segments. According to our analysis, following *SPE*, [ŋ] is derived by assimilation to a following velar consonant, but a /g/ following [ŋ] is deleted in some cases, such as *sing*, giving the velar nasal the appearance of being a contrastive segment of English.

The velar nasal [ŋ] and the postalveolar fricative [ʒ], which is an underlying segment, have a somewhat restricted distribution. Neither appears initially in native English words. This is sometimes generalized to a claim that these segments are prohibited from syllable-initial position, for example Hammond (1999: 48). This would result in *pleasure* being syllabified [pʰlɛʒ.əɹ] while *pressure* is syllabified [pʰɹɛ.ʃəɹ]. This seems quite wrong; there does not seem to be a difference in the syllabification of these two words; that is, *pleasure* should be syllabified [pʰlɛ.ʒəɹ]. Ordinarily, a single consonant between vowels is syllabified with the following syllable in English, as in most languages. The sole exception in English is [ŋ]; *singer* is probably syllabified [sɪŋ.əɹ]. Therefore the distribution of [ŋ] and [ʒ] is not as similar as it first appears. The reasons are historical. The velar nasal [ŋ] in Old English appeared only before an overt velar consonant and was not a lexical segment at that stage. The assimilation rule that changes [n] to [ŋ] before velars was then a postlexical rule. By modern English the final [g] of words like *sing* had undergone deletion and [ŋ] became a lexical segment; the assimilation rule is now a lexical rule. The source of [ʒ] may also be assimilation and deletion as in *confusion*, derived from *confuse*. Another source is borrowings from French, as in *azure, cortège, rouge, vision*. In word-initial position, such borrowings have [dʒ], as in *general*. The Norman French from which a lot of these words were borrowed had [dʒ] rather than [ʒ] in this position, although modern French does have [ʒ] in words like *général*. However, English speakers have little difficulty learning to pronounce French words like *jour, Georges, général*, where [ʒ] occurs initially. Indeed, English speakers frequently hypercorrect words like *rajah*, and Italian names like *Gigli* [dʒiʎi], substituting [ʒ] for historically correct [dʒ], presumably because it sounds more elegant. By contrast, English speakers have considerable difficulty in pronouncing, for example, the Vietnamese name *Nguyen* with initial [ŋ]. All these considerations point to a very different treatment of the sounds [ʒ] and [ŋ], despite their superficial similarity of distribution. While [ŋ] is always derived and is a lexical but not an underlying segment, [ʒ] is an underlying segment as well as a lexical segment, though in some words it is derived.

We will assume the rules in (6) for deriving [ŋ]. These rules will be somewhat revised in Section 7.4.7 of Chapter 7.

(6)   a.   n → ŋ / _____ $\begin{bmatrix} -\text{son} \\ -\text{ant} \\ -\text{cor} \end{bmatrix}$

(an alveolar nasal becomes velar before a velar stop or /h/)

b.   g → Ø / [+nasal] _____] (g is deleted after a nasal at the end of a constituent)

We defer discussion of the rules for the derivation of [ʒ] in words like *confusion* until Section 7.4.2 of Chapter 7, since the analysis is rather complex. For the moment, however, we will note that /ʒ/ is underlying in words like *azure* and *vision*, where it cannot plausibly be derived by the rules that derive it in other cases.

The glottal stop [ʔ] does not appear in (5), although it appears at the systematic phonetic level. It appears as the realization of /t/ in syllable-final position and before syllabic *n*, as in *cat*, *kitten*. It may also appear before word-initial vowels in emphatic pronunciations, for example, *I want an apple* ['ʔæpl̩], *not a pear*. We consider these pronunciations as resulting from postlexical rules, so that glottal stop is not a lexical segment in English.

In some treatments, two additional segments are added: voiceless glides [w̥] and [j̥]. The first occurs in *which*, in dialects where this is distinct from *witch*; the second occurs in *hue* where this is distinct from *you*. We take the position that these pronunciations are more properly transcribed as [hwɪʧ] and [hju], respectively, with the glides at least partially devoiced phonetically, but that the voiceless glides are not separate single lexical segments.

The dual nature of the affricates [ʧ] and [ʤ] has long been noted, and it has been suggested that affricates can be represented autosegmentally as a sequence of the features [−continuant], [+continuant] linked to a single consonant. Goldsmith (1990: 68ff) argues, however, that this is not parallel to the case of contour tones, which are typically composed of sequences of level tones that exist independently in the language. A language may have an affricate without having the corresponding stop or fricative independently, as in most dialects of Spanish, where there is [ʧ] but no independent phoneme [ʃ]. Other indications of the single-segment status of affricates comes from *phonotactics*, the study of the distribution of segments. English normally does not allow a sequence of stop plus fricative at the beginning of a word, with marginal (all borrowed) exceptions like *tsetse (fly)*. If considered a sequence of stop plus fricative, the affricates would have to be counted as systematic exceptions to this generalization. Some languages, like Polish, do allow such sequences at the beginning of a word, and in fact Polish has minimal contrasts between such sequences and affricates. The word *czy* [ʧɨ] 'whether' contrasts with *trzy* [tʃɨ] 'three.' Acoustic measurements show a considerably longer fricative portion in the stop-fricative sequence than in the affricate (Brooks 1965). Such contrasts are possible in English only at a morpheme boundary, such as *scorching* vs *courtship*. Further evidence comes from backward speech (Cowan et al. 1985). Some speakers can fluently reverse the order of phonemes in a word. When producing a word like *choice* backwards, subjects produced [soɪʧ], not [soɪʃt], showing that they perceive the affricate as a unit.

2.3 Distinctive Features

Ever since Jakobson and Halle (1956), phonology has considered the fundamental unit to be not the segment but the phonological distinctive feature. Early work on phonological features proposed features based on acoustic aspects of speech, but from *SPE* on, the features have been primarily based on articulation, with the one exception of the feature [strident]. We follow *SPE* in assuming that the features are arranged in a matrix with the columns designating segments and the rows labelled with the features, whose order is not significant. First, we will define the features that are required for the analysis of English, based mainly on *SPE*, and then provide an analysis of English segments in terms of these features.[2]

Consonantal: [+consonantal] sounds are produced with a radical constriction in the midsagittal region of the vocal tract; [−consonantal] sounds are produced without such a constriction. The midsagittal region extends along the centre of the mouth from the upper lip to the pharynx. Most English consonants are thus [+consonantal], including the flap [ɾ], but the glottal fricative [h] is [−consonantal] (because the constriction is not in the midsagittal region), and [ɹ], [w], and [j] are [−consonantal] because they have too little constriction. Abbreviated [±cons].

Sonorant: [+sonorant] sounds are produced with a vocal tract configuration in which spontaneous voicing is possible, i.e., with too little constriction to create a significant difference in the air pressure inside and outside the vocal tract; [−sonorant] sounds are produced with a

[2] The feature [distributed] ([dist]), which is nondistinctive in English, but distinguishes some segments introduced postlexically, is defined in Section 5.3.5 of Chapter 5.

vocal tract configuration that inhibits spontaneous voicing, i.e., in which there is some increase in air pressure within the vocal tract. Thus obstruents and [h] are [–sonorant], while nasals, liquids, and [w] and [j] are [+sonorant]. Abbreviated [±son].

Continuant: [+continuant] sounds are produced with an opening in the vocal tract allowing air to pass through the mouth; [–continuant] sounds involve a complete closure in the oral tract. The fricatives, liquids, vowels, [w], [j], and [h] are [+continuant], while the stops, affricates, and nasals are [–continuant]. We classify the flap [ɾ] and the trill [r] as [+continuant] despite their momentary occlusions in the oral tract because these closures are a consequence of a ballistic movement resulting from the airflow through the mouth rather than of the deliberate closing gesture that characterizes stops. We also classify [l] as [+continuant] even though the airflow is along the sides of the mouth rather than along the midsagittal region. Abbreviated [±cont].

Coronal: [+coronal] sounds are produced by raising the blade of the tongue; all other sounds are [–coronal]. Abbreviated [±cor].

Anterior: [+anterior] sounds are produced in front of the postalveolar region of the mouth, that is, forward of the sound [ʃ]. All other sounds are [–anterior]. Abbreviated [±ant].

Strident: [+strident] sounds are acoustically noisy as a result of passing the airstream over a complex path. Only fricatives and affricates can be strident. In English the (inter)dental fricatives [θ] and [ð] are [–strident]; the labiodental fricatives [f], [v], the alveolar [s], [z] and postalveolar [ʃ], [ʒ] fricatives and the affricates [ʧ] and [ʤ] are [+strident]. All sounds other than fricatives and affricates are [–strident]. Abbreviated [±strid].

Nasal: [+nasal] sounds are produced with the velum lowered, allowing airflow through the nose; [–nasal] sounds are produced with the velum raised, closing the nasal cavity. Abbreviated [±nas].

Lateral: [+lateral] sounds are produced with the sides of the tongue lowered to allow airflow along the molar teeth. All other sounds are [–lateral]. Abbreviated [±lat].

Voice: [+voice] sounds are produced with regular vibration of the vocal folds; [–voice] sounds are produced without such vibration. (In the next section we will consider some additional features for glottal states that may supersede [voice].) Abbreviated [±voice].

High: [+high] sounds are produced by raising the body of the tongue above the neutral position, defined as the position of articulation of the vowel [ɛ]; [−high] sounds are produced without such raising of the tongue body. Abbreviated [±high].[3]

Low: [+low] sounds are produced by lowering the body of the tongue below the neutral position; [−low] sounds are produced without such lowering of the tongue body. Because of these definitions no sound can be [+high, +low]; thus the features [high] and [low] define three distinct tongue body heights. Abbreviated [±low].

Back: [+back] sounds are produced by retracting the tongue body behind the neutral position; [−back] sounds are produced without such retraction. Abbreviated [±back].

Round: [+round] sounds are produced with a narrowing of the lip orifice; [−round] sounds are produced without such narrowing. Abbreviated [±round].

ATR: [+ATR] sounds are produced by advancing the tongue root, expanding the pharyngeal cavity; [−ATR] sounds are produced without such advancement. For our purposes we will regard this feature as the equivalent of *SPE*'s [tense], although there is some dispute about this identification. Abbreviated [±ATR].

The table in (7) gives a classification of English consonants in terms of distinctive features. We have omitted features relevant only to vowels. Some of these features are actually redundant, but are included for the sake of completeness.

(7)

	p	b	t	d	k	g	ʧ	ʤ	f	v	θ	ð	s	z	ʃ	ʒ	h	m	n	ŋ	l	ɹ	w	j
consonantal	+	+	+	+	+	+	+	+	+	+	+	+	+	+	+	+	−	+	+	+	+	−	−	−
sonorant	−	−	−	−	−	−	−	−	−	−	−	−	−	−	−	−	−	+	+	+	+	+	+	+
continuant	−	−	−	−	−	−	−	−	+	+	+	+	+	+	+	+	+	−	−	−	+	+	+	+
coronal	−	−	+	+	−	−	+	+	−	−	+	+	+	+	+	+	−	−	+	−	+	+	−	−
anterior	+	+	+	+	−	−	−	−	+	+	+	+	+	+	−	−	−	+	+	−	+	−	−	−
strident	−	−	−	−	−	−	+	+	+	+	−	−	+	+	+	+	−	−	−	−	−	−	−	−
nasal	−	−	−	−	−	−	−	−	−	−	−	−	−	−	−	−	−	+	+	+	−	−	−	−
lateral	−	−	−	−	−	−	−	−	−	−	−	−	−	−	−	−	−	−	−	−	+	−	−	−
voice	−	+	−	+	−	+	−	+	−	+	−	+	−	+	−	+	−	+	+	+	+	+	+	+
back	−	−	−	−	+	+	−	−	−	−	−	−	−	−	−	−	−	−	−	+	−	−	+	−

---

[3] A reader has observed that [e] could be considered [+high] under this definition. We follow *SPE* in regarding both [e] and [ɛ] as [−high, −low], differing only in that [e] is [+ATR] and [ɛ] is [−ATR].

While the feature [voice] is adequate to represent the required contrasts appearing in English at the underlying and lexical levels, there are additional contrasts in laryngeal activities that appear at the systematic phonetic level. We have already discussed aspiration; English voiceless stops may also be pronounced with simultaneous glottal closure when they appear at the end of a syllable, say the [t] at the end of *pot*. The larynx is also responsible for distinctions in tone and voice quality such as breathy voice or creaky voice, which are distinctive in some languages. Halle and Stevens (1971) proposed four features to account for these phenomena: [spread glottis], [constricted glottis], [stiff vocal cords], and [slack vocal cords]. The first two of these features define three classes of sounds, because the vocal folds can be either spread or constricted, or neither spread nor constricted, but cannot be both spread and constricted. Similarly, the third and fourth of these features define three classes, since the vocal folds can be stiff, or slack, or neither stiff nor slack, but not both stiff and slack. Together, these four features define nine classes of laryngeal activity, which are relevant to obstruents, glides, and vowels. We give the complete chart in (8) for reference, but we will only use [+constricted glottis] for glottalized consonants and [+spread glottis] for aspiration. Also we will continue to use [voice] for the voicing contrast, rather than [+stiff vocal folds] (for [–voice]) and [+slack vocal folds] (for [+voice]).[4]

(8)   *Distinctive features for glottal state (Halle & Stevens 1971)*

	1	2	3	4	5	6	7	8	9
obstruents	b₁	b	p	p*	bʰ = ḅ	pʰ	ɓ	ʔb	p'
glides	w, j				ɦ	h, ʍ, j̥	ʔ		ʔ, ʔw, ʔj
vowels	Ṽ (mid tone)	V̀ (low tone)	V́ (high tone)	voiceless vowels ḁ	breathy vowels a̤			creaky voice vowels a̰	glottalized vowels a̰ʔ
spread glottis	−	−	−	+	+	+	−	−	−
constricted glottis	−	−	−	−	−	−	+	+	+
stiff vocal folds	−	−	+	−	−	+	−	−	+
slack vocal folds	−	+	−	−	+	−	−	+	−

---

[4] The symbol b₁ represents a lax voiceless stop, as in Danish. The symbol [p*] ([pₖ] in Halle & Stevens) represents a moderately aspirated stop, as in Korean, where it contrasts with both plain [p] and with fully aspirated [pʰ]. The symbol [ʔ] represents a voiced glottal stop "that appears to be attested in Jinghpo" (Halle & Stevens 1971: 208). The symbol [ʔb] represents a preglottalized [b], for which Halle and Stevens provide no examples.

We regard the distinctive features as *universal*, that is, applicable to all languages. This does not mean that the features proposed here are the only possibility, only that whatever features are ultimately determined are applicable universally. The major application of distinctive features is to express *natural classes* of sounds. Phonological rules typically operate in terms of natural classes of sounds rather than in terms of arbitrary collections of sounds. A natural class is defined as a class of sounds which is described by fewer distinctive features than any single member of the class. If a class is natural, we can omit features that distinguish members of the class and define the class in terms of the features that all the sounds in the class have in common. For example, aspiration in English affects /p/, /t/, /ʧ/, and /k/. An inspection of the table in (7) reveals that these are all and only the sounds with the features [+cons, –son, –cont, –voice], so that this set of features defines the class of segments that undergo aspiration. We can omit some of the features common to the class, such as [–nas], since [–son] segments are all [–nas]. In fact, the features [–cont, –voice] suffice to identify this class. More specifically, we omit the features that differentiate the segments in the class in terms of point of articulation, since voiceless stops and affricates at all points of articulation are affected by the rule.

On the other hand, if we were presented with a class consisting of [p], [ɹ], [s], and [ŋ], we would not be able to describe this set as a natural class. The only feature that these segments have in common is [–lat], but this feature alone describes all the consonants of English except [l], and would not be restricted to just those four segments. Therefore the set {[p], [ɹ], [s], [ŋ]} is not a natural class.

It is sometimes proposed on the contrary that some features may have different definitions in different languages. Thus *SPE* (p. 318) and Gussenhoven and Jacobs (1998: 73) claim that [l] is treated as [–continuant] in Scottish English on the basis of the data in (9) (their transcriptions). The digraphs [ʌi] and [ae] are diphthongs and a period represents a syllable boundary.

(9) *short vowel*   *long vowel*
     including [ʌi] *including [ae]*

nʌin	'nine'	raeð	'writhe'
liθ	'Leith'	tiːz	'tease'
pis	'peace'	lʌːv	'love'
mel	'mail'	tiː	'tea'
mʌil	'mile'	fae.ər	'fire'
rod	'road'	beːʒ	'beige'
hom	'home'	kaːr	'car'

lʌif 'life'   boːr 'boar'
fud 'food'
raʃ 'rash'

It is observed that long vowels appear before voiced fricatives, [r], and vowels, while short vowels appear before other segments, i.e., before nasals, stops, voiceless fricatives, and [l]. Gussenhoven and Jacobs claim that this shows that [l] is [–continuant] here, since it patterns with the stops and nasals. But this is incorrect. It is quite easy to capture the class of sounds before which long vowels occur under the assumption that [l] is [+continuant], namely as [+voice, +continuant, –lateral]. Therefore, this example does not show that [continuant] needs to be defined differently in Scottish English than in other languages, and the universality of features can be maintained.[5]

2.4 English Vowels

Although less numerous than the consonants, the vowels present more difficulties. For one thing, there is much more dialectal variation in the vowels than in the consonants. Another thing is the fact that vowels by their very nature lack a constriction, so it is more difficult to determine their exact articulation.

2.4.1 Short Vowels

The short vowels are the most straightforward. The diagram in (10) gives these, classified in terms of distinctive features. All are [–ATR]. Examples are provided for those vowels which are fairly standard across dialects; or else examples are identified as North American English (NA) or southern British Received Pronunciation (RP), as discussed after the table.

(10)

	–back	+back	
	(–round)	–round	+round
+high –low	bit [ɪ]	[ɨ]	book [ʊ]
–high –low	bet [ɛ]	but [ə]	port [ɔ]
–high +low	bat [æ]	cot [ɑ] (NA)	cot [ɒ] (RP)

[5] See Mielke (2005) for further discussion of the ambiguity of laterals and nasals in terms of the feature [continuant].

These vowels are divided into two groups by the feature [back]. The [–back] vowels are all [–round] while the [+back] vowels are subdivided into a [–round] set and a [+round] set. The vowels are further divided according to height into three groups by the features [high] and [low], the combination [+high, +low] being excluded by the definitions of the features. Unlike some approaches to vowels, we do not recognize a separate category of 'central' vowels, intermediate between back and front vowels, since the binary feature [back] distinguishes just two classes. Unfortunately, the IPA does not provide a symbol for a lax back high nonround vowel. Accordingly, we will use [ɨ] for this purpose.[6] This vowel appears phonetically in some dialects in the adverb *just*, as in *just a minute*. It also appears in underlying representations, for example as the last vowel in *argue*, for reasons that will be discussed in Chapter 7.

We use the symbol [ə] for the vowel of *but*. This may surprise some people who are used to the symbol [ʌ] for this vowel. We reserve the latter for the tense ([+ATR]) counterpart of [ə]. The vowels in (10) are all restricted in their distribution: they cannot appear at the end of a stressed monosyllabic word. No words like those in (10) but with the final consonant removed are possible as stressed words in English, i.e., there are no words such as *[bɪ], *[bɛ], *[bæ], *[bə], or *[bʊ]. This is a consequence of their being short and lax. Since [ə] fits into this pattern, we assume that it too is short and lax. We will also use it as a reduced vowel (see Section 2.4.3).[7] The tense vowel [ʌ] does not figure (mostly) in phonetic representations but is assumed as the underlying vowel in the second syllable of *reduce*, as discussed in Chapter 7.

The vowel [ɔ] appears phonetically in English only before [ɹ], as in *port*. It appears in German as the first (stressed) vowel of *Sonne* 'sun' and in French as the vowel of *cotte* 'overalls.' The vowel appears in underlying representations, but is often converted to other vowels by various rules. The symbol [ɔ] is often used incorrectly to represent a low back tense round vowel, as in *law*, for which we use the symbol [ɒ:] (see Section 2.4.2).[8]

---

[6] We use the symbol [ɨ] for the tense ([+ATR]) counterpart of [ɨ].

[7] Hayes (1995: 12) denies the identification of the stressed vowel of *but* with the unstressed vowel of *sofa*, claiming that [ə] "is shorter, higher, and perceptually less distinct than [ʌ]." Despite these differences, which can be attributed precisely to the difference in stress, the vowels are phonetically similar and in complementary distribution, allowing them to be classed together.

[8] A lot of the confusion surrounding vowel symbols in phonology arises from the way the IPA vowel system is set up. The IPA vowel chart is based on Daniel Jones's (1966) system of cardinal vowels, which recognizes four basic degrees of height. This is difficult to reconcile with the three degrees of height defined phonologically in terms of the features [high] and [low]. This confusion is especially apparent in the symbols for "open-mid" vowels [ɛ] and [ɔ], which are sometimes identified as mid vowels and sometimes as low vowels. We take both of these to represent mid lax vowels.

The vowel [ɑ] occurs in many dialects as the vowel of *bomb*. In other dialects this word has a round vowel: [ɒ]. In both types of dialect a long tense version of the vowel [ɑ], [ɑ:] appears as the vowel of *balm*. We will consider these vowels in Section 2.4.2.

2.4.2   Length and Tenseness

In *SPE*, length and tenseness were completely correlated: all long vowels were tense, and all tense vowels were long; all short vowels were lax, and all lax vowels were short. Therefore one of these characteristics was completely redundant – *SPE* in fact used tenseness for those phonological processes where a distinction of this sort was needed, primarily for Vowel Shift and the assignment of stress. Roughly speaking, in *SPE*, tense vowels attract stress in certain positions of the word, and tense stressed vowels undergo Vowel Shift. Halle (1977), however, proposed that low back vowels could be underlyingly long without being tense. According to Halle's analysis, length is relevant to stress, while tenseness is relevant to Vowel Shift. The vowel in the penultimate syllable of *Chicago*, /ɑ:/ in the underlying representation, is long, and so attracts stress, but is lax, and so fails to undergo Vowel Shift and appears phonetically with the same quality. Phonetically it is tense, but this is because a later rule makes it so, the rule *a/o*-Tensing, given as (34) in Chapter 7, which is ordered after Vowel Shift. Similar remarks apply to the penultimate vowel of *Catawba*, /ɒ:/ in the underlying representation, stressed because it is long but not vowel shifted because it was only tensed by a later rule. The principal diagnostic for Vowel Shift is that the vowel's phonetic height is different from its underlying height; in addition, vowels that undergo Vowel Shift are diphthongized. All this results in a fairly complex system of tense vowels and diphthongs, which can be summarized in the table in (11).

(11)

		−back	+back	
		(−round)	−round	+round
+high −low	bee	[iɪ]		gnu [uw] music [juw]
			[jɨw]	
−high −low	bay	[eɪ]	[ʌw]	doe [ow] boy [oɪ]
−high +low	cow	[æw]	buy [ɑɪ] balm [ɑ:]	law [ɒ:]

The diphthongs (and two triphthongs) are consequences of the rules of Vowel Shift and Diphthongization, details of which will be discussed in Chapter 7. The triphthongs [jɨw] and [juw] result from a further rule of *j*-Insertion, (12) in Chapter 7. The two monophthongs in the back low cells are long and phonetically tense. As discussed previously, these are assumed to be lax in underlying representation, and so they do not undergo Vowel Shift. The triphthong [jɨw] appears in some dialects instead of [juw] in words like *music*. The diphthong [ʌw] is used in RP in words like *doe*, while [ow] is found in the usual pronunciation of these words in North America.

Diphthongs have a kind of dual nature similar to that of affricates as discussed in Section 2.2. While they are phonetically a sequence of two units, they behave as single units phonologically. The clearest evidence for this comes from syllabification, discussed in detail in Chapter 3. To anticipate slightly, the most basic syllable has the form CV, that is a consonant followed by a vowel. Furthermore, in most languages, a sequence ...VCV..., that is, where a single consonant appears between vowels, is syllabified before that consonant, that is, ...V.CV..., where the period indicates the syllable boundary. This is known as the Onset Principle. Now consider a word like *Toyota* in English, borrowed from Japanese. In Japanese, the word is syllabified *To.yo.ta*, following the Onset Principle. But in English the syllabification is clearly *Toy.o.ta*, apparently in violation of the Onset Principle. Similar examples are *hiatus*, *myopic*, *myopia*, *lawyer*, *allowance*. In each case where a diphthong is followed by a vowel, the glide of the diphthong belongs to the diphthong, that is, to the preceding syllable, rather than being an onset to the following syllable. We explain this by claiming that phonetic diphthongs are tense monophthongs in underlying representation. If a tense vowel is followed by another vowel, as in these examples, there is simply no available consonant to serve as an onset to the second vowel at the time syllabification applies, which is quite early in the derivation. After syllabification, stress assignment takes place, and tense vowels undergo Vowel Shift and Diphthongization after that. While Diphthongization supplies a consonant that is a potential onset, the words are not resyllabified, and so the glide remains in the syllable with the preceding vowel.

A second source of evidence for the single-unit status of diphthongs comes from backward speech, already mentioned in connection with affricates. There we pointed out that the word *choice* in backward speech is [soɪʧ]. The diphthong is preserved as such, not reversed.[9] If the

---

[9] The British slang term *yob* may be an exception, if formed by back-slang from *boy*.

diphthong were interpreted as a sequence of two segments, the backward rendition of *choice* would be [sjoʧ]. Finally we can mention the alternations of diphthongs with simple lax vowels, discussed in Section 1.1.1 of Chapter 1. The simplest explanation of these alternations is to assume simple vowels in underlying representation, for example a tense /i/ in *sublime*, which undergoes laxing in the derivative *sublimity* and undergoes Vowel Shift and diphthongization in underived *sublime*. Taken together, these three facts – syllabification, backward speech, and alternations – converge on the preferred analysis of phonetic diphthongs in English as underlying simple vowels.

2.4.3   Vowels in Unstressed Syllables

The vowels discussed to this point are all contrastive in stressed syllables. In unstressed syllables a somewhat smaller set of vowels appears. According to *SPE*, all unstressed lax vowels are realized as [ə], which may vary somewhat in different contexts. We regard this as an oversimplification. There appear to be three lax unstressed vowels, illustrated in (12).

(12)   unstressed lax vowels
        [ə]   sof**a**, **a**ppear, Lenn**o**n
        [ɪ]   **e**xact, Len**i**n, sitt**i**ng
        [ʊ]   m**u**sician

It is evident that we cannot rely on context to supply the phonetic value of these unstressed lax vowels in view of minimal pairs like *Lennon, Lenin*. We will discuss the rules required to produce the different reduced vowels in Section 7.2.3 of Chapter 7. In addition to the cases listed in (12), the unstressed lax vowel [ɪ] occurs in word final position in RP in words like *city* ['sɪtɪ].

Tense vowels may also appear in unstressed syllables. As the final segment in a word, nonlow vowels are tense in North American dialects, so that *city* is [sɪri] in these dialects. Likewise, *window, Hindu* end in phonetically tense vowels. Tense [o] also appears as the unstressed vowel in *obey*, at least in some dialects. The interesting thing about these unstressed tense vowels is that they are tense in phonetic representation but they must be lax in underlying representation. They not only fail to undergo Vowel Shift but they are unstressed. In Chapter 3 we will see a rule that makes tense vowels long as part of the syllabification process. As in Halle's (1977) analysis, we will see in Chapter 4 that long vowels are stressed. This shows that the stress rules and Vowel Shift are ordered before the rules that cause tensing of these vowels in particular environments.

2.4.4 The Underlying Vowel System

This section has been devoted to the lexical vowels of English, after the application of the lexical rules. For comparison we give the underlying vowel system in (13). We have already hinted at the justification for these underlying representations in Section 1.1.1 of Chapter 1, and will argue for them in more detail in Chapters 6 and 7.

(13) The English underlying vowel system

	$\begin{bmatrix} -\text{back} \\ -\text{round} \end{bmatrix}$		$\begin{bmatrix} +\text{back} \\ -\text{round} \end{bmatrix}$		$\begin{bmatrix} +\text{back} \\ +\text{round} \end{bmatrix}$	
	[+ATR]	[–ATR]	[+ATR]	[–ATR]	[+ATR]	[–ATR]
$\begin{bmatrix} +\text{high} \\ -\text{low} \end{bmatrix}$	/i/ divine	/ɪ/ bit, city	/ɨ/ profound	/ɪ̵/ cube, value	/u/ boy	/ʊ/ book
$\begin{bmatrix} -\text{high} \\ -\text{low} \end{bmatrix}$	/e/ serene	/ɛ/ bet	/ʌ/ reduce	/ə/ but, sofa	/o/ shoot, moon	/ɔ/ port, volcano, baud (RP)
$\begin{bmatrix} -\text{high} \\ +\text{low} \end{bmatrix}$	/æ/ sane	/æ/ bat, algebra		/a:/ balm, Chicago, spa	/ɒ/ cone	/ɒ/ bomb /ɒ:/ Catawba

2.4.5 Summary

We have now made a fairly complete catalogue of the lexical segments of English. We may well ask how this set has been determined. While it is similar in some ways to the set of sounds that would be isolated by taxonomic methods, there are important differences. As we have seen, taxonomic methods would wrongly identify nasal vowels as contrastive segments of English. Taxonomic methods might provide a first approximation to the lexical sounds of a language, but this taxonomy needs to be refined by investigating the rules of the language. It is precisely the existence of rules and, in particular, the ordering of those rules, that allows a more sophisticated analysis. Consider the nasal vowels a little more closely. An investigation of the distribution of nasal vowels shows that in a large number of cases they appear before a nasal consonant in phonetic representation. This is a clue that their appearance is a consequence of a rule. Then we observe cases like *can't* [kʰæ̃t] where the nasal consonant is not present phonetically. The taxonomic grammarian takes these cases as showing that nasal vowels contrast with oral vowels. Generative grammar seeks a way of preserving the rule by looking for some regularity behind the skewed distribution of nasal vowels. This is found by observing that nasal vowels contrast superficially with oral vowels only before voiceless obstruents. This gives a clue that there is another rule that operates in the context of voiceless consonants that interacts with the rule of Vowel Nasalization. So the method of investigating phonetic distributions is still valid, but has to be pursued in a more sophisticated way than in taxonomic phonemics.

2.5   Toward Systematic Phonemics

In determining the lexical segments of English, we have essentially made use of the method of contrast, but not mechanically in the manner of taxonomic phonemics. Ultimately the grammar decides: the segments at the lexical level are those that result from the operation of lexical rules. In this we have not considered alternations. When alternations are taken into consideration, we can achieve more abstract underlying representations in accordance with the principle that each morpheme has a single phonological underlying representation (15a in Chapter 1). This allows us to formulate the overall simplest grammar. We determine simplicity by counting the features required to state all the morphemes in their systematic phonemic representation plus the features required to state all the rules. It is simpler to have a phonological rule that predicts the phonetic forms of a large number of morphemes, where each morpheme has a single form, than listing the possible outputs of each morpheme separately. However, where no general rule can be formulated, for example in English verbs like *go, went* or *be, is*, there is no point in giving a rule for a single form; here we resort to listing each form. This is known as *suppletion* or *allomorphy*.

A fairly simple example is given in *SPE* (pp. 11–13). In (14) we give the systematic phonetic representations of three related words, already introduced in Section 1.1 of Chapter 1.

(14)   a.   telegraph   ['tʰɛlɪˌɡɹæf]
        b.   telegraphy   [tʰɪ'lɛɡɹəfi]
        c.   telegraphic   [ˌtʰɛlɪ'ɡɹæfɪk]

The stem *telegraph* appears in three different phonetic shapes. These shapes have a lot of common features but differ in terms of the vowel qualities and the location of stressed syllables. To determine the systematic phonemic, or underlying, representation of this morpheme, we decide which features are predictable and which are unpredictable. The fact that the morpheme begins with a voiceless alveolar stop is unpredictable, since English stems may begin with any consonant (except [ŋ]) or vowel. However, the fact that this stop is aspirated is predictable, as we know from the discussion in Section 1.1 of Chapter 1. Hence, the initial /t/ is part of the underlying representation, but the aspiration is not. The remaining consonants of the stem, /l/, /g/, /ɹ/, /f/, are likewise part of the underlying representation, since these are also not predictable. The vowels show alternations. Here the task is to determine, for each vowel position in the stem, what the underlying vowel should be in that position, from which the observed variants can be derived by rules whose effects are observable in many other forms. We know from Section 2.4 that certain vowels appear only in stressed syllables, among them [ɛ] and [æ]. Other vowels may appear either in stressed or unstressed syllables, among them [ɪ] and [ə]. It is fairly simple to state the rules needed to derive the quality of a vowel in an unstressed syllable if we know the quality that vowel has when stressed, since several stressed vowel qualities converge on a single unstressed quality. It would not be possible to state a rule to give the stressed quality from the unstressed, since there would be no way to choose among the possibilities in any given case. Therefore, we choose underlying vowels from stressed syllables whenever possible. In the case of (14), this implies that the underlying vowels are [ɛ], [ɛ], and [æ] for the three vowels. Putting all this together gives us the underlying representation for *telegraph* in (15).

(15)   /tɛlɛgræf/

It should be noted that this representation does not appear unchanged in any phonetic form, but it does allow us to predict the phonetic representations by means of well-motivated rules, meaning rules whose effects are observable in many other cases. All the segments in the underlying representation appear in at least one of the phonetic manifestations of this morpheme except the initial /t/, which is always aspirated phonetically. A rough outline of the sorts of rules involved is given in (16); the details of the rules will be filled out in the course of the coming chapters. In each case we start with the basic stem, then add any morphological elements, then apply the required phonological rules.

(16)   a. /tɛlɛgɹæf/   b. /tɛlɛgɹæf/   c. /tɛlɛgɹæf/
          Morphology   (none)   /tɛlɛgɹæf + i/ /tɛlɛgɹæf/ + ɪk/
          Stress rules   /ˈtɛlɛˌgɹæf/   /tɛˈlɛgɹæfi/   /ˌtɛlɛˈgɹæfik/
          Vowel Reduction   /ˈtɛlɪˌgɹæf/   /tɪˈlɛgɹəfi/   /ˌtɛlɪˈgɹæfik/
          Aspiration   /ˈtʰɛlɪˌgɹæf/   /tʰɪˈlɛgɹəfi/   /ˌtʰɛlɪˈgɹæfik/
          Systematic phonetic   [ˈtʰɛlɪˌgɹæf]   [tʰɪˈlɛgɹəfi]   [ˌtʰɛlɪˈgɹæfik]

Another example along similar lines is the words in (17a, b), whose stem
has the underlying representation (17c).

(17)   a.   atom   [ˈæɾəm]
          b.   atomic   [əˈtʰɒmɪk]
          c.   /ætɒm/

Here only one segment appears in both of the words (17a, b), the stem-
final [m]. On the basis of the principle of taking vowel qualities from
stressed positions, we arrive at the vowels in the underlying representation
(17c). We establish an underlying /t/ from its phonetic manifestations [ɾ]
and [tʰ] because we know from many other cases that neither of these
phonetic segments is underlying and that both are derived from /t/ under
certain conditions. As in the case of *telegraph*, the underlying /t/ does not
appear in any of the phonetic manifestations of the morpheme *atom*, but is
always either aspirated or flapped in phonetic representation.
      A third case is the three words in (18).

(18)   a.   electric   [ɪˈlɛktɹɪk]
          b.   electricity   [ɪˌlɛkˈtʰɹɪsɪɾi]   suffix: /ɪti/
          c.   electrician   [ɪˌlɛkˈtʰɹɪʃən]   suffix: /jæn/
          d.   /ɪlɛktɹɪk/

Here the /ɹ/ of the stem is devoiced to /ɹ̥/ in all forms; otherwise the
segments of the stem appear unchanged in the underived form. All but the
last segment of the stem are unchanged in the morphologically derived
forms. In Chapter 7 we will motivate a rule, known as Velar Softening,
that converts /k/ to /s/ when it appears before a nonlow front vowel or
glide. This accounts for the [s] in *electricity*. We will also demonstrate the
need for a rule of Palatalization that (among other effects) changes /s/ to /ʃ/
when it is followed by the glide /j/. This rule operates on underlying /s/ in
words like *pressure*, derived from *press*. In *electrician*, we assume that Velar
Softening first converts /k/ to /s/ because it is followed by the glide /j/ of
the suffix /jæn/. Then Palatalization converts this /s/ to [ʃ] because of the
same following glide. (Notice that Palatalization does not apply before the
vowel /ɪ/, so it has no effect in *electricity*.) This is simpler than proposing an

additional rule to convert /k/ to [ʃ] in *electrician*, since both Velar Softening and Palatalization are needed anyway,[10] and both together can account for *electrician* as long as they apply in this order. The glide /j/ is deleted by a later rule, as detailed in Chapter 7. This is one of many examples that show that phonological rules must be ordered, which we already saw in the discussion of Vowel Nasalization, Diphthong Shortening, and Flapping in Section 1.1 of Chapter 1. As we develop more and more rules, we will find again and again that the rules can be stated in the most general way if we assume that they are ordered, and that this ordering is part of the grammar of the language.

In some cases it is not possible to relate alternating forms of a morpheme by independently motivated rules, and we have to give in and admit that the distinct forms are allomorphs, independently listed in the lexicon. For example, nouns can be formed from verbs by the addition of the suffix *-ion*, for which we assume the underlying representation /jən/. Some examples are listed in (19).

(19) | *Verb* | *Noun* |
      |----------|------------|
      | educate | education |
      | rebel | rebellion |
      | revise | revision |

However, we must recognize four more allomorphs of the suffix on the basis of the examples in (20).

(20) a. suffix *-tion* /-t + jən/

reduce	reduction
receive	reception
destroy	destruction

  b. suffix *-ation* /-æt + jən/

realize	realization
form	formation
declare	declaration
evoke	evocation

  c. suffix *-ition* /-ɪt + jən/

repeat	repetition
add	addition
compete	competition
define	definition

---

[10] This is referred to as *independent motivation*. Rules postulated for a single case are referred to as *ad hoc* and are frowned upon.

d.   suffix *-ution* /-ʌt + jən/
     revolve   revolution
     resolve   resolution

There is a morphological uncertainty here – the suffix could simply have a
single underlying representation /jən/, preceded in (20) by a stem
extender, which is itself a meaningless morpheme. But these examples
show that some of the stems need to have allomorphs as well. For example,
there is no way to relate *destroy* and *destruc-* by regular phonological
processes in English. However, the line between allomorphs and alternants
produced by regular phonological rules is not always clear-cut. With *reduce*
and *reduction*, Rubach (1984: 29, fn. 7) claims that allomorphy is needed,
but this is not necessarily the case. The alternation between the stem-final
/s/ of *reduce* and the stem-final /k/ of *reduction* is the same as the
alternation seen in *electric* and *electricity* in (18), and so we might seek to
explain it in the same way. Indeed, *SPE* (p. 147) proposed that a number
of English words have a final /ɛ/ in underlying representation that is
ultimately deleted. This assumption allowed them to derive the stress of
certain words by means of regular rules and filled what would otherwise be
a gap in underlying representations, since otherwise /ɛ/ alone among the
lax vowels would not appear in word-final position.[11] If *reduce* is given the
underlying representation /ɹe + dʌk + ɛ/, its phonetic form follows from
rules needed elsewhere: in particular Velar Softening converts /k/ to /s/ and
subsequently /ɛ/ is deleted. This is essentially the proposal of *SPE* (p. 220).
We can even assume that /ɛ/ is a morpheme that appears at the end of
certain verbs; thus it does not appear in the nominalized form with the
suffix *-tion*. This use of /ɛ/ as a verb-forming suffix is further justified by
pairs like *use* (noun) [juws] and *use* (verb) [juwz]; if the verb is derived
from /ʌs + ɛ/, the voicing of /s/ to /z/ in the verb is a consequence of a rule
of Fricative Voicing, motivated in numerous cases (see Chapter 6).
Therefore we do not need to assume a phonological deletion of /ɛ/ in
reduction, and we also do not need to assume allomorphs, since the
alternation follows from our morphological assumptions and well-
motivated phonological rules.

   SPE (p. 201) gives a phonological account of the alternation in the suffix
-ify, as in *clarify*, which appears as *-ific-* in the nominalized form *clarification*. Assuming the suffix has the underlying representation /-ɪ + fik/,

---

[11] Our assumptions are slightly different in that we account for these apparently irregular stresses in a
different way, but the point remains.

SPE's rule in (21) derives the form of the suffix in *clarify*, and in a few other cases including *multiply* (cf. *multiplication*).

(21)   k → Ø / + C₁i___#

The tense /i/ becomes [ɑɪ] by the normal operation of Vowel Shift in words like *clarify*. However, it is not clear in the *SPE* account how the vowel is laxed in *clarification*. In extending their account to the alternation found in *satisfy, satisfaction*, they invoke an extension of Vowel Shift to certain lax vowels, which they also employ for certain cases of verb ablaut. Thus the phonological account of these alternations requires the ad hoc rule (21) and a number of ad hoc extensions of other rules. We will discuss an alternative account of ablaut verbs in Section 8.1 of Chapter 8, where this phenomenon is considered to be morphological and not simply phonological. Under these circumstances it is preferable to take the alternation seen in *clarify, clarification* and similar pairs as involving allomorphy and not to be accounted for in purely phonological terms. However, the line between allomorphy and phonologically determined alternation is somewhat difficult to draw in such cases. This must be borne in mind in subsequent chapters as we develop phonological analyses of phenomena that some would consider to be cases of allomorphy, and vice versa.

2.6   Phonology and Orthography

It is almost a cliché to refer to the vagaries of English spelling. One sound may have many spellings, for example /iː/ in *we, easy, see, police, people*. Conversely, one letter may correspond to different sounds, as in *woman, women, cone, hot, above, more*. Some sounds are represented by digraphs, that is, two letters, as in *this, thin, see, people, nation, tough*. Some letters represent no sound at all, as in *debt, mate, though, psychology*, though it can be claimed that the two letters <a> and <e> of *mate* together represent the diphthong /eɪ/. George Bernard Shaw (cited in Tauber 1963: xviii) even went so far as to suggest that the word *fish* could be spelled <ghoti> by taking the <gh> of *enough*, the <o> of *women*, and the <ti> of *nation*. Shaw, like many others, was a strong advocate of spelling reform, tending to favour a system that in our terms would correspond more closely to the lexical representation. A moment's reflection suffices to see the invalidity of Shaw's suggestion, because it does not correspond to the regularities of English orthography. The spelling <gh> spells /f/ only at the end of a word or syllable, as in *enough* or *laughter*, while at the beginning of a word it can only represent /g/, as in *ghost* or *ghetto*. The letter <o> corresponds to /ɪ/ only in the single word *women*, and <ti> can spell /ʃ/ only when it is followed by another vowel and not preceded by /s/, as in *nation, partial*. Essentially, English spelling is an alphabetic system with certain idiosyncrasies. We regard a writing system as alphabetic when its individual symbols in general correspond to segmental units. In other writing systems the individual symbols represent larger units such as a mora or a syllable, as we will discuss in Chapter 3.

Although there have been many suggestions for reforms to English spelling, none has taken hold. It cannot be pure conservatism that is responsible for this, as many other languages periodically revise their spelling systems, though usually not very drastically. *SPE* suggests that the reason for this is that English spelling corresponds to the systematic phonemic level, idiosyncrasies aside. They go so far as to say that "conventional orthography is. . .a near optimal system for the lexical representation of English words" (p. 49). The examples in the preceding section illustrate this rather well. Despite differences in stress and vowel quality among the words *telegraph, telegraphy, telegraphic*, the morpheme *telegraph* has the same spelling in each. Likewise the letter <c> has three distinct pronunciations in the words *electric, electricity, electrician*, but corresponds to the same systematic phoneme in each case. We spell *atom* the same way in *atom* and *atomic*, although the letters <a>, <t>, and <o> correspond to quite different sounds in the two words. Similarly, examples in (17) in Chapter 1 show alternations of a diphthong, for example [eɪ] in *sane*, with a monophthong, [æ] in *sanity*, where both are spelled with the letter <a>. Other examples that will appear in the course of the discussion are such pairs as *express, expression; supervise, supervision; perpetual, perpetuity; artificial, artificiality; react, reaction; medicine, medication*. In each case we will discuss the rules required for the alternation, but for now we note that common morphemes tend to have a common spelling even though the pronunciation may vary.

2.7   Exercises

2.1   Transcription

   Transcribe the following words at the systematic phonetic level, following your own pronunciation and/or that of a friend. Include indications for stress (primary and secondary), aspiration, and other features of this level. If you are unsure of a word, transcribe your best guess of its pronunciation before consulting a dictionary; remember that the dictionary may use a different transcription system from that used here. Save the results for further exercises in Chapters 3 and 4.

appliance	salicylate	seismology
amalgam	salmagundi	sclerenchyma
paraphernalia	nutmeg	interpolate
Menomini	academy	Conestoga
helicopter	devastate	palindrome
significant	broccoli	granite
shenanigan	mulligatawny	

2.2 More Transcription
Repeat exercise 2.1 using

a. your name
b. your birthplace
c. your favourite singer, actor, or other person

2.3 Distinctive Features
Each of the following classes of sounds is involved in a phonological rule of English that we will encounter in later chapters. Express each as a natural class in terms of distinctive features, using the minimal number of features necessary in each case.

a. {f, s, θ}
b. {k, g }
c. {b, g }
d. {p, t, ʧ, k}

2.4 Underlying Representations on the Basis of Alternations

a. On the basis of the alternations in the forms of the stems, determine the underlying representation of each stem and the phonological rules required to produce the given phonetic representations. For the purpose of this exercise, the stress rule can be stated simply as "stress the penultimate syllable." In addition, the last five forms in the right column have secondary stress on the first syllable. We will develop more adequate stress rules in Chapter 4. Three additional rules are required besides the stress rule(s).

atom	[ˈæɾəm]	atomic	[əˈtʰɒ̃mɪk]
metal	[ˈmɛɾəl]	metallic	[mɪˈtʰælɪk]
symbol	[ˈsĩmbəl]	symbolic	[ˌsĩmˈbɒlɪk]
organ	[ˈɔɹɡə̃n]	organic	[ˌɔɹˈgænɪk]
vocal	[ˈvowkəl]	vocalic	[ˌvowˈkʰælɪk]
magnet	[ˈmæɡnɪt]	magnetic	[ˌmæɡˈnɛɾɪk]
totem	[ˈtʰowɾĩm]	totemic	[ˌtʰowˈtʰẽmɪk]

b. Determine the underlying representation of the plural suffix and the rules required to determine the phonetic representation of the plural forms. Express the rules in terms of natural classes using distinctive features.

singular		*plural*	
cow	[ˈkʰæw]	cows	[ˈkʰæwz]
hen	[ˈhẽn]	hens	[ˈhẽnz]
dog	[ˈdɒg]	dogs	[ˈdɒgz]
chicken	[ˈʧɪkĩn]	chickens	[ˈʧɪkĩnz]
pig	[ˈpʰɪg]	pigs	[ˈpʰɪgz]
scythe	[ˈsɑɪð]	scythes	[ˈsɑɪðz]
cat	[ˈkʰæt’]	cats	[ˈkʰæt’s]
duck	[ˈdək’]	ducks	[ˈdək’s]
cuff	[ˈkʰəf]	cuffs	[ˈkʰəfs]
drip	[ˈdɹɪp’]	drips	[ˈdɹɪp’s]
horse	[ˈhɔɹs]	horses	[ˈhɔɹsɪz]
bus	[ˈbəs]	buses	[ˈbəsɪz]
wish	[ˈwɪʃ]	wishes	[ˈwɪʃɪz]
buzz	[ˈbəz]	buzzes	[ˈbəzɪz]
rouge	[ˈɹuwʒ]	rouges	[ˈɹuwʒɪz]
ostrich	[ˈɒstɹɪʧ]	ostriches	[ˈɒstɹɪʧɪz]
hedge	[ˈhɛʤ]	hedges	[ˈhɛʤɪz]

CHAPTER 3

Syllables and Moras

3.1 Syllables and Moras

The syllable is both a traditional and a popularly known element of
linguistic structure. A speaker of English can tell with no difficulty how
many syllables there are in a word, as in the examples of (1).

(1) a. cat   one syllable
     b. marmot   two syllables
     c. elephant   three syllables
     d. rhinoceros   four syllables
     e. hippopotamus   five syllables

It is more difficult to count the segments in a word. It's easy enough to
see three segments in *cat*, but less easy to see that there are five (or six, if *r*
is pronounced) in *marmot*, seven segments in *elephant*, nine in *rhinoceros*
(counting the diphthong as one, as we suggested in Chapter 2), and
eleven in *hippopotamus*. The syllable is familiar as a unit of poetry; for
example, the iambic pentameter line of Shakespeare consists of ten
syllables, frequently alternating in stress. But, for all its familiarity, the
syllable is particularly difficult to define adequately. For example,
Haugen (1956: 213) says, "[w]hile sooner or later everyone finds it
convenient to use, no one does much about defining it." And Pulgram
(1970: 11) notes that "the syllable has been employed in synchronic and
diachronic investigations without being defined—on the assumption, it
seems, that everyone knows what it is. Everyone does not know." In what
follows we will give an operational definition of the syllable; that is,
provide a procedure by which the syllabification of any English word can
be determined.

The examples in (1) illustrate syllables of varying degrees of complexity.
The simplest syllable is one that has the form CV, that is, a consonant
followed by a vowel. Every syllable requires a vowel, or a segment that can

79

function as the syllable peak, which includes consonants in certain languages, but a syllable consisting of just V is not the simplest form of a syllable. A sequence of CV syllables, as in *hippopotamus* (disregarding the final *s*), presents a rhythmic rise and fall in sonority, with the vowels as sonority peaks and the consonants as sonority valleys. Therefore, there is some preference for a CV syllable, as opposed to just V. This has been called the Onset Principle, which Itô (1989: 223) states as in (2).

(2)   Onset Principle
        Avoid [$_\sigma$ V   (i.e., avoid a syllable that begins with a vowel)

In fact, we will go beyond the Onset Principle and claim that syllables not only preferably have onsets, but that onsets are maximized, within the limits of permissible onset clusters in a given language.

The mora is also a traditional unit, perhaps not as intuitively clear as the syllable. McCawley (1968: 58, fn. 39) defines the mora as "something of which a long syllable consists of two and a short syllable consists of one." As with the syllable, we will define the mora operationally in that our procedure for syllabification will also provide moras. In line with current (and traditional) usage, we will speak of heavy syllables (rather than long) and light syllables (rather than short), reserving the terms "long" and "short" for vowels. Some poetic traditions are based on the mora, rather than on the syllable. A Japanese Haiku poem contains three lines of five, seven, and five moras, in that order. In the example in (3), from Miyamori (1932: 264), the syllables are marked by periods and long vowels are marked by a macron. The first line, though containing only three syllables, contains five moras, because the first syllable ends in a nasal, giving it two moras, and the second syllable has a long vowel, which also counts two moras.

(3)   Tom.bō ya
        Ku.ru.i-ši.zu.ma.ru
        Mi.ka no tsu.ki

        'On the rise of a crescent moon
        The dragonflies ceased their mad flight.'

Latin and Greek poetic metres have different forms, one of which is known as dactylic hexameter, where each line contains six dactylic feet. A dactylic foot consists of a heavy syllable followed by two light syllables. In most positions in the verse an equivalent foot containing two heavy syllables is permitted; the last foot of a verse in fact must have two syllables, where the first must be heavy. In general, then, in this type of verse, a heavy syllable (two moras) is equivalent to two light syllables (one mora each). The example in (4) is the opening line of Lucretius' *De rerum natura (Of the Nature of Things)*. The first line is orthographic (with long vowels indicated by macrons), the second line is a phonetic transcription, with the poetic feet set off by brackets and syllabification indicated by periods.

(4)   Aeneadum genetrīx, hominum dīvomque voluptās   (orthographic)
        [aɪ.nɛ.ɑ][dʊm.gɛ.nɛ][tri:ks.hɔ.mɪ][nʊm.di:][wɔm.kʷɛ.wɔ][lʊp.tɑ:s]
        'Mother of the Romans, delight of gods and men'

Some evidence for the mora as a linguistic unit comes from writing systems. Besides alphabetic writing systems like English there are logographic writing systems, where each symbol represents a word or a morpheme, of which Chinese is the best known example, and syllabic writing systems, where each symbol represents a syllable. Actually, it turns out that most of the writing systems that are called 'syllabic' are actually moraic in nature. The Japanese kana syllabaries are a case in point. Japanese writing is a complicated combination of logographic, using Chinese logographs for word roots, and moraic, using kana symbols for grammatical suffixes, foreign words, and other purposes. As we saw in the discussion of Japanese Haiku, Japanese syllables may be heavy (two moras) or light (one mora). A light syllable is represented by a single symbol in the kana. A heavy syllable requires two symbols. Heavy syllables are rather restricted in Japanese. Such a syllable may have a long vowel or a short vowel followed by a consonant, but not just any consonant. The consonant must be either a copy of a following consonant or a nasal homorganic with a following consonant. To show a coda consonant that geminates a following onset, the hiragana syllabary writes a small version of the symbol for *tsu* (つ); thus *kitte* 'stamp' might be written きって in hiragana. A long vowel is indicated by writing the appropriate vowel symbol after the symbol for the initial CV, thus きいと for *kīto* 'raw silk' in hiragana. There is a special symbol to represent the coda nasal, as in ほん for *hon* 'book.'[1] Thus each mora essentially has its own symbol in the kana, making it a basically moraic system. The hiragana symbols are shown in (5).

---

[1] These words would ordinarily be written in kanji, but can be written in kana, and illustrate the principles of this moraic writing system. I am indebted to the late Phil Hauptman for discussion of the Japanese data.

(5)

V	あ	a	い	i	う	u	え	e	お	o
kV	か	ka	き	ki	く	ku	け	ke	こ	ko
sV	さ	sa	し	ši	す	su	せ	se	そ	so
tV	た	ta	ち	či	つ	tsu	て	te	と	to
nV	な	na	に	ni	ぬ	nu	ね	ne	の	no
hV	は	ha	ひ	hi	ふ	fu	へ	he	ほ	ho
mV	ま	ma	み	mi	む	mu	め	me	も	mo
jV	や	ja			ゆ	ju			よ	jo
rV	ら	ra	り	ri	る	ru	れ	re	ろ	ro
	わ	wa	ゐ	wi			ゑ	we	を	wo
	ん	n								
gV	が	ga	ぎ	gi	ぐ	gu	げ	ge	ご	go
zV	ざ	za	じ	ji	ず	zu	ぜ	ze	ぞ	zo
dV	だ	da	ぢ	ji	づ	dzu	で	de	ど	do
bV	ば	ba	び	bi	ぶ	bu	べ	be	ぼ	bo
pV	ぱ	pa	ぴ	pi	ぷ	pu	ぺ	pe	ぽ	po
kyV	きゃ	kja			きゅ	kju			きょ	kjo
ʃV	しゃ	ʃa			しゅ	ʃu			しょ	ʃo
ʧV	ちゃ	ʧa			ちゅ	ʧu			ちょ	ʧo
njV	にゃ	nja			にゅ	nju			にょ	njo
hjV	ひゃ	hja			ひゅ	hju			ひょ	hjo
mjV	みゃ	mja			みゅ	mju			みょ	mjo
rjV	りゃ	rja			りゅ	rju			りょ	rjo
gjV	ぎゃ	gja			ぎゅ	gju			ぎょ	gjo
ʤV	じゃ	ʤa			じゅ	ʤu			じょ	ʤo
bjV	びゃ	bja			びゅ	bju			びょ	bjo
pjV	ぴゃ	pja			ぴゅ	pju			ぴょ	pjo

3.2 The Syllable in *SPE*

SPE did not employ the concepts of syllables and moras. In the linear system of phonological representation some other way is needed to represent the distinction of heavy and light syllables, which plays an important role in stress assignment in English. *SPE* did this with the notion of the "weak cluster." A weak cluster is defined as a linear string of the form in (6).[2]

(6) $\begin{bmatrix} -\text{tense} \\ V \end{bmatrix} C_0^1 (\begin{bmatrix} \alpha voc \\ \alpha cons \\ -ant \end{bmatrix})$

The feature system in (6) differs somewhat from ours, as introduced in Chapter 2. In particular, [vocalic] is a feature whose positive value includes vowels and liquids and whose negative value includes glides, nasal consonants, and obstruents. The Greek letter α in (6) indicates that the features [vocalic] and [consonantal] have the same value; that is, that they are either both plus or both minus. Thus the matrix at the end of (6) means a segment which is [–anterior] and which has the same value for [vocalic] and [consonantal] – glides and [ɹ].[3] This configuration forms part of the environment for the Main Stress Rule of *SPE*, which we state in (7).[4] The variable X stands for any string, the subscript A marks an adjective constituent, and + indicates a morpheme boundary.

(7) $V \rightarrow [\text{1 stress}] / [X\_\_\_C_0 (\begin{bmatrix} -\text{ATR} \\ V \end{bmatrix} C_0^1 (\begin{bmatrix} \alpha voc \\ \alpha cons \\ -ant \end{bmatrix})) + C_0 \begin{bmatrix} -\text{ATR} \\ V \end{bmatrix} C_0]_A$

This rule is intended to account for the primary stress of the adjectives in (8).[5]

(8)
I	II	III
pérsonal	anecdótal	dialéctal
máximal	adjectíval	incidéntal
medícinal	polyhédral	univérsal
ephémeral	mediaéval	abýsmal
vértebral		

---

[2] The *SPE* feature [±vocalic], which we don't use in this book, is discussed in Section 3.4.4.

[3] In *SPE* the last term in the definition of weak cluster (p. 83) appears with a subscript zero, which means there can be zero or more such terms. This appears to be an error, since in reality at most one such term can appear in a weak cluster. We have therefore put the term in parentheses, indicating optional presence.

[4] This presentation of part of the *SPE* stress system is necessarily simplified, since we will develop quite a different metrical treatment of stress in Chapter 4. Despite the complexity of (7), this is only one subcase of *SPE*'s Main Stress Rule. In (7) we have replaced *SPE*'s feature [tense] with [ATR], but we retain their feature [vocalic]. In fact the class of glides and [ɹ] can be expressed in the features introduced in Chapter 2 as [–consonantal, +sonorant], which, however, also includes vowels.

[5] An exception is *házardous*, with stress two syllables before the suffix despite the strong cluster before the suffix.

magnánimous	desírous	moméntous
polýgamous	polyhédrous	polyándrous
chívalrous		
lúdicrous		

vígilant	complaísant	repúgnant
signíficant	clairvoýant	obsérvant
recálcitrant		

díffident	antecédent	depéndent
benévolent	inhérent	contíngent
éloquent		

In *SPE*, phonological rules apply when the structural description of the rule is a submatrix of the form under consideration for application.[6] If we match elements of the rule in (7) to a form from column I of (8), for example *personal*, we obtain the display in (9). Because the weak cluster (6) is in parentheses in the structural description of rule (7), it may either be present or absent. The *SPE* convention on the interpretation of parentheses requires that the rule first be tried with the parenthesized material present, and if the rule can apply that way, then the possibility without the parenthesized material is skipped. Only if the longer expansion, containing the parenthesized material, is unable to apply is the shorter expansion, without this material, tried for application.

(9)   Structural $[\![$ X   V C_0 $\begin{bmatrix} -\text{ATR} \\ V \end{bmatrix}$ C_0^i $\left(\begin{bmatrix} \alpha\text{voc} \\ \alpha\text{cons} \\ -\text{ant} \end{bmatrix}\right)$ + C_0 $\begin{bmatrix} -\text{ATR} \\ V \end{bmatrix}$ C_0 $]\!]_A$
      description
      of (7)

      $[\![$ p   e   rs   o   n $\emptyset$ + $\emptyset$ a   l $]\!]_A$
Structural   [1 stress]
change

The box in the structural description in (9) encloses the weak cluster, which can be matched to the string *on* in the adjective *personal*. The final matrix of this weak cluster is itself in parentheses, and so it can be matched with nothing in the form under consideration. This term finds a match in the liquid *r* when the rule is tested for application to *ludicrous*, as shown in (10).

---

[6] See Stanley (1967: 413). A matrix M is a submatrix of N if, whenever M has a specification, + or −, in a given position, N has the same specification in the corresponding position (but not necessarily the converse). *SPE* (p. 337) claims that a rule applies to strings which are nondistinct from its structural description. This definition has the same effect, as long as additional material is admitted before and after the elements specified in the rule's structural description, as implied by the ellipses (. . .) before and after the string under consideration for the application of the rule in *SPE*'s definition. Since a rule generally does not contain as many units in its structural description as the items to which it is applicable, the submatrix interpretation is preferable.

(10) Structural description of (7)

$$[\ X \quad V \quad C_o \quad \begin{bmatrix} -\text{ATR} \\ V \end{bmatrix} \quad C_o^! \quad \left(\begin{bmatrix} \alpha\text{voc} \\ \alpha\text{cons} \\ -\text{ant} \end{bmatrix}\right) \quad + \quad C_o \quad \begin{bmatrix} -\text{ATR} \\ V \end{bmatrix} \quad C_o \quad]_A$$

Structural change

[l	u	d	i	c	r	+	Ø	ou	s	]_A
[1 stress]										

However, such a match is impossible with the adjectives of columns II and III. The diagram in (11) illustrates the attempt to match forms from these two columns with the longer expansion of rule (7). The heavy outline shows the failed match in each case.

(11) Structural description of (7)

$$[\ X \quad V \quad C_o \quad \begin{bmatrix} -\text{ATR} \\ V \end{bmatrix} \quad C_o^! \quad \left(\begin{bmatrix} \alpha\text{voc} \\ \alpha\text{cons} \\ -\text{ant} \end{bmatrix}\right) \quad + \quad C_o \quad \begin{bmatrix} -\text{ATR} \\ V \end{bmatrix} \quad C_o \quad]_A$$

[an	e	cd	o [+ATR]	t	Ø	+	Ø	a	l	]_A
[di	a	l	e	c	t $\begin{bmatrix} -\text{voc} \\ +\text{cons} \end{bmatrix}$	+	Ø	a	l	]_A

In column II the forms have a tense ([+ATR]) vowel in the position that requires a lax vowel. In column III the forms have a sequence of two consonants where the second is neither a glide nor [ɪ]. Under these conditions, when the long expansion of the rule cannot be matched to the form, the parenthesized material is omitted and the match is tried again. The results are shown in (12) for *anecdotal* and in (13) for *dialectal*. Recall that the variable X stands for any string.

(12) Structural description of (7)

$$[\ X \quad V \quad C_o \quad + \quad C_o \quad \begin{bmatrix} -\text{ATR} \\ V \end{bmatrix} \quad C_o \quad]_A$$

Structural change

[anecd	o	t	+	Ø	a	l	]_A
[1 stress]							

Here the term V in the structural description is any vowel, not restricted in terms of tenseness, and so can be matched to the [+ATR] vowel spelled *o* in *anecdotal*.

(13) Structural description of (7)

$$[\ X \quad V \quad C_o \quad + \quad C_o \quad \begin{bmatrix} -\text{ATR} \\ V \end{bmatrix} \quad C_o \quad]_A$$

Structural change

[dial	e	ct	+	Ø	a	l	]_A
[1 stress]							

Here the term C_0 can be matched to any string of consonants and so can be matched to *ct* of *dialectal*.

This discussion shows that defining a weak cluster for the purpose of stress assignment in English in terms of the linear string is quite complex. In fact, the weak cluster as in (6) appears not only in the Main Stress Rule of *SPE* but also in two additional rules. Chomsky and Halle note that "this repetition indicates that we have failed to capture important properties of strong and weak clusters and thus points to a defect in our theory that merits further attention" (*SPE*: 241, fn. 3). Clearly, proceeding in this manner is similar to accounting for vowel shift by directly relating pairs of alternating segments such as [ɪ] and [aɪ], resulting in fairly complex statements (cf. Section 1.1.1 of Chapter 1). The description of these alternations can be greatly simplified by separating the statements that govern the distribution of tense and lax vowels (expressed as tensing and laxing rules in various environments) from the rules that express the phonetic realization of the tense vowels, as argued in Section 1.1.1 of Chapter 1. Similarly, separating syllable structure from rules of stress assignment allows considerable simplification of the rules that account for these aspects of phonological structure. The definition of a weak cluster requires a lax vowel followed by at most one consonant, optionally followed by a glide or [ɹ]; that is, a lax vowel followed by a cluster that can begin a syllable in English. As we will show in detail in Section 3.4, syllable onsets are maximized if there is any ambiguity as to the division of consonants between syllables. The words in column I of (8), where stress falls on the antepenultimate syllable (that is, the third from the end) have light syllables in penultimate position (second from last); i.e., the penultimate syllable ends in a lax vowel. Thus *per.so.nal, ver.te.bral, lu.di.crous, e. lo.quent* are syllabified as shown, where the period indicates the syllable boundaries. The stress rule can skip a light syllable in this case, and so the stress falls on the syllable before. When the penultimate syllable is heavy, either because it contains a tense vowel, as in column II of (8), or because it ends in a consonant, as in column III, this syllable cannot be skipped and so is stressed. This is the case with *a.nec.do.tal* and *di.a.lec.tal*, respectively.[7]

---

[7] The syllabic account encounters problems in two cases where *SPE* fares better. One is *chi.val.rous*, syllabified as shown, where the stress is antepenultimate despite the penultimate being heavy. Note that the sequence *alr* meets *SPE*'s definition of a weak cluster. The second involves more complex clusters, as in *or.che.stral*. Here, the principle that onsets are maximized gives the syllabification shown, where *str* constitutes the syllable onset since this cluster appears initially in such words as *strike*. Nevertheless, *orchéstral* is stressed on the (light) penultimate syllable. (But compare *órchestra*, regular in syllabic terms, but irregular in the *SPE* treatment.)

3.3 Other Early Approaches to the Syllable

3.3.1 The Syllable Boundary Approach

The simplest approach to the syllable is to insert syllable boundaries into a string of segments and syntactic boundaries of *SPE*. This approach is therefore still linear. Hooper (1972), for example, observes that certain rules of Spanish are more concisely and more insightfully stated in terms of strings that contain syllable boundaries. Consider the examples in (14).

(14)   *assimilation*   *no assimilation*

within   ámbar ['ɑmbɑɾ] 'amber'   muevo ['mweβo] 'I move'
words   ancho ['ɑn̠ʧo] 'width'   nieto ['njeto] 'grandson'
                banco ['bɑŋko] 'bank'   nuevo ['nweβo] 'new'
                                                miel ['mjel] 'honey'

across   un beso [um'beso] 'a kiss'
word   un charco [uɲ'ʧɑrko] 'a pool'
boundaries   un gato [uŋ'gɑto] 'a cat'
                un huevo [uŋ'weβo] 'an egg'
                un hielo [uɲ'jelo] 'an ice'

Harris (1969) found that nasals assimilate before obstruents in the same word or across word boundaries, but that nasals assimilate before glides only across word boundaries. Without syllable boundaries, Harris was unable to provide a single rule for this phenomenon. With syllable boundaries, Hooper writes a single rule that assimilates a nasal to a following consonant (obstruent or glide) only if a syllable boundary intervenes. The cases in (14) where no assimilation takes place have the nasal and the following glide in the same syllable, whereas, where assimilation takes place, there is always a syllable boundary after the nasal.

While English speakers have no difficulty in determining the number of syllables in words like those in (1), there may be some hesitation as to where the boundaries are between the syllables. Is the first syllable of *elephant* *e* or *el*? Most dictionaries (e.g., *American Heritage* 1969 and *Collins* 1979) give it as *el*, but the Onset Principle (2) fixes it as *e*, in order that the second syllable can have an onset. Even when the Onset Principle is not at issue, there can be various possibilities consistent with the constraints on onsets and codas within a syllable; for example, *extra* could be syllabified *ek.stra*, *eks.tra*, or *ekst.ra*. The decision can be based on the segmental effects that syllabification may have, for example, on the allophonic properties of segments. Hoard (1971), for example, proposes rules for English that insert syllable boundaries at word boundaries and within words depending on the position of stress. Before a stressed vowel, his rules insert a syllable boundary before the maximal cluster that can form a syllable onset preceding that vowel. Before an unstressed vowel, his rules insert a syllable boundary immediately before the vowel, regardless of the number or type of consonants intervening. This, rather implausibly, results in the syllabification *extr.a*, even though [kstɪ] is not a possible syllable coda. The Onset Principle would require that at least one consonant be syllabified with the second syllable, ruling out Hoard's syllabification. Kiparsky (1979) proposes that, in such cases, the onset of the second syllable is maximized at the expense of the coda of the first syllable, thereby fixing the syllabification *ek.stra*. This is a stronger version of the Onset Principle, which we will refer to as *Onset Maximization*.

Hoard proposes further rules that refer to syllable boundaries, dealing with such matters as aspiration, assimilation, and vowel length. These rules give reasonably accurate results as far as they go, but these matters are not necessarily best treated in terms of syllable structure. As discussed in Kiparsky (1979), many of these phenomena receive better formulations in terms of foot structure, and we will follow Nespor and Vogel (1986) in using higher prosodic categories in dealing with some of these facts (see Chapter 5). Naturally, such explanations are not available within a linear theory, even augmented with syllable boundaries.

3.3.2   The Autosegmental Approach

Kahn (1976) proposed an autosegmental theory of the syllable. However, this is not really an appropriate use of autosegmental formalism, inasmuch as syllable structure is an organization of segmental units rather than a representation of certain segmental properties (such as tone) on an independent phonological tier. At the same time, it breaks away from the linear treatments of *SPE* and the syllable boundary approach. It still retains the feature [syllabic] – his rules first associate a syllable to a segment with the feature [+syllabic]. Nonsyllabic segments to the left of a syllabic segment are next associated with the same syllable up to the maximal onset clusters permitted in the language. Finally, the rules associate leftover consonants to the syllable on the left. The chief difference between the linear treatment and that of Kahn lies in the autosegmental possibility of one-to-many association, so that not only can a syllable be linked to more than one segment but also a segment can be linked to more than one syllable. Kahn argues extensively for such *ambisyllabicity* in accounting for phenomena such as flapping. He gives representations of words like *butter* as in (15) (our symbols).

(15)

σ σ
/\ /\

b ə ɾ ə ɪ

When the full range of facts is considered, Kahn's approach is unable to account for all types of stop allophony. One case where it fails is in words like *Mediterranean*, where the [t] at the start of the third syllable is aspirated, even though it is in the environment for flapping according to Kahn's rules. We will show in Chapter 5 that the full range of facts concerning stop allophony can be predicted in terms of prosodic structure and that ambisyllabicity can be entirely dispensed with (cf. Jensen 2000).

A more elaborate autosegmental approach appears in Clements and Keyser (1983), which employs three tiers. We give their representation of *Jennifer* in (16).

(16)

σ σ σ
/\ /\ /\
C V C V C V C
| | | | | \/
dʒ ɛ n ɪ f ɹ

This representation not only makes the [n] and [f] ambisyllabic but links the final [ɹ] to both a V and a C, giving it the character of both a syllabic sonorant and a syllable coda. This theory can dispense with the feature [syllabic], partly encoding this in terms of the CV tier. Clements and Keyser argue extensively for this independence of the CV tier, which does not simply mirror the intuitive sense of consonants and vowels. In fact, they use this tier as a kind of diacritic to express what might otherwise be considered irregularities. In Turkish, for example, the dative suffix has an initial [j] when it follows a vowel-final stem (17a) and no [j] when it follows a consonant-final stem (17b). Some stems that end in a long vowel in the uninflected form have [j] in the dative (17c), while others have no [j] (17d).

(17)

		nominative	*plural*	*dative*
a.	'room'	oda	odalar	odaja
b.	'stalk'	sap	saplar	sapa
c.	'la (music)'	la:	la:lar	la:ja
d.	'mountain'	da:	da:lar	daa

Clements and Keyser propose that the choice of dative suffix is sensitive to the CV tier, not to the segmental tier. Because 'mountain' appears to act like a consonant-final stem, they represent the stem as ending in C (18a). This C functions as an unpronounced onset of the second syllable in the dative *daa*; in the nominative it is associated to the preceding vowel, yielding a long vowel *da:*. For 'la,' the musical note, they give it the representation (18b), ending in V on the CV tier, and so taking the dative form associated with other vowel-final forms like 'room.'

(18)   a. 'mountain'   b. 'la'

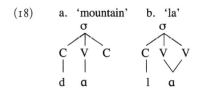

That is, forms which are segmentally similar may differ on the CV tier, and this influences their phonological behaviour. We note in passing that 'mountain' in Turkish spelling is *dağ*, with a final unpronounced consonant that here, as often, symbolizes a lengthening of the preceding vowel. This use of C as a diacritic for an irregularity is suspect, though.

Although we will use a moraic rather than an autosegmental approach, we will make some use of autosegmental formalism in Section 3.3.4. A single consonant can be linked to both a final mora of one syllable and the initial mora of the following syllable if the consonant is phonetically geminate, as in the Japanese *kitte* 'stamp' (22). We will also allow a single vowel melody to link to both moras of the same syllable, thus expressing a long vowel, as in the Japanese *sensee* 'teacher' (23).

3.3.3   The Constituent Structure Approach

This approach uses constituent structures analogous to those in syntax. The syllable is divided initially into two parts, the onset and the rhyme, with the rhyme in turn divided into a peak and a coda. This is illustrated in (19).

(19)

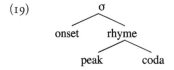

The syllable peak is the vowel or diphthong. The rhyme is relevant to stress assignment in many languages, including English. The *SPE* notion of weak cluster can be expressed in this approach as a syllable with a simple, i.e., nonbranching, rhyme (that is, there is no coda) and whose peak is also nonbranching (i.e., contains a short, lax vowel). We call this a light syllable. A heavy syllable is one whose rhyme contains a branching structure; that is, either the rhyme branches into peak and coda, or the peak branches (that is, contains two syllabic positions, representing a long vowel or diphthong). These characterizations are still somewhat complex, however. We will see that the moraic approach allows this to be further simplified, in that a heavy syllable is one which branches into two moras, and a light syllable is one that does not branch and contains only a single mora. The rhyme is also a unit of poetry in English and other languages. In English, two monosyllabic words rhyme if their rhymes, in the syllable structure sense discussed above, are identical, as in the words *rhyme, time, lime, mime*. Clements and Keyser (1983) point out, however, that the rhyming of longer words does not involve any such unit: the rhyme pairs *city, pity* and *felicity, domesticity* simply involve identity of the stressed vowel and all that follows it in the word.

Levin (1985) offers a constituent structure approach to the syllable inspired by the X-bar theory of syntax. This theory not only dispenses with the feature [syllabic], but also discards C and V elements, replacing both by X. Levin argues that syllabicity is determined entirely by syllable position – in particular, the peak of a syllable is dominated by a node N (for nucleus), and the rhyme is dominated by a node N′ (read: N-bar), with the coda, as it were, the complement of the nucleus. The N′ is in turn dominated by N″ (read N-double-bar), which also dominates the onset, as it were, the specifier. This is illustrated in (20).

(20)

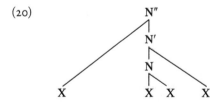

Selkirk (1982b) gives a constituent structure analysis of the syllable labelling the constituents with distinctive features, where the onset is [–syll]([+son]), the nucleus is [+syll]([+son]), the coda is [+cons]([–son]), and both onset and coda are optional.

We will use a moraic approach rather than a constituent structure approach, but nevertheless we can use the terms 'onset' and 'coda' informally to mean a sequence of consonants in a syllable before and after the vowel, respectively.

3.3.4 The Moraic Approach

In both the autosegmental approach and the constituent structure approach, the syllable contains heterogenous units. In keeping with the overall organizational approach governed by the prosodic hierarchy, it will be preferable to integrate the syllable into that hierarchy by having homogeneous units, as is the case with the other units in the hierarchy. As with most other units of the hierarchy, we restrict branching to binary, where one branch is labelled s (strong) and its sister is labelled w (weak). For this purpose we adapt a unit proposed by Hyman (1985) that he calls the *weight unit* and we will call the *mora*, symbolized m.[8]

The moraic approach combines the advantages of the constituent structure approach with the advantages of the autosegmental approach, without, we hope, the disadvantages of either. In it, a syllable consists of one or two moras. The first or only mora of a syllable must contain a vowel (or other syllabic segment); in addition it may contain one or more consonants that we can call the onset.[9] If there are two moras, the first is strong and the second weak (although we will not always mark them as such, for typographical convenience). The second mora, if present, dominates either the vowel that is already contained in the first mora, or one or more consonants that we can call a coda, or possibly both. There are four types of syllables, which can be illustrated in (21).[10]

[8] Some authors use μ for *mora*, but this Greek letter is more appropriate for *morpheme* (Greek derived) and is often so used, e.g., McCarthy (1981). *Mora* is a Latin word (literally 'delay') and appropriately represented by a Roman letter.

[9] In some versions of moraic phonology, such as Hayes (1989a), the onset if present is attached directly to the syllable rather than to the first mora. In Hayes's approach, the syllable consists of heterogenous units, which is not consistent with the prosodic hierarchy. None of Hayes's results are lost under the assumption that the onset belongs to the first mora of a syllable.

[10] A fifth syllable type appears in Eastern Cheremis, where only syllables with a long vowel count as heavy. Thus, instead of (21c), we have (i) in Eastern Cheremis. See the discussion in Section 4.2 of Chapter 4.

(i) σ
     |
     m
   C_0 V C_1

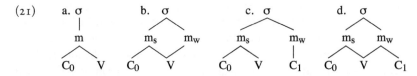

(21)
a. σ
|
m
⌢
C₀   V

b. σ
⌢
m_s   m_w
⌢   ⌢
C₀ V C₀ V

c. σ
⌢
m_s   m_w
⌢ |
C₀ V C₁

d. σ
⌢
m_s   m_w
⌢   ⌢
C₀ V C₁

Of the four syllable types in (21), the first is light, while the remainder are heavy. The first (21a) contains an onset of zero or more consonants followed by a short vowel. The second (21b) contains an onset of zero or more consonants followed by a long vowel, where the vowel is linked to both moras. The third (21c) contains an onset of zero or more consonants followed by a short vowel (as one mora) and a coda of one or more consonants constituting the second mora. The fourth (21d) combines these possibilities – an onset of zero or more consonants followed by a long vowel (linked to both moras), followed in turn by a coda of one or more consonants, where the vowel and the coda are both linked to the second mora.

While our approach to the syllable is primarily metrical, there are two possibilities for the use of autosegmental formalism. The first is one we have just illustrated, where a long vowel is shown as linked to the two moras of a syllable. This expresses the vowel length without an explicit feature [+long] or a geminate vowel. It will be further illustrated by the example from Japanese in (23), with the long vowel in the second syllable of *sensee* 'teacher.'

The second possibility is consonantal gemination, as we saw in the examples of Japanese kana. The word *kitte* 'stamp' could be represented as in (22).

(22)
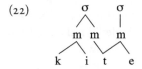
σ   σ
/\ |
m m m
⌢\ ⌣ \
k i t e

In terms of syllable boundaries, the word could be syllabified *kit.te*. Because of the limitations on Japanese codas, discussed in Section 3.1, the coda of the first syllable could only be [t] (a gemination of the following onset) or /N/, a nasal homorganic with the following onset. Therefore, it makes sense to link the [t] both to the second syllable as an onset and to the first syllable as a second mora. In a sense, there is only one feature matrix [t] that forms part of two syllables. We claim this is a legitimate structure for gemination. Similar structures are used for

ambisyllabic segments, a notion we rejected earlier. The gemination in
(22) is a strengthening phenomenon: the segment [t] is held for approximately double the time required for a single [t]. Ambisyllabicity has been
used for the opposite: the [t] of English *butter*, claimed to be ambisyllabic
by Kahn (1976) and others, is weakened in its realization as a flap. It is
illegitimate to use many-to-one linking both for strengthening and weakening – we will therefore restrict it to gemination and other forms
of strengthening.

In addition to gemination, Japanese allows a nasal consonant in the
coda, but no other coda consonants are possible. The coda nasal must be
homorganic with a following obstruent – that is, produced at the same
point of articulation. Here we can consider the word *sensee* 'teacher,' whose
structure we give as (23).

(23)

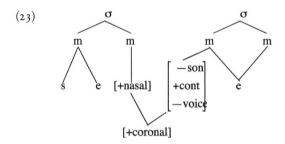

The segments [n] and [s] are separate segments and require separate feature
matrices. However, they are partially alike – they share the feature [+cor-
onal], which gives their common point of articulation. We can factor this
feature out of the two matrices and give it once, autosegmentally linking it
to both segments. This expresses the requirement that a coda nasal be
homorganic to a following obstruent, as also illustrated in (23). The long
vowel in the second syllable of *sensee* is shown as a single [e] linked to both
moras of the syllable. Although we write a geminate vowel in the transcription, the moraic formalism more clearly shows that it is a single long
vowel by writing the vowel features only once but linking them to both
moras of the syllable.

3.3.5   Conditions on Onsets and Codas

Many languages, including English, permit fairly complex syllables. For
example, several consonants may appear before or after the vowel, giving
complex onsets or codas. However, not all possible combinations of
consonants can appear as onsets or codas, so we need a way of restricting

these possibilities to ones that may actually occur in the language. Commonly, possible onsets and codas are governed by the Sonority Hierarchy. The vowel, or peak, of a syllable is the most sonorous segment in the syllable; that is, produced with a fairly open vocal tract. The sonority, or openness of the vocal tract, tends to diminish both before and after the vowel, or, stated differently, tends to increase from the beginning of the syllable until the vowel is reached, then to diminish up to the end of the syllable. If we represent sonority on a vertical scale and the components of the syllable horizontally, the diagram in (24) roughly represents this rise and fall of sonority in a typical syllable.

(24)

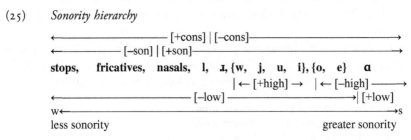

onset peak coda

We can say that the peak is literally the sonority peak of the syllable. We give the Sonority Hierarchy in (25), from Kiparsky (1979).

(25)   *Sonority hierarchy*

```
←─────────────── [+cons] | [−cons]─────────────────────→
←────────── [−son] | [+son]──────────────────────────→
stops,   fricatives,   nasals,   l,   ɹ, {w,   j,   u,   i}, {o,   e}   a
                                      | ← [+high] →   | ← [−high] ──────→
←──────────────────────── [−low] ──────────────────→| [+low]
w←──────────────────────────────────────────────────→s
less sonority                                greater sonority
```

Kiparsky also uses weak and strong labelling within the syllable, as we do for higher metrical structures; however, we will not use these labels for relative sonority within syllable onsets and codas. For the relative sonority of segments within the syllable, Selkirk (1984b: 116) proposes the Sonority Sequencing Generalization (26).

(26)   *Sonority Sequencing Generalization (SSG)*
         In any syllable, there is a segment constituting a sonority peak that is preceded and/or followed by a sequence of segments with progressively decreasing sonority values.

Some examples of well-formed syllables according to the SSG, which happen also to be English words, are given in (27).

(27)   brand, print, grind, snark, snarl, swarm

Note that *Karl* [kɑɹl] is a single syllable, with its coda of decreasing sonority, while *collar*, with a reversal of the last two segments, must be

disyllabic [kɑl̩ɹ] (North American pronunciation), since the last two segments rise in sonority. (Some might prefer the transcriptions [kɑlɔɹ] or
[kɑlɚ].)

However, not all sequences which are allowed by the SSG are well-
formed onsets in English. For example, English words cannot begin with a
stop plus a nasal, so there can be no word *bnick*, although this is allowed by
the SSG, and such words are well formed in French, as in *pneu* 'tyre.' On
the other hand, English words can begin with the sequence [s] plus
voiceless stop, as in *stop*, which is contrary to the SSG. We will provide
a more extensive list of conditions on the onset in English in the
next section.

Similarly not all sequences allowed by the SSG are well-formed codas in
English and other languages. Itô (1986) discusses the rather restrictive coda
conditions of Japanese, Finnish, and Italian. We will present these here,
because of their interest for syllabification in general, and because of the
link they show between word-internal codas and the onset of a following
syllable. Then we will show how this approach applies to English in
Section 3.4.

Itô (1986: 18ff.) illustrates various possibilities for syllable structure in
Japanese, given in (28). Syllable boundaries are indicated with periods;
geminate vowels are to be interpreted as long (our transcriptions).

(28)   a.   ka.mi.ka.ze   'divine wind'
             i.ke.ba.na   'flower arrangement'
        b.   kai.soo   'seaweed'
        c.   sen.see   'teacher'
             kam.pai   'cheers'
             min.na   'everyone'
             kon.ni.ʧi.wa   'good afternoon'
             am.ma   'masseur'
        d.   sek.ken   'soap'
             gak.koo   'school'
             kap.pa   'legendary being'
             tos.sa   'impulsively'
             toot.te   'passing'

The words in (28a) consist of light, open syllables; in (28b) we have heavy
syllables of the CVV type; in (28c) we have syllables closed by a nasal; and
in (28d) syllables closed by an obstruent. Itô points out that the free
permutation of the syllables of the words in (28) does not necessarily
produce well-formed words in Japanese, and that the hypothetical words of
(29) are ungrammatical.

(29)   *kɑp.toot
        *sek.pɑ
        *kɑp.sek
        *te.gɑk

Recall that a syllable in Japanese is well formed if it ends in a vowel (whether short, long, or a diphthong), if it ends in a nasal, or if it ends in an obstruent which is identical to the following onset. Itô offers an explanation involving several proposals from previous work. One that she adopts is syllable representations along the lines of Clements and Keyser (1983), illustrated in (16) and (18), but she notes that other representations would serve her purposes as well. For ease of exposition, we will recast her representations in terms of our moraic structures. The important thing for our purposes is that geminate consonants are represented as a single consonant melody linked to two syllabic positions. For example, *gak.koo* 'school' has the representation in (30).[11]

(30)

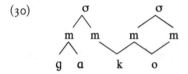

The second theoretical element that Itô brings to the analysis of codas is Hayes's (1986) Linking Constraint. Hayes observes that a phonological rule that freely applies to a single segment may fail to apply to a geminate segment that otherwise meets the rule's structural description. One example he discusses is Spirantization in Tigrinya, which he formulates as in (31), in terms of the CV theory of Clements and Keyser (1983). This rule converts velar stops into the corresponding fricatives when they follow a vowel.

(31)   *Spirantization (Tigrinya)*

$$\begin{bmatrix} -son \\ +back \end{bmatrix} \longrightarrow [+cont] \, / \, \underset{\underline{\quad\quad}}{\overset{\displaystyle V \;\; C}{ \mid}}$$

Hayes illustrates the operation of this rule with the examples in (32) (his transcriptions).

---

[11] Note that the [k] in (30) is interpreted as a geminate, not as ambisyllabic. In our representations, a consonant linked to two syllables is necessarily a geminate, since we rejected ambisyllabicity of simple segments in Section 3.3.2.

(32)   a.   kʌlbi   'dog'
             ʔaxalɨb   /ʔakalɨb/   'dogs'
        b.   gʌnʔi   'pitch'
             ʔaɣaniʔ   /ʔaganiʔ/   'pitches'
        c.   k'ʌbʌrʌ   'to bury'
             yɨx'ʌbbɨr   /yɨ + k'ʌbbɨr/   'he buries'

However, Spirantization does not apply to geminate /kk/, where both
segments belong to the same morpheme, as shown in (33).

(33)   a.   fʌkkʌrʌ   *fʌxxʌrʌ   *fʌxkʌrʌ   'he boasted'

        b.   V C C
                 \/
                 k

If the structure of the relevant portion of (33a) is (33b), Spirantization will
not apply if the Linking Constraint is assumed as a universal condition on
rules that are stated in terms of two or more autosegmental levels. We give
this constraint in (34).

(34)   *Linking Constraint* (Hayes 1986: 331)
        Association lines in structural descriptions are interpreted as exhaustive.

Since the association line in Spirantization (31) links the rule's focus with a
single C, the Linking Constraint (34) blocks its application in (33), given
the structure (33b) where a single segment [k] is linked to two C positions.
Interestingly, Spirantization does apply correctly to what Hayes calls 'fake
geminates,' that is, geminates that arise by morpheme concatenation. This
is illustrated in (35).

(35)   a.   /mɨrak + ka/ → mɨraxka 'calf 2 sg. masc.'

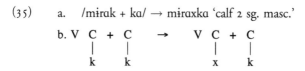

This is because each morpheme is provided with association lines before
morpheme concatenation.[12] The single association line associated with the
morpheme-final /k/ of *mɨrak* satisfies the structural description of
Spirantization (31), which can thus apply to this form.

---

[12] The Obligatory Contour Principle (OCP, Section 1.5.1 of Chapter 1), originally proposed for tone
in Leben (1973) and formulated explicitly by Goldsmith (1976: 36), requires that geminates within
morphemes be multiply linked to a single melody, as in (33), but allows individual linking of
identical segments separated by a morpheme boundary, as in (35).

Itô (1986: 27) makes the novel proposal that the Linking Constraint applies to conditions, such as the Coda Condition, as well as to phonological rules. This allows a maximally simple statement of the Coda Condition for Japanese, as in (36).

(36)   *Coda Condition (Japanese)*

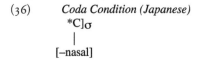

Condition (36) disallows any nonnasal segment in the coda of Japanese. By the Linking Constraint (34), however, the doubly linked /k/ in (33) is exempt from (36) so that a geminate consonant is allowed in syllable-final position, in addition to a nasal.[13]

Fairly restrictive limitations on the onset and the Japanese Coda Condition together imply a rather restricted set of syllables in the language. Japanese syllables have onsets of zero, one, or two consonants, but onsets of two consonants are restricted to those whose second element is /j/, as reflected in the kana (5). This fact makes the kana a successful way of representing Japanese sounds; a moraic writing system for English would be much more cumbersome owing to the far greater variety of syllables that are possible in English. Japanese borrowings from English in fact conform to the syllable structure of Japanese, so that 'sprinkler' appears as *supuriŋkuraa*. (See Don C. Bailey 1962 for more examples.) Observe that vowels are inserted to avoid clusters that are not permitted in Japanese, and that [l] is replaced by [r] in the last syllable, since these two liquids do not contrast in Japanese.

Finnish is another language with a fairly restricted syllable structure. Syllable onsets can have at most one consonant, and codas have at most two consonants, which must fall in sonority according to the scale in (25). Stops are not permitted as the second consonant in a coda unless they are part of a geminate. The examples in (37a–c) are possible (and actual) Finnish words conforming to these constraints, while (37d–e) show some hypothetical words that violate these constraints. Syllable boundaries are indicated by periods. Forms are in Finnish orthography, where <a> = [ɑ], <y> = [y], <ö> = [ø], <ä> = [æ], and long vowels are written as geminates, from Itô (1986: 40ff).

---

[13] This condition does not account for the requirement that syllable-final nasals be homorganic with a following obstruent or [+coronal] if word final.

(37) a. lap.si   'child'   (one consonant in coda of first syllable)
          uk.si   'door'
          lat.va   'top'
          jat.ka   'continue'

      b. pyrs.tö   'fish- or   (two consonants of falling sonority in coda
                        bird-tail'   of first syllable, the last one not a stop)
          kons.ti   'trick'
          sals.kea   'slender'

      c. help.po   'easy'   (two consonants of falling sonority in the
          polt.ta   'burn'   coda of the first syllable, the last one a
          tark.ka   'exact'   stop identical to the following onset)
          kynt.ti.lä   'candle'

      d. *laps.ka   (sonority rises in the coda of the first
                                      syllable)

          *uks.ta

      e. *pyrk.sö   (two consonants of falling sonority in the
          *tolp.ko   coda of the first syllable but ending in a
          *kont.po   stop that is not part of a geminate)

Once again the Linking Constraint allows a fairly compact statement of
the Coda Condition for Finnish, which Itô (1986: 42) gives as (38).

(38)   *Coda Condition (Finnish)*

        *CC]σ
          |
        [–cont]

This condition excludes stops from final position in two-consonant codas,
but the Linking Constraint exempts stops in this position when they are
part of a geminate.

The Finnish Coda Condition has a few exceptions. Kiparsky (1979:
436) cites *hamst.raa* 'he hoards.' In addition, the restriction of the onset to
a single consonant is violated in a few recent loans, e.g., *frak.ki* 'dress
coat.'[14]

The last example we will examine in terms of coda conditions is
Italian, which presents some additional interesting complications (Itô
1986: 35ff). In Italian, the maximal syllable is CCVC. If there are two
consonants in the onset, their sonority profile must be rising; indeed, it is

---

[14] Kiparsky argues from examples like *hamst.raa* that Finnish maximizes the coda, as opposed to
English, which maximizes onsets. We will claim that all languages maximize the onset, regarding
Finnish as a language that limits onsets to a single consonant (in most cases).

mostly limited to a sequence [–son][+son]. Coda consonants are limited to sonorants and [s]; obstruents other than [s] can appear in the coda only if they are geminated. These conditions are illustrated in (39) (our transcriptions).

(39) a. in.fles.'si.bi.le   'inflexible'   (coda a sonorant or [s])
          'al.tro   'other'
          bur.'gra.vio   'castle lord'
          em.'blɛ.ma   'emblem'
          es.'prɛs.so   'express'

      b. 'lab.bro   'lip'   (obstruent coda as part of a
                                                     geminate)
          'grap.pa   'brandy'
          ap.plaw.'di.re   'clap, applaud'
          'tut.to   'all'
          e.'lɛt.tri.ko   'electric'
          rad.dridz.'dza.re   'straighten'
          ak.kre.di.'ta.bi.le   'creditable'
          ag.glo.me.'ra.re   'agglomerate'

      c. *it.fles.si.bi.le   (obstruent other than [s] in
                                                     coda that is not geminated)
          *ap.tro
          *bud.gra.vi.o
          *eg.blɛ.ma
          *ek.prɛs.so

Itô (1986: 38) expresses the Italian Coda Condition as (40).

(40)   *Coda Condition (Italian)*
        *C]σ
         |
        [–cont]
        [–son]

Once again the Linking Condition permits apparent violations like (39b), where the geminate is considered doubly linked.

   Some additional stipulations are required to complete the picture of Italian syllable structure. One is that clusters of [s] or [z] plus obstruent are permitted word initially, as in splen.'do.re 'brilliance,' and 'skri.ve.re 'to write,' and 'zba.ʎo 'mistake.' But such clusters are divided within words, as in 'pas.ta 'pasta.' One piece of evidence is that stressed vowels are lengthened in open syllables, but the first vowel of 'pas.ta is not lengthened, as would be expected if the syllabification were pa.sta. In addition, words like pelsto are excluded in Italian, which is predicted by the syllabification *pels.to*, since there can only be one consonant in the coda.[15] Words beginning with clusters of [s] or [z] plus obstruent have the peculiarity of requiring an allomorph of the definite article. The masculine singular article is generally *il*, but before such clusters the form *lo* is required, shown in (41).

(41)   il libro   'the book'
       il coltɛllo   'the knife'
       lo stɑto   'the state'
       lo spɛkkio   'the mirror'
       lo zbaʎo   'the mistake'

A second problem that Itô points out with this analysis is that the Coda Condition (40) wrongly predicts that the other fricatives of Italian, [f] and [ʃ], could occur ungeminated in coda position. She suggests possibly revising (40) by dropping the feature [−cont] but notes that this would wrongly rule out singly linked [s] in codas, as in *es.prɛs.so*. Noting that only sonorants, and not [s], are allowed as word-final consonants, a special and uniform treatment should be developed for the properties of [s] in word-initial and word medial positions before a consonant that would also disallow it word finally; however, she does not suggest what that special treatment might be.

Finally, we should note that there is a fairly large number of exceptions to the Coda Condition in Italian, more than in Finnish. Blevins (1995: 228) notes the following: *kakto* 'cactus,' *kɔpto* 'coptic,' *kamtʃatka* 'Kamchatka,' *fiat* 'fiat,' *wɔt* 'watt,' to which we can add *film* 'film.'[16] Such words do not appear to present difficulties to Italian speakers. It is not easy to determine which gaps in distribution reflect genuine regularities in the language and which are simply accidental. In Section 2.2 of Chapter 2, we suggested that the general absence of [ʒ] in word-initial position in English is accidental and not the result of a special constraint against this segment in syllable-initial position. With respect to coda conditions, it appears that there may be such general constraints but that individual words may violate them without causing too much distress. We will see certain examples of this in English in Section 3.4.

---

[15] See Goad (2012) for further discussion of medial *s*C clusters in Italian and other languages.
[16] Thanks to Lisa Di Domenico for discussion of the Italian data. I have adjusted some of Blevins's examples in deference to Di Domenico's native-speaker intuitions.

3.4   The Syllable in English

With this background we are now ready to examine the syllable in English. We will start by examining possible onsets at the beginnings of words and possible codas at the ends of words. We will then examine sequences of syllables within words, where possible codas are much more limited, and develop a Coda Condition for English on that basis. This will include restrictions involving the interaction of vowel length and coda possibilities. Finally, we will look at some problematic questions and suggest ways of accounting for them, some of which will be further developed in later chapters.

3.4.1   *The Onset*

Syllable onsets may consist of from zero to three consonants in English. Vowel-initial syllables have zero or no onset. Any single underlying consonant can form a single consonant onset. This excludes only /ŋ/ from syllable-initial position. This segment does not appear in underlying representations but is derived from an underlying sequence of a nasal followed by a velar consonant, and its exclusion from syllable-initial position follows from the exclusion of clusters consisting of a nasal plus obstruent in this position, which follows from the Sonority Hierarchy. Unlike some analyses, we do not exclude /ʒ/ from syllable-initial position, regarding its rarity there as accidental (see Section 2.2 of Chapter 2).

Possible two-consonant onsets are best set out in a tabular format, as in (42). The first consonant of the cluster is in the left column and the second is listed across the top. A blank indicates that the cluster does not occur; shaded cells indicate marginal clusters. A prefixed [%] indicates variation, i.e., pronunciations found in some speakers but not others. The heavy line separates clusters conforming to the Sonority Sequencing Generalization (26) (to the right of the line) from those that do not conform (to the left). The significance of the double line separating the *j* column from the rest of the table will be discussed below.[17]

---

[17] Thanks to a reader for some additional examples in the C*w* column.

(42)

	p	t	k	f	v	s	θ	m	n	l	ɹ	w	j
p										pl	pɹ	pw	pj
b										bl	bɹ	bw	bj
t						ts				tl	tɹ	tw	tj
d											dɹ	dw	dj
k					kv					kl	kɹ	kw	kj
g										gl	gɹ	gw	gj
f										fl	fɹ	fw	fj
v										vl	vɹ	vw	vj
s	sp	st	sk	sf			sθ	sm	sn	sl		sw	sj
z										zl		zw	
θ											θɹ	θw	θj
ʃ	ʃp	ʃt						ʃm	ʃn	ʃl	ʃɹ	ʃw	
ʒ												ʒw	
h												hw	hj
m												mw	mj
n												nw	nj
l												lw	lj

We list some exemplifications of these clusters in (43).

(43)   play, pray, pueblo, pure, (Pyongyang)
         blade, braid, bwana, beauty
         tsetse, Tlingit, trim, twin, tune
         dry, dwell, dune
         kvass, clan, cry, quick cute
         glow, green, guava, linguistics, gules, angular
         fly, fry, foie gras, few, (fjord)
         Vladimir, vroom, voilà, view
         speak, steak, scan, Sphinx, sthenic, smile, snow, slow, swarm, suit
         zloty, $^{\%}$zwieback
         three, thwart, thulium
         spiel, shtick, schmalz, schnapps, schlep, shrink, schwa
         joie de vivre

%which, %hue
moiré, mute
moisette, new
%Loire, lute, lieu

We can extract a few generalizations from the table of onsets. Most of the two-consonant clusters that occur conform to the Sonority Sequencing Generalization, but not all clusters conforming to that generalization in fact occur. The clusters that do occur but do not conform to this generalization begin with [s] or [ʃ]; of these only [sp], [st], and [sk] are nonmarginal. The most robustly attested clusters are those that begin with an obstruent followed by a liquid or [w].

As we will justify in greater detail later on (especially in Chapter 4), when (possible) word-initial clusters come between vowels, the principle that onsets are maximized attaches the full cluster to the following vowel rather than splitting it between syllables. Therefore, a word like *a.ppli.ance* is syllabified as shown; since [pl] is a possible onset, as in *play*, this cluster is syllabified as an onset to the second syllable. A test that helps to demonstrate this principle uses the allophones of various consonants: in *ma.ttress*, for instance, the [t] is pronounced quite differently than in *but.ler*. This may not be the case for the clusters we have designated as marginal in (42), but it is difficult to test, since these clusters occur rarely in word-internal position also, and the allophony is less clear in these cases. My impression is that such clusters are divided word medially; for example *as.phyxiate* rather than *a.sphixiate* despite words like *Sphinx*. These allophones will be discussed further in Chapter 5.

The rightmost column in (42) is separated from the rest of the table by a double line to reflect the fact that clusters whose final element is [j] occur at the lexical level and at the systematic phonetic level but do not occur at the underlying level, where syllabification takes place. These clusters occur only before the vowel [u] or [ʊ], as the examples in (43) show.[18] We take these instances of *j* to be inserted by a rule of *j*-Insertion, formulated as in (12) of Chapter 7. Before other vowels, English speakers generally reject C*j* clusters. For example, the Japanese name *Kyoto* is pronounced as three syllables in English: *Ky.o.to*, <y> pronounced [i], although in Japanese it is two syllables: *Kyo.to*. C*j* clusters are the only onset clusters permitted in Japanese, and there is even a set of special kana characters for such clusters,

---

[18] Thanks to a reader for pointing out a few exceptions to this generalization in borrowed words, where *j* must be assumed to be underlying, given in parentheses in (43).

as we saw in (5). When such clusters occur medially in English, as in *million*, the syllable division is between the consonant and the *j*: [mɪl.jən].

Kiparsky (1979) proposes that there are specific *constraints* in each language to rule out onset clusters that, although conforming to the Sonority Sequencing Generalization, are not found in that language. He also proposes specific *dispensations* that allow certain clusters that do appear in the language, even though they do not conform to the Sonority Sequencing Generalization. We give the most important of these constraints and dispensations for English onsets here.[19] First we list some constraints in (44). The (C) that appears in some constraints indicates that the restriction applies to the second and third consonants of three-consonant onsets as well as to the two consonants of two-consonant sequences.

(44)   Constraints on English onsets

a. $*[_\sigma$ (C) [–cont][–cont]

b. $*[_\sigma$ (C) $\begin{bmatrix} +cor \\ -strid \end{bmatrix}$ l

c. $*[_\sigma(C) \begin{bmatrix} C \\ +son \end{bmatrix} \begin{bmatrix} C \\ +son \end{bmatrix}$

d. $*[_\sigma$ (C) [–cont] $\begin{bmatrix} -son \\ +cont \end{bmatrix}$

e. $*[_\sigma\ C_1^2\ j$

f. $*[_\sigma$ (C) $\begin{bmatrix} -cont \\ +strid \end{bmatrix}$ C

g. $*[_\sigma$ (C) $\begin{bmatrix} C \\ +cont \\ +voice \end{bmatrix}$ C

Constraint (44a) rules out syllable-initial sequences of a stop plus a nasal, such as a hypothetical word *bnick*. This implies that such sequences within words will be divided, e.g., *obnoxious*. It also rules out a sequence of two oral stops, as in hypothetical *ptick*. However, such sequences are already ruled out by sonority sequencing, since two stops cannot present rising sonority. Both types of sequences appear in French, for example *pneu* 'tyre,' *ptomaïne* 'ptomaine.' The former shows that French does not have constraint (44a); the latter requires a special dispensation.

Constraint (44b) excludes syllable-initial sequences *tl*, *dl*, and *θl*. The only example of word-initial *tl* is *Tlingit*, which we considered marginal in (42). Such clusters are distinctly divided within words, as in *butler*, *bedlam*, *athlete*.

[19] Some of these are adapted from other sources, especially Hammond (1999).

Constraint (44c) excludes a sequence of two sonorant consonants as onsets (with a few exceptions noted in 43). By the Sonority Sequencing Generalization we might expect some of these, such as *ml, mr, mw, nl, nr, nw, lr*. The reverse of these clusters are valid codas, as in *elm, form, kiln, barn, gnarl*.[20] The cluster *lr* seems to be divided word internally, as in *walrus*. As we discussed in Section 3.2 (see Footnote 7), the sequence *lr* meets *SPE*'s definition of a weak cluster (6), which is convenient for the correct stressing of *chivalrous*. Since we do not allow *lr* as a syllable-initial cluster, we will have to regard *chivalrous* as exceptional for stress in Chapter 4.

Constraint (44d) excludes syllable-initial sequences of a stop plus a fricative (which is another reason to consider affricates as simple segments, as discussed in Section 2.2 of Chapter 2). This has only marginal exceptions, such as *tsetse*. Such combinations are divided within words, as in *flotsam*.

Constraint (44e) excludes syllable onsets of two or three consonants that end in *j*, i.e., the rightmost column of (42), with the exceptions noted in (43). Otherwise, when such clusters occur (which is only before [u] or [ʊ], as in *stew*), the *j* is in fact inserted by a rule that follows syllabification. The rules involved will be detailed in Chapter 7.

Constraint (44f) excludes affricates from onset clusters. Constraint (44g) excludes voiced fricatives from such clusters, with marginal exceptions such as *Vladimir, vroom, zloty*. Such clusters seem to be divided internally, as in *grizzly*.

Kiparsky also proposes that the grammar may contain *dispensations* that allow certain sequences that violate the Sonority Hierarchy. He specifically proposes the dispensation in (45).

$$(45) \quad [_\sigma \ s \begin{bmatrix} -\text{son} \\ -\text{cont} \\ -\text{voice} \end{bmatrix} \ldots \text{ is OK}$$

This dispensation allows the syllable-initial sequences *sp, st, sk*. There are several reasons for giving these sequences special treatment. First, some languages, such as Spanish, lack these clusters, while allowing clusters that conform to the Sonority Hierarchy. Second, other languages that do permit such clusters treat them differently from other clusters. In Old English, these clusters alliterate as units in verse. Old English poetry requires alliteration, or identity of the beginnings of words, rather than rhyming, which is identity of the ends of words. Outside of the clusters *sp*,

---

[20] We leave out the onsets starting with [w], e.g., *wr, wl, wn*, since [w] would be part of a diphthong in the reverse order.

st, *sk*, two words alliterate if they begin with the same consonant, regardless
of whether the consonant is alone or followed by another consonant before
the vowel. Vowel-initial words alliterate regardless of the quality of the
vowels. But if a word begins with *sp*, *st*, or *sk*, it requires another word with
the same initial cluster for alliteration. Some examples of alliteration are
given in (46). Alliterating consonants and clusters are italicized.

(46)   Þā *st*ōd on *st*æðe   *st*īþ-līċe clipode
        *w*iċinga ār   *w*ordum mǣlde
        'Then a messenger of the vikings stood on the shore and called out
        sternly, spoke with words. . .' (The Battle of Maldon, lines 25–26)

        *cr*ēad *cn*earr on flot,   *c*yning ūt ʒewāt
        on *f*ealone *f*lōd,   *f*eorh ʒenerude
        '. . .the ship hastened to sea, the king went out on the dark flood, saved
        his life.' (The Battle of Brunanburg, lines 35–36)

        Hē ǣrest sċōp   *ie*lda barnum
        *h*eofon to *h*rōfe   *h*āliʒ sċieppend
        'He, the holy creator, first created heaven as a roof for the sons of
        men. . .' (Caedmon's Hymn, lines 5–6)

In Gothic and Sanskrit, among other Indo-European languages, the
preterite (in Gothic) and perfect (in Sanskrit) tenses may be formed by
partial reduplication. In most cases the initial consonant of the stem plus a
short vowel, [ɛ] in Gothic, [a] in Sanskrit, is prefixed to the stem. In
Gothic, if the verb stem begins with [s] plus a stop, the entire cluster is
copied in the reduplication. In Sanskrit, the second (rather than the first)
of the two consonants of the stem is copied when the Sonority Hierarchy is
violated. Some examples are given in (47).

(47)   *Gothic*

        Infinitive   *preterite*   *gloss*
        háita   [haɪta]   haí-háit   [hɛhaɪt]   'be called'
        grēt-an   [greːtan]   gaígrōt   [gɛgroːt]   'weep'
        skáid-an   [skaɪdan]   skaí-skáiþ   [skɛskaɪθ]   'divide'

        Sanskrit

        present   *perfect*   *gloss*
        tanoti   tataːna   'stretch'
        smarati   sasmarːa   'remember'
        spr̥çati   pasparça   'touch'

Thus, reduplication in these languages is another kind of evidence for a
special treatment of clusters consisting of [s] plus a stop.

We do not propose a dispensation to allow the marginal clusters *ſt, ſp, sf, sθ*, in word-initial position. These should be divided medially, as in *asphalt, aesthetic*.

Three-consonant onsets in English are limited to those listed in (48a). Those in (48b), with *j* as their final member, are not formed in the initial syllabification but are the result of *j*-Insertion, as is the case of the two-consonant onsets ending in *j* (right column of 42).

(48)   a.   [spl]   splice   b.   [spj]   spew
             [spɹ]   sprite   [stj]   stew
             [stɹ]   stray   [skj]   skew
             [skl]   sclera   [slj]   sluice
             [skɹ]   scream
             [skw]   squeak

Three-consonant onsets are in effect an overlap of two two-consonant onsets: the first two consonants form a possible two-consonant onset, and the last two consonants also form a possible two-consonant onset. Two-consonant onsets following the Sonority Hierarchy all consist of an obstruent plus *l, r,* or *w* (leaving out *j*). These sonorants *l, r, w* do not appear as the first member of two-consonant onsets. The only two-consonant onsets containing two obstruents are those consisting of [s] plus a voiceless stop. Because of these limitations, three-consonant onsets are limited to those consisting of [s] plus voiceless stop plus sonorant *l, r, w*, with *stl* excluded because of the constraint ruling out *tl*. These constraints also ensure that no onset clusters exceed three consonants. Up to this limit, onsets are maximized within words, as long as all the constraints are satisfied.

3.4.2   The Coda

Codas at the systematic phonetic level are more complex than onsets. Part of this complexity results from the addition of inflectional suffixes, giving rise to quite complex coda clusters, seen at a maximum in *sixths* [sɪksθs]. Inflectional suffixes are attached at stratum 2 of the lexicon, and are therefore not present at the stage of initial syllabification. In addition, codas can contain clusters of two stops or two sonorants, which, as we have seen, are excluded from onsets. Finally, the most complex codas appear only after short vowels, so a complete characterization of codas is possible only by including a consideration of the moraic structure of the syllable. However, the most complex codas specifically appear only in word-final position. Hence, given the principle that onsets are maximized, we will be able to give a fairly simple characterization of the possible codas word internally.

We will start with the observation that any single underlying consonant in English, except *h*, can constitute a coda. We continue by cataloguing the possible two-consonant codas in (49). In (50) we list words containing these codas. Codas below and to the left of the heavy line in (49) conform to the Sonority Sequencing Generalization; those above and to the right do not. A double line in (49) surrounds those clusters that are found only where the final consonant is an inflectional suffix. Examples containing such clusters are italicized in (50). The significance of the shaded combinations will be explained below.

(49)

	p	b	t	d	k	g	ʧ	ʤ	f	v	θ	s	z	ʃ	m	n	l
p			pt								pθ	ps					
b				bd									bz				
t											tθ						
d											dθ		dz				
k			kt									ks					
g				gd									gz				
ʧ			ʧt														
ʤ				ʤd													
f			ft								fθ	fs					
v				vd									vz				
θ			θt									θs					
ð				ðd									ðz				
s	sp		st		sk												
z				zd													
ʃ			ʃt														
ʒ				ʒd													
m	mp		mt						mf				mz				
n			nt	nd	nk	ng	nʧ	ndʒ			nθ	ns	nz				
ŋ =/ng/				ŋd	ŋk	ŋg					ŋθ		ŋz				
l	lp	lb	lt	ld	lk		lʧ	ldʒ	lf	lv	lθ	ls	lz	lʃ	lm	ln	
ɹ	ɹp	ɹb	ɹt	ɹd	ɹk	ɹg	ɹʧ	ɹdʒ	ɹf	ɹv	ɹθ	ɹs	ɹz	ɹʃ	ɹm	ɹn	ɹl

(50) apt, depth, copse
      robed, robes
      eighth
      width, adze
      act, axe
      sagged, sags
      watched
      judged
      soft, fifth, *laughs*
      loved, loves
      pithed, deaths
      smoothed, smooths
      rasp, last, bask
      gazed
      wished
      portaged
      lamp, dreamt, lymph, Thames
      paint, hint, pained, hand, lunch, lunge, tenth, flounce, tense, lens
      ringed, link, ring, length, *rings*
      gulp, bulb, bolt, fold, bulk, mulch, bulge, elf, twelve, health, pulse,
          Wells, Welsh, helm, kiln
      harp, herb, heart, hard, bark, morgue, arch, gorge, surf, carve, hearth,
          farce, Mars, marsh, form, barn, snarl

We should note that the [ŋ] in the line of codas with that as their first
member is not present at the initial stage of syllabification. As we have
discussed in Section 2.2 of Chapter 2, the segment [ŋ] is always derived by
assimilation; consequently, at the stage where syllabification takes place,
we have syllable-final clusters /nk/, /ng/, but no /ŋ/. The word *ring* has the
underlying representation /ɹɪng/, which becomes [ɹɪŋ] by assimilation and
deletion of /g/. We will detail these rules in Chapter 7. Meanwhile this line
of clusters is included for completeness, but the clusters on this line other
than *ŋk, ŋg*, should really be considered three-consonant clusters, since the
underlying representation of *ringed*, for example, is /ɹɪng + d/. For this
reason, we have shaded those cells in (49).

Three-consonant codas are more limited. The list in (51) is probably
exhaustive, excluding inflections.

(51) | /dst/ | midst | /lpt/ | sculpt |
     |-------|-------|-------|--------|
     | /kst/ | next | /lkt/ | mulct, milked |
     | /ksθ/ | sixth | /lks/ | calx, balks, milks |
     | /mpt/ | tempt | /lfθ/ | twelfth |
     | /mps/ | mumps | /ɹkt/ | infarct |
     | /nst/ | against | /ɹmθ/ | warmth |

/ŋst/ < /ngst/	amongst	/ɹpt/	exerpt
/ŋkt/ < /nkt/	instinct	/ɹps/	corpse
/ŋks/ < /nks/	lynx		

The final cluster in *amongst* is actually a four-consonant cluster, on the assumption that [ŋ] is always derived from /n/ followed by a velar. The possibility exists that -*st* is a suffix here (likewise in *midst*, *against*). The [θ] occurring after a numeral is also a suffix, as in *sixth*. Otherwise, four-consonant codas are limited to cases where the three-consonant codas in (51) are followed by an inflectional suffix, as in *sixths, instincts, sculpts, excerpts*.

It should be noted that the last consonant in all the examples of (51) is a voiceless coronal obstruent: *t*, *s*, or *θ*. Even the two-consonant codas in (50) mostly end in coronals. With few exceptions, the words in (50) and (51) have short lax vowels. A long vowel (or diphthong) may occur before a two-consonant cluster if the cluster contains only coronals but not otherwise: *paint* but not **paimp*. Long vowels do not occur before three-consonant clusters at all (except in the case of inflectional suffixes). This suggests that we develop a Coda Condition for English along the lines of what we did for Japanese, Finnish, and Italian in Section 3.3.5.

3.4.3   The Coda Condition

One striking fact about the codas investigated in Section 3.4.2 is that they are all *word final*. If we look at codas internal to the word, we find that they are considerably more limited. If the vowel of a nonfinal syllable is long (or a diphthong), i.e., bimoraic, it tends to be in an open syllable, as in the examples of (52).

(52)   me.te.or, fi.nal, li.bra.ry, foi.ble, vo.cal, au.thor, pow.der

If a nonfinal syllable is closed, it tends to have a short, lax vowel. In (53) we give some examples where two consonants appear between vowels. Where these two consonants cannot form an onset to the second syllable, the two consonants are divided between the two syllables, the first consonant forming the coda of the first syllable, and the second consonant forming the onset of the second syllable. As a result, the first syllable is closed.

(53)   in.ter.nal, cap.tain, tem.per, pan.ther, sel.dom, Az.tec, At.kins, Af.ghan,
         From.kin

In cases where the first syllable is closed and contains a long vowel, its closing consonant is most frequently a sonorant *homorganic* (i.e., sharing its point of articulation) with a following consonant. The examples in (54) illustrate this. In *ointment*, the homorganic obstruent is in the same syllable as the sonorant; in the other examples, the obstruent begins the following syllable.

(54)   cham.ber, an.gel, dain.ty, laun.der, moun.tain, oint.ment

Examples with a long vowel followed by two nonhomorganic consonants in nonfinal position are extremely rare, the list in (55) being (probably) exhaustive.

(55)   deictic, deixis, seismic, peascod, fo'c'sle, zeugma, folksy

We find numerous examples with two consonants between vowels where both consonants belong to the second syllable. These are cases where the two consonants make a well-formed onset. In these cases, both long and short vowels are found in the first syllable, and the stress may be either on the first or the second syllable.

(56)

	stress on first syllable	*stress on second syllable*
first vowel short	whi.sper, ci.trus	de.spair, di.sturb, e.scape, su.blime
first vowel long	A.pril, sa.cred, aw.kward	se.crete, re.quire

Likewise, if three consonants between vowels form a possible onset, they belong to the second syllable. These all begin with /s/, as we saw in (48), and the vowel of the first syllable may be long or short.

(57)   mi.stress, di.stress, pa.stry, pa.stra.mi, boi.strous

If the three consonants cannot form an onset, the last two form an onset if they can. Here again, the vowel of the first syllable is typically short.

(58)   pam.phlet, coun.try, pil.grim, an.thrax, in.stant, textile [tɛk.stɑɪl]

Long vowels are found in this environment only in the examples in (59), according to Borowsky (1989).

(59)   Cam.bridge, laun.dry, scoun.drel, foun.dry, wain.scot

The syllable division is after the second of three consonants when the last two cannot form an onset (and the first two *can* form a coda). The first vowel is usually short here too, and the coda consonants are homorganic.

(60)   ant.ler, emp.ty, func.tion, pump.kin, part.ner, vint.ner

Long vowels in this position appear to be limited to words in *-ment*.

(61)   ointment, appointment

Four consonants between vowels usually have the last three from the set in (48a), forming an onset to the second syllable (62a). Only a few four-consonant sequences seem to have the division after the second consonant (62b).

(62)   a.   in.stru.ment, ob.struct, express [ɛk.spɹɛs], exclaim [ɛk.skleɪm],
                extra [ɛk.stɹə], mon.strous
          b.   dump.ster, prank.ster

This suggests a very simple formulation of the Coda Condition for English, considering only syllables that are not word final. Recall the four syllable types in (21). Most of the facts presented in (52)–(62) can be accounted for by excluding (21d), that is, syllables whose second mora branches, where the right branch of this mora is singly linked. We state this in (63).

(63)   *English Coda Condition*

An open syllable with a long vowel, as in (52), for example the first syllable of *final*, has the structure of (64), which conforms to (63), since the second mora does not branch.

(64)

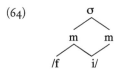

A closed syllable with a short vowel, as in (53), for example, the first syllable of *internal*, has the structure of (65), which also conforms to (63), since the second mora does not branch.

(65)

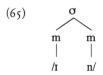

Cases like *antler* and *Cambridge* seem to violate the Coda Condition. We appeal to the Linking Constraint (34) to account for these. We give the structure of *antler* in (66).

(66)

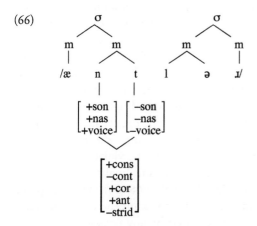

The features shared by /n/ and /t/ have been given in a matrix linked to both segments, while the features that are different are listed separately for each segment. Because the English Coda Condition excludes syllables with a branching second mora only when the right branch of this mora is singly linked, the double link to the common features of these two segments exempts the structure from the Coda Condition, and so (66) is acceptable.

The story is similar for *Cambridge*, the only difference being that the double linking joins the two syllables, as shown in (67).[21]

(67)

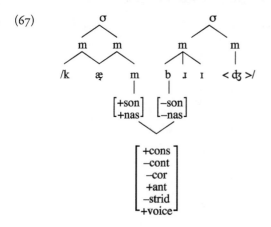

Because the matrix for /m/ is linked to another matrix of the features it shares with /b/, the Coda Condition is not violated. Where there is no such

---

[21] The /æ/ in *Cambridge* is the underlying representation of the vowel of the first syllable. This becomes [eɪ] by Vowel Shift and other rules discussed in Chapter 7.

double linking, as with hypothetical *Camkridge* (with a long vowel in the first syllable) or *amtler*, where the consonants differ in point of articulation, the Coda Condition is violated and these structures are excluded.[22]

We must still allow some exceptions to the Coda Condition in English, just as we observed for Finnish and Italian. The words in (55) are exceptions to the Coda Condition, and we will see others in later chapters. For such words we assume it is the Coda Condition rather than the conditions on the onset that are violated; that is, the syllabification must be *deic.tic*, violating the Coda Condition rather than *dei.ctic*, where the prohibition of two stops in an onset (44a) would be violated.

As an alternative to the Coda Condition for word-final syllables, we give the constraint in (68), based on Kiparsky (1982: 68–69). The interpretation is that the second mora may contain a sonorant, here interpreted as including the glide of a diphthong, followed by any consonant, followed by a coronal appendix. The appendix can be any single coronal consonant or, exceptionally, one of the two sequences [st], [sθ]. Examples are given in systematic phonetic representation.

(68)   *Maximal word-final syllable*

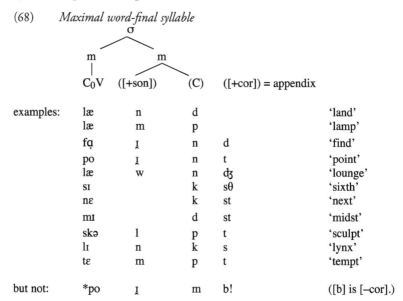

examples:	læ	n	d		'land'
	læ	m	p		'lamp'
	fǫ	ɪ̯	n	d	'find'
	po	ɪ̯	n	t	'point'
	læ	w	n	dʒ	'lounge'
	sɪ		k	sθ	'sixth'
	nɛ		k	st	'next'
	mɪ		d	st	'midst'
	skə	l	p	t	'sculpt'
	lɪ	n	k	s	'lynx'
	tɛ	m	p	t	'tempt'
but not:	*po	ɪ̯	m	b!	([b] is [–cor].)

---

[22] A formal problem for the Linking Constraint is that the shared features must include point of articulation features [coronal], [anterior]. The /m/ and /k/ of hypothetical *Camkridge* share the features [+cons, –cont, –cor, –strid, +voice], but this does not exempt the first syllable from the Coda Condition. In fact, attested violations of the Coda Condition seem to be restricted to homorganic nasal plus stop sequences. This problem would not be resolved by adopting a more highly articulated approach to features, such as feature geometry (Section 1.5.1, cf. Clements & Hume 1995).

Inflectional suffixes are permitted beyond this limit, as in *sixths, instincts, sculpts, twelfths, excerpts.*

3.4.4 Rules for Syllabification in English

We have now developed all the background needed to state the rules for English syllabification. Before we do so, we need to discuss three points. The first has to do with the representational difference between consonants and vowels. The second is concerned with the status of certain word-final consonants. Finally, we will have to consider the relationship between vowel tenseness (coded in the feature [±ATR]) and vowel length.

In *SPE*, where representations are linear and do not include organizational units like the syllable, syllabicity is represented in terms of distinctive features. In chapter 7 (cf. p. 303) of *SPE*, the major class features [±consonantal] and [±vocalic] cross-classify to define four classes of segments, as in (69).[23]

(69)		liquids	nasals and obstruents	voiced vowels	glides
consonantal		+	+	−	−
vocalic		+	−	+	−

In chapter 8 of *SPE*, Chomsky and Halle (1968: 354) propose a modification to this system in which the feature [±vocalic] is eliminated and the feature [±syllabic] is introduced, where any segment that functions as a syllable peak is [+syllabic] and all other segments are [−syllabic]. Such a modification was required in any case in the *SPE* framework for those languages in which consonants such as liquids and nasals can function as syllable peaks, as in Czech *prst* 'finger.'

In our framework, we do not need features like [±vocalic] or [±syllabic], since syllabicity can be determined from syllable position; i.e., a vowel is the rightmost segment dominated by the first mora of a syllable. In general, syllabicity can be determined in any sequence of segments by finding segments which are *local sonority peaks,* meaning an element surrounded on both sides by less sonorant elements (or word boundaries). This in turn means that a syllabic segment, like the *r* of Czech *prst,* does

---

[23] In *SPE* [±sonorant] is also included among the major class features. It and [±consonantal] have the same definitions as in Section 2.3 of Chapter 2. Voiceless vowels in *SPE* are given the same feature composition as the corresponding glides, i.e., [−consonantal, −vocalic].

not differ in feature composition from the same segment used as a consonant, for example, the *r* of Czech *ruka* 'hand.' Thus, our rules for English syllabification must include a search for sonority maxima as defined by the Sonority Hierarchy (25).

Nevertheless, there are certain instances where we will need to distinguish between vowels and consonants in underlying representations, in order to account for certain facts about English stress. For example, in *gálaxy*, stress is on the first syllable rather than on the second. Nouns in English are usually stressed on the penultimate syllable if it is heavy (i.e., bimoraic), as in *appéndix*. In addition, the final syllable of nouns is generally ignored in determining their stress. This would lead us to expect stress on the second syllable of *galaxy*. However, stress is placed correctly if the final segment of this word is a glide rather than a vowel, for then the final syllable of *galaxy* is *laxy* at the time stress is assigned. In *SPE*, this was a simple matter of assigning the feature [–vocalic] (or [–syllabic]) to the final segment of *galaxy*. For us it is less simple: since [ɪ] and [j] do not differ in distinctive features, the final segment of *galaxy* is a local sonority peak in any event. We will regard this final segment as the glide [j] in underlying representation, temporarily adopting the idea of CV phonology (Section 3.3.2) that [j] is linked to a C node in underlying representation. In practice we will simply transcribe it as /j/ when it must be considered a consonant.

The need to disregard certain final elements for the purpose of some phonological rules goes by the name *extrametricality*. We will make extensive use of extrametricality in developing the rules for English stress in Chapter 4. Thus when we say that a final syllable of a noun is disregarded in assigning stress, as in the previous paragraph, we formalize this by saying that the final syllable is extrametrical. An extrametrical element is one that is temporarily removed from consideration for metrical rules, though ultimately it is returned to structure and so is ultimately pronounced. We will mark extrametrical elements by enclosing them in angled brackets (< >). In addition to the extrametricality of the final syllable of nouns, a single final consonant is extrametrical for purposes of stress assignment in all word classes. A verb, for example, is stressed on its final syllable if that is heavy, but a single word-final consonant does not make the syllable heavy, as in *astónish*, stressed on the penultimate syllable. A final syllable ending in two consonants is heavy and stressed, as in *molést*. If the final consonant is marked extrametrical, the final syllable of *astonish* is not heavy when stress is assigned, but the final syllable of *molest* is. We consider that final consonants are made extrametrical before syllabification, so that the final syllable of *astonish* is assigned only one mora. (Some earlier treatments, such as Hayes (1982) and Jensen (1993), had syllabification before extrametricality.) Like the underlying distinction between [ɪ] and [j], extrametricality will be fully justified and discussed in detail in Chapter 4.

Finally, as discussed in Section 2.4.2 of Chapter 2, we assume that vowels in underlying representation are distinguished in terms of tenseness, i.e., [±ATR]. This is the distinction assumed in *SPE* also, although much recent work has assumed that the difference between the vowels of *beet* and *bit* is one of length rather than of tenseness, representing the difference autosegmentally in terms of linking a vowel matrix to one versus two V slots (or moras). However, we noted in Section 2.4.2 of Chapter 2 that both length and tenseness have to be seen as distinctive in English vowels, based on Halle (1977), who noted that the vowels [ɑ:] of *Chicago* and [ɒ:] of *Catawba* are stressed (and hence long) but do not undergo Vowel Shift (hence lax in underlying representation).[24] To capture this idea in the present framework, we mark the vowels in question underlyingly as [–ATR] and with a mora in underlying representation. We then formulate the rules for syllabification in such a way that a mora is attached to each vowel, with an additional mora being attached to a vowel that is [+ATR]. The vowel of *beet* receives two moras because it is underlyingly [+ATR], while the vowel of *bit* receives only one because it is [–ATR]. The vowels [ɑ:] and [ɒ:] are underlyingly [–ATR] and so receive only one mora by the rule, but they have an underlying mora, so they emerge from syllabification with two moras. They are thus long, and so their syllables are heavy and so stressed by the stress rules, but still lax ([–ATR]), so they retain their quality and do not undergo Vowel Shift.

The rules for Consonant Extrametricality and Syllabification are given in (70). These are in fact the first rules of the phonology of English, in order of application.

(70)   *Rules for English syllabification*
        Consonant Extrametricality
            A word-final consonant is extrametrical.

[24] They are phonetically [+ATR] as a consequence of a later rule, *a/o*-Tensing, (34) in Chapter 7.

Syllabification
1. Assign a mora to the string C_0V, where V is a local sonority maximum according to the Sonority Hierarchy (25) and C_0 is a possible (maximal) onset according to the Sonority Sequencing Generalization (26) and the restrictions and dispensations on onsets (44), (45).
2. If V in step 1 is [+ATR], assign a second mora to it. Join the two moras attached to this vowel as one syllable.
3. A string C_1 which does not belong to an onset must be a coda. Adjoin such a string to the second mora of a bimoraic vowel; assign it a mora of its own after a monomoraic vowel. This mora must be joined to the syllable dominating the mora preceding it.

Before proceeding to the examples, some comments on these rules are in order. Consonant Extrametricality makes any word-final consonant extra-metrical, including certain consonants that ultimately become vowels, such as underlying word-final [j] in words like *galaxy* and underlying word-final [ɹ] in words like *metre*. We will fully justify considering these segments as underlying consonants in later chapters.

The local sonority maximum referred to in part 1 of Syllabification will in practice always be a vowel, although it could in principle include syllabic sonorants like the final segment of *metre*. These will however always be extrametrical by Consonant Extrametricality. Part 2 of syllab-ification adds a second mora to tense vowels only, and so not to the vowel of *bit* nor to the [–ATR] (long) vowels of *Chicago* and *Catawba*, since these vowels are [–ATR]. Finally, part 3 of syllabification adjoins any consonants remaining after parts 1 and 2 to a second mora, if there is one, or creates a second mora to contain them. The consequence of our statement of parts 2 and 3 of syllabification is that a syllable will never contain more than two moras, although it may contain only one and always contains at least one.

The examples in (71) illustrate the operation of these rules on some of the words we considered in (8) of Section 3.2, along with another example not introduced there. Notice that we can now state the gener-alization for the stress of words such as those in (8) even more simply. These words receive penultimate stress only when the penultimate sylla-ble contains two moras (II, III), otherwise the antepenultimate syllable is stressed (if there is one: I). The example *extra* shows the attachment of the multiple onset consonants to the mora of the syllable peak in the second syllable.

(71)

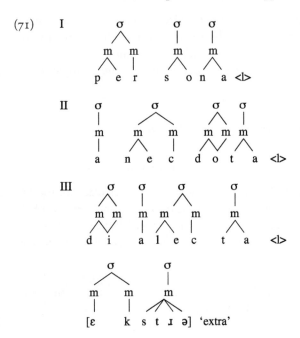

3.5 Exceptions, Real and Apparent

There are a few genuine counterexamples to the Coda Condition. We have already mentioned the words in (55), which contain a long vowel followed by a consonant that is not linked to an adjacent consonant for place features. There are also a few words with short vowels before a cluster of three consonants and another vowel, where no adjacent pair of consonants can be linked to common place features and the first two consonants must be regarded as a coda. We give some of these in (72).

(72)   arctic, sculpture, absorption

Borowsky (1989: 163) lists fifteen words of this type, but some of her examples do not belong in this group. For example, in *mixture* and *fixture* only the first consonant [k] of the intervocalic cluster belongs to the coda of the first syllable. This further reduces the list of relevant counterexamples.[25] In fact, *absorption* is nearly unique as a derived noun in *-tion* added

---

[25] Borowsky apparently considers the syllabification of *mixture* to be [mɪks.tjʊɹ], but by our rules it is [mɪk.stʃʊɹ] (in underlying representation /mɪkstɹɪ/).

to a stem-final cluster which cannot be place linked (two others being *infarction* and *excerption*). Ordinarily, such stem-final clusters require the allomorph *-ation*,[26] as in *usurpation, exculpation, inculcation*.

The examples in (73) should not be considered counterexamples to the Coda Condition.

(73)   *Compounds*
        worldwide, bandsman, helmsman, tribesman

        Stratum 2 suffixes
        childhood, apartment, cowardly, eventful, tasteless, worldly

In the theory of Lexical Phonology, syllabification takes place on the first stratum of the lexicon. Derivations formed on the second stratum of the lexicon, including compounds, have no effect on syllabification. This is in contrast to words like *sculpture* and *absorption* from (71), which are formed by stratum 1 suffixes.

There are a number of apparent exceptions to the principle that onsets are maximized, but most can be explained in terms of the theory of Lexical Phonology. Consider the words in (74).

(74)   *Compounds*
        hat rack, map library, mass transit

        Stratum 2 suffixes
        sleep.less.ness, luck.less, fin.ger.ing, sap.ling

As we have seen, clusters *tr, pl, str* are acceptable onsets in words like *mattress, amplify, monstrous*. But these clusters are divided in *hat rack, map library, mass transit* so that the first consonant belongs to the first syllable. In terms of Lexical Phonology, the individual words, *hat, rack, map*, etc., are syllabified in stratum 1 of the phonology, and the compounds *hat rack*, etc., are formed subsequently, in stratum 2 of the morphology. We will simply assume that no resyllabification takes place after stratum 2 morphology.[27] The same explanation holds for words formed with stratum 2 suffixes like *sleeplessness*. Although *pl* and *sn* are acceptable onsets, they are divided in *sleeplessness*, the syllabification of the individual morphemes being retained in the derivatives. This is especially evident with vowel-initial suffixes such as *-ing*. Although *gr* is

---

[26] This allomorph violates the Coda Condition itself, since its underlying representation is /æt + jən/.
[27] Some resyllabification will occur in conjunction with stratum 2 phonological rules that delete vowels or vocalize glides, as detailed in Chapter 7.

an acceptable onset, it does not make a complex onset to the suffix -*ing* in
fingering, where *r* can be syllabic. Similarly, in *sapling*, *p* is a coda rather
than part of the onset. There is a minimal contrast between *twinkling*,
with three syllables, from the verb *twinkle*, and *twinkling* 'instant,' with
two syllables. This is in contrast to a stratum 1 suffix like -*ic*, which does
get syllabified with a preceding cluster, as in *me.tric*, derived from *metre*,
with a syllabic *r*. Again we assume that stratum 2 morphology, both
affixation and compounding, induces no resyllabification, whereas stratum 1 morphology is accompanied by resyllabification, in accordance
with the predictions of the theory of Lexical Phonology. The details of
this model are expanded in Chapter 6.

   Finally, we can point out that a number of names are exceptions either
to the Coda Condition or to the requirement that onsets be maximized.
A representative sample is given in (75).

(75)   *Names: Coda Condition exceptions*
        Carls.berg, Kings.ley, Blooms.bury, Salz.burg

        Names: medial onsets not maximized[28]
        Ack.royd, Ack.ron, Rock.land, Lock.wood, At.will, At.wood,
        At.water, Att.ridge, Dopp.ler, Kap.lan

Names are often deviant with respect to a number of phonological phenomena. Many of these names appear to be compounds or other stratum 2
derivations; others appear to be foreign; many fall in both categories.
Consequently, we do not need to consider them exceptional, but more
work may be required to determine their phonological status.

3.6   Exercises

3.1   Syllabification
        Divide the words from exercises 2.1 and 2.2 into syllables. Show
        the metrical structure of each syllable using the moraic approach of
        Section 3.3.4. Save the results for a further exercise in Chapter 4.
3.2   Possible Words
        Which of the following are impossible as hypothetical English
        words, and why?

---

[28] There are a few examples in this category that are not names, like *mush.room*. But, interestingly,
note the slang form *shroom*.

a. blick   [blɪk]
b. bnick   [bnɪk]
c. warmk   [wɒɹmk]
d. tyarm   [tjɑɹm]
e. sagdleen   [sægdliịn]
f. mring   [mɹɪŋ]
g. chlamp   [ʧlæmp]
h. zrool   [zɹuwl]]
i. taymprel   [teịmprɛl]
j. reemklint [ɹiịmklɪnt]

3.3 More Impossible Words

Make up three more impossible English words, and show why they are so.

3.4 Moraic Writing

Write your name in the Japanese Hiragana syllabary in (5). Discuss the types of difficulties you encounter, if any.

CHAPTER 4

English Stress

English stress has an apparent contrastive (or distinctive) function in a small number of cases. These cases can be divided into two types. In the first type, the words are unrelated and are simply accidentally similar in segmental properties, differing only in the position of the main stress. Some cases like this are illustrated in (1).[1]

(1) *final* *nonfinal*
     deféct   défect
     belów   bíllow
     refér   réefer
     defér   díffer
     abýss   ábess

The majority of cases where English stress appears to function contrastively are ones where the words are related, in that one is a verb with final stress and the other is a noun with a meaning related to the verb and nonfinal main stress. Some of these are illustrated in (2).

(2) *verb*   *noun*   *gloss of noun*
     tormént   tórmènt   'consequence of being tormented'
     conflíct cónflìct 'result of things conflicting'
     impórt   ímpòrt   'that which is imported'
     expórt   éxpòrt   'that which is exported'
     permít   pérmìt   'that which permits something'

Pairs like those in (2) form a major part of the evidence for Lexical Phonology, which will be treated in greater detail in Chapter 6. For the

---

[1] We mark stresses informally with the acute accent (´) for primary stress and grave accent (`) for nonprimary stress, disregarding the relative strength of nonprimary stresses for the time being. These differences are important in English and will be represented more accurately when necessary.

present we note that these pairs exhibit a considerable degree of regularity, which suggests that it would be fruitful to seek rules for stress in English. This chapter is devoted to that task. It will be clear in the course of the discussion that there are also a considerable number of idiosyncrasies. We will note these also and try to find the most economical way of dealing with them.

To place the English stress system in context, we will first develop a *parametric* approach to stress systems in general, based on the work of Hayes (1980; 1982; 1995). A *parameter* is a grammatical property that admits of two possible settings, and each setting has far-reaching consequences for the grammar as a whole. For example, in syntax, there is a parameter which determines the position of the *head* of a phrase. Some languages, such as English and Italian, have the head at the left end of a phrase, and are called *head-first* languages. Other languages, including Japanese and Korean, have the head at the right end of the phrase, and are called *head-last* languages. Fixing this one parameter has wide implications for the word order in these languages. Similarly, fixing certain parameters concerned with the shape and positioning of stress feet goes a long way in describing the stress system of a language.

As discussed in Section 1.2 of Chapter 1, we will develop a metrical approach to stress using trees. This involves rules that construct feet and that organize the feet into word trees. As discussed in Section 3.4.4 of Chapter 3, word-final consonants are generally *extrametrical*, or temporarily kept out of consideration, for the purpose of constructing syllables. We will also allow certain syllables to be extrametrical while stress trees are being constructed. Some rules of *destressing* are also necessary; these remove feet. Extrametrical syllables and syllables that have had their dominating feet removed are known as *stray* syllables. We will propose a procedure for adjoining stray syllables to adjacent feet so that ultimately all syllables belong to feet. Although Hayes (1995: 108–109) claims that adjunction is not necessary, we will show that it is essential for at least three segmental rules, none of which can be adequately accounted for otherwise.

4.1   Parameters of Stress

We will list the parameters in (3), then discuss some of the ways in which various settings combine in the description of actual language stress systems.

(3)   *Parameter 1*: Foot construction is *Quantity Sensitive* or *Quantity Insensitive*.
       Parameter 2: Stress feet are either *maximally binary* or *unbounded*.
       Parameter 3: Stress feet are either *left branching and left strong* or *right
       branching and right strong*.
       Parameter 4: Stress feet are constructed either *right to left* or *left to right*.
       Parameter 5: The phonological word tree that groups the feet of a word
       together is either *left branching* or *right branching*.

To begin with we will consider quantity-insensitive systems, in which foot
construction does not consider syllable weight. Later, we will look at
quantity-sensitive systems. So, for now, all systems have parameter 1 set
at *quantity insensitive*.

Parameter 2 concerns the size of feet. If feet are maximally binary, they
cannot be larger than two syllables. A foot containing a single syllable may
be formed in a system where feet are constrained to be maximally binary.
Such a foot is called a *degenerate* foot. These are illustrated in (4). The
terminals are syllables, which would dominate syllable trees like those we
saw in Chapter 3.

(4)   *Binary feet*   *Degenerate foot*
       left strong   *right strong*

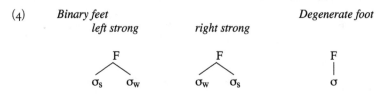

Within the foot all branching is binary (or unary); that is, no node
dominates more than two daughter nodes. A branching node dominates
two positions, one labelled *strong* (s) and the other labelled *weak* (w).
The position of the strong nodes follows from parameter 3 so that left-
dominant feet have the strong nodes on the left and right-dominant feet
have the strong nodes on the right. The strong and weak labelling can be
considered analogous to a magnet. A magnet has both a north and a south
pole. If you break the magnet in half, each half still has a north and a south
pole; you cannot break a magnet in such a way as to isolate the north and
south poles from each other. Similarly, each strong node in a metrical tree
has a corresponding weak sister, and vice versa. Because a degenerate foot
is not branching, the syllable cannot be labelled either strong or weak,
since it has no sister.

The other possible setting of parameter 2 is unbounded. An unbounded
foot can have many syllables, subject to other limitations. Parameter
3 again determines whether it is left or right nodes that are labelled strong.

Here it is necessary to restrict the types of structure that the foot can have. We assume the constraint on foot construction stated in (5).

(5)   *Constraint on foot construction*
       Within the foot only strong nodes may branch.

The effect of (5) on basic feet is to ensure uniformity of branching, either right or left, in feet of more than two syllables. This allows left-branching feet of the type in (6a) and right-branching feet of the type in (6b). Note that strong intermediate nodes are not labelled as to category.

(6)   a. Left branching feet, left nodes labelled strong

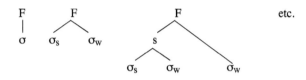

       b. Right branching feet, right nodes labelled strong

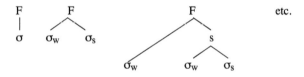

Since parameter 2 has only two settings, there is no way for a language to have basic feet of up to three syllables but no more. Selkirk (1980b) proposed such a maximal three-syllable foot template to account for English stress. However, Hayes argues that three-syllable feet in English are always derived from basic, maximally binary feet, either by adjunction or by syllabification of a nonsyllabic segment, and so the more restrictive version of this parameter can be maintained.

Parameter 4 governs the direction of foot construction. If foot construction is right to left, a foot is first constructed at the right edge of the word, then a second foot is constructed adjacent to the first foot, and additional feet are constructed in a similar manner as long as the word contains enough syllables. If foot construction is left to right, an analogous procedure is followed starting at the left edge of the word.

Parameter 5 governs the way in which the feet of a word are joined together in the word tree. The word tree is unbounded. Word trees are either left branching or right branching. In addition, it is necessary to specify the manner in which the word tree is labelled. Left branching word trees may be labelled left strong, or they may be labelled left strong if and only if branching. Similarly, right-branching word trees may be labelled right strong or right strong if and only if branching. This gives four types of word tree, illustrated in (7) for a structure of three feet. The branching or nonbranching nature of crucial feet is indicated. (The expression *iff* is to be read "if and only if.")

(7)   a. Left branching word tree. Left strong.

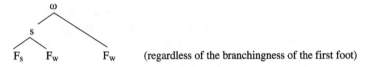

(regardless of the branchingness of the first foot)

b. Left branching word tree. Left strong iff branching.

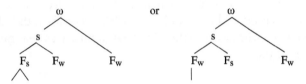

c. Right branching word tree. Right strong

(regardless of the branchingness of the first foot)

d. Right branching word tree. Right strong iff branching.

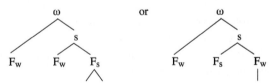

Let us consider an example of how setting these five parameters accounts for the stress system of an actual language, Maranungku (data from Tryon 1970). In this language, primary stress is on the initial syllable, with secondary stress falling on alternate syllables after that, as in the examples of (8).

(8)   a.   tíralk   'saliva'
       b.   mérepèt   'beard'
       c.   yáŋarmàta   'the Pleiades'
       d.   láŋkaràtetì   'prawn'
       e.   wélepènemànta   'kind of duck'

Hayes accounts for this pattern with the parameter settings in (9).

(9)   *Maranungku stress*
       Parameter 1: Foot construction is quantity insensitive.
       Parameter 2: Stress feet are maximally binary.
       Parameter 3: Stress feet are left branching and left strong.
       Parameter 4: Stress feet are constructed left to right.
       Parameter 5: The word tree is left branching, labelled left strong.

This is all that needs to be said about Maranungku stress. We give the word tree for *mérepèt* 'beard' in (10), where the first foot is binary and the second is degenerate. Constructing maximally binary feet means that a degenerate foot is produced when only one syllable remains at the edge of a domain. Below the word we give the *SPE* stress numbers, as determined by the algorithm in (20).

(10)

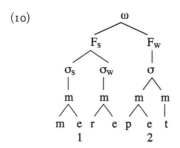

As a second example, consider Latvian (Lazdiņa 1966; Andronov 2002). With a few exceptions, Latvian words have stress on the initial syllable, regardless of the length of the word or the weight of syllables, and there is no secondary stress, as in the examples in (11).

(11)   a.   ['galts]   'table'
       b.   ['maːja]   'house'
       c.   ['fizika]   'physics'
       d.   ['gravitaːtsija]   'gravity'
       e.   ['popularitaːte]   'popularity'

This is described by setting the parameters as in (12).

(12)   *Latvian stress*
        Parameter 1: Quantity insensitive.
        Parameter 2: Unbounded feet.
        Parameter 3: Stress feet are left dominant.
        Parameter 4: Inapplicable.
        Parameter 5: Inapplicable.

In Latvian, each word contains only one stress foot, since there is only one stress per word, and the feet are unbounded. In this case, parameters 4 and 5 are inapplicable. The word node (ω) dominates the single foot of each word.

As a third example, the data in (13) show the stress pattern of Warao (Osborn 1966).

(13)   a.   yàpurùkitànehásе   'verily to climb'
        b.   nàhoròahàkutái   'the one who ate'
        c.   yiwàrabáe   'he finished it'
        d.   enàhoròahàkutái   'the one who caused him to eat'

Hayes analyzes these data in terms of the parameter settings in (14).

(14)   *Warao stress*
        Parameter 1: Quantity insensitive.
        Parameter 2: Maximally binary feet.
        Parameter 3: Stress feet are left branching and left strong.
        Parameter 4: Stress feet are constructed from right to left
        Parameter 5: The word tree is right branching, labelled right strong.

However this is not quite sufficient, since it would imply that the initial syllables of (13c, d) would be stressed, since degenerate feet would be constructed on these syllables. This would result in two consecutive stressed syllables, a situation known as *stress clash*, which seems to be avoided in many languages. There are potentially two ways of avoiding this stress clash in Warao: either not to assign a stress on the initial syllable in the first place, or to remove this stress after it has been assigned. To prevent assigning stress, parameter 2 would need to be revised to allow three options: maximally binary feet, binary feet only, or unbounded feet. Warao would then choose the second option, which would not permit degenerate feet. Hayes (1980: 52) proposes a destressing analysis. Leaving the parameter as it is, and assigning maximally binary feet in Warao, Hayes proposes a destressing rule that we will write as (15).

(15)   *Destressing (Warao)*

$F_w \rightarrow \varnothing$

The vertical line under the foot indicates that it is nonbranching; the subscript *w* indicates that it is a weak foot. So this means "delete a nonbranching weak foot." We will express all destressing rules with this sort of notation. It is understood that only the foot node is deleted by such rules, not any of the material that it dominates.

Once a foot is deleted, the syllable or syllables that it dominated are left *stray*. In different versions of metrical phonology, stray syllables are either left stray or are incorporated into the metrical structure. Hayes assumes that stray syllables in Warao are incorporated directly into the word tree. Another possibility is to incorporate the stray syllable into an adjacent foot by adjunction. We will show that adjunction to a foot is necessary in English. We have no direct evidence for adjunction in Warao, but let us assume that adjunction is the regular procedure for stray syllables in all languages. A preliminary version of Stray-Syllable Adjunction (SSA) is stated in (16). More specific conditions will be incorporated into our analysis of Stray-Syllable Adjunction in English (see 75).

(16)   *Stray-Syllable Adjunction* (cf. Hayes 1982: 235)
         Adjoin a stray syllable by Chomsky Adjunction as a weak member of an adjacent (maximal) foot.[2]
         Chomsky Adjunction of a node x to a node A involves the creation of a new node A that dominates the original node A and the adjoined node x. Schematically,

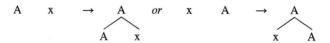

Therefore, following the parameters, the structure in (17a) is produced for (13d) *enàhoròahàkutái* 'the one who caused him to eat.' This is subject to Destressing (15), which produces (17b). This in turn is subject to Stray-Syllable Adjunction (16), which gives the final result, (17c), which also shows the *SPE* stress numbers as determined by (20).

---

[2] The term 'maximal foot' is defined in (19).

(17) a.

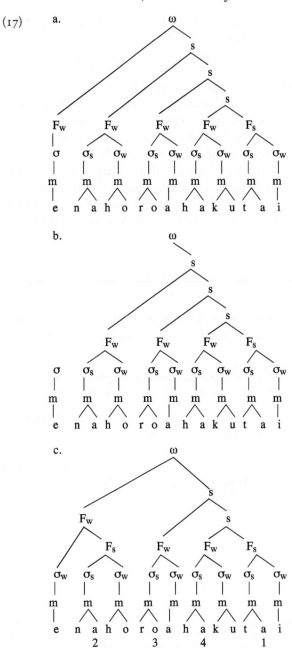

When a syllable is Chomsky adjoined to a foot, a new foot is created that dominates both the syllable that is adjoined and the original foot, as seen in (17c). In Chapter 5, when we develop the complete prosodic hierarchy, we will observe that the normal case is for each unit in the hierarchy (in this case, feet) to dominate only units of the next lower rank (in this case, syllables). However, a specific rule may create recursive structures in which a unit dominates another unit of the same type. Such structures prove necessary for certain rules that have the foot as their domain, as will be shown in detail in Chapter 5. Recursion is restricted, however, in that the definition of the foot is maintained as a unit that contains just one stressed syllable. As seen in (17c), both the lower foot and the foot that dominates it each contain only one stressed syllable. The lower foot in addition contains one unstressed syllable, while the higher foot contains two unstressed syllables.

(18)   *Foot (definition)*
A *foot* is a unit containing one and only one stressed syllable, along with possibly one or more unstressed syllables.

It is useful to have some terminology to distinguish embedded from nonembedded feet. We offer the definitions in (19).

(19)   *Definitions*
A *maximal* foot is a foot that is not dominated by another foot.
A *minimal* foot is a foot that does not dominate another foot.

The stressed syllable within a foot is marked strong (s), unstressed syllables are marked weak (w). Similarly, in the word tree, one foot is marked strong, and the others are marked weak. The strong foot corresponds to the main stress of the word. The weak feet correspond to different lower degrees of stress. The more deeply a foot is embedded in the word tree, the lesser its degree of stress. Liberman and Prince (1977: 259) propose an algorithm for determining the degree of stress in terms of *SPE* numbers from a word tree. We paraphrase their algorithm in (20), repeated from (31) of Chapter 1.[3]

---

[3] Liberman and Prince stated this algorithm in terms of terminal nodes, rather than feet (cf. (31) in section 1.2 of Chapter 1). It seems that this procedure would assign stress numbers to unstressed syllables also. We have therefore restated it in terms of (the stressed syllables of) feet. In fact, since adjunction creates nested feet, this algorithm can be applied to *maximal* feet only; that is, feet that are not embedded within a higher foot. This concept is developed further in Section 5.3.3 of Chapter 5.

(20)   *Determining* SPE *stress numbers from the tree:*
a.   If a (maximal) foot is labelled *s*, the stress number of its stressed (strong) syllable is equal to the number of nodes dominating the first *w* node dominating the foot, plus one.
b.   If a (maximal) foot is labelled *w*, the stress number of its stressed (strong) syllable is equal to the number of nodes dominating the foot plus one.

Applied to (17c), this algorithm gives primary stress on the penultimate syllable, secondary stress on the second syllable, tertiary stress on the fourth syllable, and quaternary stress on the sixth syllable, as shown under the tree. The *SPE* numbers are merely a guide to the pronunciation, not a part of the structure.

4.2   Quantity Sensitivity

In a quantity-sensitive stress system, syllable weight plays a role in the construction of feet.[4] Quantity sensitivity can be stated as in (21).

(21)   *Quantity sensitivity*
In a quantity-sensitive system, syllables marked weak must be monomoraic.

The first quantity-sensitive system we will examine is Eastern Cheremis (Hayes 1980: 57). The syllable structure of this language is a little different from English as described in Chapter 3. In Eastern Cheremis, syllable weight is determined entirely by the character of its vowel. A syllable with a long (sometimes called 'full') vowel is heavy, and a syllable with a short vowel (transcribed as [ə]) is light, regardless of whether or not it has a coda consonant. That is, Eastern Cheremis syllables have the forms of (22). Syllable type (22c) is monomoraic, whereas syllable type (21c) in Section 3.3.4 of Chapter 3 is heavy.

(22)   a. σ   b. σ   c. σ   d. σ

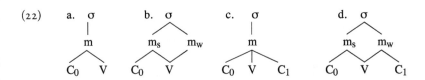

[4] Quantity sensitivity should more accurately be called 'weight sensitivity.' We retain the term 'quantity sensitivity' as the one in general use.

Eastern Cheremis stress is described in terms of parameters as in (23).

(23)   *Eastern Cheremis stress*
       Parameter 1: Quantity sensitive.
       Parameter 2: Unbounded feet.
       Parameter 3: Stress feet are left branching and left strong.
       Parameter 4: Stress feet are constructed right to left.
       Parameter 5: The word tree is right branching, labelled right strong.

The effect of these parameter settings is to place primary stress on the last full vowel of a word or on the first syllable if there are no full vowels. We give some examples in (24).

(24)   a.   ['pyːgəlmə]   'cone'
       b.   ['kiːdəʃtəzə]   'in his hand'
       c.   ['tələzən]   'moon's'
       d.   [ˌʃiːn'ʧaːm]   'I sit'
       e.   [ˌʃlaːˈpaːʒəm]   'his hat (accusative)'

Unlike Latvian (12), we have to specify a value for parameter 4 in Eastern Cheremis. Because Latvian stress is quantity insensitive, constructing an unbounded foot means constructing a foot over the whole word so that there is no chance to construct additional feet. Because Eastern Cheremis stress is quantity sensitive, unbounded feet do not necessarily cover the whole word. The construction of a foot must stop when a heavy syllable is encountered; otherwise, there would be a bimoraic syllable in the weak position of a foot. To see this, consider [ˌʃiːn'ʧaːm] 'I sit.' The tree built for this word in accordance with the parameters in (23) is (25a). If a foot were formed over the entire word, the result (25b) would violate quantity sensitivity, since the weak second syllable is bimoraic.

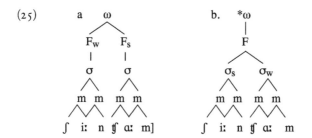

Hayes in fact constructs only a single foot at the right edge of the word. We have assumed iterative foot construction. There is little information on secondary stress in Eastern Cheremis – the initial foot in (25a) implies a secondary stress on the first syllable – but, according to Hayes (1980: 57–58), the foot is the domain of vowel harmony in Eastern Cheremis. Unfortunately, Hayes does not represent the results of vowel harmony in his examples (our 24), but implies that it has the effect of assimilating reduced vowels in backness and roundness to the nearest preceding full vowel – which is stated most perspicuously as an assimilation within the foot.

A second example of quantity-sensitive stress is Classical Latin (Hayes 1980: 66ff). Syllable weight in Latin is determined in a way similar to English: a heavy syllable either contains a long vowel or has one or more coda consonants. In words of three or more syllables, main stress falls on the penult (next-to-last syllable) if it is heavy, otherwise the antepenult receives main stress. The final syllable is not stressed (except in words of one syllable), regardless of weight. We give some examples in (26).

(26) a. ['anɪmɑl]   'animal'
      b. [anɪ'malɪa]   'animals'
      c. ['karmɪna]   'songs'
      d. ['arbɔre:s]   'trees'
      e. [lɛ'o:nɪs]   'lion (genitive)'
      f. [ɔrna:'mɛntum]   'embellishment'
      g. [aɪdɪ'fɪkɪum]   'building'
      h. [rɛ'fɛktus]   'restored (masc. sg. participle)'
      i. [rɛ'fe:kɪt]   'restored (perfect 3rd singular)'
      j. ['rɛfɪkɪt]   'restores (present 3rd singular)'
      k. ['ɔs]   'bone'

One way to describe this pattern would be to construct maximally ternary feet, where the second of three syllables cannot be bimoraic. This would not only not be in accord with Hayes's theory, it would leave the irrelevance of the weight of the word-final syllable unexplained. Hayes adopts a different approach, suggested by Liberman and Prince (1977: 293). This is to allow certain elements to be *extrametrical*; that is, ignored temporarily by the stress rules. We already proposed that word-final consonants in English be treated as extrametrical. For Latin, we require that word-final syllables be extrametrical (except in words of one syllable). Then Latin stress can be described in terms of maximally binary feet, which are within the scope of Hayes's approach. We describe Latin stress in (27).

(27)   *Latin stress*
        Extrametricality: a word-final syllable is extrametrical.
        Parameter 1: Quantity sensitive.
        Parameter 2: Maximally binary feet.
        Parameter 3: Stress feet are left branching and left strong.
        Parameter 4: Stress feet are constructed from right to left.
        Parameter 5: The word tree is right branching, labelled right strong.

As with Eastern Cheremis, we have little information on secondary stress in Latin. With our statement of parameters 4 and 5 we leave open the possibility of secondary stresses.

Extrametricality receives additional support from the stress system of Winnebago. In this language, primary stress falls on the third mora from the beginning of the word. Secondary stresses appear on every second mora after that, as in *haakítujikshanà* 'I pull it taut (declarative)' (Hayes 1980: 72). If we expanded the foot inventory to include ternary feet, we would need to construct a ternary foot at the beginning of the word, then construct binary feet after that from left to right. With Hayes's more restricted foot inventory, we can mark the first mora extrametrical and simply construct binary feet from left to right.

Not just any element can be extrametrical, though. Hayes proposes the restrictions in (28) on extrametricality.

(28)   *Restrictions on extrametricality*
        a.   Extrametricality can only be marked on a single unit (e.g., segment (consonant), mora, syllable).
        b.   The unit marked extrametrical must be at an edge (left or right, more often on the right).
        c.   Extrametricality cannot mark an entire domain extrametrical.

Restrictions (28a, b) are self-explanatory. Restriction (28c) allows stress to be assigned to a monosyllabic word in Latin like ['ɔs] 'bone' (26k). Word-final syllables are generally extrametrical in Latin, but not in a monosyllabic word, where extrametricality would remove the entire word from the domain of stress assignment, rendering it unstressable.

Like syllables made stray by foot deletion, extrametrical syllables must be adjoined into the prosodic structure. We can illustrate this with the derivation of *reficit* 'restores.' In (29a) we give the structure that results from extrametricality and construction of a maximally binary, quantity-sensitive left-dominant foot. We adopt the convention of enclosing extrametrical elements in angle brackets (<>). In (29b) we show the result of adjunction and construction of the word tree.

(29)

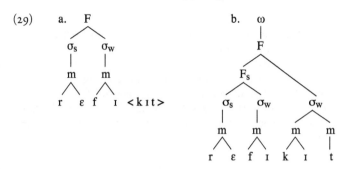

We assume Chomsky Adjunction here as well. Prince (1980) suggests that structures of this sort are needed for the description of Estonian gradation. He further suggests that the minimal foot, i.e., a foot with no foot embedded within it, is universally the domain for weakening processes, citing the obligatory flapping of *t* in *pity* vs the optional flapping of *t* in *unity*. While our account of flapping is somewhat different (see Chapter 5, Section 5.3.8), this seems to be a correct observation.

4.3 English

We now have all the ingredients necessary for a description of English stress. This poses some additional challenges to the parametric approach, since English has (apparent) ternary feet not only in word-final position (30a), like Latin, but also in other positions of the word, as shown in (30b).

(30)   a.   *Ternary feet in word-final position*
           América, lábyrinth

       b.   *Ternary feet in nonfinal position*
           detérioràte, Nèbucadnézzar, héterodòx, pàraphernália

However, like Latin, we can describe English in the framework of a parametric theory. We will add both extrametricality, such as we saw in Latin, and destressing, such as we saw in Warao. We will also have to recognize a certain amount of lexical idiosyncrasy. The basic analysis of English stress is given in (31). Following that, we will fill in the details. Apparently ternary feet in (30a) are a consequence of extrametricality with subsequent adjunction; apparently ternary feet in (30b) are a consequence of destressing (or other rules) with subsequent adjunction.

(31) *English stress*
      Extrametricality of final consonants and some word-final syllables.
      Parameter 1: Quantity sensitive.
      Parameter 2: Maximally binary feet.
      Parameter 3: Stress feet are left branching and left strong.
      Parameter 4: Stress feet are constructed from right to left.
      Parameter 5: The word tree is right branching. Word tree labelling is
      right strong if branching and under certain other conditions (to be
      specified).

4.3.1   The Rightmost Stress

Discussions of English stress generally start with the assignment of the
rightmost stress in the word, which is often but not always the main word
stress. The assignment of additional stresses is generally treated separately
under the heading of 'retraction.' For ease of exposition we will follow this
usual descriptive practice in this section, introducing the rightmost stress
in the treatment based on Hayes (1980), Liberman and Prince (1977), and
ultimately on *SPE*. We then show that the same rule, quantity-sensitive,
iterating right to left, produces all the required remaining stresses as well,
obviating the need for any retraction rules (essentially following Kager
1989). Though some excess stresses are assigned in this manner, the
unneeded stresses can be trimmed back with independently motivated
destressing rules.

The simplest case of assignment of the rightmost stress is that of verbs
and unsuffixed adjectives. These are stressed on the final syllable if it has a
long vowel or ends in a string of at least two consonants[5]; otherwise the
penultimate is stressed. Hayes (1982: 238) gives the examples in (32).[6]

---

[5] By 'long vowel' we mean a vowel that has been assigned two moras by the rules of English
syllabification given in Section 3.4.4 of Chapter 3. These are generally diphthongs phonetically,
derived by rules to be discussed in Chapter 7. Similarly, a 'short vowel' is one assigned a single mora
by the rules of Chapter 3.

[6] Hammond (1999: 251–252) notes that adjectives like *honest*, *modest*, and *earnest* do not have final
stress (contrasting with *robust*). He suggests that these have the suffix *-est*, which usually marks
superlative (cf. *biggest*), although not here. They would then be subject to Adjective (Syllable)
Extrametricality, in our terms. This is difficult to accept; we may simply have to mark these
adjectives as (irregularly) subject to extrametricality. It is somewhat easier to accept his suggestion
that adjectives like *silent* and *second* end in a suffix *-ent*, *-ant*,*-end*, *-ond* (here attached to bound
stems) that otherwise attaches to words *(dividend)* or stems *(vacate, vacant)*. Adjectives like *orange*,
damask, and many verbs *(challenge, harvest)* that also end in clusters without having final stress may
be considered to be derived from the corresponding nouns by zero derivation (Section 6.1.3 of
Chapter 6) on stratum 2 and so have stress assigned on the initial syllable by the rules for nouns.

(32)

		long vowel in final syllable	two or more final consonants	other
a.	*verbs*	obéy	molést	astónish
		atóne	usúrp	devélop
b.	*adjectives*	divíne	robúst	cómmon
		discréte	ovért	illícit

To account for this pattern, we can assume that a single word-final consonant is extrametrical, as indeed we already proposed in our rules for English syllabification in (70) in Section 3.4.4 of Chapter 3. Thus, a final syllable ending in a single consonant preceded by a short vowel (right column of 32) is not heavy at the point where stress is assigned, but a final syllable ending in two or more consonants is heavy. A final syllable with a long vowel is heavy regardless of how many consonants are in the coda. We give partial derivations of four words from (32) in (33). While other stressing and destressing rules apply, in these cases, this preliminary rule already results in the actual stress pattern of the word (though not the final word tree).

(33)

	a. atone	b. molest	c. develop	d. obey
underlying representation	/ætɒn/	/mɔlɛst/	/dɪvɛləp/	/ɔbæ/
Consonant Extrametricality	ætɒ<n>	mɔlɛs<t>	dɪvɛlə<p>	ɔbæ

Syllabification

The patterns of nouns are slightly more complex. A common pattern in nouns whose final syllable does not contain a long vowel is to stress the penult if it is heavy, otherwise the antepenult. In these cases the weight of the final syllable does not matter. This is shown in the examples of (34).

(34)

	long vowel	consonant-final
light penult	*in penult*	*penult*
América	Manitóba	agénda
díscipline	factótum	appéndix
lábyrinth	elítist	amálgam

The situation with these nouns is very similar to the Latin examples in (26). Hayes (1982: 240) proposes Noun Extrametricality to account for these. We give a slightly different version of this rule in (35).[7]

(35)   *Noun Extrametricality*
        Mark the final syllable extrametrical in nouns whose final syllable does not contain a long vowel.

We therefore assume the derivation in (36), where the same English Stress Rule applies after Noun Extrametricality. For now, we show the derivation only as far as the construction of the main word stress.

(36)   a. labyrinth   b. Manitoba   c. agenda

        underlying representation   /læbɯnθ/   /mænɪtɒbə/   /ədʒɛndə/

        Consonant Extrametricality læbɯn<θ>   mænɪtɒbə   ədʒɛndə

        Syllabification   σ σ   σ   σ σ σ σ   σ σ   σ
                                    | | /\ | | /\ | | /\ |
                                    m m m m   m m m m m   m m m m
                                    | | | | | | \/ | | | | |
                                    læ bɪ ɹɪ n<θ>   mæ nɪ tɒ bə   ə dʒɛn də

        Noun Extrametricality   læ bɪ <ɹɪn<θ>>   mæ n ɪ tɒ <bə>   ə dʒɛn <də>

        English Stress Rule (first F   F   F
        application; structures   /\ | |
        abbreviated)   læ bɪ <ɹɪn<θ>>   mæ nɪ tɒ <bə>   ə dʒɛn <də>

We have stated Noun Extrametricality differently from Hayes in that we exclude final syllables that contain a long vowel. If such syllables were extrametrical, as they are by Hayes's rule, then we would expect that nouns would never have final stress, which is incorrect. Nouns with a long vowel in the last syllable have stress on this syllable, either secondary (37a) or primary (37b).

(37)   a. Mánitòu   cávalcàde   mísanthròpe   vétò
        b. mònsóon   ènginéer   sèrenáde   trùstée

---

[7] In (42) we will combine this rule with Adjective Extrametricality (40) into the single rule of Syllable Extrametricality, which will be refined in Section 4.6. In Section 4.7 we will see that, in some cases, final syllables of nouns and suffixed adjectives need to be extrametrical even when their final syllable contains a long vowel.

Hayes accounts for this with a special rule of Long-Vowel Stressing, ordered before Noun Extrametricality. However, this rule appears to duplicate the effect of the English Stress Rule, in that it places stress on a heavy syllable. We will pursue an alternative analysis in which such words are exempt from Noun Extrametricality and receive stress by the normal operation of the English Stress Rule.

Some nouns with a short vowel in the final syllable also receive final stress, somewhat idiosyncratically. Hayes cites the examples in (38).[8]

(38) a. *final syllable*   b. *final syllable*
         stressed   *unstressed*

      mániàc   Ísaac
      pársnìp   kétchup
      prótòn   ápron
      ínsèct   súbject
      gýmnàst   témpest
      nárthèx   hélix

Hayes accounts for these with a foot on the final syllable in the underlying representation. We can, however, assume that these too are stressed by the English stress rule on the final syllable if these nouns are marked as exceptions to Noun Extrametricality, and, if they end in a single consonant (38a), also exceptions to Consonant Extrametricality. This will also account for words like *ellipse* without the need of a final vowel ε that is subsequently deleted, as it is analyzed in *SPE*.[9]

Adjectives formed with suffixes follow a pattern similar to nouns in that they have antepenultimate stress if the penult is light, and penultimate stress if the penult is heavy, as in (39).[10]

(39)   *long vowel*   *consonant-final*
      light penult   *in penult*   *in penult*

      munícipal   àdjectíval   fratérnal
      màgnánimous   desírous   treméndous
      signíficant   clairvóyant   relúctant
      ínnocent   complácent   depéndent
      prímitive   condúcive   expénsive

[8] *Gymnast* does not have final stress for (most) Canadian speakers. *Subject* may have final stress as a noun but not as an adjective (as in the phrase *subject to*).
[9] A final ε will be invoked in Chapter 6 to account for alternations such as *bath, bathe*, and in Chapter 7 to account for alternations like *reduce, reduction*.
[10] Final *-al, -ous, -ent, -ive, -ant* are regarded as suffixes even if the stem to which they are attached is not an independent word.

Hayes accounts for these with a rule of Adjective Extrametricality, which marks a suffix extrametrical at the end of an adjective. It seems more correct to mark the final *syllable* that contains the suffix extrametrical. We give our statement of this rule in (40).

(40)   *Adjective Extrametricality*
        Mark the final syllable extrametrical in adjectives formed with a suffix if this syllable does not contain a long vowel.

We can illustrate this with some derivations in (41).

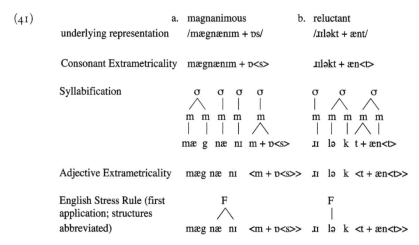

(41)   a. magnanimous   b. reluctant
        underlying representation   /mægnænɪm + ɒs/   /ɹɪləkt + ænt/

        Consonant Extrametricality   mægnænɪm + ɒ<s>   ɹɪləkt + æn<t>

        Syllabification   σ   σ   σ   σ   σ   σ   σ
                                     /\\ | | | | /\\ /\\
                                      m m m m   m   m m m m m m
                                      | | | | /\\ | | | |/\\ |
                                     mæ g næ nɪ m + ɒ<s>   ɹɪ lə k t + æn<t>

        Adjective Extrametricality   mæg næ nɪ <m + ɒ<s>> ɹɪ lə k <t + æn<t>>

        English Stress Rule (first   F   F
        application; structures   /\\ |
        abbreviated)   mæg næ nɪ <m + ɒ<s>> ɹɪ lə k <t + æn<t>>

The suffix *-ic* is an exception to Adjective Extrametricality. Consequently, words like *atomic* are stressed on the syllable before this suffix, as a consequence of building a foot over the last two syllables, including the suffix.

In view of the close similarity between Noun Extrametricality and Adjective Extrametricality, we combine these into a single rule, which we call Syllable Extrametricality, given in (42).

(42)   *Syllable Extrametricality*
        In adjectives formed with a suffix and in nouns, mark the final syllable extrametrical if it does not contain a long vowel

4.3.2   The English Stress Rule: Further Iterations

We will now show that the English Stress Rule, in the form of the parameters in (31) iterates from right to left to assign additional stresses in longer words. Indeed, it would be strange, given the parametric approach, to assume that different principles are needed for stresses in different positions of the word. Nevertheless, assignment of stresses after the first stress on the right edge of the word has been referred to as retraction, historically, since in some respects it behaves somewhat differently than the assignment of the rightmost stress. We can examine the question from this point of view in this section, and then show how retraction can be reduced to the iterative application of the same rule that assigns the rightmost stress.

Liberman and Prince (1977) identify three modes of retraction, which they refer to as weak retraction, strong retraction, and long retraction. In their analysis, a particular mode of retraction is triggered by certain types of words or by certain suffixes.

Weak retraction places a stress two syllables before an existing stress if the syllable before that stress is light but on the syllable immediately before an existing stress if that syllable is heavy (or the only one available). Liberman and Prince show that the suffixes in (43) show this pattern. In fact, this can be regarded simply as a second iteration of the same quantity-sensitive English stress rule.

(43)   Weak retraction

	light penult	heavy penult	one syllable before suffix
-oid	pyrámidòid	ellípsòid	líthòid
	càrtiláginòid	sàlamándròid	óvòid
-ite	molýbdenìte	stalágmìte	sámìte
	dýnamìte	staláctìte	
-on	pósitròn	eléctròn	léptòn
	báryòn		
-ode	pálinòde	eléctròde	cáthòde
-ide	cýanìde	peróxìde	nítrìde
-i	Géminì	alúmnì	fócì
-ology	phenòmenólogy	aràchnólogy	
		òdòntólogy	
		Ègýptólogy	

Liberman and Prince's strong retraction places stress two syllables before an existing stress regardless of the weight of the second syllable, or one syllable before an existing stress if it is the only one available. Liberman and Prince claim that this mode of retraction is characteristic of verbs in -*ate* and a number of miscellaneous forms. They give examples like those in (44).

(44)   *Strong retraction*
   -*ate*   manípulàte   sálivàte   rótàte
           artículàte   défecàte   óràte
           oríginàte   désignàte
           hydrógenàte   exácerbàte

   misc.   ánecdòte   ádversàry   ínfantìle
           pálindròme   sédentàry   mércantìle
           cávalcàde   vóluntàry   býzantìne
           Árkansàs   mómentàry   árgentìne

Hayes (1982: 247) in fact claims that strong retraction is the normal mode of retraction. However, a great many cases in (44) could be accounted for by weak retraction as well – this is the case where the syllable before the suffix is light, as in the first column of words in -*ate*, (e.g., *manipulate*) and all forms with only one syllable before the suffix (e.g., *rotate*). The cases where the syllable before the suffix is closed by a sonorant (e.g., *exacerbate, adversary*) can have this syllable destressed by Sonorant Destressing (Section 4.4.3) and so might also come under weak retraction, with this syllable first being stressed and then subsequently destressed. Cases of apparent retraction over an underlying long vowel (*salivate, defecate*; cf. *saliva, faeces*) require a special shortening and destressing rule that also applies when assigning the rightmost stress in derived words (e.g., *aspirant, resident*; cf. *aspire, reside*). This is Minor Relabelling (104). The only remaining cases that seem to require strong retraction are those where the syllable before the suffix (or stressed syllable) is closed by an obstruent (*designate, anecdote*). Kager (1989) points out that there are actually very few of these and suggests that these too might be subject to a destressing rule, Arab Destressing (Section 4.4.4). If these alternatives can be maintained, the motivation for strong retraction is greatly weakened.

Liberman and Prince's final retraction mode is long retraction, which retracts stress to the *third* syllable before a stress, across a light syllable plus another syllable. Such a form of retraction entails forming a ternary foot, which is excluded by Hayes's parameters. Fortunately these are also subject to reanalysis, as Hayes shows. The forms in (45) are given by Liberman and Prince to illustrate this possibility.

(45) Long retraction (to be reanalyzed)
      weight of syllable two before rightmost stress (underlined)
      light   heavy

	light	heavy
Noncomplex	Tàtamagoúchi	Monòngahéla
	àbracadábra	
	Wìnnepesaúkee	
	Kàlamazoó	
$\breve{V}\breve{V}$	tóreadòr	
	detérioràte	
	amélioràte	
	ìdeológical	
	méteoroìd	
Greek	héteronỳm	larýngoscòpe
	hélicogràph	
	aútomobìle	
-atory	hallúcinatòry	compénsatòry
	artículatòry	condémnatòry
misc.	péregrinàte	
	véterinàry	
	óxygenàte	

Hayes (1982) accounts for the noncomplex forms by Poststress Destressing (Section 4.4.2): *Tatamagouchi* is initially assigned three feet: (ta)(tama) (gouchi), and the second foot is removed. Hayes (1982: 266) shows that the examples under $\breve{V}\breve{V}$ are actually all cases where the first vowel is [i], and proposes that these cases derive from forms where this sequence appears as / jV̆/, with subsequent vocalization of /j/. The Greek forms can be regarded as compounds ⟦hetero⟧⟦nym⟧, where each part is stressed separately. The forms in *-atory* are to be derived cyclically from forms in *-ate* (e.g., *hallucinate*), with *-ate* destressed by *-ate* Destressing (78 in Chapter 6). The miscellaneous group may also be subject to Poststress Destressing; *oxygenate* is entirely regular with a cyclic derivation (see the end of Section 4.5). Given these reanalyses, the motivation for long retraction seems very weak.

    In conclusion, stress retraction is the iterative application of the English Stress Rule from right to left across a word. This procedure builds binary feet if it can, when the rightmost syllable under consideration is light, otherwise it builds degenerate feet. It may also build a degenerate foot on the initial syllable, if this is the only syllable left when the right-to-left sweep reaches that stage. Some of the feet constructed by this procedure

may be eliminated by destressing rules (Section 4.4). Before we discuss
those, however, we will show how the word tree is constructed.

4.3.3   Word-Tree Construction

Parameter 5 for English stress in (31) states that the word tree is right
branching, labelled right strong if branching and under certain other
conditions. Let us first illustrate cases where the right nodes are labelled
strong if branching, and where there is no destressing. Given the word
hàmamèlidánthemum, three feet are derived by Consonant and Syllable
Extrametricality and the English Stress Rule operating from right to left:
(hama)(meli)(danthe)mum. Stray-Syllable Adjunction (75) adjoins the last
syllable to the rightmost foot. Forming a right-branching word tree
involves first joining the two feet on the right into a constituent, labelling
the right foot strong because it branches. This constituent is then joined
into a word constituent with the initial foot, with the right node again
labelled strong because it branches. Labelling a right node strong automatically entails marking its sister weak, whether it branches or not. This
produces the structure in (46). We adopt a convention of attaching an
extrametrical consonant to an existing mora, if present, with a dashed line,
otherwise to the syllable node. On the last line we give the *SPE* stress
numbers as derived by the algorithm in (20).

(46)

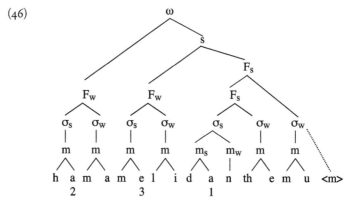

This mode of tree labelling accounts for the stress pattern of a great many
English words. For example, it predicts the common observation that the
main stress of a word is its last stressed syllable that is not the last syllable of
the word. Two common names illustrate this basic pattern. *Ísidòre* has two
feet and the rightmost is labelled weak because it is nonbranching. But

Ìsidóra has a branching right foot, labelled strong, and thus main stress on the penultimate syllable. The trees in (47) demonstrate this.

(47)

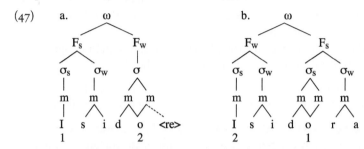

Liberman and Prince (1977: 304ff) identify a number of other environments where right feet are labelled strong, even when nonbranching. One case concerns a number of 'endings' (not necessarily actual suffixes), largely of French origin, that have final main stress. We give these in (48). We assume that word-tree labelling is sensitive to these endings and assigns the label *strong* to the foot dominating them.

(48)

-ier, -eer	èngineér, fròntiér, veneér, càvaliér, chàndeliér
-oon	pàntaloón, òctoroón, tỳcoón, baboón, poltroón
-ique	uníque, àntíque, bezique, Mòzambíque
-oo	tattoó, kazoó, shàmpoó, bàmboó, canoé
-ise	chemíse, valíse, èxpertíse
-ade	sèrenáde, càscáde, grenáde, stòckáde, blòckáde
-ette	nòvelétte, cìgarétte, vignétte, còrvétte
-ee	dèporteé, àddresseé, trùsteé, ábsenteé, Tènnesseé
-elle	bágatélle, mosélle, vìllanélle
-air	affaír, còrsaír, dèbonaír
-che	càrtoúche, pàstíche, brióche, panáche
-esce	àcquiésce, rècrudésce, ìncandésce, èffervésce
-ane	mùndáne, trànspadáne, ùltramòntáne, chicáne
-ar	guitár, bizárre, cigár, bazaár
-eau	flàmbeaú, tàbleaú, chàteaú, pòrtmànteaú
-esque	pìcturésque, gròtésque, stàtuésque, ròmanésque

Another case where Liberman and Prince find unexpected nonbranching strong right branches is with certain words of two syllables whose initial syllable is light, such as those in (49).

(49)   Julý, manúre, attíre, patról, lamént, obéy

There is a certain amount of lexical idiosyncrasy in this class of items; other words of similar structure have the right node weak, since it is nonbranching, as in (50).

(50)   sátìre, éssày, rábbì

The suffixes of the words in (43) are also correctly labelled by this rule. The monosyllabic ones (that is, all except -*ology*) are labelled weak, while -*ology* (branching) is labelled strong.

A third case of unexpected strong labelling of nonbranching right nodes includes disyllabic verbs and adjectives such as those in (51).

(51)   maintain, caress, harass, advance, bombard, torment, discourse, infer, rotund, overt, august, robust, obey, atone, molest, divine, discrete

For this class of cases the first syllable need not be light, as was the case in (49). This case has very few exceptions (*cómment,*[11] *ríbald*) and includes a number of verb-noun pairs in which the noun has main stress on the first syllable, while the verb has main stress on the last syllable. We give a few of these in (52).

(52)   *verbs*   *nouns*
        survéy   súrvèy
        detaíl   détaìl
        transfér   tránsfèr
        permít   pérmìt
        expórt   éxpòrt
        protést   prótèst

For the verbs, we can say that the right node is marked strong in spite of being nonbranching. In North American English, this provision does not apply in the case of the suffixes -*ize* and -*ate*, although these do receive primary stress in British English, at least in some words like *donate* and *baptize*. The nouns are derived cyclically from the corresponding verbs, which accounts for their having stress on both syllables.[12] Cyclicity will be discussed in detail in Section 4.5 and in Chapter 6. However, a few nouns are labelled strong on the right, such as those in (53).[13]

(53)   advánce, abúse, constraínt, deláy, lamént, excúse, suspénse, descént, offénce, pursuít, desígn, accórd, exhaúst

The fourth and final case of nonbranching right strong labelling occurs in verbs that contain a latinate stem. These are stems derived from Latin, whose meaning in English is not always transparent. Some of these cases are listed in (54).

[11] *Comment* might be a verb derived from a noun, like *pattern*. Cf. Chapter 6, Section 6.1.3.
[12] In some of the examples in (52) the form with initial main stress may be used as a verb, such as *tránsfèr* and *éxpòrt*. These may be derived from the corresponding nouns (cf. Section 6.1.3 of Chapter 6).
[13] Nouns like *exhaust* may be derived from verbs on stratum 2 by zero derivation. See Section 6.1.3 of Chapter 6.

(54)   ìntervéne, ìnterséct, ìnterspérse, ìnterpóse, ìntercépt, sùperpóse, còmprehénd, sùpervéne, cìrcumvént, pèrsevére

There are occasional exceptions such as *súpervìse, círcumcìse*. Adjectives with this structure follow the regular pattern of right weak when non-branching, i.e., *círcumspèct*.

We can now summarize the rules for Word-Tree Construction in (55). We give specific examples to illustrate the various cases; these represent a large number of additional cases.

(55)   *Word-Tree Construction (WTC; parameter 5)*
Construct a right-branching word tree over the feet of a word.
Within the word tree the right branches are labelled strong if any of the following conditions is met:
a.   The right node branches.
b.   The right node immediately dominates one of the endings in (47) (*engineer*).
c.   In disyllables where the first syllable is light and the right node does not dominate a suffix (*July* vs *lithoid*).
d.   In verbs and adjectives (and specially marked nouns) of two syllables, where the right node does not dominate *-ize, -ate* (North American English) (*omit, advance*).
e.   In verbs where the right node dominates a latinate stem (*intervene*).
Otherwise, right nodes are labelled weak.

This accounts for the majority of cases. Some words are marked as exceptions to individual clauses of (55). For example, *Ládefòged* can be marked as [−55a]; since none of (55b–e) is applicable to this word, its rightmost foot will be labelled weak.

Our account of English stress to this point has provided a way of constructing feet over an entire word of any length and the organization of these feet into a word tree. However, some of the syllables stressed by these rules do not remain stressed. In the next section we will discuss the rules that remove certain stresses and the way in which the syllables involved are incorporated into the prosodic structure.

4.4 Destressing Rules

4.4.1 Initial Destressing

The leftward iteration of the English Stress Rule ensures that every syllable belongs to a foot (unless it is extrametrical). Some syllables stressed by this procedure are actually phonetically unstressed, so we need a means to remove stresses in certain cases, usually when two stressed syllables are adjacent – a stress clash. It is easier to trim back excess stresses than to try to modify the rules assigning stress so that they do not place stress in these positions.

One effect of applying stress iteratively right to left is that a stress will always be assigned to the first syllable of a word. But word-initial light syllables (and some others) are frequently unstressed if followed by a stressed syllable (56a), which is not necessarily the main word stress. Word-initial heavy syllables, either with a long vowel (56b) or with a closing consonant (56c), retain their stress.

(56)   a. *light*   b. *heavy (long vowel)* c. *heavy (closed)*

a.	b.	c.
banána	psỳchólogy	bàndána
Monòngahéla	tòtálity	làctátion
balloón	Dàytóna	pòntoón
aspáragus	neùtrálity	sèctárian
mosquíto	tìsáne	Càrtésian
astrónomy	maìntaín	tèchníque

Light word-initial syllables are not destressed when they carry the main word stress, as in the examples of (50), already cited as words whose right foot is labelled weak by the normal operation of Word-Tree Construction (55). Hayes (1982: 257) proposes a general constraint on destressing rules, stated in (57).

(57)   No foot labelled strong can be deleted by destressing.

This prevents destressing the initial syllable of (50). On the other hand, there are some exceptions to initial destressing, partly depending on dialect, such as (58).

(58)   ràccoón, tàttoó, sètteé

Some words with an underlying tense vowel in the initial syllable do undergo destressing of this syllable (59a). Liberman and Prince (1977: 284) assume that these words undergo a minor shortening rule prior to destressing. The underived words in (59b) show a long vowel in this position. We can rather assume that the words in (59a) are specially marked to undergo Initial Destressing; they are subsequently subject to Auxiliary Reduction (69).

(59)   a. phonólogy b. phónate

a.	b.
schemátic	schéma
banálity	bánal (if pronounced [beɪnəl]

legálity	légal
maníacal	mániàc
labórious	lábour
varíety	váry

Initial syllables containing a latinate or Celtic prefix are also destressed when followed by a stronger stress. They do not destress when followed by an unstressed syllable or by a weaker stress.

(60)

prefix unstressed followed by stronger stress	*prefix stressed followed by weaker stress*	*prefix stressed followed by unstressed syllable*
condénse	còndènsátion	cóntemplàte
advánce	àdvàntágeous	ádulàte
absúrd	àbnòrmálity	ábnegàte
prodúctive	pròdùctívity	pròclamátion
reláx	rèlàxátion	réplicàte
expéct	èxpèctátion	èxplanátion
MacDónald		Mácintòsh

In a few monomorphemic words, initial syllables closed by a sonorant are destressed. These will have to be marked as exceptionally undergoing the rule. We give a few examples of this type in (61). The normal case is for such syllables to retain their stress, as shown by examples like *bandana* in (56c).

(61)   Kentúcky, Vermónt, Berlín

We can formulate Initial Destressing as in (62). This rule replaces Hayes's rule of Prestress Destressing. Unlike Hayes, we restrict this rule to word-initial position. Hayes's formulation allowed for the possibility of applying this rule in medial position, such as the destressing of *-ize* in *fraternization*, which we will ascribe to a different rule (Medial Destressing, Section 4.4.5). Similarly, the destressing of *-ate* in *migratory* (see Section 6.4 of Chapter 6) is probably effected by a special rule particular to this suffix, *-ate* Destressing (78 in Chapter 6) and not by Initial Destressing (cf. Nanni 1977).

(62)   *Initial Destressing (postcyclic)*

$$F \rightarrow \emptyset \; / \; [\underline{\quad\quad} F$$
$$|$$
$$\sigma$$

where the syllable dominated by the foot to be eliminated is monomoraic (*banana*), is (part of) a latinate prefix (*condense*), or in specially marked words (*Kentucky, maniacal*).

The explanation for the destressing of the prefix in *expect* versus retention of stress on the prefix in *expectation* comes from the postcyclic ordering of Initial Destressing. This is explained fully in Section 4.5. Briefly, the English Stress Rule is cyclic. In the lexical theory of phonology, as applied to English, the phonology of stratum 1 applies cyclically, that is, once to an underived lexical item and then again after each layer of derivation. Initial Destressing, however, is postcyclic, and applies on stratum 2 after all cyclic rules have applied. Stratum 2 rules apply only once, after all affixation on that level. If Initial Destressing applied cyclically, it would destress the prefix in *expect* before the affixation of *-ation*. As a postcyclic rule, its operation is delayed until after affixation has taken place and another rule (the Rhythm Rule (83)) has applied marking as strong the foot that dominates the syllable of the prefix.

Stray syllables from extrametricality or destressing are adjoined into the metrical structure by Stray-Syllable Adjunction (16), to be revised as (75). We assume that this rule applies both in the cycle on stratum 1, before Word-Tree Construction, and after each destressing rule on stratum 2. As an illustration, consider the derivation of *asparagus* in (63).

(63)   underlying   /əspæɹəgəs/
         Stratum 1
              Consonant Extrametricality   əspæɹəgə\<s>
              Syllabification   ə.spæ.ɹə.gə\<s>
              Syllable Extrametricality   ə.spæ.ɹə\<gə\<s>>

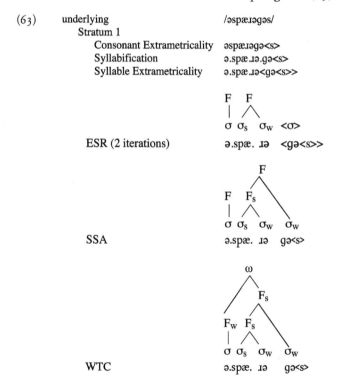

         ESR (2 iterations)   ə.spæ. ɹə   \<gə\<s>>

         SSA   ə.spæ. ɹə   gə\<s>

         WTC   ə.spæ. ɹə   gə\<s>

Stratum 2

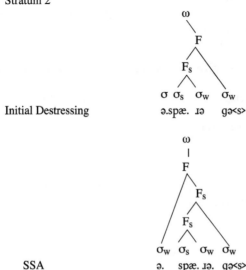

Initial Destressing

SSA

No segmental rules are involved, so this is essentially the final form of this word.

4.4.2 Poststress Destressing

Poststress Destressing removes stress from an open syllable that is between a stronger stress on its left and an unstressed syllable on its right. It is best formulated as a rule that eliminates a binary foot after a stronger foot that is nonbranching. This applies in two major classes of words. One is made up of the apparent cases of long retraction in the noncomplex cases of (45). We can eliminate these cases of long retraction by constructing maximally binary feet from right to left and then eliminating the binary foot over the second and third syllables of such words. We give a formulation of this rule in (64). This rule is also postcyclic, on stratum 2. Like all destressing rules, it is restricted by (57) not to apply to a foot marked strong. It does not apply in examples like *Monongahela*, where the second syllable is closed; here Initial Destressing destresses the first syllable. The subscripts are merely for reference, not part of the structure.

(64)   *Poststress Destressing (postcyclic)*

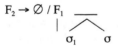

Conditions:
1. F_1 is stronger than F_2: either F_1 is labelled strong or is less deeply embedded than F_2.
2. σ_1 is open

As an example, we give the derivation of *abracadabra* in (65).

(65)   underlying   /æbɹəkədæbɹə/
        Stratum 1
            Syllabification   æ.bɹə.kə.dæ.bɹə

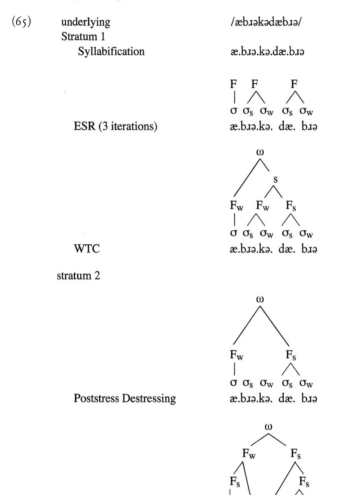

        ESR (3 iterations)

        WTC

        stratum 2

        Poststress Destressing

        SSA

Because Stray-Syllable Adjunction (16) requires adjunction to an *adjacent* foot, the second syllable *bra* is adjoined to the foot dominating the first syllable, and the third syllable *ka* is adjoined to the foot dominating the last two syllables. In this we follow Withgott (1982) rather than Hayes (1982: 263), who adjoined both stray syllables from Poststress Destressing to the foot on the left. He claimed that this was a kind of structure preservation, in that basic feet are strong on the left. However, the split adjunction illustrated is empirically superior, in that it places the /k/ at the beginning of the third syllable in foot-initial position, where it is aspirated, according to rules developed in Chapter 5.

Actually, Initial Destressing is also potentially applicable to the structure that results from Word-Tree Construction in (65). We will ensure that Poststress Destressing applies by ordering it before Initial Destressing. Once Poststress Destressing has applied, Initial Destressing is no longer applicable.[14]

The second class of cases where Poststress Destressing occurs is with the suffixes *-ary* and *-ory*. These have secondary stress when they follow an unstressed syllable (66a) but are unstressed after a stressed syllable (66b).

(66) a. tránsitòry   b. advísory
          prómissòry   cúrsory
          plánetàry   plénary

Since Poststress Destressing (64) is formulated to apply after a nonbranching foot, but not after a branching foot, it will correctly apply in (66b) but not in (66a).

Because these suffixes have two syllables phonetically, there might be a question as to why they are not marked strong by Word-Tree Construction, and thus ineligible for destressing. Hayes argues that the suffixes actually have the glide /j/ in underlying representation rather than the vowel [ɪ]. The vowel preceding *r* is underlyingly tense. They are stressed by Long-Vowel Stressing in Hayes's system before being made extrametrical by Adjective Extrametricality. However, since we have eliminated Long-Vowel Stressing, we can let these suffixes be stressed by the normal application of the English Stress rule. Adjective Extrametricality (i.e., Syllable Exrametricality) does not apply to these suffixes because they contain a long vowel. Assuming quantity-sensitive retraction ensures that the syllable before the suffix is stressed if it is heavy, otherwise stress is assigned two syllables before the suffix. We still

[14] It may be possible to formulate a principle by which, with two adjacent weak feet that are both potentially subject to destressing, it is the weaker (i.e., more deeply embedded) one that is actually destressed.

assume that the suffixes end in an underlying glide, in order to ensure that the foot dominating them is labelled weak by Word-Tree Construction. This requires a rule to syllabify the final glide, ordered before Poststress Destressing. More generally, final sonorants are syllabified after consonants, as in (67a). We will analyze this as insertion of /ə/ between the consonant and the sonorant at the end of the word. The sequence of schwa plus sonorant is optionally converted to a syllabic sonorant by Compensatory Syllabification, (35) in Chapter 5. That the examples in (67a) have no underlying vowel before the final sonorant is shown by the stratum 1 derivatives in -*ic*. In contrast, the words in (67b) have an underlying vowel in this position, since their derivatives in -*ic* also have a vowel there, where it is stressed.

(67)

		underlying	phonetic	derivative	
a.	rhythm	/ɹɪðm/	['ɹɪðəm] ~ ['ɹɪðm̩]	rhythmic	['ɹɪðmɪk]
	metre	/metɹ/	['miɹɾəɹ] ~ [·miɹɾɹ̩]	metric	['mɛtɹɪk]
	cycle	/sikl/	['səɪkəl] ~ ['səɪkl̩]	cyclic	['sɪkl̩ɪk]

b.	atom	/ætɒm/	['æɾəm] ~ ['æɾm̩]	atomic	[ə'tʰɒmɪk]
	Homer	/hɒmɛɹ /	['howməɹ] ~ ['howmɹ̩]	Homeric	[ˌhow'mɛɹɪk]
	vocal	/vɒkæl/	['vowkəl] ~ ['vowkl̩]	vocalic	[ˌvow'kʰælɪk]

We give this rule, known as Sonorant Syllabification, in two parts, in (68). In each case, the rule creates a stray syllable, which gets adjoined by (16), (75).

(68)   *Sonorant Syllabification*

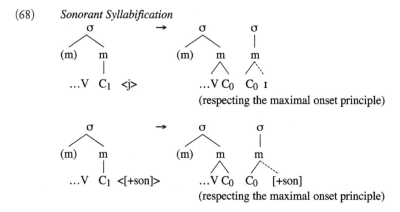

When a syllable containing a long vowel is destressed, as in the suffixes -*ary* and -*ory*, its vowel is laxed and shortened by Auxiliary Reduction, which we formulate in (69).

(69)   *Auxiliary Reduction* (cyclic; also after destresssing on stratum 2)

V → [–ATR]

i.e., detach the second mora of a bimoraic vowel in a weak syllable and simultaneously lax the vowel.

One final point needs to be mentioned. The first vowel of the suffix *-ary*, although tense for the purpose of stress, is lax phonetically. We assume, with *SPE* (p. 136), that there is a special laxing rule for this suffix, given in (70).

(70)   *-ary Rule*
        æ → ɛ in the suffix *-ary*

In (71) we give a summary of the stress rules so far, in order.

(71)   a.   *Cyclic rules (stratum 1)*

              Consonant Extrametricality (70 of Chapter 3)
              (Re)Syllabification (70 of Chapter 3)
              Syllable Extrametricality (42)
              English Stress Rule (Parameters 1–4 of 31)
              Stray-Syllable Adjunction (16; revised as 75)
              Word-Tree Construction (55)
              Auxiliary Reduction (69)

        b.   *Postcyclic rules (stratum 2)*

              Sonorant Syllabification (68)
              Poststress Destressing (64)
              Initial Destressing (62)
              -ary Rule (70)

4.4.3   Sonorant Destressing

When we consider additional forms with the suffixes *-ary* and *-ory*, we find that most have stress on the syllable preceding the suffix if this syllable is heavy (72a); otherwise stress falls two syllables before the suffix, as in (66a). However, stress also falls two syllables before the suffix when the syllable before the suffix is closed by a sonorant. Compare (72a) with (72b).

(72)   a. òlfáctory   b.   dýsentèry
            trajéctory   vóluntàry
            perfúnctory   désultòry

Kiparsky (1979, 428) proposes that the two cases are initially stressed in the same way, but that the forms in (72b) undergo Sonorant Destressing, which we give in (73).

(73)   *Sonorant Destressing*

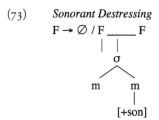

This rule removes a nonbranching foot whose syllable dominates a vowel followed by a sonorant when it is between two other feet, the first of which is nonbranching. This will correctly remove the medial foot in (72b), with the resulting stray syllable adjoined to the preceding foot by Stray-Syllable Adjunction. Let us illustrate with the derivation of *desultory* in (74).

(74)   underlying   /dɛzəltɳɹj/
        stratum 1
            Consonant Extrametricality   dɛzəltɳɹ<j>
            Syllabification   dɛ.zəl.tɳɹ<j>

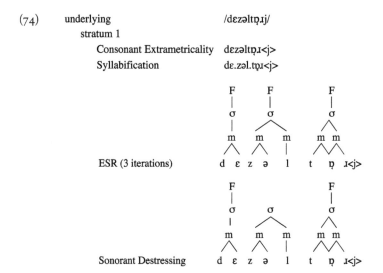

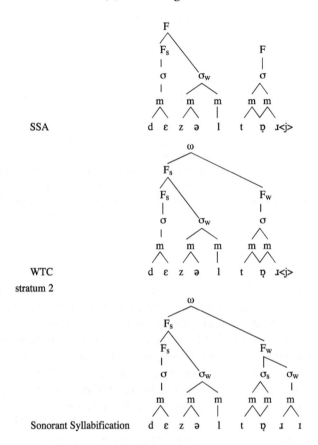

Notice that Sonorant Destressing applies *before* Word-Tree Construction. If WTC applied first, it would result in the foot dominating the syllable /zəl/ being labelled *strong*, and thus ineligible for destressing. Constraint (57) prevents feet labelled strong from being deleted; it allows deletion of feet labelled weak, or, in this case, not yet labelled.

Notice also that Stray-Syllable Adjunction adjoins the destressed sonorant-final syllable to the left. This is the first case where the instruction to adjoin a stray syllable to an adjacent foot is ambiguous: this syllable is adjacent to a foot on both sides. We resolve this ambiguity in this case by adjunction to the left. We will state the final form of Stray-Syllable Adjunction in (75). Structures derived by adjunction will be seen to be relevant to three segmental rules. Underlining in the examples indicates the syllable(s) being adjoined. Some of these cases will be examined as we develop additional destressing rules.

(75)   *Stray-Syllable Adjunction (final form; stratum 1 and after each destressing rule and Sonorant Syllabification)*

Adjoin a stray syllable by Chomsky adjunction as a weak member of an adjacent (maximal) foot.

a.   Two stray syllables between feet: one goes each way (*abracadabra*)
b.   A single syllable is adjoined to a preceding monosyllabic foot (*desultory, migratory, proclamation*)
c.   A single syllable between feet adjoins to the right if the preceding foot is binary (*militaristic, sanitization, opportunistic*)
d.   Any syllable on an edge adjoins to the left (iteratively in *advisory*) or to the right if there is no syllable to the left (*potato, banana*)

4.4.4   Arab Destressing

Arab Destressing destresses a syllable closed by an obstruent when it follows a stressed, light syllable. It takes its name from the word *Arab*, which illustrates these conditions, in having a light stressed first syllable and a stressless second syllable, in contrast to *Ahab*, with secondary stress on the second syllable and a long vowel in the first syllable. This is something of a misnomer, however. Like Sonorant Destressing, Arab Destressing requires a further foot to the right of the foot to be destressed, so it would not affect the word *Arab* itself. We retain the term as the one in use (Fidelholtz 1967; Ross 1972; Hayes 1982: 256). This rule destresses the second syllable of the words in (76a), but not in (76b), where the first syllable is heavy.

(76)   a.   désignàte   b.   tìcktàcktoé
             récognìze   Tìmbùktú
             ánecdòte
             mónophthòng
             pálimpsèst
             pároxỳsm
             Àlexánder
             gélignìte
             rèsignátion

The verbs in (76a) are the main motivation for strong retraction in the analyses of Liberman and Prince (1977) and Hayes (1982). However, the majority of words with this pattern are nouns, which causes difficulties for those analyses. They can generally be treated in those theories by considering the words to be exceptions to Noun Extrametricality. The word *resignation* is derived cyclically from *resign*, which has stress on the final syllable (cf. Section 6.4 of Chapter 6). A rule like Arab Destressing is needed in any case for this word. We formulate the rule in (77).

(77)   *Arab Destressing*

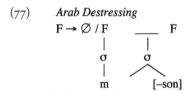

Like Sonorant Destressing, Arab Destressing must be ordered before Word-Tree Construction. The reason is the same: Word-Tree Construction would label the syllable *sig* of *designate* strong, and hence ineligible for destressing.

4.4.5   Medial Destressing

Medial Destressing removes a foot containing a single open syllable with a long vowel between two feet where the following foot is the main word stress. There are two main cases to consider. After a binary foot, there is optional destressing in words like *fraternization, sanitization*. These are derived cyclically from *fraternize, sanitize*, each of which is assigned two feet on the first cycle. When the suffix is added, a foot is assigned to it, which is marked strong because it is branching. This produces a structure like (78).[15]

(78)

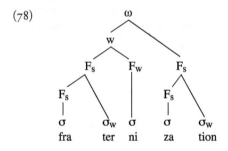

---

[15] The structure in (78) reflects the effects of Sonorant Destressing on the first cycle on *fraternize* and the subsequent adjunction of the second syllable to the first foot.

Medial Destressing removes the middle foot. We formulate the rule in (79).[16]

(79)   *Medial Destressing (cyclic)*

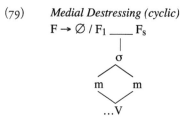

$$F \rightarrow \emptyset \,/\, F_1 \_\_\_ F_s$$

Conditions: 1. Optional if F_1 is branching (*fraternization*)
                2. Obligatory if F_1 is degenerate (*proclamation*)

After medial destressing, the syllable *ni* is left stray. According to (75c) this syllable is adjoined to the foot on the right (contrary to Hayes's assumption that it adjoins to the left), producing the structure in (80).

(80)

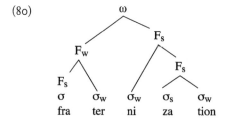

Evidence that the stray syllable is attached to the right in these cases is the aspiration of /t/ in *sanitization*. The context for Aspiration is initial position in a foot, as discussed more fully in Section 5.3.3 of Chapter 5.

Hayes (1982: 252) proposes that Medial Destressing is just a medial application of his Prestress Destressing (our Initial Destressing). However, it is necessary to separate these two rules because Medial Destressing must precede Trisyllabic Laxing (35 of Chapter 6), which is cyclic, while Initial Destressing, as we have seen, is postcyclic. The cyclic nature of Medial Destressing is seen in *proclamation*, where the destressing of the second syllable *cla* creates the conditions for Trisyllabic Laxing, which can apply to *pro* only if the following syllable is unstressed. We will discuss this ordering in greater detail in Section 6.4 of Chapter 6.

---

[16] *Satirize* is a problem under this analysis: the middle foot cannot be removed by (79) because the final foot is marked weak.

The second case of Medial Destressing is after a degenerate foot. *Proclamation* is derived cyclically from *proclaim*, with two feet of which the right is marked strong by (55d). Since there are additional rules involved, we defer full discussion of this case until Section 6.4 of Chapter 6.

4.5 Cyclicity and Stress

We encountered the concept of cyclicity briefly in Section 1.1.4 of Chapter 1 in discussing stress rules in the *SPE* framework. In English, the phonological rules of stratum 1 apply cyclically, which means that this sequence of rules applies to an underived item, and, if an affix or other morphological operation applies, the same sequence of rules applies again to the derived form, and so on, applying after each layer of derivation until no more morphological derivation takes place. Rules of stratum 2 are postcyclic and apply all in one block after all affixation or other morphology on that stratum. We illustrated this with the word *theatricality* in (25) of Chapter 1. Of the stress rules discussed so far in this chapter, only Sonorant Syllabification (68), Poststress Destressing (64), and Initial Destressing (62) are postcyclic; the rest are cyclic. One effect of the cycle is that a stress assigned on an early cycle may be retained in a derivative form. A word of similar segmental composition to that derivative form but without an internal cycle would not have stress on the syllable in question. In (81a) we give the base forms and in (81b) their corresponding derivatives. Compare (81c) with similar words but without an inner cycle, whose inner cycle does not assign stress to the second syllable, or where a stress has been removed from this position.

(81)	a.	eléstic	b.	èlàstícity	c.	Cònestóga
		condénse		còndènsátion		còmpensátion
		expéct		èxpèctátion		dèsignátion

The stress assigned to the second syllable on the first cycle to the words of (81a) is retained (though reduced) on the same syllable in the derivative in (81b), but the words in (81c) of similar segmental composition to those of (81b) have no stress in that position, either because no stress was placed there to begin with *(Conestoga)* or it was removed by a destressing rule (Sonorant Destressing in *compensation*; Arab Destressing in *designation*).

Let us consider the derivation of *expect* and *expectation* in detail, since these derivations illustrate the Rhythm Rule, which plays an important

role in English stress and intonation both within words and in phrases.[17]
The derivation of *expect* is quite straightforward, according to the rules
already discussed. Two feet are assigned and the right one is labelled strong
by (55d). Postcyclically, Initial Destressing removes the stress on the first
syllable, which is adjoined to the following foot.

The derivation of *expectation* is the same on the first cycle: starting with
expect, we assign two feet and label the right one strong. On the second
cycle, the affix is added, and the English Stress Rule applies again, placing a
foot on the suffix.[18] The structure at this point looks like (82).

(82)

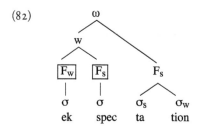

The Rhythm Rule applies to reverse the relative prominence of the first
two feet, shown in boxes. We formulate the Rhythm Rule in (83) (cf.
Section 1.2 of Chapter 1).

(83)   *Rhythm Rule* (Kiparsky 1979: 424)

Intuitively, the Rhythm Rule applies to resolve a clash of stresses that
results when a strong stress is followed by a stronger stress. The strong
stress on the final syllable of *expect* clashes with the stronger stress on the
suffix added on the second cycle. The Rhythm Rule resolves this clash by
reversing the labelling of the first two feet. The stresses are not removed –
unlike the case with destressing rules – but are merely reversed in prominence. Not all stress clashes can be resolved. If there is no destressing rule
that can apply and the Rhythm Rule is inapplicable, a clash of stresses

---

[17] Phrasal application will be considered in detail in Chapter 5, Section 5.3.6.
[18] Since English word formation generally involves suffixes, this procedure leads to a left-branching
tree, rather than a right-branching tree, which is actually characteristic only of long
monomorphemic words by parameter 5.

simply remains in the form. The result of applying the Rhythm Rule to (82) is (84).

(84)

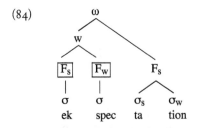

Notice that it is not possible simply to compare the *outputs* of *expect* and *expectation*. Both must be related to an abstract intermediate form of *expect* that has two stresses – i.e., two feet. In *expect*, the first of these feet is removed; in *expectation*, the relative prominence of the two feet is reversed; in neither is the exact pattern of that abstract form phonetically realized.

The derivation of *condensation* follows exactly the same pattern as that of *expectation*. Sonorant Destressing might be expected to destress the second syllable in *condensation*; however, Sonorant Destressing is ordered before the Rhythm Rule. At the time Sonorant Destressing is applicable, the second syllable of *condensation* is marked strong and so is ineligible for destressing. This is a counterfeeding interaction of these two rules: the Rhythm Rule creates the input for Sonorant Destressing in such cases, but too late for the latter to apply. In a few lexically marked cases, such as *information*, we stipulate that the Rhythm Rule applies before Sonorant Destressing. Here the order is feeding, and Sonorant Destressing is able to apply.

The Rhythm Rule is subject to the constraint in (85) (Kiparsky 1979: 425).

(85)   The Rhythm Rule (83) (usually) does not apply when it would create a metrical structure of the form (i) within the (minimal) phonological word, where the first *s* is nonbranching.

(i)

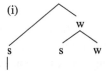

Intuitively, the interpretation of this restriction is that the Rhythm Rule does not resolve one clash only to create another. This restriction blocks the operation of the Rhythm Rule on the last cycle in the derivation of *sensationality*. This derivation runs as in (86).

(86)

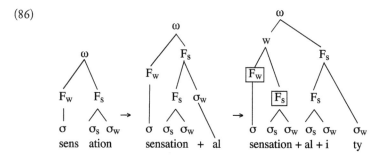

Although the boxed feet in (86) are in the context of the Rhythm Rule, the application of this rule would produce the structure in (85i), and so it is blocked. This restriction does not prevent the Rhythm Rule from applying in (82), since the weak boxed foot there (after the Rhythm Rule applies) is nonbranching.

The cyclic assignment of stress is subject to the proviso that previously assigned stresses are retained except that the structure may be changed to the extent that is necessary to accommodate newly added morphological material. This point has been the source of confusion in some of the previous literature. Cyclic assignment of stress does not *necessarily* change previous stresses. It depends on the nature of the suffix involved. There are two cases to consider. If the suffix can be completely incorporated into the new metrical structure on its own, there is generally no change in the previously assigned structure, other than relabelling the word tree. If the suffix is unable to be completely metrified on its own, then the metrical structure must be minimally modified in order to accommodate the suffix. In (87) we give a few examples of suffixes of each type.

(87)   a.   *suffixes that can be completely metrified on their own*
              -ate, -ize, -ation, -ary, -ory

        b.   *suffixes that require a change in metrical structure*
              -ity, -ic, -al, -ent, -ify

Suffixes that contain a long vowel, such as *-ate*, can be given a monosyllabic foot, with resyllabification of a stem-final consonant as the onset of the syllable. Consequently, there is no change in the foot structure assigned to the base words in (88a) with the addition of a suffix from (87a), giving the derived words in (88b)

(88) a. *base*   b. *derived word*
          óxygen   óxygenàte
          hóspital   hóspitalìze
          skéleton   skéletonìze
          nátural   náturalìze
          expéct   èxpèctátion

In the cyclic derivation of *oxygenate*, for example, the base *oxygen* is first provided with a foot. With the addition of -*ate* on the second cycle, the final *n* of *oxygen* is resyllabified as an onset, and a foot is built over this syllable. This foot can be labelled weak (since it is nonbranching) in a new word tree, and the final structure for the word is achieved. The situation is similar for words in -*ize* and -*ation*. The derivation of the word *expectation* involves the Rhythm Rule, as we have seen, but this requires only relabelling of the two feet assigned on the first cycle to *expect*, not any change in the feet themselves.

The suffixes in (87b) cannot fully support their own metrical structure, and consequently require some adjustments in previously assigned structure on the second cycle of stress assignment. This results in a shift of stress in the examples of (89).

(89)   a. *base*   b. *derived word*
       -ity   símilar   sìmilárity
                méntal   mèntálity
       -ic   átom   atómic
                órgan   òrgánic
       -al   médicine   medícinal
                órigin   oríginal
                párent   paréntal
       -ify   sólid   solídifỳ
                pérson   persónifỳ

On the first cycle, the last syllable of *similar* is extrametrical (as containing an adjective suffix) and a binary foot is built on the first two syllables, following which the extrametrical syllable is adjoined. On the second cycle, -*ity* is attached, and its final syllable is made extrametrical, since this derivation results in a noun. The penultimate syllable *ri*, with a short vowel, cannot support a foot by itself. Therefore, a foot is built on the two syllables *lari*, removing the last syllable of the base from the structure built on the first cycle. The foot on the first two syllables remains, however. After the adjunction of the final syllable and word-tree labelling, which marks the final foot strong, the correct stress pattern is achieved.

A technical detail needs to be discussed at this point. Since Stray-Syllable Adjunction (75) is by Chomsky Adjunction, we may have superfluous structures in certain derivations. In *similar*, for example, the final (extrametrical) syllable is Chomsky adjoined to the foot constructed on the first two syllables (90a). When the suffix *-ity* is added on the second cycle, the last syllable <ty> is extrametrical and a binary foot is constructed on *lari*, incorporating the syllable previously adjoined to the foot on *simi*. This leaves the embedded foot on *simi* without a sister, as shown (boxed) in (90b), after adjunction of <ty> to the final foot, but before Word-Tree Construction.

(90)   a.   b.   c. ω

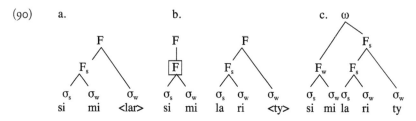

We assume that such embedded nodes are *pruned* from the structure before Word-Tree Construction, producing the result in (90c). In other words, embedded feet resulting from adjunction are removed when they no longer have a sister, since such vacuous embedding serves no function in the structure.

In *atomic*, the suffix *-ic* is an exception to Syllable Extrametricality, but, with a short vowel (and the extrametricality of the final consonant), it is unable to support a foot by itself. Therefore, a foot is built on the last two syllables, which is labelled strong by Word-Tree Construction. The first syllable, being light, is destressed by Initial Destressing, giving the final form. With *solidify*, a verb, the last syllable of the suffix, which contains a long vowel, can support a foot on its own, but the first syllable of the suffix is light and cannot support its own foot, so a foot is built on the *fy* and then on *lidi*, removing the final syllable of the base *solid* from the foot built on *solid* on the first cycle. The first syllable, being a light syllable in a weak foot, is destressed, giving the final stress pattern.

In a number of cases, the suffixes in (87b) do not cause a shift in stress, such as the examples in (91).

(91)   a. *base*   b. *derived word*
        -ity   sane   sanity
        -ic   cone   conic
        -al   person   personal
        -ify   note   notify

These examples are completely consistent with the cyclic derivation of stress being developed here. It is simply the case that the structure assigned on the second cycle of the examples in (91b) duplicates, or does not modify, the structure already assigned on the first cycle. Where the structure of the word is such that a different structure is assigned on the second cycle, the stress changes, as in (89b).

In some cases, attachment of a suffix from (87a) does result in a change in stress with respect to the base, such as (92).

(92) a. políticìze
      b. hỳdrógenàte

The words in (92) are stressed as if they were not derived cyclically from *politic* and *hydrogen*, respectively. In other words, although they include suffixes, they are derived in a single cycle, like words such as *municipal*, which was one of the principal examples of Adjective Extrametricality in (39). Our approach will indeed be to analyze these cases similarly. That is, *municip-* in *municipal* is a bound stem, and bound stems do not undergo a separate cycle: *municipal* is derived in a single pass through the stress rules. Similarly, we can consider *politic-* a bound stem in *politicize*: the word *politicize* does not mean 'to make politic,' but rather 'to make political.' We therefore regard both *political* and *politicize* as both derived from a stem *politic-*, which is related to but not identified with the independent word *politic*. Such an analysis is more difficult to maintain with *hydrogenate*, since *hydrogen* is part of the meaning in this case, but it is interesting to note the alternative pronunciation *hýdrogenàte*. A common assumption is that the words in (88b), *oxygenate*, etc., have to be treated as irregular in some way; for example, Kager (1989: 152) suggested that they are irregularly affixed at stratum 2 (in our terms), since stratum 2 affixation generally does not induce stress shift. On the contrary, these forms are perfectly regular examples of stratum 1 cyclic stress assignment under our analysis, where the salient property of cyclic stress assignment is *retention* of previously assigned stresses rather than overriding of them, subject to the restrictions imposed by the necessity of assigning a foot including suffixes of various metrical types. We will discuss some of these issues further in Section 6.2.1 of Chapter 6.

To complete this picture of stress assignment in English, we need a rule on stratum 2 to build a word tree after the addition of stratum 2 affixes and in compounds. This rule is relatively straightforward, as shown in (93).

(93)   *Word-Tree Construction* (stratum 2)
        Construct a word tree respecting the structure of a compound and
        incorporating all new morphological elements added on stratum 2.
        Label right nodes strong if branching, or if dominating a stem while
        their sister dominates an affix, or if dominating a suffix from (48).

Some stratum 2 affixes are stressed, such as *-ship* in *kingship*, *-like* in *lifelike*,
-hood in *childhood*, and *un-* in *unnatural*. Mohanan (1986: 19–20) proposes
that such affixes are assigned stress on stratum 1 before being attached to
stems on stratum 2. Their relative degree of stress is determined by their
labelling by (93). Unstressed stratum 2 affixes are listed as exceptions to the
stress rules, and their syllables are adjoined (iteratively) to adjacent feet in
accordance with the normal operation of Stray-Syllable Adjunction (75).

4.6   Summary of the Stress Rules

In this section we give a summary of the stress rules developed so far, along
with their ordering. Following the standard convention of generative
phonology, an arc joining two rules indicates that the top rule is crucially
ordered before the lower one.

(94)   a.   *Cyclic rules (stratum 1)*

              Consonant Extrametricality (70 of chapter 3)
              (Re)Syllabification (70 of chapter 3)
              Syllable Extrametricality (42)
              English Stress Rule (Parameters 1–4 of 31)
              ⎰ Arab Destressing (77)
              ⎱ Sonorant Destressing (73)
              Stray Syllable Adjunction (75)
              Word Tree Construction (55)
              Rhythm Rule (83) and (85)
              Medial Destressing (79)
              Auxiliary Reduction (69)

        b.   *Postcyclic rules (stratum 2)*

              WTC for compounds and stratum 2 affixes (93)
              Minor Relabelling (104)
              Sonorant Syllabification (68)
              Poststress Destressing (64)
              Initial Destressing (62)
              -ary Rule (70)
              Special *j*-Vocalization (101)

As noted in (42), we have combined Noun Extrametricality and Adjective Extrametricality into a single rule called Syllable Extrametricality. This rule is subject to a certain amount of lexical idiosyncrasy, as will be discussed in the next section. There are also certain cases where Arab Destressing or Sonorant Destressing apply *after*, rather than before, the Rhythm Rule. Arab Destressing applies after the Rhythm Rule in *resignation* on the second cycle, since, before the Rhythm Rule, the second syllable is marked strong and so ineligible for destressing. Similarly, in *information*, Sonorant Destressing applies after the Rhythm Rule, for the same reason. These have to be lexically marked, as the order given in (94) predicts that the second syllable stress assigned on the first cycle should remain, as indeed it does in words like *annexation* and *condensation*.

Cyclic rules are subject to the Strict Cycle Condition, which restricts their operation. We give a preliminary statement of this Condition in (95) (Mascaró 1967; Kiparsky 1982: 41), reserving a more formal discussion for Chapter 6, Section 6.2.1.

(95) Strict Cycle Condition (preliminary formulation)
Cyclic rules may change structure only in derived environments.

A form is considered *derived* if it results from morphological operations on a particular stratum or if it has been changed by phonological rules on that stratum. If a form is underlying, or if it has been changed by phonological or morphological operations on a previous stratum, it is considered underived. The Strict Cycle Condition does not prevent cyclic rules from adding structure in underived environments, as we have assumed is the normal case for stress rules.

4.7 Exceptions

Our stress rules predict the correct stress patterns of the vast majority of English words. However, a number of exceptional cases remain. A few of these may require brute-force lexical listing of metrical structure, but we try to make as much sense of the exceptions as possible. In many cases, a word is simply marked not to undergo a particular rule, and its stress pattern follows from the remaining rules. In other cases it may be possible to adjust the underlying representation so that the stress will come out right. This method suffers from arbitrariness and introducing unmotivated abstractness, unless some independent motivation can be found for the underlying representations proposed.

SPE relied on the method of adjusting underlying representations. For example, for *vanilla*, *SPE* proposed an underlying representation with a geminate /ll/: in our terms /vənɪllə/ (with a remarkable similarity to the orthographic representation of this word). This provides a strong cluster (in our terms, a heavy syllable) in penultimate position, resulting in main stress on that syllable. Such adjustments to underlying representations necessarily require a rule or some rules that bring the form into line with its actual pronunciation. In this case, there is a rule of Degemination that is needed independently, since morphological combinations can produce geminates, as /nn/ in *in+nocuous*, which are realized as single consonants phonetically. However, since the word *vanilla* is monomorphemic, there is no motivation for a geminate *in this word* outside of predicting the stress.

Kiparsky (1982: 50) proposes that words like *vanilla* have a foot present in the underlying representation, as in (96).[19]

(96)

va   ni   lla

The English Stress Rule, as a cyclic rule, is not able to override the existing foot in Kiparsky's analysis due to the Strict Cycle Condition (95). The problem with this proposal is that there is no restriction on where feet can be located in underlying representations. For example, under this proposal there could be an underlying representation with five light syllables, each of which has an underlying foot. Such exceptional cases are entirely absent. A more constrained view of exceptions takes *vanilla* simply to be an exception to Syllable Extrametricality, otherwise allowing the rules to apply normally. Then, the English Stress Rule places a foot on the last two syllables and another one on the first syllable, which is then deleted by Initial Destressing, which, after adjunction, gives the correct form. In this way, we account for the fact that the stress pattern of exceptional words is largely similar to the regular pattern, not wildly different from it.

Selkirk (1984a: 93) also accounts for cases like *vanilla* by assuming that their final syllables are not extrametrical. Halle and Vergnaud (1987) object to this analysis, preferring the assumption of an underlying stress (in their bracketed grid framework, a line one asterisk) in words like

---

[19] The structure in (96) does not include predictable syllabic structure, which, however, is presupposed by the presence of a lexical foot.

Kentucky and *Mississippi*. Their objection to marking these as exceptional to extrametricality concerns derivatives like *Kentuckian, Mississipian,* "where main stress falls on the antepenult and not on the penult, as might have been expected if these stems caused Extrametricality to be blocked" (1987: 232). This objection is invalid. The stems are themselves exceptions to Syllable Extrametricality, but this has no effect on the derivatives, since extrametricality is possible only in word-final position and Syllable Extrametricality affects the final syllable of the suffix in these cases, not any part of the stem. So the approach using exceptions to extrametricality applies to *Kentucky* and *Mississippi* also, and is more constrained than Halle and Vergnaud's underlying stress, since they have no restrictions on where underlying line one asterisks can be placed.

Nouns with stress on the final syllable when this syllable does not contain a long vowel are treated in a similar way. A sample is given in (97a); similar examples in (97b) are not stressed on the final syllable (repeated from (38)).

(97)   a.   mániàc, pársnìp, prótòn, ínsèct, gýmnàst, nárthèx, pálimpsèst
          b.   Ísaac, kétchup, ápron, súbject, témpest, hélix

Hayes (1982: 239) appeals to underlyingly marked stresses to account for (97a). A better approach is to say that these words are exceptions to Syllable Extrametricality and also to Consonant Extrametricality for those that end in only one consonant. The last syllable then gets stress in the normal way by the English Stress Rule. Other exceptions to Consonant Extrametricality are adjectives such as *parallel* and *agog* and verbs like *begin, attack, caress.* These words also must have the right branch marked strong in Word-Tree Construction by (55d) (except *parallel*).

The adjective suffix *-ic* generally requires stress on the preceding syllable, as in *acídic, àrtístic, tèlegráphic.* We can say that the suffix *-ic* is an exception to Syllable Extrametricality. Exceptions to the exception are *Árabic, chóleric, cátholic.*

A number of nouns need to undergo Syllable Extrametricality even if they have a long vowel in their final syllable ([+ATR] in the underlying representation). We can ascertain that the final syllable contains an underlying tense vowel when there is a verb of the same segmental composition whose final syllable gets a secondary stress and so keeps a bimoraic vowel. A sample of such pairs appears in (98) (Kiparsky 1983).[20]

[20] The adjective *désignàte* has a similar analysis, contrasted with the verb *désignàte*.

(98)   *noun*   *verb*
        ádvocåte   ádvocàte
        ággregåte   ággregàte
        assóciåte   assóciàte
        subórdinåte   subórdinàte

Some words are exceptions to Sonorant Destressing, like *òdóntòid, Tridéntìne, chìmpànzée, ìncàntátion*. The stress on the second syllable of the last of these cannot be attributed to a cyclic derivation, as we did in *condensation*, because there is no word **incant*.[21]

Some words are exceptions to Poststress Destressing, such an *amànuénsis, apòtheósis*. In these cases Initial Destressing applies.

Certain words derived from Greek that have unexpected stress patterns, such as (99), can be treated as compounds.

(99)   hélicogràph, síderoscòpe, héteronỳm, eléctrogràph, larýngoscòpe, kaléidoscòpe, hómonỳm

If these are treated as compounds with a recursive prosodic word structure, as ⟦ ⟦helico⟧$_\omega$ ⟦graph⟧$_\omega$ ⟧$_\omega$, and each part is stressed separately, undergoing Syllable Extrametricality where appropriate, the correct pattern is derived by the postcyclic rule of WTC for compounds and stratum 2 affixes in (93), which labels right nodes strong if they are branching (and under certain other conditions). The ω on the right branch counts as nonbranching in the examples of (99). Some evidence that this compound analysis is correct comes from the tensing of the final *o* in prefixes like *helico*, like the final *o* of *buffalo*. These final *o*s are not underlyingly tense, since they do not get stressed. The rule involved is Stem-Final Tensing, discussed in Chapter 7, Section 7.2.2.

A number of words have ternary feet that cannot be derived by Poststress Destressing, like the examples in (100).

(100)   detérioràte, álienàte, váriegàte

Following Hayes (1982: 266) we assume these to have the glide /j/ in underlying representation (e.g., /dɪteɪjɒɪæt/). This /j/ becomes the vowel /ɪ/ by a postcyclic vocalization rule, which we give as (101).[22]

---

[21] A reader points out that *incant* is attested in the Oxford English Dictionary with a frequency between 0.01 and 0.1 times per million words, the same range as *nocuous*. Speakers whose lexicons include *incant* can account for the secondary stress on the second syllable of *incantation* by a cyclic derivation just like *condensation*.

[22] We call this Special *j*-Vocalization to distinguish it from a more general *j*-Vocalization rule developed in Section 7.4.2 of Chapter 7.

(101)   *Special* j-*Vocalization*

$$j \rightarrow \imath / \begin{bmatrix} V \\ +\text{ATR} \end{bmatrix} C\_\_\_V$$

The second syllables in the examples in the right column of (102) undergo laxing and destressing with the addition of an affix to the corresponding word in the left column.

(102)   *base form*   *with suffix*
confíde   cónfident
ignóre   ígnorant
maìntáin   máintenance
admíre   ádmirable
vagína   váginal
resíde   résident
confíde   cónfident
presíde   président
salíva   sálivàte
refér   réferent   réference

base form   *with prefix*
píous   ímpious
pótent   ímpotent
fínìte   ínfinite
fámous   ínfamous
mígràte   émigràte

In contrast, other words retain the base stress with the same suffixes and prefixes, as in (103).

(103)   *base form*   *with affix*
cohére   cohérent   cohérence
exíst   exístent   exístence
resíst   resístant   resístance
consíst   consístent
pátient   impátient   impátience

The irregularity in (102) seems to reside not in a special type of laxing and destressing, but rather in the labelling of the feet in the derived form. By the rules developed so far, the words *confide* and *cohere* will have two feet after the first cycle, labelled right strong by (55e). This labelling is retained in the derivative *coherent*, as expected. If the labelling is reversed in *confident*, destressing will be effected by Poststress Destressing and laxing (where the second syllable has a long vowel) by Auxiliary Reduction. It is not the regular Rhythm Rule that does this relabelling, since these forms do not meet its structural description. We propose a special relabelling rule for the cases in (102), given in (104).

(104)   *Minor Relabelling*
        in F_w F_s
        reverse the strong and weak labels in specially marked derived forms.

We assume that Minor Relabelling applies at stratum 2, before Poststress Destressing in a feeding relation in cases like (102). With further derivation, as in *confidential*, the regular Rhythm Rule (83) applies, and Medial Destressing (79) removes the middle foot.

Two types of irregular penultimate stress are discussed by Pater (1994). These have primary stress on a light penultimate syllable, with the final syllable ending in a consonant cluster or having a tense vowel, as in (105).

(105)   a. *final syllable*   b. *final syllable with*
            with tense vowel   *consonant cluster*
            Ulíssès   lieuténant
            Achíllès   àdoléscent

There seem to be very few examples in these categories, and even other Greek names have more regular stress, like *Sócratès*. We cannot simply analyze (105) as exceptions to Syllable Extrametricality, because the final syllable would be stressed in (105b) and in both cases the antepenult would get main stress since the penultimate is light. Pater opts for an analysis that provides the consonant following the penultimate vowel with an underlying mora, making the penultimate syllable honorarily heavy, so that it attracts stress. In fact, he uses this analysis for the *vanilla* type as well, which, however, we have analyzed as exceptions to Syllable Extrametricality. We can tentatively adopt his suggestion for (105), but we reject it for the *vanilla* words.

Some words, originally compounds, can have the second element destressed, such as (106). Some of these words were mentioned as apparent counterexamples to the Coda Condition in (73) of Chapter 3, where we invoked their stratum 2 derivation as a reason for the apparent exceptionality.

(106)   bandsman, helmsman, tribesman, Iceland

Finally, we consider examples like *amànuénsis, hallúcinàte*, which unexpectedly undergo Initial Destressing rather than Poststress Destressing. Hayes (1982: 261) suggests that these words irregularly have a left-branching word tree. However, this is quite out of character with the rest of the English stress system. It is far preferable simply to mark such words as exceptions to Poststress Destressing.

4.8 SBG Revisited

At the end of Section 1.2 of Chapter 1 we briefly introduced the simplified bracketed grid (SBG) approach to metrical representations. We can now investigate how this system might be applied in an account of English stress, considering only the regular case of noun stress, following Dresher (2016). Dresher assumes three lines of grid marks, where the first line, line 0, has a mark for each syllable. He considers the seven rules in (107), somewhat paraphrased here for clarity.

(107) a. Quantity Sensitivity (QS). Place a left parenthesis to the left of a heavy syllable on line 0.
  b. Edge marking. Place a right parenthesis to the left of the rightmost mark on line 0 (coded RLR: encodes our Syllable Extrametricality).
  c. Iterative Constituent Construction (ICC). From right to left insert a left bracket to the left of each pair of elements on line 0. Constructs binary feet.
  d. Line 0 heads. Constituents on line 0 receive a line 1 mark over their leftmost elements.
  e. Edge marking on line 1. Insert a right parenthesis to the right of the rightmost element (RRR) on line 1.
  f. Line 1 heads. Constituents receive a line 2 mark over their rightmost elements.
  g. Phonetic realization. Line 2 marks are realized as main stress; other line 1 marks are realized as secondary stress.

Dresher illustrates the operation of these rules with the derivation of the stress patterns of some English nouns, as in (108). The H (heavy) and L (light) indications are for reference and do not form part of the structure.

(108) a. QS. Place a left parenthesis to the left of a heavy syllable on line 0.

```
x  x  x  x        x  x  (x  x       x  (x  x   Line 0
L  L  L  L        L  L  H  L        L  H  L    Syllables
i. A me ri ca   ii. Ma ni to ba   iii. a gen da
```

  b. Edge marking RLR on line 0.

```
x  x  x  )x       x  x  (x  )x      x  (x  )x  Line 0
A  me ri  ca      Ma ni to  ba      a  gen da
```

c.   ICC right to left.

```
x  (x  x  )x      (x  x  (x  )x      x  (x  )x   Line 0
A  me ri  ca      Ma ni  to  ba      a  gen da
```

d.   Line 0 heads.

```
      x               x   x                  x       Line 1
x  (x  x  )x      (x  x  (x  )x      x  (x  x      Line 0
A  me ri  ca      Ma ni  to  ba      a  gen da
```

e.   Edge marking RRR on line 1.

```
   x)                x   x)                x)       Line 1
x  (x  x  )x      (x  x  (x  )x      x  (x  x      Line 0
A  me ri  ca      Ma ni  to  ba      a  gen da
```

f.   Line 1 heads

```
   x                     x                 x        Line 2
   x)                x   x)                x)       Line 1
x  (x  x  )x      (x  x  (x  )x      x  (x  x      Line 0
A  me ri  ca      Ma ni  to  ba      a  gen da
```

g.   Phonetic realization

América   Mànitóba   agénda

This is only a sketch of the way this approach would work for English stress, and much more would have to be said to account for all that we have described in terms of destressing rules, cyclic stress assignment, multiple degrees of nonprimary stress, and the interaction with segmental rules. The procedure Iterative Constituent Construction only constructs binary feet: if only one syllable remains, no foot is constructed, as in *America* and *agenda*. In these two examples the initial syllable remains outside of any constituent. In this respect it differs from our iterative English Stress rule which creates a degenerate foot on a single remaining syllable. We argue that this, along with destressing and Stray-Syllable Adjunction, ensures that all syllables are part of feet and higher prosodic structure and that this is necessary for the operation of certain segmental rules.

A reader has suggested that Simplified Bracketed Grid theory provides a means of accounting for exceptions that avoids the criticism in Section 4.7 of the theories that account for exceptional stresses in terms of underlying stresses. In fact SBG theory, like ours, allows for several ways of accounting for such exceptions. Indeed, Dresher assumes that accented syllables project a left or right parenthesis, which amounts to marking stress in underlying representations. Similarly, Halle (1997) assumes that morphemes in Russian and some of the other languages that he discusses may be marked with a parenthesis in underlying representation to provide a lexical stress. In Russian, the lexical stress can appear on any syllable, at least in foreign borrowings, as shown by his examples *síntaksis, akvárium, temperáment, koloratúra, avtomobíl'*. Idsardi (1992) appeals to different parameters of edge marking. Macedonian, for example, regularly has antepenultimate stress, as in *vodéničar* 'miller.' This is subject to a line o edge marking RLR as in English that with ICC from right to left gives antepenultimate stress, just as in English *America* in (108). Some exceptional forms have final stress, as *kandidát* 'candidate,' while others have penultimate stress, as *televízor* 'television.' Forms with final stress are subject to the line o edge marking LLR; forms with penultimate stress lexically stipulate that no edge marking applies to them when they appear alone, but the normal edge marking applies in derived forms. ICC from right to left then yields penultimate stress in the stem when it appears alone and (regular) antepenultimate stress in derived forms. This could be the SBG analysis of English *vanilla*, though this is essentially equivalent to our proposal that such forms are simple exceptions to the rule of Syllable Extrametricality.

4.9 Conclusion

In this chapter we have developed an analysis of the stress patterns of English, in terms of rules that construct feet. Despite some variety in the surface patterns, the stress system of English is basically describable in terms of a setting of Hayes's parameters, such that maximally binary, quantity-sensitive, left-strong feet are constructed from right to left across a word, with a right-branching word tree constructed over the resulting feet. We have rejected the proposal of much previous work that the rightmost stress and subsequent stresses are assigned by distinct rules, claiming that a single iterative rule is responsible for the initial assignment of stress to English words. Consonant and Syllable Extrametricality sometimes have the effect of shifting the pattern one syllable to the left. The labelling of word trees generally marks right branches strong when branching; otherwise weak. There are a number of cases where right nonbranching nodes are marked strong (55b–e), having the effect of shifting the main stress to the right, but still retaining the basic pattern of stress assignment.

We account for exceptions by marking certain morphemes as exceptions to rules, rejecting proposals that allow for unrestricted lexical marking of exceptional stress. This allows for even exceptional stress to fall within the basic pattern, aside from the nonapplication of one or more rules.

4.10 Exercises

4.1 Garawa (Furby 1974)

In Garawa, main stress (marked with the acute accent) falls on the initial syllable, secondary stress (marked with the grave accent) falls on the penultimate (in words of four or more syllables), and tertiary stresses (marked with the macron) appear on alternate syllables preceding the penult (in long-enough words). However, nonprimary stress never appears on a syllable directly following the main stress. The following forms are suggestive. The symbols [tj] and [nj] are digraphs representing lamino-alveolar stop and nasal respectively, the symbol [ř] is a trill, [y] = IPA [j]; otherwise the symbols are those used in this book. Set the parameters in (3) so that the correct stress patterns are produced. Also state a destressing rule needed to complete the analysis. Your rules will give more than three degrees of stress for words of eight or more syllables.

yámi	'eye'
púnjala	'white'
wátjimpàŋu	'armpit'
kámalařìnji	'wrist'
yákalākalàmpa	'loose'
ŋánkiřikīřimpàyi	'fought with boomerangs'
ŋámpalāŋinmūkunjìna	'at our many'
nářiŋinmūkunjīnamìřa	'at your own many'
nímpalāŋinmūkunānjimìřa	'from your own two'

4.2 Stress Derivations

Show how the stress pattern of each of the words you transcribed in exercises 2.1 and 2.2 and syllabified in exercise 3.1 is derived using the rules of this chapter. Note that some phonetic tense [i] vowels are lax in underlying representation, such as the penultimate vowel in *paraphernalia* and the final vowel in words like *Menomini*. In addition, *helicopter* is an exception to (55a).

4.3   Cyclic Derivations
       Discuss the cyclic derivation of the following sets of words.

civil	civilize	civilization
theatre	theatrical	theatricality
annex	annexation	
relax	relaxation	
advise	advisory	
element	elemental	
experiment	experimental	
electric	electricity	
object	objective	objectivity
metre	metrical	metricality
proclaim	proclamation	

CHAPTER 5

Prosodic Phonology

5.1   Prosodic Constituents

Prosody is the study of the structure of verse, literally, the study of the accompaniment to song (from Greek προσῳδία *prosōidíā* 'song sung to music'). In phonology, the term refers to the larger organization of speech sounds. Although *SPE* employed syntactic structure to establish the domain of certain phonological rules, the authors acknowledged that there is some difficulty with this idea. For example, in discussing sentences like (1), they point out that the intonational structure does not reflect the syntactic structure.

(1)   This is [$_{NP}$the cat that caught [$_{NP}$the rat that stole [$_{NP}$the cheese]]]

To quote *SPE*:

> Clearly the intonational structure of the utterance does not correspond to the surface structure. Rather the major breaks are after *cat* and *rat*; that is, the sentence is spoken as the three-part structure *this is the cat—that caught the rat—that stole the cheese* (*SPE*: 372).

SPE proposes to derive the correct intonation contour by means of a readjustment rule. This rule would convert (1), "with its multiply embedded sentences, into a structure where each embedded sentence is sister-adjoined to the sentence dominating it." They do not, however, provide any explicit structures or rules for achieving this. But they claim that

> it can certainly be plausibly argued that this "flattening" of the surface structure is simply a performance factor, related to the difficulty of producing right branching structures. . .Hence it can certainly be argued that these problems do not belong to grammar—to the theory of competence—at all (*SPE*: 372).

However, in discussing such structures, Chomsky himself (1965: 10–15) stresses that it is repeated nesting, and especially self-embedding, that contributes to unacceptability whereas left-branching and right-branching structures can be recognized by "an optimal perceptual device, even with a bounded memory," suggesting that right branching is not a problem at all in (1). Thus it seems undesirable, even within the context of *SPE* theory, to attribute the discrepancy between the syntactic structure and the intonation structure of (1) to performance factors alone.

In addition to such theoretical considerations, we must consider an empirical fact – the robustness of the intonation that *SPE* observes. That pattern, with intonation breaks after *cat* and *rat*, is the only way to break the sentence into intonation contours. Uttering (1) with intonation breaks at any of the NP brackets would seem wholly unnatural. This provides further evidence that intonation breaks must be considered as aspects of competence, rather than being attributed to vague performance factors.

Besides intonation, a number of other aspects of pronunciation depend on structures that are neither syntactic nor segmental. One is concerned with the allophones of English voiceless stops, which may be aspirated, glottalized, unreleased, or (for alveolars) flapped, under certain conditions. *SPE* did not treat this aspect of English, but a number of studies which appeared soon after *SPE* introduced the concept of syllable as one means of accounting for these aspects of English pronunciation. Kahn (1976) is especially representative of this trend. His syllabifications however do not account for all the facts and rely on a particularly problematic concept, that of ambisyllabification, in order to account for the flapping of alveolar stops. Kiparsky (1979) considerably improved the empirical coverage by including the foot among the categories relevant for the determination of stop allophones. However, some processes that Kiparsky attributed to the foot are better stated in terms of higher prosodic structures. The theory of prosodic phonology, developed most extensively in Nespor and Vogel (1986), provides a complete set of prosodic categories and demonstrates the relevance of each category to a variety of phonological phenomena in a number of different languages. These categories include the word-internal categories we have already discussed: the mora,[1] the syllable, the foot, and the phonological word.[2] In accordance with the theory of Lexical Phonology, we assume that these categories are formed in the lexicon by the rules of syllabification developed in Chapter 3 and the rules of stress developed in Chapter 4. The theory of Lexical Morphology and Phonology will be developed more fully in Chapter 6. Above the

---

[1] Nespor and Vogel do not explicitly discuss the mora, however.
[2] Also known as the prosodic word.

phonological word are prosodic categories derived from syntactic structure. These are necessarily constructed in the postlexical phonology, after lexical structures are inserted into the syntax. These higher-level prosodic categories are not necessarily isomorphic to the syntactic categories from which they are derived. Nespor and Vogel demonstrate that in each such case it is the prosodic category, rather than the syntactic category, that is relevant to the phonology. Indeed, some phonological processes may involve a prosodic unit larger than the sentence. Since the sentence is the largest syntactic unit, such processes must necessarily involve the prosodic, rather than the syntactic, structure. Nespor and Vogel argue that this is the case with Flapping in North American English and *r*-Insertion in nonrhotic dialects of English. The rules developed in this chapter are all postlexical, in the terminology of Lexical Phonology, regardless of whether the categories are formed in the lexicon or postlexically on the basis of syntax.

5.2   The Prosodic Hierarchy

The essential proposal of prosodic phonology is that there is a hierarchy of prosodic units. These units form a hierarchy in the sense that each unit is a member of the next higher unit and each unit dominates one or more of the next lower unit. First, we list the elements of the prosodic hierarchy in (2), along with the symbols we will use for each.

(2)   *The prosodic hierarchy*
        a.   U   phonological utterance
        b.   I   intonation phrase
        c.   ɸ   phonological phrase
        d.   C   clitic group
        e.   ω   phonological word
        f.   F   foot
        g.   σ   syllable
        h.   m   mora

Following Selkirk (1984a: 26) Nespor and Vogel assume that the prosodic hierarchy is governed by the strict layer hypothesis, which we give in (3).

(3)   *Strict layer hypothesis*
        a.   A given nonterminal unit of the prosodic hierarchy, X^P, is composed of one or more units of the immediately lower category, X^{P-1}.

        b.   A unit of a given level of the hierarchy is exhaustively contained in the superordinate unit of which it is a part.

In other words, every unit in the hierarchy (except the highest, the utterance) is contained in the next higher unit, along with possibly one or more sister units of the same type, and each unit in the hierarchy (except the lowest, the mora) exhaustively contains one or more units of the next lower rank, with no overlapping. Strict layering appears to be true of the basic construction of prosodic units. However, some derived structures may violate this hypothesis. We have already encountered one such violation in the analysis of English stress in Chapter 4. When a syllable is Chomsky-adjoined to a foot, a new foot is created that dominates the original foot along with the syllable being adjoined. Since, according to (3a), a foot should dominate only syllables, this constitutes a violation of strict layering. In subsequent discussion we will see some examples of a prosodic word dominating other prosodic words. We will claim that violations of strict layering are possible only in derived structures, where a specific rule produces a structure violating the condition, but that it is strictly observed in basic structures.

It is also necessary to determine the nature of the branching and labelling of prosodic constituents. With binary branching, each nonterminal node dominates at most two daughter nodes. If a given category dominates more than two terminal nodes, there will necessarily be a number of intermediate nodes between the category and some of the terminals. With n-ary branching, a given category can directly dominate any number of terminals. This difference is illustrated in (4), with five terminal nodes for an arbitrary category X. The binary branching diagram has been made uniformly right branching; uniformly left branching or nonuniform branching would also be possible.

(4)   a. binary branching   b. n-ary branching

For the syllables and feet within a word, we assumed that all branching is binary. Within binary feet the left syllable is labelled strong in English. Word trees are labelled right strong if branching (and under certain other conditions). This left us with some nodes within a word labelled strong or weak but without a constituent label. Nespor and Vogel propose that branching is n-ary in prosodic categories and indeed present a fairly convincing argument that intonation phrases have a flat structure (n-ary branching) rather than a binary branching structure (see Section 5.3.7). But we will show that the phonological phrase has to have binary branching (essentially following the syntactic structure) for the purpose of the phrasal application of the Rhythm Rule. So we will continue to assume binary branching up to the level of the phonological phrase, but follow Nespor and Vogel and allow n-ary branching for intonation phrases and utterances. For these, we also follow their convention whereby one node of a multiply-branching structure is labelled strong, with the others labelled weak. (The magnet analogy of Section 4.1 of Chapter 4 breaks down here.)

Following Selkirk (1980a), Nespor and Vogel distinguish three types of phonological rules in terms of the role of boundaries in the rules. A *domain span* rule simply specifies the prosodic category within which a rule applies, that is, within which the entire structural description of the rule must fall in order for the rule to apply. This is schematically represented in (5).

(5)   *Domain span rule (schematic)*
        $A \rightarrow B \; / \; [\dots X\_\_\_Y\dots]_{D_i}$

An example in English is the rule of Nasal Consonant Deletion, informally introduced as (8b) of Chapter 1, which can be expressed in terms of this scheme as in (6), discussed in Section 5.3.3.

(6)   *Nasal Consonant Deletion*

$$\begin{bmatrix} +\text{cons} \\ +\text{nasal} \\ \alpha\text{anterior} \\ \beta\text{coronal} \end{bmatrix} \rightarrow \emptyset \; / \; [\dots V\_\_\_ \begin{bmatrix} -\text{son} \\ -\text{voice} \\ \alpha\text{anterior} \\ \beta\text{coronal} \end{bmatrix} \dots]_F$$

That is, a nasal consonant is deleted when it follows a vowel and precedes a homorganic voiceless obstruent, provided all these elements are included within the domain of a foot, regardless of what other elements may precede or follow these elements. The rule does not apply when any of the required elements is not in the same foot as the others, even if all the elements occur in the correct order. See Section 5.3.3 for further exemplification of this rule.

A *domain limit* rule specifies that a rule applies at the right or left edge of a prosodic constituent. Here, the edge of the prosodic domain is part of the conditioning environment for the rule. This is expressed schematically in (7), where in (7a) the rule applies at the right edge of the domain and in (7b) it applies at the left edge.

(7)   *Domain limit rule (schematic)*
        a.   A → B / [...X____Y]$_{D_i}$
        b.   A → B / [X____Y...]$_{D_i}$

An example in English is the Aspiration of voiceless stops in foot-initial position, as in (8).

(8)   *Aspiration (preliminary)*

$$\begin{bmatrix} -\text{cont} \\ -\text{voice} \end{bmatrix} \rightarrow [+\text{spread}] / [\underline{\quad}...]_F$$

For examples and discussion see Section 5.3.3, where we will generalize this rule to one that strengthens all consonants in foot-initial position, in view of the fact that a number of other rules are either triggered or blocked in this context.

The third type of prosodic rule is the *domain juncture* rule, which applies to an element in a particular category, where part of the conditioning environment is in an adjacent category of the same type and both of these smaller categories are contained within a larger category. Such rules have the schematic representations in (9), where in (9a) the rule applies at the right edge of the leftmost of the two smaller domains with reference to an environment at the left edge of the rightmost of the two smaller domains, while in (9b) the rule applies at the left edge of the rightmost of the two smaller domains with reference to an environment at the right edge of the leftmost of the two smaller domains.

(9)   *Domain juncture rule (schematic)*
        a.   A → B / [...[...X____Y]$_{D_j}$ [Z...]$_{D_j}$ ...]$_{D_i}$
        b.   A → B / [...[...X]$_{D_j}$ [Y____Z...]$_{D_j}$ ...]$_{D_i}$

I have been unable to find any examples of this type of rule in English. In Spanish, a nasal at the end of one syllable assimilates in point of articulation to a consonant at the beginning of the next syllable (Harris 1969; Hooper 1972), a rule that was illustrated in (14) of Chapter 3, repeated here as (10).

(10)

	assimilation	*no assimilation*
within words	ámbar ['ambaɾ] 'amber'	muevo ['mweβo] 'I move'
	ancho ['aṅʧo] 'width'	nieto ['njeto] 'grandson'
	banco ['baŋko] 'bank'	nuevo ['nweβo] 'new'
		miel ['mjel] 'honey'

across word   un beso [um'beso] 'a kiss'
boundaries   un charco [uɲʧarko] 'a pool'
                     un gato [uŋ'gɑto] 'a cat'
                     un huevo [uŋ'weβo] 'an egg'
                     un hielo [uɲ'jelo] 'an ice'

We can state this rule as in (11).

(11)   Nasal Assimilation (Spanish)

$$[\text{+nasal}] \rightarrow \begin{bmatrix} \alpha\text{ant} \\ \beta\text{cor} \end{bmatrix} / [\ldots[\ldots\underline{\quad}]_\sigma \, [\begin{bmatrix} C \\ \alpha\text{ant} \\ \beta\text{cor} \end{bmatrix} \ldots]_\sigma \ldots]_C$$

Since all the examples of assimilation across word boundaries involve the clitic indefinite article *un*, we have stated the rule in terms of the juncture of two syllables within the clitic group.

The following section illustrates prosodic rules in all the prosodic categories of (2), starting from the mora and working up to the utterance. Examples are from English and other languages, in order to demonstrate the generality of the phenomena. The rules discussed here are postlexical, hence the input is drawn from the lexical level, as discussed in Chapter 2, and the output is the systematic phonetic level.

5.3   Exemplification of Prosodic Categories

5.3.1   *The Mora*

Since the mora is not always identified as a prosodic category, not many rules have been proposed having it as their domain. Nespor and Vogel (1986: 12–13) explicitly deny that subsyllabic constituents such as onset and rhyme are part of the prosodic hierarchy, and claim that all rules formulated in terms of onset and rhyme can be reformulated with reference to the syllable. In the constituent structure approach to syllable structure (Section 3.3.3 of Chapter 3), a syllable consists of one onset and one rhyme, that is, one each of two distinct daughter categories, whereas prosodic structures are composed of one or more daughter units of the same type. Their claims concerning onset and rhyme do not apply to the mora, which we consider part of the prosodic hierarchy, since, in our treatment, a syllable consists of one or two moras, consistent with (3). One rule that has been claimed to have the mora as its domain is *l*-Velarization in English, as discussed by Zec (1988: 9). She states that "*l* is velarized if and only if it is the most sonorous segment within a mora." An *l* is most sonorous within its mora if it is syllabic, as in the second syllable of *bottle*, if it is the only segment in its mora, as in *pill*, or if it is followed by less sonorant segments in a coda, as in *film*. One problem for this proposal is words like *feel*, where a coda *l* follows a glide *j* in the lexical representation, since *j* is more sonorous than *l*. Consider the structures in (12).

(12)   a. 'bottle'   b. 'pill'   c. 'film'   d. 'feel'

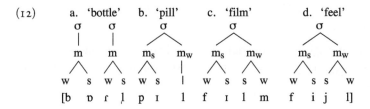

If *l* is velarized in *feel*, this is not captured by Zec's formulation. *L*-Velarization can also be formulated in terms of the rhyme: *l* is velarized in the rhyme, but, as we have noted, the rhyme cannot be considered a prosodic constituent. Therefore, in order to stay within the realm of prosodic constituents, we can reformulate *l*-Velarization in terms of the syllable or the mora. Indeed, we will provide several formulations, some referring to the foot, since the rule is quite variable in different dialects of English.

A number of other rules have been formulated in terms of the rhyme, and Nespor and Vogel reanalyze each in terms of the syllable, as is necessary within their approach. The postulation of the mora as a prosodic constituent opens up additional possibilities for these rules as well. For example in certain dialects of Spanish, /n/ is velarized to [ŋ] in the rhyme, according to the analysis of Harris (1983), as in the examples in (13), where the period represents a syllable boundary.

(13)   a.   cantan   [kaŋ.taŋ]   'they sing'
       b.   instituto   [iŋs.ti.tu.to]   'institute'
       c.   constante   [koŋs.taŋ.te]   'constant'

Unlike English, Spanish does not allow [s]+stop in the syllable onset; accordingly, the first syllable of (13b, c) ends not in the nasal but in [s]. The /n/ that undergoes velarization is in the rhyme in each case of (13); however, in prosodic phonology rules cannot refer to rhymes. Nespor and Vogel (1986: 74) therefore reformulate the rule as a domain limit rule referring to the syllable, as in (14).

(14)   n-*Velarization (Spanish; syllable domain limit formulation)*
       n → ŋ / ____C_0]$_\sigma$

One might question the use of the term C_0 in this rule, which may seem to violate the spirit, if not the letter, of the concept of a domain limit rule, since the segment undergoing the rule may not be strictly at the limit of the syllable domain. The /n/ in question is always contained in the weak mora of the syllable, and so it is possible to reformulate the rule as a domain span rule on the weak mora, as in (15).

(15)   n-*Velarization (Spanish; weak mora domain span formulation)*
        n → ŋ / [..._____...]$_{m_w}$

Some rules of English traditionally given a syllable-based context may also be reformulable in terms of moras, as we will note in the following subsection.

5.3.2   The Syllable

A number of phonological processes have the syllable as their domain. However, some processes formerly attributed to the syllable must be reformulated in terms of the foot or the phonological word. Some may also be amenable to reformulation in terms of the weak mora, as discussed for Spanish *n*-Velarization at the end of the previous subsection.

Nespor and Vogel (1986: 77ff.) discuss the glottalization of voiceless stops in English, observing that this occurs in syllable-final position (16). We have added a few examples in order to exemplify some additional points. We represent unreleased glottalized *t* by the symbol [t']; for many speakers this can be replaced by the glottal stop [ʔ]. The other voiceless stops are also glottalized (and unreleased) in the same environment, but the effect is less pronounced and they cannot be realized by glottal stop alone.[3]

---

[3] These are not ejective stops, another type of articulation for which these symbols are frequently used. In forms like (16g) *button*, Glottalization is fed by Compensatory Syllabification (35). I suggest that a kind of 'mora preservation' is at work, represented schematically as in (i). From the lexical representation we first get Compensatory Syllabification, after which the stranded mora dominating [t] is attached to the preceding syllable putting the [t] in syllable-final position where it can undergo Glottalization.

(i)

(16) a. grea*t*   [ˈɡɹeɪʔ]
      b. quar*t*   [ˈkwɒɹʔ]
      c. plian*t*   [ˈpʰlɑɹənʔ]
      d. bu*t*ler   [ˈbətˈləɹ]
      e. ca*t*s   [ˈkʰæts]
      f. wi*t*ness   [ˈwɪtˈnɪs]
      g. bu*tt*on   [ˈbətˈn̩]
      h. grea*t* party   [ˌɡɹeɪʔ ˈpʰɑɹi]
      i. grea*t* reunion [ˌɡɹeɪʔ ɹiˈjuwnjən]
      j. grea*t* wonder   [ˌɡɹeɪʔ ˈwəndəɹ]

Glottalization does not apply if *t* is preceded by an obstruent, as in *act*. The *t* need not be in absolute syllable-final position, as shown by *cats* (16e). This suggests a formulation of the rule analogous to Spanish *n*-Velarization, either as a domain limit rule with C_o (17a) or as a domain span rule within the weak mora (17b).[4]

(17)   *Glottalization*

      a. $\begin{bmatrix} -\text{cont} \\ -\text{voice} \end{bmatrix}$ → [+constr] / [...[+son] ____C_o]$_\sigma$

      b. $\begin{bmatrix} -\text{cont} \\ -\text{voice} \end{bmatrix}$ → [+constr] / [...[+son] ____...]$_{m_w}$

A second rule with the domain of the syllable is Sonorant Devoicing. A sonorant is devoiced after a voiceless consonant within the same syllable, as in the examples of (18a). When the sonorant is not in the same syllable as a preceding voiceless consonant, the rule does not apply, as in (18b).

(18) a. c*r*y
          p*l*ay
          st*r*ay
          t*r*ain
          t*w*in
          pure   [pʰjuwɹ̥]
          matt*r*ess
          app*l*y
          Is*l*ip
          eye s*l*ip

      b. At*l*as
          ice *l*ip
          hat *r*ack

---

[4] Glottalization often fails to apply if the next word begins with a vowel, as in *great idea*. This is due to the prior application of Flapping, a domain span rule on the phonological utterance. See Section 5.3.8.

We can formulate Sonorant Devoicing as a domain span rule as in (19).

(19)   *Sonorant Devoicing*

$$\begin{bmatrix} C \\ +son \end{bmatrix} \rightarrow [-voice] \ / \ [\ldots[-voice] \ \underline{\quad} \ldots]_\sigma$$

Both Kiparsky (1979: 440) and Nespor and Vogel (1986: 93) mistakenly formulate this rule as having the foot as its domain. If the foot were the domain, the *l* in *Atlas* would be devoiced.

Alveolar and velar stops are affected by a following *r* in the same syllable and, when the stops are voiceless, the *r* undergoes devoicing by (19), a combined effect that Kiparsky (1979: 439) refers to as "mutual assimilation." However, it is better to treat these processes separately. First, consider the velars. Velars are fronted before *r* in the same syllable, as shown in (20a), but not in (20b), where the velar and the following *r* are not in the same syllable.

(20)   a.   *c*rew   [ḵ]
             ìn*c*réase_V
             ín*c*rèase_N
             in*c*rement
             *g*rew   [g̟]

             in*g*ratiate

        b.   ba*ck* rub
             co*ck* roach
             fi*g* rack

We therefore formulate Velar Fronting as a syllable span rule as in (21).[5]

(21)   *Velar Fronting*

$$\begin{bmatrix} -son \\ -cont \\ -cor \\ -ant \end{bmatrix} \rightarrow [-back] \ / \ [\ldots\underline{\quad}\text{ɹ}\ldots]_\sigma$$

Alveolar stops, on the other hand, assimilate to the retroflex articulation of a following *r* in the same syllable, as in (22a). Again, the rule fails to apply if the *r* is in a different syllable (22b).

---

[5] In effect, the velars become palatals, and might be written [c] and [ɟ]. The symbols in (20) may be clearer for our present purposes.

(22)   a.   *t*reat   [t]
            s*t*reet
            re*t*rieve
            ci*t*rus
            des*t*roy
            ni*t*rate
            *d*ream   [d]
            ma*d*rigal

       b.   nigh*t* rate   [ʔ] ~ [t']
            ra*t* race
            cu*t* rate
            tigh*t* rope
            ma*d* regal   [d]

We can formulate Alveopalatalization as a syllable span rule as in (23).

(23)   *Alveopalatalization*

$$\begin{bmatrix} \text{cont} \\ +\text{cor} \end{bmatrix} \rightarrow [-\text{ant}] \; / \; [\ldots \underline{\quad}\text{\i}\ldots]_\sigma$$

As a final example of a rule with a syllable domain, we consider the rule of
æ-Tensing in certain dialects of American English, specifically those spo-
ken in the cities of New York and Philadelphia (Kiparsky 1995: 648–651).
This rule tenses the low front vowel [æ] when it is followed by certain
consonants within the same syllable. Its effects can be observed in (24a),
but not in (24b), where the consonant is in the following syllable.[6]

(24)   a.   pass   [æ̯]
            passing

       b.   passive   [æ]
            acid

We formulate the rule as in (25).

(25)   *æ-Tensing*
       æ → [+ATR] / [\ldots \underline{\quad}[s]]_σ

---

[6] Here we give examples where the consonant inducing tensing is [s]. In fact, there can be other
consonants involved, depending on the dialect, and these form a hierarchy, not necessarily
phonetically motivated, such that, if tensing takes place before any consonant in the hierarchy, it
also takes place before all the consonants below it on the hierarchy, but not necessarily vice versa. See
C.-J. Bailey (1973) for discussion.
   Kiparsky (1988; 1995) claims that æ-Tensing is cyclic on stratum 1. This cannot be correct.
Cyclic æ-Tensing would apply on the first cycle to *pass*, prior to affixation of *-ive*, incorrectly
predicting tense [æ] is *passive*.

It should be observed that æ-Tensing applies before stratum 2 suffixes, as in *passing*, but not before stratum 1 suffixes, as in *passive*. This is predicted by our observation in Chapter 3 (Section 3.5) that there is no resyllabification after stratum 2 morphology. Resyllabification following suffixation on stratum 1 removes the [s] in *passive* from the syllable containing [æ], which bleeds the postlexical rule of æ-Tensing.

5.3.3 The Foot

The foot is the prosodic context for a number of phonological rules in English. We have already noted that foot-initial position is where voiceless stops are aspirated in English (see (8)). For a second example, note that /h/ can be realized only in foot-initial position, as in *vehicular, hilarious*, but not in *vehicle*.[7] A minimal contrast occurs in the place names Birmingham ['bɜːmɪŋəm] in England (West Midlands) and Birmingham ['bɹɪmɪŋˌhæm], Alabama. In fact, foot-initial position is a position of 'strengthening' for several processes in English. This includes the initial position in feet derived by adjunction, as discussed in Chapter 4, and so foot-initial position is not limited to initial position in stressed syllables. We will discuss these other rules in Chapter 7. The special nature of foot-initial position suggests that we mark consonants located here by a particular label. We will assign such consonants the feature [+tense] by a tensing rule (26); all other consonants will have the feature [−tense].[8]

(26)   *Consonant Tensing*
       C → [+tense] / [_____ . . .]$_F$

Aspiration can then be reformulated as in (27).

(27)   *Aspiration (revised)*
$$\begin{bmatrix} -cont \\ -voice \\ +tense \end{bmatrix} \rightarrow [+spread]$$

The combination of Consonant Tensing and Aspiration correctly predicts aspiration of the italicized voiceless stops in (28a), given the rules of foot

---

[7] *Vehicle* can have secondary stress on the second syllable in some dialects, in which case the *h* is pronounced.
[8] If it is objected that this feature is excessively abstract, in that it has no direct phonetic correlates, the rules that refer to it can easily be reformulated with reference to the foot, though with greater redundancy. This analysis is somewhat reminiscent of Kiparsky's (1979: 437) ad hoc feature [+lax], which he assigns to consonants that are *not* foot initial.

construction, including adjunction, and correctly predicts nonaspiration of the italicized voiceless stops in (28b). Foot constituents are shown by brackets.⁹

(28)   a.   [*t*ime]
            [*t*una]
            [*t*y][phoon]
            [*t*e[rrain]]   (first syllable unstressed, adjoined to following foot)
            [en[*t*ire]]
            [sa][*t*ire]
            [*p*o[*t*ato]]
            [*t*ree][*t*oad]

       b.   [s*t*ing]
            [ab[s*t*ain]]
            [af*t*er]
            [sha*tt*er]
            [hos*p*i*t*al]
            [nigh*t*] [owl]

As an example of a rule that relies on the default [–tense] feature associated with nonfoot initial consonants, consider *r*-Tapping in British English, discussed in different terms by Rubach (1996: 220).¹⁰ This rule converts the approximant [ɹ] into a flap [ɾ] when it is between vowels and not initial in a foot, as in (29a). When these conditions are not fulfilled, the approximant appears phonetically, as in (29b).

(29)   a.   [ɾ]   b.   [ɹ]
            ve*r*y   *r*educe
            cou*r*age   cou*r*ageous
            sto*r*y   *r*ed
            pe*r*iod   b*r*ight
            so*rr*y   Hen*r*y
            ba*r*on   wal*r*us
            lau*r*el   su*rr*ound
            fo*r* example   to *r*emember
            the othe*r* end   to *r*ead

We state the rule in (30), which presumes prior application of Consonant Tensing (26).

---

⁹ Both Kiparsky (1979: 438) and Nespor and Vogel (1986: 91–2) consider that the initial syllables of words like *terrain, entire, potato* constitute a 'stressless foot.' This apparently contradictory notion is avoided by our proposed adjunction procedures in Chapter 4 (Stray Syllable Adjunction, (75) in Section 4.4.3).

¹⁰ Rubach claims that this rule provides evidence for ambisyllabicity. Our reanalysis in terms of the foot, however, shows that it offers no such support.

(30)   r-*Tapping* (British English)

$$\begin{bmatrix} \text{ɹ} \\ -\text{tense} \end{bmatrix} \rightarrow \text{ɾ} \ / \ V\_\_\_V$$

Two rules that apply within the domain of the foot (domain span) and do
not refer to Consonant Tensing are Nasal Consonant Deletion and
Compensatory Syllabification. Nasal Consonant Deletion was briefly
introduced in Chapter 1, Section 1.1, to demonstrate the need for rule
ordering (see (8b) of Chapter 1). Here we give a more careful formulation
in (31) and show the need for the foot domain (repeated from (6)).

(31)   *Nasal Consonant Deletion*

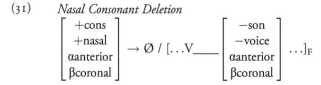

This rule is illustrated in (32). Vowel Nasalization applies before Nasal
Consonant Deletion, so the examples in (32a) all have a nasalized vowel,
even when the conditioning nasal consonant is deleted.

(32)   a. n *deleted*   b. n *retained*
            sent   ['sɛ̃t]   [den]F [tition]F
            central   centrality   [ˌsɛ̃n'tʰɹælɪɾi]
            painter   pontoon
                                                entangle
            antler   ['æ̃ɾ'ləɹ]   anterior
            mental   ['mɛ̃ɾ̃əl]   mentality
                                                van top

As a final example of a rule that applies within the foot domain, we
consider Compensatory Syllabification, discussed by Rubach (1996:
220–221). This rule optionally converts a sequence of schwa plus a
sonorant consonant into a syllabic sonorant in an unstressed syllable.
This is illustrated in (33).

(33)   nation   ['neɪʃən] ~ ['neɪʃn̩]
        bacon   ['beɪkən] ~ ['beɪkn̩]
        (told) them   [ðəm] ~ [ðm̩]
        Italy   ['ɪɹəli] ~ ['ɪɾ̩i]
        gluttony   ['glətəni] ~ ['glət'n̩i]
        animal   ['ænɪməl] ~ ['ænm̩əl] ~ ['ænm̩l̩]

The forms in (34) may also have a syllabic sonorant for some speakers. Rubach denies this possibility, and indeed his analysis, which relies on the coda status of the sonorant before it becomes syllabic, cannot derive syllabic sonorants in (34).

(34)   aroma   [əˈɹowmə] ~ [ɹ̩ˈowmə]
        Jerome   [dʒɪˈɹowm] ~ [dʒɹ̩ˈowm]
        Gerard   [dʒɪˈɹɑɹd] ~ [dʒɹ̩ˈɑɹd]
        anaemic   [əˈniɪmɪk] ~ [n̩ˈiɪmɪk]
        velocity   [vɪˈlɒsɪɾi] ~ [vl̩ˈɒsɪɾi]
        Amelia   [əˈmiɹliə] ~ [m̩ˈiɹliə]

The rule in (35) accounts for the appearance of syllabic sonorants in (33) and (34). In autosegmental notation, this says to detach a vowel from the mora of a weak (unstressed) syllable and attach that same mora to a following sonorant consonant, while at the same time detaching that sonorant consonant from its own mora. All elements involved must be in the same foot.[11]

(35)   *Compensatory Syllabification*

        Condition: F is minimal (if the rule is to be blocked in (34)).

Since our approach to prosodic phonology allows a limited amount of recursion, we have the opportunity to exploit this possibility in rules. One example of such recursion occurs when a syllable is adjoined to a foot, creating a new foot dominating the adjoined syllable and the original foot. Such an adjoined structure occurs in *potato*, as in (36).

(36)

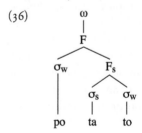

---

[11] Compensatory Syllabification feeds Glottalization in words like *button*. See Footnote 3.

In discussing Aspiration, we noted that the [p] of the first syllable and the
[t] of the second syllable are both foot initial in the structure of (36), and
consequently both are aspirated. We can, however, distinguish the two
species of feet, by offering the definitions in (37), repeated from (19) in
Chapter 4.[12]

(37)   *Definitions*
        A *maximal* foot is a foot that is not dominated by another foot.
        A *minimal* foot is a foot that does not dominate another foot.

In (36) the foot dominating the two syllables *tato* is a minimal foot; the
higher foot dominating *potato* is a maximal foot. Where no recursion is
involved, as in the examples of (33), the foot is both a minimal foot and a
maximal foot. The word *aroma* has the same prosodic structure as *potato*
(36). If the condition that F be minimal is imposed on Compensatory
Syllabification (35), the rule cannot apply to *aroma* since the initial vowel
is outside the minimal foot, and so the entire structural description of the
rule is not contained in the domain required for the rule. If this condition
is not imposed, the entire structural description is found within the
maximal foot, and so the rule can apply.

   Another rule that refers to a distinction between minimal and maximal
feet (in certain dialects) is *l*-Velarization, already alluded to in Section 5.3.1
as a possible example of a rule on the domain of the weak mora. The
operation of this rule is quite variable across English dialects. According to
Wells (1982: 74), in Irish English, *l* is clear in all environments. In some
Scottish varieties, *l* is dark (velarized) in all environments (Wells 1982:
411). In RP, according to Wells (1982: 43), *l* is light before a vowel or [j],
including cases where this context is in a following word, as in *let, blow,
valley, million, fall off*; otherwise it is dark. Rubach (1996: 222–223) claims
that *l* is light in onsets, including onsets resulting from ambisyllabicity, in
cases like *fall off*. However, he regards [lj] as a complex onset in *million*,
which is not correct. As in other dialects, onsets of the form Cj appear only
before the vowels [u] and [ʊ], where the *j* is inserted by a rule (to be
discussed in Chapter 7, Section 7.1.2).[13] Where /j/ is underlying, we gave
a constraint ((44e) in Chapter 3) that disallows complex onsets containing
/j/. Consequently, [l] is in the coda in *million*. It appears that syllabic
conditioning does not account for the distribution of light and dark *l* in

---

[12] Analogous definitions apply to other prosodic categories that allow recursion, such as the
phonological word.
[13] We noted a few marginal word-initial exceptions like *Pyongyang* and *fjord* in Section 3.4.1 of Chapter 3.

RP. Here we have to be content with the segmental environment as stated by Wells.

North American dialects appear to fall into three groups with respect to this rule. In one group, *l* is dark in the rhyme (38b), otherwise light. This is the dialect described by Halle and Mohanan (1985: 65–66).

(38)   a.   *light [l]*   b.   *dark [ł]*
              let   milk
              light   belt
              blow   dull

As we noted in Section 5.3.1, rules with a rhyme domain are expressed in prosodic terms either as domain limit on the right edge of the syllable with the term C_0 or as domain span on the weak mora. In (39) we give both alternatives of *l*-Velarization as exemplified in (38).

(39)   l-*Velarization*
        a.   l → [+back] / ____$C_0]_\sigma$
        b.   l → [+back] / [...____...]$_{m_w}$

In a second group of North American dialects, *l* is light only at the beginning of a foot, maximal or minimal, so that *l* is dark in (40a) in addition to (38b), but light in (40b).

(40)   a.   va*ll*ey
              si*ll*y
              ye*ll*ow

        b.   a*l*arm
              ve*l*ocity

For these dialects we can have the rule in (41).

(41)   l→ [+back] / [X____...]$_F$ (X≠∅)   *or* $\begin{bmatrix} l \\ -tense \end{bmatrix}$ → [+back]

For the third group, *l* is dark except at the beginning of a *maximal* foot. Here, *l* is dark in (40b) in addition to (40a) and (38b). For these dialects we have rule (41) with the addition of a restriction to the maximal foot.[14] Notice that (40b) is also a context (like 34) where *l* can be syllabic by Compensatory Syllabification (35), without the restriction to the minimal foot. It is clear that reference to the foot is needed to account for

---

[14] The third group of dialects could also be described by a rule making *l* dark if it is [–tense]. Cf. C-Tensing (26).

l-Velarization in some of these dialects and that the syllable alone, even with ambisyllabicity, is not adequate.

5.3.4 The Phonological Word

The phonological word is the highest prosodic constituent constructed in the lexicon. We have already discussed the rules for its construction in Chapter 4 . Essentially, an ω node is provided as the top node in a word tree at the end of stratum 1 of the lexicon. We need to make a few refinements to this notion for a more complete picture. On stratum 2 additional affixes may be added or compounds may be formed. The simplest assumption to make for compounds is to retain the ω on each compound element. Thus a compound of two words consists of two phonological words. This assumption is supported by the rule of Diphthong Shortening, which we argue has the phonological word as its domain. Thus, the phonological word need not correspond directly to any syntactic constituent. Syntactically, a compound is a single unit, but its components can be treated as separate units for phonological purposes. This possibility appears in other languages also. Nespor and Vogel argue that stress and vowel harmony in Turkish have the phonological word as their domain. In our terms, this will be the minimal phonological word, since compounds are represented with the nested phonological word structure in (42).

(42)   [[ ]ω [ ]ω]ω

Stress in Turkish is normally on the final syllable, as in (43).

(43)   a. ʧoˈdʒuk   'child'
        b. ʧodʒukˈlar   'children'
        c. ʧodʒuklarɨˈmɨz   'our children'
        d. ʧodʒuklarɨmɨˈzɨn 'of our children'

In compounds, however, the main stress is on the last syllable of the first member of the compound, with secondary stress on the last syllable of the last member of the compound, as illustrated in (44) (examples from Nespor & Vogel 1986: 120). The final vowel in each compound is a possessive suffix, which is included in the phonological word defined by the second compound element.

(44)   a. dyˈjynʧiʧeˌji   'buttercup'
            dyˈjyn   'feast'
            ʧiˈʧek   'flower
            ʧiʧeˈji   'its flower'

b. ˈʧɑɪ eˌvi   'tea house'
    ˈʧɑɪ   'tea'
    ˈev   'house'
    eˈvi   'its house'

Therefore, each element of the compound receives final stress separately. Compound stress labels the first element strong, and the second weak, resulting in the primary stress of the second element being reduced to secondary.

Vowel harmony in Turkish and Hungarian is limited to the domain of the minimal phonological word. We can illustrate with some Hungarian examples. Normally, a monomorphemic word has only back vowels or only front vowels. A compound can be made of two words with opposite harmonic properties, each of which retains its individual harmony within the compound. Any suffix attached to the compound harmonizes to the last member of the compound. This is illustrated in (45).

(45)   a. køɲvtaːr   'library'
            køɲv   'book'
            taːr   'repository'
            køɲvtaːrbɒn   'in library'

        b. laːtkeːp   'view'
            laːt   'see'
            keːp   'picture'
            laːtkeːpynk   'our view'

The syntactic structure and the prosodic structure of the suffixed words in (45) are incompatible, since the suffix belongs with the entire compound syntactically but only to the final element prosodically. These structures are illustrated in (46).

(46)   syntactic   [[køɲvtaːr]$_N$bɒn]$_N$
        prosodic   [[[køɲv]$_ω$[taːrbɒn]$_ω$]$_ω$

We also assume that the entire compound constitutes a phonological word; that is, this category also can be recursive. For languages such as Turkish, Hungarian, and English, Nespor and Vogel (1986: 121) define the phonological word as in (47).

(47)   ω domain
        a. The domain of ω consists of a stem and any linearly adjacent string of affixes.
        b. Any unattached element forms a ω on its own.

We will also assume recursion of the prosodic word with stratum 2 affixes in English; that is, *sleepless* has the structure [[sleep]$_\omega$ less]$_\omega$. and *bookshelves* has the structure [[book]$_\omega$ [shelves]$_\omega$]$_\omega$. Some support for this position will be adduced when we discuss *r*-Insertion in nonrhotic dialects of English in Section 5.3.8.

Nespor and Vogel do not give any examples in English of rules having the phonological word as their domain. The rule of Diphthong Shortening, briefly introduced in Chapter 1, Section 1.1 is one, however. Nespor and Vogel accept Kiparsky's (1979: 440) characterization of this rule as one with the foot as its domain. However, it must in fact have the phonological word as its domain, since the diphthong is shortened in (48a), but remains long in (48b).

(48)   a.   *Diphthong shortened [əɪ]*
           n*i*ght
           *i*ce
           *i*ce lip
           *I*slip
           n*i*ght rate
           n*i*trate
           *i*ce cream
           *Ei*ffel

      b.   *Diphthong remains long [ɑɪ]*
           eye
           eye#ful
           eye slip
           N*ye* trait
           I scream

Kiparsky correctly argues that Diphthong Shortening cannot be a syllable-based process, since it affects diphthongs followed by a voiceless consonant in another syllable in examples like *I.slip* and *ni.trate*. But examples like *nitrate* show that it cannot be foot based either, for the same reason. The word *nitrate* has two feet (each syllable is stressed, and so constitutes a foot). Yet Diphthong Shortening applies in the first syllable. Note that ambisyllabicity would not help here. The *t* of *nitrate* cannot be ambisyllabic, because of the stress on the following syllable. We therefore formulate Diphthong Shortening as a rule on the (minimal) phonological word domain, as in (49).[15]

---

[15] Chambers (1973) claims that the rule is blocked if the diphthong has nonprimary stress and is followed by a stress as in *biséxual, citátion*. The failure of shortening in *biséxual* might be attributed

(49)   *Diphthong Shortening*

$$V \rightarrow \begin{bmatrix} -low \\ -ATR \end{bmatrix} / [\ldots\underline{\hspace{1cm}}[-cons][-voice]\ldots]_\omega$$

As a matter of fact, all vowels are somewhat shorter and laxer before voiceless consonants within the phonological word domain. We can express this informally as (50).

(50)   *Vowel Shortening*
         $V \rightarrow$ 'shorter' / $[\ldots\underline{\hspace{1cm}} [-voice]\ldots]_\omega$

Thus [i] is shorter in *beet* than in *bee* or *bead*, etc.

5.3.5   The Clitic Group

The next prosodic category in the hierarchy is the Clitic Group (C). This category is motivated in a number of languages by the need for a category larger than the phonological word but smaller than the phonological phrase, for the application of certain phonological rules. Normally, this category contains one full word and may include one or more clitics. A *clitic* is a (normally) unstressed element that is more independent than an affix but not as independent as a full word – it cannot stand on its own but needs to lean on an adjacent word (from Greek *klinein* 'to lean'). A *proclitic* leans on the following word, while an *enclitic* leans on the preceding word. It is the unstressed character of clitics that causes a problem in terms of the prosodic hierarchy. That is, a clitic group is composed of one or more of the next lower unit, the phonological word. Each phonological word in turn is composed of one or more feet, each of which contains one stressed syllable. This would seem to imply that a clitic should have stress, although by definition it is stressless. For this reason it is sometimes proposed that clitics should be considered unstressed elements of phonological words. However, there seem to be a number of cases where a category intermediate between affix and word – a clitic – is unavoidable.

Classical Latin has a number of units that fit the definition of clitic; one example is -*que* 'and.' Latin clitics affect the stress of the words they attach

to the phonological-word status of the prefix in this case (Footnote 19); in fact, in my speech, there is shortening in *citation*. There is also the possibility that some words, like *Cyclops*, may be lexical exceptions to (49). This is a problem for Lexical Phonology, since postlexical rules should not have lexical exceptions in this theory. The conditions on the rule in various dialects require further investigation.

to: the stress falls on the syllable before the clitic, regardless of the quantity of that syllable. As discussed in Chapter 4 (Section 4.2), Latin words of three or more syllables without clitics have quantity-sensitive stress: the penultimate syllable is stressed if it is heavy, otherwise the antepenultimate syllable is stressed. The words in (51) illustrate this, given orthographically with the addition of certain diacritics. The acute accent marks stress, long vowels are indicated with a macron (̄), short vowels with a breve (̆), and syllable boundaries are marked where relevant. Note that Latin syllable onsets do not allow *s*+stop clusters medially in a word, although this is allowed word initially, as in *studium* 'zeal.'

(51) amícus   'friend'
      amīcórum   'friends" (genitive plural)
      molés.tus   'troublesome'
      fácĭ.lis   'easy'
      facílĭor   'easier'
      pópŭ.lus   'people'
      populáris   'popular'

When a clitic is attached to a word, stress falls on the syllable before the clitic, regardless of the quantity of that syllable, as shown in (52).

(52) rósă   'rose (nom.)'
      rosáque   'and rose (nom.)'
      *rósăque

      fḗmină   'woman (nom.)'
      fḗminá que   'and woman (nom.)'
      *fḗmínăque

This shows that clitics are not simply suffixes, since suffixes participate in the quantity-sensitive stress of (51), nor are they full words, since they shift the stress of their hosts, which full words do not do. Clitics must therefore be assigned to an intermediate category between suffixes and words.

Turning to clitics in English, Hayes (1989b: 207) defines the clitic group "roughly as a single content word together with all contiguous grammatical words in the same syntactic constituent." More precisely, a grammatical word is adjoined as a clitic to the left or right of the content word with which it is most closely bound syntactically; the content word serves as a host to the clitic(s). A content word is a noun, verb, adjective, or adverb, while a grammatical word is a pronoun, article, auxiliary, or preposition. For example, given the syntactic structure (53a), Hayes assigns the division into clitic groups (53b). It should be noted that the clitic groups *he kept it* and *in a large* are not isomorphic to any syntactic constituent.[16]

(53)   a.

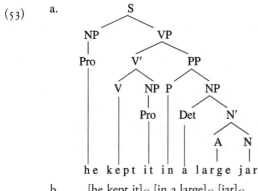

          b.   [he kept it]_C [in a large]_C [jar]_C

Hayes discusses two phonological rules in English that have the clitic group as their domain of application. The first of these deletes a word-final [v] before a consonant-initial word in certain lexical items. He gives the examples in (54), where the clitic groups are bracketed.

(54)   a.   [Please]_C [leave them]_C [alone]_C
                 [liị]
          b.   [Will you save me]_C [a seat?]_C
                 [seị]
          c.   [John]_C [would have left]_C
                 [wʊdə]
          d.   [a piece]_C [of pie]_C
                 [ə]

But where the triggering consonant occurs in a separate clitic group, [v] cannot be deleted, as shown in (55).

(55)   a.   [Please]_C [leave]_C [Maureen]_C [alone]_C
                 [liịv]
          b.   [Will you save]_C [those people]_C [a seat?]_C
                 [seịv]

---

[16] It is interesting to note that *SPE* anticipated this idea. Chomsky and Halle (1968: 367–8) offer a definition of "word" as the domain of noncyclic rules, under which the sequence *was in an unlikely* is a word in the sentence *The book was in an unlikely place.*

    c.   I can't do it this week, [but I would have]$_C$ [last]$_C$ [week]$_C$
                      [hæv]
    d.   [It was thought of]$_C$ [constantly]$_C$
           [əv]

There is no way to reanalyze this rule using the syllable, whether or not ambisyllabicity is invoked, since the [v] to be deleted (or that remains) and the consonant that could trigger deletion will always be in separate syllables.

A second rule that applies within the clitic group is a rule of palataliza-tion that converts [s] or [z] to [ʃ] or [ʒ] respectively before [ʃ] or [ʒ]. At normal rates of speech this rule applies only within the clitic group, as in (56). At faster rates or in sloppy speech it can also apply across clitic groups, as in (57).

(56)   a.   [his shadow]$_C$
            [ʒ]
       b.   [Is Sheila]$_C$ [coming?]$_C$
           [ʒ]
       c.   [as shallow]$_C$ [as Sheila]$_C$
           [ʒ]   [ʒ]

(57)   a.   [Laura's]$_C$ [shadow]$_C$
            [ʒ] (fast or sloppy speech only)
       b.   [he sees]$_C$ [Sheila]$_C$
           [ʒ] (fast or sloppy speech only)
       c.   [those boys]$_C$ [shun him]$_C$
           [ʒ] (fast or sloppy speech only)

In these examples from Hayes, the syntactic host of the clitic is also its phonological host. However, Klavans (1982; 1985) shows that this is not always the case, by providing examples where the clitic attaches phono-logically to an element with which it is less closely bound syntactically than with another element. One example involves auxiliary contraction in English. Auxiliary contraction does not take place if a syntactic gap appears to the right of the auxiliary, as in the examples in (58), from Klavans (1985: 110).

(58)   This won't have the effect on us
                              a. that it will have on you
                              b. that it will____on you
                              c. that it'll have on you
                              d. * that it'll____on you

It might be thought that the gap deprives the auxiliary of a host, but the phonological attachment of clitics in English is to the left, as is clear from voicing assimilation in examples like (59).

(59)   Jack's a fool ([dʒæks], *[dʒækz])

Klavans suggests the partial structure in (60) to account for the dual clitic nature of the contracted auxiliary in (58c).

(60)

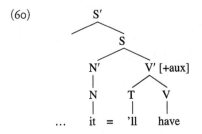

In this structure, the equals sign (=) shows phonological cliticization to the left. Syntactically, however, the clitic *'ll* is placed initially in the V', before the verb. This shows that phonological cliticization need not always follow the direction of syntactic cliticization.

Another rule that applies within the clitic group is Nasal Assimilation. We illustrate this with various pronunciations of the preposition *in* in prepositional phrases in (61a–f) and within words (61g–l).

(61)   a.   in Alberta   [ɪn]   g.   dentition   [ˌdẽnˈtɪʃən]
        b.   in Toronto   [ɪn]   h.   menthol   [ˈmẽn̪θɒl]
        c.   in Thrace   [ɪn̪]   i.   lymphatic   [ˌlĩɱˈfæɾɪk]
        d.   in France   [ɪɱ]   j.   impossible   [ĩmˈpɒsɪbl̩]
        e.   in Paris   [ɪm]   k.   Winchester   [ˈwɪn̠ˌʧɛstəɹ]
        e.   in Germany   [ɪn̠]   l.   increase (N)   [ˈɪŋˌkɹiɪs]
        f.   in Canada   [ɪŋ]

Nasal Assimilation assimilates a nasal to the point of articulation of the following consonant. It is interesting that it assimilates to the exact point of articulation, not just points of articulation that are distinctive for nasals in English. In other words, this rule introduces nondistinctive nasal segments: the dental [n̪], the labiodental [ɱ], the postalveolar [n̠], and the velar [ŋ]. Not all of these distinctions can be made with the features we introduced in Section 2.3 of Chapter 2. The major points of articulation are distinguished by the features [anterior] and [coronal]; these two are the only ones needed for the distinctive points of articulation in English. For the fricatives, we used [strident] to distinguish the dental [θ] [–strident] from the alveolar [s] [+strident]. But all nasals are [–strident], so we cannot use this feature to describe the alternation in (61). We will use [distributed] for this purpose. According to *SPE*, "[d]istributed sounds are produced with a constriction that extends for a considerable distance along the direction of the air flow; nondistibuted sounds are produced with a constriction that extends only for a short distance in this direction" (p. 312). The additional points of articulation distinguished with this feature are given in (62). The feature [distributed] is redundant for nonanterior consonants but needs to be specified for the purposes of the rule of Nasal Assimilation.

(62)

	examples		[anterior]	[coronal]	[distributed]
Bilabial	[p]	[m]	+	–	+
Labiodental	[f]	[ɱ]	+	–	–
Dental	[θ]	[n̪]	+	+	+
Alveolar	[t]	[n]	+	+	–
Postalveolar	[ʧ]	[n̈]	–	+	(–)
Velar	[k]	[ŋ]	–	–	(–)

With these feature specifications, we can express the Nasal Assimilation that applies in the phrases of (61) as in (63).

(63)   *Nasal Assimilation (postlexical)*

$$n \rightarrow \begin{bmatrix} \alpha\text{anterior} \\ \beta\text{coronal} \\ \gamma\text{distributed} \end{bmatrix} / [\ldots \underline{\qquad} \begin{bmatrix} C \\ \alpha\text{anterior} \\ \beta\text{coronal} \\ \gamma\text{distributed} \end{bmatrix} \ldots]_C$$

Since this is a postlexical rule, it can be nonstructure preserving; that is, it can introduce segments that are noncontrastive in English. We will meet other rules of nasal assimilation in Chapters 6 and 7 that apply within the lexicon. These rules are necessarily structure preserving, according to the principles of Lexical Phonology, which are developed fully in Chapter 6.

5.3.6   The Phonological Phrase

Like the clitic group, the phonological phrase is defined with reference to syntactic structure but is not necessarily coextensive with any syntactic unit. In addition, the phonological phrase, and the next two higher units in the hierarchy, may optionally be subject to *restructuring*, which further reduces their congruity with syntax. We will discuss the details of restructuring when we consider the phrasal application of the Rhythm Rule in English.

The definition of the phonological phrase is related to the position of syntactic heads, identified as a parameter at the beginning of Chapter 4. In languages like English and Italian, the head is at the left end of a phrase, so we call these languages head-first languages. On the other hand, languages like Japanese and Korean have the head at the right end of a phrase and are called head-last languages. We will be concerned only with head-first languages here. These languages can also be called *right recursive*, since the phrases that depend on a head are introduced to the right of that head within its phrase. The phonological phrase is constructed leftward from lexical heads in right-recursive languages. A lexical head includes the same syntactic constituents that Hayes called "content words" in the definition of the clitic group, that is, nouns, verbs, adjectives, and adverbs. We give Nespor and Vogel's (1986: 168) principle of phonological phrase formation in (64), modified in parts II and III to require binary-branching constituents, where they assumed n-ary branching. We will justify the return to binary branching in the discussion of the English Rhythm Rule.

(64)   *Phonological phrase formation*
        I.   φ domain
              The domain of φ consists of a C which contains a lexical head (X) and all Cs on its nonrecursive side up to the C that contains another head outside the maximal projection of X.

        II.   φ construction
              Join all Cs included in a string delimited by the definition of the domain of φ into a binary branching φ, right branching in right-recursive languages and left branching in left-recursive languages. In ambiguous cases branching follows the syntactic structure.

        III. φ relative prominence
              Label φ trees strong on the right in right-recursive languages; label φ trees strong on the left in left-recursive languages.

Freely paraphrased, (64) creates phonological phrases by grouping a lexical head with all syntactic material to its left, up to but not including the next lexical head outside its maximal projection. This next lexical head begins a new phonological phrase. Let us consider a simple example from Italian. In (65) the syntactic structure of the sentence is given on top, in terms of X-bar notation, while the division into phonological phrases is given underneath (Nespor & Vogel 1986: 171).

(65)

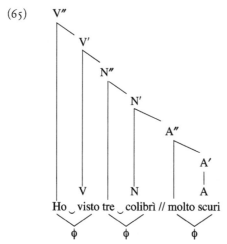

'I saw three very dark hummingbirds.'

The final phonological phrase corresponds to the syntactic phrase A″, but the first two phonological phrases do not correspond to any single syntactic constituent. Nespor and Vogel use the structure in (65) to argue for the phonological phrase as the domain of the rule of Italian traditionally called *Raddoppiamento Sintattico (RS)*. This rule lengthens a consonant at the beginning of a phonological word if it follows a word-final stressed vowel in the preceding phonological word, provided that the two phonological words are contained within the same phonological phrase. It thus qualifies as a domain juncture rule. We give Nespor and Vogel's formulation in (66).[17]

(66)   *Raddopiamento Sintattico (Italian)*

$$\sigma_{(s)}$$
$$|$$
$$C \rightarrow [+\text{long}] / [\ldots[\ldots V]_\omega [\underline{\hspace{1cm}} \begin{bmatrix} +\text{son} \\ -\text{nas} \end{bmatrix} \ldots]_\omega \ldots]_\phi$$

---

[17] Nespor and Vogel mark the final vowel of the first phonological word with the feature [+DTE], where DTE stands for 'designated terminal element,' in the terminology of Liberman and Prince (1977: 259) for main stress. Since [DTE] is not a proper phonological feature but the result of finding the terminal node in a stress tree that is not dominated by any weak node, I have replaced this designation with the requirement that the vowel in question be dominated by a syllable which is optionally strong; i.e., it is either a strong syllable or the only syllable within the foot.

The subscripted curves (‿) in (65) show where the requirements of RS are met, and thus lengthening occurs in the initial [v] of *visto* and the initial [k] of *colibrì*. RS is inhibited at the double slash (*//*), since this marks the boundary of two phonological phrases. The [m] of *molto* is not lengthened, despite the preceding stressed vowel, because these two segments are in distinct phonological phrases, as shown.

Turning now to English, Nespor and Vogel discuss two rules that apply within the domain of the phonological phrase: the Rhythm Rule[18] (in its phrasal manifestation) and the Monosyllable Rule. We saw the Rhythm Rule in its word-internal application in Section 4.5 of Chapter 4. The formulation in (67) for phrasal application is stated with the symbol Z instead of F, where Z stands for a prosodic category F or higher. The application of this rule where Z = ω will be shown in (70).

(67)   *Rhythm Rule (phrasal)*

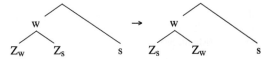

Condition: all elements are contained in the same phonological phrase.

Like the word-internal version of this rule, the phrasal version is subject to the constraint in (68) (Kiparsky 1979: 425).

(68)   The Rhythm Rule (67) (usually) does not apply when it would create a metrical structure of the form (i) within the (minimal) phonological word, where the first *s* is nonbranching.

(i)

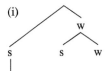

The phrasal effect of the Rhythm Rule is the same as within words, but we have made a slight modification to the definition. To begin with, we claim that, for phrasal application, the entire structural description of the rule must fall within a phonological phrase. In addition, the weak node need not directly dominate two feet but may dominate higher nodes, which we

---

[18] Liberman and Prince (1977: 319) and Nespor and Vogel (1986: 177) refer to this rule as "Iambic Reversal."

214 Prosodic Phonology

denote by Z in (67). Application within the phonological phrase is illustrated in (69), where $Z = F$.

(69)

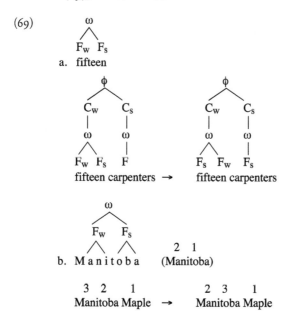

Relabelling of nodes at the prosodic word level is illustrated in (70), where the boxed nodes are the ones whose labelling is reversed by the Rhythm Rule. This example also illustrates recursion of prosodic word nodes within compounds. *SPE* stress numbers as calculated by algorithm (31) in Chapter 1 (=(20) in Chapter 4) are added for convenience.

(70)

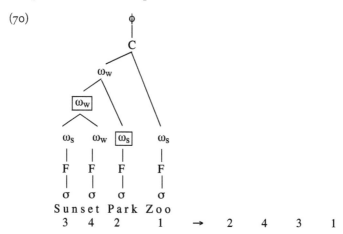

Constraint (68) is illustrated by the operation of the Rhythm Rule in (71a) versus its nonapplication in (71b).[19] This example also illustrates our claim that branching is binary within the phonological phrase, and that the branching follows the syntactic structure. If branching were n-ary, as proposed by Nespor and Vogel, the configuration for the Rhythm Rule would not be present.

(71)   a.   well-funded bank
             transnational banking
             bisexual leanings
             cross-cultural studies

        b.   Alberta bank
             sensational claim

The word *Alberta* has the prosodic structure in (72).

(72)

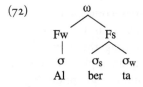

It is clear that, if the two feet in (72) had their strong and weak labellings reversed when in the phrase *Alberta bank*, the disallowed configuration of (68i) would result within the ω. On the other hand, the phrase *well-funded* has the structure in (73a); the structure of the phrase *well-funded bank* is shown in (73b), before the Rhythm Rule applies.

(73)   a.   b.

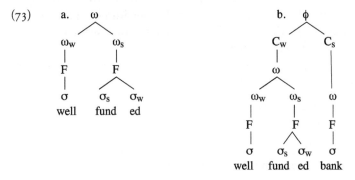

[19] Examples from Kiparsky (1979: 425–426, fn. 2). Stressed prefixes like *trans-* and *bi-* are assumed to have phonological word status.

Since *well-funded* consists of two phonological words, the Rhythm Rule
does not create the configuration of (68i) within the minimal phonological
word, and so it applies.

The Rhythm Rule does not apply to just any sequence of words with the
stress pattern of (67). For example, the rule applies to the italicized words in
(74) but not in (75) (examples from Nespor & Vogel 1986: 178 et passim).
The acute accent indicates the primary stress of the relevant words.

(74)   a.   More than *fifteen* cárpenters are working in the house. (<fiftéen)
        b.   A *kángaroo's* life is full of surprises. (<kangaróo)

(75)   a.   When she was *fiftéen*, cárpenters rebuilt the house. (*fífteen)
        b.   *Kangaróos* carry their young in pouches. (*kángaroos)
        c.   John *persevéres* gládly and díligently (*pérseveres)
        d.   Rabits *reprodúce* véry quickly. (*réproduce)

The explanation for the difference between (74) and (75) lies in the
phonological phrase. In (74a) *fifteen carpenters* is contained within a
phonological phrase consisting of the head *carpenters* and everything to
its left within the maximal projection N″, including the word *fifteen*.
Since restriction (68) is inapplicable here, the rule can apply. By contrast,
the sequence *fifteen carpenters* does not fall within a single phonological
phrase in (75a). Each of these words heads its own phonological phrase,
and so the Rhythm Rule is blocked. In (74b) *kangaroo's life* falls within a
single phonological phrase, since the head is *life* and the maximal projection, consists of the entire N″ *a kangaroo's life*. But in (75b), *kangaroos*
and *carry* each head their own maximal projection, and cannot be
grouped together as a phonological phrase, so the Rhythm Rule again
is blocked. Similarly, in (75c, d), the verb constitutes a phonological
phrase separate from the adverb phrase that follows, again preventing
application of the Rhythm Rule.

There are some cases, superficially similar to (75c, d), where the
Rhythm Rule does apply, as in (76).

(76)   a.   John *pérseveres* gládly. (<persevéres)
        b.   Rabbits *réproduce* quíckly. (<reprodúce)

Nespor and Vogel (1986: 173) propose that phonological phrases can
optionally be *restructured* by the rule in (77).

(77)   φ *Restructuring* (optional)
        A nonbranching φ which is the first complement of X on its recursive
        side is joined into the φ that contains X.

The term "complement" is not employed strictly in the usual syntactic sense in this definition. Nespor and Vogel give a number of examples of phonological phrase restructuring in Italian, of which we cite the two in (78).

(78)   a.   [I caribù]$_\phi$ [nani]$_\phi$ [sono estinti]$_\phi$
            'Dwarf caribous are extinct.'

        b.   [Se prenderà]$_\phi$ [qualcosa]$_\phi$ [prenderà]$_\phi$ [tordi]$_\phi$
            'If he catches something, he will catch thrushes.'

Nespor and Vogel propose that the phrase *i caribù nani* in (78a) and the phrase *prenderà qualcosa* in (78b) can each be (optionally) restructured as a single phonological phrase, making it possible to apply Raddoppiamento Sintattico in both. In (78b), *qualcosa* 'something' is a complement in the strict sense, in fact, the direct object of the verb. But in (78a) *nani* 'dwarf' is an adjective modifying *caribù* 'caribou' (adjectives normally follow the noun they modify in Italian). This is not strictly a complement. But, in both cases, the nonbranching φ contains a C which is contained within the maximal projection of the phrase to its left, and it is in this sense that we must understand "complement" in the definition (77). Returning to the English examples in (76), Nespor and Vogel propose that *perseveres gladly* (76a) can be restructured as a single φ, and likewise *reproduce quickly* (76b), even though the expressions *quickly* and *gladly* are adverbial modifiers, not strictly complements. This allows the application of the Rhythm Rule in these cases. Similar restructuring is blocked in (75c, d), because the adverbial modifier is branching. Such restructuring is blocked in English in the case of genuine complements, at least of a noun phrase that is the direct object of a verb. Kiparsky (1982: 32) observes that the phrase *maintáin órder* cannot be pronounced **máintain órder*; that is, it cannot be subject to the Rhythm Rule, which in our terms indicates that the two phonological phrases *maintain* and *order* cannot be restructured as one, despite the latter being a nonbranching complement on the recursive side of the former.

The second example of a phonological rule with the phonological phrase as its domain is the Monosyllable Rule, which Nespor and Vogel take from Selkirk (1978). This rule reduces monosyllabic words that are not members of the major lexical categories N, A, V, but only if the monosyllable in question is labelled *w* with respect to an *s* syllable in the same φ. According to the labelling conventions in (64III), the monosyllable in question will be labelled *s* if it is final within its φ, otherwise it will be labelled *w*. This accounts for Selkirk's examples in (79), where the prosodic labelling is Nespor and Vogel's.

(79)   a.   [The sluggers]$_\phi$ [boxed]$_\phi$ [in the crowd]$_\phi$ (reduced *in*)
        b.   [The cops]$_\phi$ [boxed in]$_\phi$ [the crowd]$_\phi$ (unreduced *in*)

In (79a), the preposition (or particle or adverb) *in* is marked *w* within its ϕ, and so reduced. In (79b), the preposition (or particle) *in* is marked *s* within its ϕ, and so cannot be reduced.

Nespor and Vogel demonstrate that the phonological phrase is the domain of liaison in French. Liaison is the phonetic realization of a word-final consonant before a vowel in the next word, a consonant that would be silent in phrase-final position. The examples in (80a) show the application of liaison within the phonological phrase. The examples in (80b) show that liaison does not apply between words that belong to two different phonological phrases, and those in (80c) show that liaison does not apply between the head of a phrase and the first nonbranching complement on its recursive side (the right, in French). As Nespor and Vogel note, (80c) demonstrates that French does not allow restructuring of phonological phrases (examples from Nespor & Vogel 1986: 179). A subscripted curve (‿) indicates that liaison takes place; a double slash (//) indicates that it is blocked.[20]

(80)   a.   Cette famille a [trois beaux ‿ enfants]$_\phi$ [bo.zɑ̃.fɑ̃]
              'This family has three beautiful children'

              Les ‿ enfants [sont ‿ allés]$_\phi$ à l'école   [sɔ̃.tæ.le]
              'The children went to school'

        b.   Jean a [des livres]$_\phi$ // [assez nouveaux]$_\phi$ [liv.ʁæ.se]
              'John has some rather new books'   *[liv.ʁə.zæ.se]

              Nos ‿ invités [sont ‿ arrivés]$_\phi$ // [en retard]$_\phi$ [tæ.ʁi.ve.ɑ̃]
              'Our guests arrived late'   *[tæ.ʁi.ve.zɑ̃]

        c.   [Les maisons]$_\phi$ // [italiennes]$_\phi$ coûtent beaucoup   [mɛ.zɔ̃.i.tæ.ljɛn]
              'Italian houses are expensive'   *[mɛ.zɔ̃.zi.tæ.ljɛn]

              Le garçon [les ‿ aidait]$_\phi$ // [activement]$_\phi$ [zɛ.dɛ.æk.tiv.mɑ̃]
              'The boy helped them actively'   *[zɛ.dɛ.tæk.tiv.mɑ̃]

---

[20] This discussion of liaison in French applies to the colloquial style only. In more elevated styles, liaison can apply in a wider range of contexts, partly morphologically determined, including some of the contexts where we have excluded liaison in (80). Thanks to Marie-Hélène Côté for discussion.

The plural adjective *beaux* in (80a) is pronounced [bo] in phrase-final position; before a vowel-initial word within the phonological phrase it is pronounced [boz], with the [z] syllabified with the following vowel, as shown. But the plural [z] in *livres* is not pronounced in (80b), even though a vowel follows, because the following vowel belongs to a word in the following phonological phrase, as is also the case in (80c).

5.3.7 The Intonation Phrase

Selkirk (1978: 130) defined the intonation phrase as the domain over which an intonation contour is spread. Nespor and Vogel demonstrate that, in addition, the intonation phrase constitutes the domain of a number of segmental rules in Italian, Spanish, and Modern Greek. They give no examples of segmental rules in English with the intonation phrase as their domain. The primary criterion is that the end of an intonation phrase is a position where one may pause in the utterance of a sentence. In many cases, an entire sentence can be pronounced as a single intonation phrase but, as with the phonological phrase, the possibility exists for restructuring the intonation phrase. And like the other prosodic categories, the intonation phrase is constructed out of one or more units of the immediately subordinate prosodic category, in this case, the phonological phrase. However, certain syntactic constructions obligatorily form intonation phrases on their own. These include "parenthetical expressions, nonrestrictive relative clauses, tag questions, vocatives, expletives, and certain moved elements" (Nespor & Vogel 1986: 188), illustrated in (81a–f), to which we can add (81g), an appositive.

(81) a. Lions [as you know]$_I$ are dangerous. (parenthetical)
  b. My brother [who absolutely loves animals]$_I$ just bought himself an exotic tropical bird. (nonrestrictive relative)
  c. That's Theodore's cat [isn't it]$_I$ (tag question)
  d. [Clarence]$_I$ I'd like you to meet Mr Smith. (vocative)
  e. [Good heavens]$_I$ there's a bear in the back yard. (expletive)
  f. They're so cute [those Australian koalas]$_I$ (right dislocation)
  g. Jennifer [our neighbour]$_I$ discovered a nest of squirrels in her attic. (appositive)

Nespor and Vogel suggest that the common element uniting this rather disparate class of items is that they are all external to the root sentence with which they are associated. A root sentence, as defined by Emonds (1976), includes a matrix sentence and any subordinate clauses embedded within it; however, conjoined sentences are separate root sentences. Nespor and

Vogel (1986: 189) claim that an intonation phrase can be no longer than a root sentence. Thus, conjoined sentences necessarily form separate intonation phrases, while subordinate clauses can be part of a larger intonation phrase. The contrast in (82), first discussed by Downing (1970), illustrates this rather vividly.

(82)   a.   [Billy thought his father was a merchant]$_I$ [and his father was a
                secret agent]$_I$
        b.   [Billy thought his father was a merchant and his mother was a
                secret agent]$_I$

In (82a) two root sentences are conjoined, and so they form separate intonation phrases, as indicated by the bracketing. In (82b), however, two subordinate clauses are conjoined within a single subordinate clause within the root sentence, which can form a single intonation phrase.

It should also be noted that those phrases that obligatorily form I do so regardless of where they occur in the sentence. Because of the basic assumptions of the theory, the parts of the sentence outside the obligatory I form separate Is on one or both sides. This becomes clearer as we examine some of Nespor and Vogel's examples in (83). The phrase *as you know* is a parenthetical, which can occur in various places in the sentence. As a parenthetical, it forms an obligatory I. Whatever is left over forms additional Is, which are not (necessarily) themselves isomorphic to any syntactic constituent, although they do contain phonological phrases (ϕs).

(83)   a.   [As you know]$_I$ [Isabelle is an artist]$_I$
        b.   [Isabelle]$_I$ [as you know]$_I$ [is an artist]$_I$
        c.   [Isabelle is]$_I$ [as you know]$_I$ [an artist]$_I$
        d.   [Isabelle is an artist]$_I$ [as you know]$_I$

Nespor and Vogel speculate that, in right-recursive languages such as English, Is that are not also isomorphic to syntactic constituents, such as the *I Isabelle is* in (83c) may appear only to the left of an obligatory I, here the *I as you know*. This may have to do with where adverbials may be inserted into a syntactic structure. Jackendoff (1972) suggests that, in English, parentheticals may only be inserted such that they are dominated by the root sentence, that is, at the beginning of the sentence, as in (83a), at the end of the sentence, as in (83d), or between major constituents of the sentence. In (83b) the parenthetical occurs after the subject NP, and in (83c) it occurs after the auxiliary verb *is*. These positions are both between major constituents of the sentence. But parentheticals cannot occur between a verb and its direct object in English, as shown by the ungrammaticality of *Isabelle read, as you know, a book*.

Examples such as (83) lead Nespor and Vogel (1986: 189) to propose the algorithm in (84) for constructing intonation phrases. For the intonation phrase we accept Nespor and Vogel's proposed n-ary branching.

(84)   *Intonation phrase formation*
    I.   *I* domain
         An *I* domain may consist of
         a.   all the ϕs in a string that is not structurally attached to the sentence tree at the level of s-structure, or
         b.   any remaining sequence of adjacent ϕs in a root sentence.
    II. *I* construction
         Join into an n-ary branching *I* all ϕs included in a string delimited by the definition of the domain of *I*.

The relative prominence of ϕs within *I* is somewhat different from the other prosodic categories we have considered up to now. Instead of uniform right- or left-strong labelling, Nespor and Vogel suggest the algorithm in (85).

(85)   *Intonation phrase relative prominence*
        Within *I*, a node is labelled *s* on the basis of its semantic prominence; all other nodes are labelled *w*.

Nespor and Vogel illustrate this with the sentence in (86). Any one (but only one) of the five ϕs can be labelled *s*; all others are weak.

(86)   [[My sister]$_\phi$ [sells]$_\phi$ [fresh fruit]$_\phi$ [at the market]$_\phi$ [on Monday]$_\phi$]$_I$

Nespor and Vogel argue that the flexibility of the position of the strong ϕ within *I* provides an argument for n-ary branching over binary branching for the *I* constituent. If uniform binary branching is assumed, a structure with five ϕs embedded within *I* could have one of the two structures in (87).

(87)   a.   I   b.   I

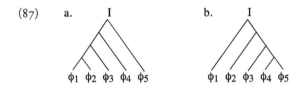

In a left-branching tree like (87a), the usual labelling conventions would either label left nodes strong (in which case ϕ_1 would be labelled strong and the other terminal ϕs would be labelled weak) or label the left node strong if and only if branching (in which case ϕ_2 would be labelled strong and the other terminal ϕs would be labelled weak). The reverse would apply to a right-branching tree like (87b). Labelling right nodes strong would label ϕ_5 strong and the others weak; labelling right nodes strong if and only if branching would label ϕ_4 strong and the others weak. These labelling conventions would have no way of labelling ϕ_3 as strong, which, however, is a possible pronunciation of (86) if the phrase *fresh fruit* receives semantic prominence. The same would be true for binary branching structures that are not uniform. More generally, for longer sequences of ϕs, only the first two or the last two could be labelled strong by the usual labelling conventions for binary branching trees.

Like the phonological phrase, intonation phrases can be restructured. Unlike ϕ, where restructuring results in longer units, however, I restructuring consists of breaking an I up into smaller Is. A variety of factors play a role in I restructuring, including the length of I, speech rate, speech style, and contrastive prominence. The longer an I is, the more likely it is to be broken down into smaller Is. A related factor is the rate of speech. The faster the speech rate, the less the likelihood of breaking long Is into shorter ones. Conversely, the more formal or pedantic the style of speech, the slower it is likely to be and the greater the likelihood of I restructuring. Nespor and Vogel speculate that "there is a tendency to establish Is of more or less uniform, 'average' length, although at this point we are not able to characterize this ideal length more precisely" (1986: 194).

Semantic and syntactic factors also play a role in I restructuring. One semantic factor is that of contrastive prominence, discussed by Bing (1979: 210ff.). A sentence like (88a) is assigned one I, since it is dominated by a single root sentence.

(88)   a.   [Paul called Paula before Carla called Carl]$_I$
         b.   [Paul called Paula]$_I$ [before *she*]$_I$ [called *him*]$_I$

But the presence of the pronouns in (88b) forces a specific interpretation in which the pronouns are coreferential to the nouns so that (88b) cannot be interpreted in the same way as (88a). This interpretation is realized phonologically as extra prominence on the pronouns, which in turn causes the single I to be restructured as three smaller Is, as indicated in (88b). This is another indication of the independence of the prosodic structure from the syntactic structure, since both sentences in (88) have identical syntactic structures but differ in prosodic structure.

One syntactic factor is the tendency to restructure I so that the final ϕ of the new I ends in a noun. This can be observed in a sentence like (89), where (89a) gives a partial syntactic structure, (89b) gives the division into

ϕs (as a single *I*, as a single root sentence), and (89c) gives the division into restructured *I*s, where the division does not respect syntactic constituents, but where the first smaller *I* does end in a noun. The examples are from Nespor and Vogel (1986: 197–198).

(89) a. [I would never have believed [the children of John and Mary to be able to become so ill mannered]$_{S'}$]$_{S'}$.

  b. [[I would never have believed]$_\phi$ [the children]$_\phi$ [of John and Mary]$_\phi$ [to be able to become]$_\phi$ [so ill mannered]$_\phi$]$_I$

  c. [I would never have believed the children of John and Mary]$_I$ [to be able to become so ill mannered]$_I$

Similar considerations apply to sentences like (1) at the beginning of this chapter, which we repeat as (90a), with the addition of the division into phonological phrases in (90b) and the possible *I* restructuring in (90c).

(90) a. [This is [the cat [that caught [the rat [that stole [the cheese]$_{NP}$]$_{S'}$]$_{NP}$]$_{S'}$]$_{NP}$]$_{S'}$
  b. [[This is]$_\phi$ [the cat]$_\phi$ [that caught]$_\phi$ [the rat]$_\phi$ [that stole]$_\phi$ [the cheese]$_\phi$]$_I$
  c. [This is the cat]$_I$ [that caught the rat]$_I$ [that stole the cheese]$_I$

Nespor and Vogel (1986: 197) claim that there is "a general tendency to avoid restructuring an *I* in any position other than at the end of a noun phrase." The restructuring in (90c) does just that, however – it interrupts noun phrases. In support of their claim, they cite sentences such as (91).

(91) [[My friend's neighbour's aunt's mother]$_\phi$ [knows]$_\phi$ [a famous writer]$_\phi$]$_I$

Restructuring the *I* in (91) is possible only with a division after *mother*. Any division within the subject noun phrase would violate this general tendency. But the subject noun phrase is a single ϕ in any case; they incorrectly assume that it could be four ϕs, one ending in each noun of the subject noun phrase.[21] But since *my friend's*, *neighbour's*, and *aunt's* are all within the maximal projection of the head *mother*, there is no reason for their assumption that this "general tendency" holds. Since in fact noun phrases can be interrupted by restructuring, as in (90c), it is better simply to require that, in these cases of restructuring, the shorter *I*s end in a ϕ which terminates in a noun.

---

[21] Nespor and Vogel (1986: 219, fn. 7) claim that "in strings of such pre-head modifiers some type of restructuring takes place so that these modifiers may form ϕs on their own," without further specifying that type of restructuring.

Another type of *I* restructuring occurs with lists, regardless of the syntactic category of the listed items. This is actually a problematic case, because it involves breaking up ϕ as well as *I*. One of Nespor and Vogel's examples is (92), given first with its initial analysis into phonological phrases and then with the proposed restructured intonation phrases.

(92)   a.   [[The big fat ugly nasty beast]$_\phi$ [scared away]$_\phi$ [the children]$_\phi$]$_I$
         b.   [The big]$_I$ [fat]$_I$ [ugly]$_I$ [nasty beast]$_I$ [scared away the children]$_I$

By the principle of strict layering, the first ϕ in (92a) has to be converted into smaller ϕs before it can be made into smaller *I*s. When the listed items are noun phrases, this problem does not arise, as in the restructured *I*s of (93). An intonation break is inserted after each of the listed items (but not before the first).[22]

(93)   [They own two cats]$_I$ [three dogs]$_I$ [four parakeets]$_I$ [and a turtle]$_I$

If the list is separated from the matrix sentence to a greater extent, a new intonation break is inserted even before the first item in the list, as in (94).

(94)   [Let's invite]$_I$: [Arnold]$_I$ [Arthur]$_I$ [Archibald]$_I$ [and Zachary]$_I$

For these cases, Nespor and Vogel (1986: 201) propose List Restructuring (95).

(95)   *List Restructuring (optional)*

         In a sequence of more than two constituents of the same type X, i.e., x_1, x_2, ... x_n, an intonation break may be inserted before each repetition of the node X (including the first occurrence x_1 when separated from the matrix sentence).

5.3.8   The Phonological Utterance

The final prosodic unit is the highest: the phonological utterance. Nespor and Vogel define the phonological utterance in terms of the highest node in a syntactic tree: X^n. This is often a root sentence, but may be a different syntactic unit such as a noun phrase. People don't always speak in complete sentences! We give their rules for the construction of the utterance in (96).

---

[22] Nespor & Vogel are not explicit about the analysis of conjunction. If *gladly and diligently* is a single ϕ in (75c), then perhaps *two cats, three dogs, four parakeets, and a turtle* is all one ϕ in (93), in which case the same problem does arise.

(96)   *Phonological utterance formation*
I.   *U* domain
    The domain of *U* consists of all the *I*s corresponding to the highest
    X^n in the syntactic tree.
II.   *U* construction
    Join into an n-ary branching *U* all *I*s included in a string delimited
    by the definition of the domain of *U*.
III.   *U* Relative Prominence
    The rightmost node dominated by *U* is strong; all other nodes are weak.

The *U* domain is relevant to two segmental processes in English: flapping
in North American English and the rules responsible for the distribution of
word-final *r* in nonrhotic dialects. We will consider Flapping first.
Flapping affects alveolar stops, converting them into the sonorant flap
[ɾ]. We will also see that it may apply to the alveolar nasal [n] producing a
nasalized flap [ɾ̃]. The segmental environment can be stated quite generally
if we assume that Aspiration (27), or more exactly Consonant Tensing
(26), precedes Flapping. We state Flapping in (97).

(97)   *Flapping*

$$\begin{bmatrix} +\text{cor} \\ -\text{strid} \\ -\text{cont} \\ -\text{tense} \end{bmatrix} \rightarrow \begin{bmatrix} +\text{cont} \\ +\text{son} \\ +\text{voice} \end{bmatrix} / [\ldots[-\text{cons}] \underline{\quad\quad} V \ldots]_U$$

On the left side of the segmental environment, the specification [–cons]
allows the rule to apply after vowels, glides, and [ɹ], but not after other
sonorants, nor after obstruents. This is shown in (98).

(98)   *Flapping applies*   *No Flapping*
    bu*tt*er   ac*t*or
    wri*t*er   cin*d*er
    Car*t*er   al*t*er

The restriction of the input to [–tense] segments prevents Flapping in
Foot-initial position, but allows it in other positions in the foot, regardless
of the syllabic position of the segment in question, as long as the other
conditions are met. This is shown in (99) (Nespor & Vogel 1986: 224).

(99)   *Flapping applies*   *No Flapping*
    a*t*om   a*t*omic
    a*t* issue   a *t*issue
    a*dd*er   a*d*ore
    I'*d* ascribe   I *d*escribe

The examples in (100) show that Flapping can apply within words, whether simple, affixed, or compound, and between words within sentences (Nespor & Vogel 1986: 224–225).[23]

(100) a. wa*t*er
       b. ri*d*er
       c. whi*t*ish
       d. hea*d*ache
       e. a hundre*d* eggs
       f. whi*t*e owl
       g. grea*t* idea
       h. My mother bough*t* a parrot
       i. A very dangerous wild ca*t*, as you know, escaped from the zoo.
       j. Ichabo*d*, our pet crane, usually hides when guests come.
       k. Pa*t*, I'd like you to meet Joe.

Examples (100i, j, k) show that the domain of Flapping must be larger than the Intonation phrase, since the parenthetical *as you know*, the appositive *our pet crane*, and the vocative *Pat*, are among the syntactic units that form obligatory *I*, so that the conditions for Flapping are spread across two adjacent *I*s in these examples.

As Kahn (1980: 102) observed, Flapping can apply across sentence boundaries, as in (101). The first example is from Kahn; the others are from Nespor and Vogel (1986: 237ff.).

(101) a. Have a sea*t*. I'll be right back.
       b. Turn up the hea*t*. I'm freezing.
       c. It's la*t*e. I'm leaving.
       d. You invite Charlo*tt*e. I'll invite Joan.
       e. That's a nice ca*t*. Is it yours?
       f. Where's Pa*t*? I need him.
       g. Martha didn't invite Pa*t*. I did.

Nespor and Vogel propose that more than one syntactic unit of the type X^n can be grouped together to form a single phonological utterance. As with the phonological phrase and the intonation phrase, they refer to this process as restructuring. Notice that U restructuring is like ϕ restructuring in that both join two or more original units into one larger unit, and unlike I restructuring, which breaks an I up into two or more shorter units. However, as the examples in (102) show, not every sequence of two

---

[23] Prince (1980: 545) suggests that Flapping is obligatory when it is within the domain of the minimal foot, otherwise optional.

sentences can be restructured into a single *U*. The italicized segments would most likely be realized as glottalized rather than flapped.

(102) a.   Have a sea*t*. It's warm in here.
       b.   It's la*te*. I'm Larry.
       c.   That's a nice ca*t*. Is it after eight already?
       d.   Turn up the hea*t*. I'm Frances.
       e.   Stop tha*t*. I'll leave otherwise.
       f.   It's la*te*. I'm not leaving, though.

Nespor and Vogel (1986: 240ff.) postulate a number of conditions on *U* restructuring. First, they propose two pragmatic conditions, given in (103). These conditions must be met in order for restructuring to take place.

(103) *Pragmatic conditions*
       a.   The two sentences must be uttered by the same speaker.
       b.   The two sentences must be addressed to the same interlocutor(s).

Then they propose two phonological conditions, given in (104). These must also be met in order for restructuring to take place.

(104) *Phonological conditions*
       a.   The two sentences must be relatively short.
       b.   There must not be a pause between the two sentences.

Both (101) and (102) meet these pragmatic and phonological conditions. However, the difference between them is that there is a close syntactic or semantic relation between the two sentences in each of the examples in (101) which does not hold in (102). Nespor and Vogel argue that either one of the syntactic conditions in (105) or one of the semantic conditions in (106) must hold between two sentences in order for *U* restructuring to join them into a single utterance.

(105) *Syntactic conditions:*
       a.   Anaphora (a pronoun in one sentence refers to a full noun phrase in the other).
       b.   Ellipsis (one sentence contains a syntactic gap that implies material from the other sentence).

(106) *Semantic conditions:*
       The sentences are related explicitly or implicitly by one of these logico-semantic connectors:
       a.   and
       b.   therefore
       c.   because

For example, the two sentences in (101a, b) are related by the implied connector *because*.[24] In (101c) they are related by *therefore*, and in (101d) by *and*. In (101e) the pronoun *it* refers to *cat*, and in (101f) the pronoun *him* refers to *Pat*. These are instances of anaphora. Finally, (101g) is an example of ellipsis. The second sentence, *I did*, is short for *I invited Pat*. Thus, each of these discourses fulfils one of the syntactic or semantic requirements for *U* restructuring, and the restructured *U* contains the context for Flapping, which can apply. On the other hand, the two sentences of each example of (102) do not exhibit these relationships. In (102a–d) the two sentences of each example are entirely unrelated. In (102e) the logico-semantic relation could be expressed by *or*, which is not a possible connector for restructuring to occur. In (102f) the relation is *but*, also not a connector that allows restructuring. Therefore, we predict that the italicized alveolar stops in (102) are not eligible for Flapping.

The segmental conditions on Flapping (97) require that the segment before the focus be [–cons]. This includes not only vowels and glides but also the liquid [ɹ]. Indeed Flapping applies after *r*, as in *carder* and *Carter*, both pronounced ['kɑɹɾəɹ]. The other liquid in English, [l], is [+consonantal] and does not permit Flapping, so that *alter* and *alder* remain distinct. Nasals are also [+consonantal], so that /d/ remains a stop in *cinder*, which does not become homophonous with *sinner*. But *winter* can be homophonous with *winner*, in some dialects, because of the interaction of Flapping with Nasal Consonant Deletion. The formulation of Flapping in (97) includes the alveolar nasal as a possible input. The result of flapping the nasal /n/ is a nasal flap [ɾ̃]. We give the derivations of *winter* and *winner* in (107). The outputs are identical, if we assume that nasalization spreads from the vowel to the flap in *winter*. Compare the derivation of *cinder*, with a voiced stop, and hence no Nasal Consonant Deletion.

(107)		'winter'	'winner'	'cinder'
	lexical representation	/wɪntəɹ /	/wɪn + əɹ/	/sɪndəɹ/
	Vowel Nasalization (7a in Chapter 1)	ĩ	ĩ	ĩ
	Nasal Consonant Deletion (31)	Ø	– – –	– – –
	Flapping (97)	ɾ	ɾ̃	– – –
	Nasalization Spread	ɾ̃	– – –	– – –
	Output	[wĩɾ̃əɹ]	[wĩɾ̃əɹ]	[sĩndɹ]

Another rule that has the phonological utterance as its domain is *r*-Insertion in some nonrhotic dialects of English, such as RP and Eastern Massachusetts. Oversimplifying somewhat, in these dialects, *r* is

---

[24] In (101a) the connector could be *and*.

not pronounced at the end of words in isolation or before a consonant, but is pronounced when a vowel follows, within a word (before stratum 2 suffixes) or across word boundaries. As with Flapping, it can also apply across sentence boundaries, when restructuring is possible according to the conditions in (103)–(106). This is illustrated in (108). The symbol ɍ represents an orthographic *r* that is not pronounced in these dialects; we write [ɹ] for an *r* that is inserted in the pronunciation in these dialects, whether or not it is present orthographically (cf. Nespor & Vogel 1986: 226ff.).

(108) a. clea ɍ   /kleɹ/
       b. clea[ɹ]est
       c. gnaw   /nɒ:/ (/ɒ:/ is long but [–ATR]; cf. Section 2.4.2)
       d. gnaw[ɹ]ing
       e. Wanda
       f. Wanda[ɹ] arrived
       g. that spider is dangerous   →   ...spide[ɹ] is...
       h. the panda eats bamboo   →   ...panda[ɹ] eats...
       i. It's my mother. I have to go →   ...mothe[ɹ] I...
       j. Try that sofa. It's softer   →   ...sofa[ɹ] It's...

We give the rule of *r*-Insertion in (109).[25]

(109) r-*Insertion*

$$
\emptyset \rightarrow \text{ɹ} / [\ldots[\ldots
\begin{bmatrix}
\text{V} \\
\text{–ATR} \\
\text{–high} \\
\text{+back}
\end{bmatrix}
\underline{\qquad}]_\omega \text{ V }]_U
$$

For *clearest, gnawing*, we assume a nested prosodic word structure [[clear]ω est]ω, as suggested in Section 5.3.4.

However, *r*-Insertion is not possible between any pair of sentences, as shown in (110).

(110) a. It's my mother. I have two cats   ↛   *...mothe[ɹ] I
       b. Try that sofa. It's after midnight   ↛   *...sofa[ɹ] It's...

The examples in (108i, j) meet the semantic conditions for restructuring: the logico-semantic connector is *therefore* in (108i), and *because* in (108j). These conditions are not met in (110), so that here restructuring is not possible, and hence there is no *r*-Insertion.

---

[25] Notice that this rule does not fall into any of Nespor and Vogel's types of prosodic rules: domain span, domain limit, or domain juncture. It applies at the limit of one prosodic unit (ω) within the span of a larger unit (U).

McCarthy (1991) argues that *r*-Deletion is needed in Eastern Massachusetts (and other nonrhotic dialects) in addition to *r*-Insertion. This is because underlying *r* is retained before stratum 1 suffixes, but no *r* is inserted in this context, as shown in (111).

(111)   a. Homer   ['howmə]   Homeric   [ˌhow'mɛɹɪk]
        b. algebra ['ældʒɪbɹə]   algebraic   [ˌældʒɪ'bɹeɪɪk]   *[ˌældʒɪ'bɹeɪɹɪk]

We formulate *r*-Deletion in (112).

(112)   r-*Deletion*
        ɹ → Ø / V ____ ...]σ

To complicate matters further, words with a high vowel before *r* or *l* are pronounced with a schwa between the vowel and the liquid, as in the examples of (113).

(113)   a. fear   [fiɪə(ɹ)]   /feɹ/
        b. feel   [fiɪəl]   /fel/

To account for this, McCarthy proposes a rule of *ə*-Insertion, which we give as (114).

(114)   *ə-Insertion*

$$[_F \ldots \sigma \ldots]$$

$$\Large \diagup\diagdown$$

m   m
| |

$$\varnothing \to ə / \quad V \quad [+high] \quad \underline{\quad\quad} \quad \begin{bmatrix} +son \\ -nas \\ -high \end{bmatrix}$$

In more casual speech in McCarthy's dialect, this schwa can be deleted. This deletion can also affect schwa from other sources, such as a reduced vowel. Some examples are in (115).

(115)   feeling   ['fiɪəliŋ]   or   ['fiɪliŋ]   /fel/
        realize   ['ɹiɪəˌlɑɪz]   or   [ɹiɪˌlɑɪz]   /ɹeæl/   (cf. *reality*)

The underlying representation of *real* must contain two vowels: the second vowel appears unreduced when stressed in a derived form such as *reality*. The rule of schwa Deletion for McCarthy's casual speech is given in (116).

(116)   σw
        |

$$ə \to \varnothing / \begin{bmatrix} -cons \\ +high \end{bmatrix} \underline{\quad\quad} \begin{bmatrix} +son \\ -nas \\ -high \end{bmatrix}$$

5.4 The Ordering of the Rules

In (117) we give a summary of the rules developed in this chapter for English, in order of application. Not all orderings are crucial; we mark crucial orderings with the conventional curved line. Pairs of rules not so connected could have been listed in the opposite order. We will then discuss the motivation for the crucial orderings. All these rules are postlexical, except Consonant-Tensing and ə-Insertion, which apply on stratum 2 of the lexicon. The rules ɔ-Lowering, Low Back Lengthening, a/o-Tensing, and ɒ-Unrounding are discussed in Chapter 7.

(117)   a.   *Lexical, stratum 2*

Consonant Tensing (26)
ə-Insertion (114)

b.   *Postlexical*

C, φ, I, U Formation, Restructuring
⌠Diphthong Shortening (49)
⌡Vowel Shortening (50)
Aspiration (27)
Vowel Nasalization (8a in chapter 1; domain = ω)
Nasal Assimilation (63)
Nasal Consonant Deletion (31)
Flapping (97)
Compensatory Syllabification (35)
Glottalization (17)
Sonorant Devoicing (19)
Velar Fronting (21)
Alveopalatalization (23)
l-Velarization (39), (41)
Palatalization (47 in chapter 7)
r-Deletion (nonrhotic dialects, 112)
r-Insertion (nonrhotic dialects, 109)
ɔ-Lowering (9 in chapter 7)
Low Back Lengthening (35 in chapter 7)
a/o-Tensing (34 in chapter 7)
ɒ-Unrounding (37 in chapter 7)
r-Tapping (British English, 30)
ə-Deletion (optional, casual 116)
æ-Tensing (25)
v-Deletion (examples in 54)
Palatalization of /s/, /z/ (examples in 56 amd 57)
Rhythm Rule (phrasal. 67, with restriction 68)
Monosyllable Rule (examples in 79)
h-Deletion (70 in chapter 7)

The derivations in (107) illustrate the ordering of Vowel Nasalization, Nasal Consonant Deletion, and Flapping. Vowel Nasalization must apply before Nasal Consonant Deletion, since the latter rule eliminates the context for the former rule. In addition, Nasal Consonant Deletion must apply before Flapping, since the former rule creates the context for the latter. Prior to the operation of Nasal Consonant Deletion, the *t* in *winter* is preceded by /n/ which is [+cons] and so not a context for Flapping. After Nasal Consonant Deletion, the *t* in *winter* is preceded by /ĩ/, which is [–cons], and which therefore provides an appropriate context for Flapping. This situation, where a rule creates the context for a subsequent rule that did not previously exist, is known as *feeding* order.

We also order Flapping (97) before Glottalization (17). In (16h) we observed that /t/ is glottalized in the phrase *great party*. In (100g) we observed that /t/ is flapped in the phrase *great idea*. In fact, the /t/ initially fulfils the conditions for Glottalization in both phrases, since it is syllable final in both. However, the prior application of Flapping removes /t/ from the domain of Glottalization in *great idea* by making it [+voice]. This situation, where a rule destroys the context for a subsequent rule, making it no longer applicable, is known as *bleeding* order.

In (14) of Chapter 1 we observed the ordering of Diphthong Shortening and Flapping. In *writer*, Diphthong Shortening applies because it is followed by a voiceless consonant, /t/. However, the subsequent application of Flapping changes this same voiceless consonant into a voiced one, a flap. If Flapping were to apply first, it would destroy the context for Diphthong Shortening. This situation, where a rule destroys the context of a previous rule, but the previous rule has had the chance to apply anyway because it is ordered first, is known as *counterbleeding* order. The ordering of Vowel Nasalization and Nasal Consonant Deletion in (107) is also a counterbleeding order, since Nasal Consonant Deletion eliminates the Nasal Consonant that triggers Vowel Nasalization.

5.5   Conclusion

This chapter has discussed a number of rules of English whose domains are defined in terms of prosodic categories. The prosodic categories are established both lexically and postlexically. Lexically, the rules of syllabification and stress at stratum 1 produce syllable structure, foot structure, and phonological words. Recursion of phonological words occurs at stratum 2 with the addition of the affixes at that level. Postlexically, after words have been concatenated into sentences, higher prosodic categories are

assigned, to which postlexical phonological rules have access. The phonological rules at each lexical stratum and postlexically are ordered. We will
encounter more rule ordering in Chapters 6 and 7, where we investigate
the lexical rule systems in greater detail.

5.6 Exercises

5.1 Application of Allophonic Rules
The following words and phrases illustrate the rules determining
consonant and vowel allophones (Diphthong Shortening,
Aspiration, Vowel Nasalization, Nasal Consonant Deletion,
Flapping, Glottalization, Sonorant Devoicing, Velar Fronting, and
Alveopalatalization). Determine which rules apply in each and give a
phonetic transcription of each.

a.	treat	j.	ice peak
b.	mighty	k.	I speak
c.	atlas	l.	saw Ted
d.	deictic	m.	sought Ed
e.	night train	n.	might rain
f.	my train	o.	micrometer (measuring instrument)
g.	like rain	p.	mice treat
h.	lye crane	q.	my street
i.	my tea	r.	citation

5.2 Rhythm Rule
Discuss the possibility of applying the Rhythm Rule to the
following phrases.

a. overdone steak
b. artificial intelligence
c. kangaroo rider
d. achromatic lens
e. bamboo tables
f. Japanese bamboo
g. interior decorator
h. Ontario Legislature

5.3 Phonological Phrases and Intonation Phrases
Divide the following sentences into phonological phrases and
intonation phrases. Indicate obligatory intonation phrases and

discuss the possibilities of restructuring. (Examples based on Nespor & Vogel 1986: 194–200 passim.)

a. My friend's baby hamster always looks for food in the corners of its cage.
b. The adult orangutan, according to this article, constructs a nest every evening out of leaves and twigs.
c. Our next-door neighbour, Clarence, truly believes that black cats bring bad luck.
d. Ducks, geese, swans, and coots inhabit this lake.
e. The giant panda, which lives mainly in China, eats only one type of bamboo in its natural habitat.

5.4 Flapping across Sentence Boundaries

Discuss the possibility of flapping across sentence boundaries (i.e., converting the final alveolar stop of the first sentence into a flap) in the following examples. Assume that the pragmatic and phonological conditions are met and concentrate on the syntactic and semantic conditions.

a. Take your coat. It's cold out.
b. Take your coat. It's a full moon tonight.
c. This coffee's too sweet. I won't drink it.
d. Don't call Pat. I want to.
e. I'm short. I'll get in the front.
f. It's late. I won't stop until I'm finished, though.

CHAPTER 6

Lexical Phonology: The Cyclic Rules

This chapter has three main goals. One is to expand and clarify the concepts of the theory of Lexical Phonology, introduced in Section 1.4 of Chapter 1. The second is to develop a number of segmental rules that apply in stratum 1 of the lexicon, integrate these into an ordered set with the stress rules that we developed in Chapter 4, and expand on the principles governing the application of these rules. The third is to investigate the way in which phonology interacts with morphology in terms of this model.

6.1 Principles of Lexical Phonology

In the linear model of *SPE*, a phonological representation consists of a sequence of segments and boundaries. Certain grammatical morphemes may have an abstract semantic representation at the output of the syntax, such as the past tense morpheme, represented in *SPE* as 'past.' This had to be converted to phonological substance by readjustment rules that preceded phonological rules; either 'past' triggered an internal change in the case of verbs like *sing*, changing this to *sang*, or it was replaced by /d/ following regular verbs, like *mend*, which was subject to further phonological operations – in this case, Epenthesis gives the final form *mended*. Roughly speaking, *SPE* divides morphology between syntax and phonology, the former manipulating items, the latter spelling them out.

Lexical phonology takes a quite different approach. It provides fully specified words prior to syntactic operations, regarding the appropriate past tense forms as a matter for the lexicon rather than either syntax or phonology. In this model, the lexicon is more than a list of items; it is an active, generative component of the grammar. The lexicon still contains a list of morphemes, to be sure, but it also includes morphological operations and certain phonological operations. A diagram of the model was provided in Figure 1.1 in Section 1.4.1 of Chapter 1, repeated here as Figure 6.1.

235

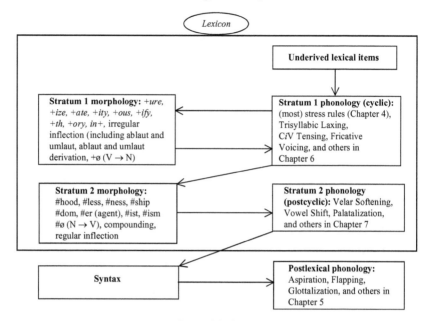

Figure 6.1   The model of Lexical Phonology

The diagram shows two lexical strata for English, each of which includes both a morphological and a phonological component. The first stratum is cyclic, while the second is noncyclic, or postcyclic, since its operations follow the cyclic stratum. It allows for the application of stratum 1 phonological rules before the morphological operations of that stratum, and then the reapplication of cyclic phonology after each morphological operation. On stratum 2, all affixes are added before any phonological operations, and all phonological rules follow the addition of affixes at this stratum. In addition, there is a component of postlexical phonology, which applies after lexical items have been processed by the syntax.

6.1.1   Criteria for Morphological Strata

There are a number of criteria for assigning morphological operations to stratum 1. It follows from the organization in Figure 6.1 that stress rules, for example, reapply after each layer of affixation on stratum 1. Therefore, as was discussed in Section 4.5 of Chapter 4, stress may be affected by the addition of stratum 1 affixes, as shown in (1a). We use the plus sign (+) as an informal indication that an affix belongs to stratum 1. Stratum 1 affixation does not necessarily result in a stress shift, as shown by (1b).

(1)   a.   sólid   solíd+ify
              tótal   tòtál+ity
              órigin   orígin+al, orìgin+ál+ity
        b.   desíre   desírous
              légal   légalìze
              óxygen   óxygenàte

In contrast, stratum 2 affixes do not result in a shift in stress, as in (2). The crosshatch (#) is an informal indication of stratum 2 affixation.

(2)   válue, válue#less, válue#less#ness

As will be shown in Section 6.2, Trisyllabic Laxing is another stratum 1 phonological rule that does not apply to the result of stratum 2 affixation, although such forms seem superficially to be subject to those rules.

Another consequence of the model in Figure 6.1 is the ordering of affixes: if affixes from both strata are attached to a stem, the stratum 1 affixes are nearly always closer to the stem than those from stratum 2. For example, the stratum 1 suffix *-ian* attaches to nouns to form adjectives and the stratum 2 suffix *-ism* attaches to either nouns or adjectives to form nouns, and they can attach only in this order, as shown in (3).[1]

(3)   a.   Mendel+ian#ism
        b.   Mongol+ian#ism
        c.   *Mendel#ism+ian
        d.   *Mongol#ism+ian

There are other characteristics of stratum 1 affixes that do not directly follow from the model. One is that stratum 1 affixes may induce *allomorphy* of the stem they attach to, whereas this does not happen with stratum 2 affixes. Recall from Chapter 1, Section 1.1 (and Footnote 1 of Chapter 1), that we use the term *allomorph* to refer only to phonologically unpredictable variants of a morpheme. The examples in (4) illustrate allomorphs with stratum 1 affixes.[2]

---

[1] See Section 8.2.1 of Chapter 8 for some discussion of apparent counterexamples and an explanation of them within the model.

[2] In some instances it may not be obvious whether or not allomorphy is involved. In Section 2.5 of Chapter 2 and Section 6.3.1, for example, we show that the stem alternation in *reduce* vs *reduction* is phonologically conditioned, not a case of allomorphy (pace Rubach 1984: 29, fn. 7).

(4)   receive, reception
        resolve, resolution

Stratum 1 affixes themselves sometimes exhibit allomorphy, as in (5), whereas this does not occur with stratum 2 affixes.[3]

(5)   *alternations*   *underlying representation of suffix*
        reduce, reduc+tion   /t + jən/
        educate, educat+ion   /jən/
        repeat, repet+ition   /ɪt + jən/
        realize, realiz+ation   /æt + jən/
        resolve, resol+ution   /ʌt + jən/

Stratum 1 affixes may attach to bound stems, that is, stems that do not occur as independent words, as in (6). There are only rare examples of this with stratum 2 affixes, such as *uncouth, unkempt, ruthless, grateful, gruesome* (cf. Giegerich 1999: 50).

(6)   in+ept, *ept
        re+ceive
        vac+ate, vac+ant
        nomin+ate, nomin+ee

Finally, we should note that affixation on stratum 2 is generally more semantically transparent than affixation on stratum 1, where the meaning is liable to be more idiosyncratic.

On the basis of these criteria, we can list some of the morphological operations of the two lexical strata in English in (7). Some of these are discussed further with more information bearing on their stratal affiliation. They are listed in no particular order; morphological operations are not considered to be ordered beyond belonging to a particular stratum. Their operation is restricted by the type of stem they attach to, the semantics, and sometimes other factors.[4]

---

[3] The suffix illustrated in (5) is underlyingly always /jən/, possibly preceded by a stem extender. Less abstract allomorphs, such as /ʃən/ in *reduction*, might be thought preferable. However, back-formations like *(self)-destruct* seem to argue against this possibility.

[4] This section is by no means intended as a complete account of English morphology, which would require a book in itself. It is merely a sample of the morphological operations that we will need for the discussion of the phonology. See Marchand (1969) for a thorough discussion of English morphology.

(7) a. *Stratum 1 morphology*

affix or process	underlying representation	attaches to	result	examples
in+	/ɪn/	adjective, stem	negation	indecent, inept
be+	/be/	noun	verb	becloud, bewitch
en+	/ɛn/	noun	verb	empower
in+	/ɪn/	stem	verb	insist
re+	/ɹe/	stem	verb	resist
pro+	/pɹɒ/	stem, verb, adjective	verb	proclaim, prolong
de+	/de/	stem	verb	design
con+	/kɒn/	stem	verb	consist
+ous	/ɒs/	noun, stem	adjective	poisonous, pious
+ious	/iɒs/	noun, stem	adjective	laborious, odious
+ious	/jɒs/	noun, stem	adjective	rebellious, ferocious
+al	/æl/	noun, stem	adjective	anecdotal, municipal
+ial	/ɪæl/	noun, stem	adjective	baronial, filial
+ial	/jæl/	noun, stem	adjective	facial, initial
+ual	/ʉæl/	noun, stem	adjective	factual, annual
+ar	/æɹ/	noun, stem	adjective	molecular, lunar
+iar	/ɪæɹ/	noun, stem	adjective	linear, peculiar
+an	/æn/	noun, stem	adjective	Tibetan, Tuscan
+ian	/ɪæn/	noun, stem	adjective	reptilian, Dravidian
+ian	/jæn/	noun, stem	adjective	Egyptian, Elysian
+ic	/ɪk/	noun, stem	adjective	acidic, ethnic
+ity	/ɪtɪ/	adjective, stem	noun	density, dignity
+ion	/jən/	verb, stem	noun	impression, fraction
+ation	/æt + jən/	verb, stem	noun	realization, implication
+tion	/t+ jən/	verb, stem	noun	description, reduction
+ition	/ɪt + jən/	verb, stem	noun	repetition, dentition
+ution	/ʌt + jən/	stem	noun	resolution
+ure	/ʉɹ/	verb, stem	noun	pressure, future
+ent	/ɛnt/	verb, stem	noun, adjective	resident, affluent
+ence	/ɛns/	verb, stem	noun	dependence, science
+ize	/iz/	adjective, stem	verb	realize, eulogize
+ate	/æt/	noun, stem	verb	originate, migrate
+ant	/ænt/	verb, stem	noun, adjective	defendant, reluctant
+ance	/æns/	verb, stem	noun	guidance, elegance
+ify	/ɪfi/	adjective, noun, stem	verb	solidify, codify, dignify
+th	/θ/	numeral	adjective	fifth
+th	/θ/	adjective, stem	noun	warmth, length
+ory	/ŋɹj/	verb, noun, stem	noun, adjective	migratory, sensory, illusory
+ary	/æɹj/	noun, stem	noun, adjective	planetary, auxiliary
+ive	/ɪv/	noun, verb, stem	adjective	objective, responsive receptive
+y	/j/	noun	noun	advocacy
+an	/ən/	noun	noun	librarian
+able	/əbɪl/	verb, stem	adjective	préferable, perceptible
+ee	/e/	verb, stem	noun	appointee, nominee
+t	/t/	verb	past, participle	slept
+d	/d/	verb	past, participle	told, fled, heard
+e	/ɛ/	noun	verb	bathe
+Ø		verb	noun	increase
umlaut		noun	plural	feet, mice
umlaut		noun	verb	feed (<food)
ablaut		verb	past, participle	sang, sung

b. *Stratum 2 morphology*

affix or process	underlying representation	attaches to	result	examples
un#	/ən/	adjective	negative	unequal
anti#	/æntɪ/	various	adjective, noun	antireligious

re#	/ɹe/	verb	verb	rewire
mis#	/mɪs/	verb	verb	mistrust
non#	/nɒn/	adjective	negative	nontoxic
de#	/de/	noun	verb	denature
#ful	/fʊl/	noun (verb)	adjective	peaceful, resentful
#ish	/ɪʃ/	noun, adjective	adjective	boyish, greenish
#ed	/d/	noun	adjective	moneyed
#ment	/mɛnt/	verb	noun	enjoyment
#ism	/ɪzm/	adjective, noun	noun	socialism, Marxism
#ist	/ɪst/	adjective, noun	adjective, noun	socialist, Marxist
#ly	/lɪ/	noun, adjective	adjective	ghostly, deadly
#ly	/lɪ/	adjective	adverb	cheaply
#er	/əɹ/	verb	noun (agent)	singer
#er	/əɹ/	noun	noun	prisoner
#ing	/ɪŋ/	verb	noun	singing
#ing	/ɪŋ/	verb	participle	singing
#dom	/dəm/	noun	noun	kingdom
#ness	/nɪs/	adjective	noun	kindness
#age	/ɪdʒ/	noun, verb	noun	orphanage, steerage
#less	/lɪs/	noun	adjective	childless
#ship	/ʃɪp/	noun	noun	championship
#hood	/hʊd/	noun	noun	neighbourhood
#al	/əl/	verb	noun	withdrawal
#en	/ɪn/	adjective (noun)	verb	whiten, lengthen
#able	/əbəl/	verb, stem	adjective	understandable, perceivable
#d	/d/	verb	past, participle	mended
#er	/əɹ/	adjective	comparative	bigger
#est	/ɪst/	adjective	superlative	biggest
#z	/z/	noun	plural	cats
#z	/z/	verb	3 singular	sings
#Ø		noun	verb	pattern
#Ø		verb	noun	exhaust

compounding (all categories)

6.1.2   Affixes Sensitive to Stress

The stratum 2 suffix *#al*, which forms nouns from verbs, as in *withdrawal*, has two additional restrictions on its use (Siegel 1974: 164–168). First, it attaches only to verbs that have final stress. Second, the verb must end in a vowel or sonorant or a [+anterior] consonant; if the verb ends in a consonant cluster, however, this can only be a sequence of a sonorant followed by a [+anterior] consonant.[5] In (8a) we give some examples of well-formed derivatives of this type, while in (8b, c, d) are some impossible formations using this suffix.

---

[5] Recall from (7) of Chapter 2 that [+anterior] includes labial and alveolar consonants but excludes palatoalveolars such as [ʃ]. It is interesting that this class cannot be captured in those versions of feature geometry that rely on articulator nodes, such as the one discussed at the end of Section 1.5.1 of Chapter 1.

(8) a. *vowel final*   *labial final*
         deny   denial   retrieve   retrieval
         withdraw   withdrawal   arrive   arrival
         renew   renewal   survive   survival
         avow   avowal   remove   removal
         betray   betrayal   approve   approval
         try   trial
         portray   portrayal

         alveolar final   *sonorant final*
         appraise   appraisal   procure   procural
         propose   proposal
         dispose   disposal
         acquit   acquittal
         refuse   refusal

         two consonants
         rehearse   rehearsal   reverse   reversal
         disperse   dispersal   rent   rental

     b. *not final stressed*
         develop   *developal   abandon   *abandonal
         promise   *promissal   edit   *edital

     c. *ending in [–anterior]*
         palatoalveolar   *velar*
         final   *final*
         begrudge   *begrudgeal   rebuke   *rebukal
         impeach   *impeachal

     d. *ending in two obstruents*
         accept   *acceptal   resist   *resistal

Not all verbs that meet the stated criteria admit of suffixation with *#al* – for example, there are no words *derival, *convinceal, *forceal*. However, all verbs that do allow such suffixation conform to the criteria above, with one exception: *bury*. We could consider the final <*y*> of this word to be a glide underlyingly, so that it would have final stress prior to stratum 2 affixation and prior to the vocalization of the [j] by Sonorant Syllabification ((68) of Chapter 4). However, we would still have the problem that [j] is neither an obstruent nor [+anterior]. However, the stress condition on this affixation implies that certain phonological rules, namely those assigning stress, must apply prior to some morphological operations, in this case *#al* suffixation, and just this sequence of events is permitted in Lexical Phonology but not in the *SPE* model.

Another suffix that requires a base with final main stress is the adjective-forming *#ful*, as discussed by Siegel (1974: 168–174). This suffix attaches to a large number of monosyllabic nouns (9a), disyllabic nouns with final stress (9b), trisyllabic nouns with final stress (9c), a few disyllabic nouns that do not have final stress (9d, e, f), and even fewer verbs with final stress (9g). Most nouns whose main stress is nonfinal exclude suffixation with *#ful*, as in (9h)

(9)				
a.	peace	peaceful	dread	dreadful
	law	lawful	play	playful
b.	suspense	suspenseful	neglect	neglectful
	deceit	deceitful	event	eventful
c.	disrespect	disrespectful	disregard	disregardful
d.	pleasure	pleasureful	worship	worshipful
	purpose	purposeful	sorrow	sorrowful
e.	fancy	fanciful	pity	pitiful
	mercy	merciful	plenty	plentiful
f.	wonder	wonderful	master	masterful
g.	venge	vengeful	resent	resentful
	invent	inventful	forget	forgetful
	mourn	mournful		
h.	firmness	*firmnessful	judgement	*judgementful
	tension	*tensionful		

Siegel concludes that only words with final stress allow *#ful* suffixation, with the sole exception of the four words in (9d).[6] The words in (9e) can be regarded as having final stress if the final orthographic <y> is regarded as nonsyllabic in underlying representation, as with the final <y> of *bury* and numerous other examples. The final <r> of *wonder, master*, can also be regarded as nonsyllabic underlyingly, as shown by stratum 1 derivations like *wondrous*. While *#ful* normally attaches only to nouns, it attaches to a small number of verbs (9g). Siegel argues that the stress requirement of the suffix is stronger than the syntactic requirement that it should attach to nouns: if the corresponding nouns *(vengeance, resentment, invention)* do not have final stress, or if there is no corresponding noun *(forget, mourn)*, the suffix attaches to the corresponding verbs, which do have final stress.[7]

Another suffix where a phonological requirement is stronger than a syntactic one is the verb-forming suffix *-en*, although stress is not involved in this case. This suffix regularly attaches to monosyllabic adjectives that

---

[6] A reader notes that the Oxford English Dictionary also lists *feelingful, adventureful,* and *challengeful.*
[7] *Venge* is archaic for *avenge*. Siegel also notes that *#ful* does not attach to words ending in /f/, /v/: *loveful, *griefful.*

end in an obstruent, as in *whiten, blacken, redden, stiffen, broaden*. It does not attach to polysyllabic adjectives *(*morosen, *afraiden)* or adjectives that end in sonorant consonants or vowels *(*greenen, *thinnen, *bluen, *greyen)*. However, it can attach to a noun that meets the phonological requirements (monosyllabic, obstruent final) when the corresponding adjective does not. So we get *heighten (*highen), lengthen (*longen), strengthen (*strongen), frighten (*afraiden)*.[8]

6.1.3 Zero Derivation

In (2) of Chapter 4 we encountered a number of noun–verb pairs that differ only in stress (and possibly in segmental properties that depend on stress). We repeat some of these in (10).

(10)

verbs	nouns
survéy	súrvèy
detáil	détàil
transfér	tránsfèr
permít	pérmìt
expórt	éxpòrt
protést	prótèst

Two ways have been proposed for accounting for these. Both *SPE* and Kiparsky (1982) propose that the verb is basic and that it undergoes stress rules appropriate to verbs. The noun is derived from the verb by a zero suffix (on stratum 1 in Kiparsky's lexical treatment), which then undergoes stress rules again according to the cyclic principle, yielding the noun stress pattern. Later, Kiparsky (1983) suggested a different treatment, according to which neither noun nor verb is basic, but rather both are derived on stratum 1 from a stem unspecified for lexical category. The lexical category may be specified either as a noun or a verb, and the form then undergoes the stress rules appropriate for its category. This implies that, when specified as nouns, the forms in (10) are marked as exceptions to Consonant Extrametricality and Syllable Extrametricality in our approach. Kiparsky notes that a treatment in which lexical category is not specified is needed anyway for pairs such as those in (11).

---

[8] *Long* and *strong* end in a sonorant at the lexical level but in an obstruent /g/ at the underlying level. These fall under the stated generalization only after the application of stratum 2 phonology, which lends some support to Borowsky's (1986) suggestion that stratum 2 phonology applies *before* the morphology of that stratum.

(11)

	nouns	*verbs*
a.	expérimènt	expérimènt
	régimènt	régimènt
b.	ádvocàte	ádvocàte
	ággregàte	ággregàte
	assóciàte	assóciàte
	subórdinàte	subórdinàte

Kiparsky points out that there is no way to remove the stress on the last syllable of these nouns if they are derived from the corresponding verbs. If the nouns and verbs are independently stressed according to the rules for their category, the correct stresses are assigned, as long as we assume that Syllable Extrametricality (42 in Chapter 4) does apply to the nouns in (11); in the case of (11b), this is in spite of the underlying tense vowel in the last syllable.

There are two other patterns of noun–verb pairs, in both of which there is no difference in stress between the noun and the verb. In the first of these, shown in (12), both noun and verb follow the stress pattern that is expected for a noun.

(12)

noun	*verb*
páttern	páttern
poíson	poíson
ránsom	ránsom
cómfort	cómfort
pícture	pícture
fócus	fócus

Kiparsky (1982; 1983) argues that the noun is basic in this case and that the verb is derived from it by zero affixation on stratum 2. A word like *pattern* would be expected to have final stress if it were a basic verb, like *cavórt, usúrp*. There is also a semantic criterion: the verbs in (12) can be paraphrased in terms of the noun, roughly 'to do something with N,' as *to pattern* is 'to do something after a pattern.' This is in contrast to the semantics of pairs like (10), where the noun is best paraphrased in terms of the verb, that is 'something which V*s*' or 'that which is V*ed*,' as *an export* is 'that which is exported.'

Kiparsky (1983) points to a third category, where the verb is basic and the noun is derived from the verb at stratum 2. These have the stress pattern appropriate for verbs in both the verb and the noun and a consistent semantic relation in which the noun is paraphrasable in terms of the verb. We give some examples in (13).

(13)   exhaúst, consént, refórm, resúlt, resérve, revérse, retúrn, despaír, debáte

These zero affixation processes interact in predictable ways with overt morphological operations. For example, when both the noun and the verb are derived at stratum 1, both can take overt morphology from stratum 1, as shown in (14).

(14)   a.   *verbs*   *derivative (stratum 1)*
              rebél   rebéllion
              contráct   contráction
              expérimènt   expèrimèntátion

        b.   *nouns*   *derivative (stratum 1)*
              rébel   rebéllious
              cóntràct   còntráctual
              expériment   expèriméntal
              ádvocate   ádvocacy

When the verb is derived from the noun on stratum 2, as in (12), the noun but not the verb can undergo stratum 1 affixation, as shown in (15).

(15)   a.   *nouns*   *derivative (stratum 1)*
              poison   poisonous

        b.   *verbs*   *no derivative at stratum 1*
              pattern   *patternation
              poison   *poisonation

When the noun is derived from the verb on stratum 2 (13), the verb but not the noun can undergo stratum 1 affixation, as shown in (16).

(16)   a.   *verbs*   *derivative (stratum 1)*
              exhaust   exhaustion

        b.   *nouns*   *no derivative at stratum 1*
              exhaust   *exhaustious
              consent   *consentual

Compounding is especially interesting in this regard. Compound nouns can become verbs by zero derivation, as in (17). Both compounding and zero derivation of nouns to verbs are stratum 2 operations.

(17)   to grandstand, to wallpaper, to snowball, to quarterback

Kiparsky (1982) claimed that compound verbs cannot become nouns by zero derivation, citing the examples in (18). This follows from his claim that nouns are zero derived from verbs only on stratum 1.

(18)   *an air-condition, *a stage-manage

However, Kiparsky (1983) acknowledges the possibility of verb-to-noun zero derivation on stratum 2 (see 13), and indeed proposes some compounds that undergo this process, as in (19).

(19)   a deep-freeze, a winter-kill, a broadcast

Kiparsky points out that these are not simply compounds formed with a basic noun in the second position, since the nouns do not occur on their own with the same meaning. A *deep-freeze* is a device, but a *freeze* is an event; *winterkill* is a process but a *kill* is a single act or a result. Nor can we take *freeze, kill, cast* as basic nouns, entering into the compounds of (19), and derive the verbs from the nouns (possible only on stratum 2), since the verbs *freeze, cast* have stratum 1 inflection (*frozen* (ablaut), *cast* (+*t*, with degemination)) and this form of inflection is possible only with basic verbs. The only possibility for (19) is to form compound verbs on stratum 2 and derive the compound nouns from the verbs.

Kiparsky (1982) observes that verbs formed by affixation at stratum 1 do not have a corresponding zero-derived noun, as shown by the ungrammaticality of the examples in (20).

(20)   *a publicize, *a demonstrate, *a clarify

He also observes that nouns formed with stratum 2 suffixes do not have corresponding zero-derived verbs, although this is also a stratum 2 process, as shown in (21).

(21)   *to singer, *to reading, *to freedom, *to promptness, *to championship, *to alcoholism, *to nationalist, *to sisterhood

In both (20) and (21) we observe a failure of zero derivation in forms with an affix assigned at the same stratum. Kiparsky (1982) proposes the constraint in (22) to block these derivations.[9]

(22)   *Constraint on zero derivation*
         *] X] Ø] (X≠Ø)

However, nouns formed at stratum 1 by overt affixation readily undergo zero affixation to verbs on stratum 2, as shown in (23).

---

[9] If stratum 1 noun-verb pairs are formed from unspecified stems, as in Kiparsky (1983), then constraint (22) will not block (20). However, they are blocked anyway, since *publicize* is not a stem but a verb that has already had its stress pattern assigned.

(23)   to pressure, to picture, to commission, to proposition, to requisition, to
        trial, to engineer, to reverence, to reference

To account for these, Kiparsky proposes that the output of every stratum
is a *lexical item*. Thus, lexical items are the underived lexical items in the
top box in Figure 6.1 plus the output of every lexical stratum. To
implement this idea, Kiparsky proposes the procedure of Bracket
Erasure, stated in (24).

(24)   *Bracket Erasure*
        Erase all internal brackets at the end of a stratum.

This ensures that morphological and phonological rules have access to
word-internal structure only when it has been assigned at the same
stratum. Under this assumption, the verb *to pressure* is derived as
in (25).

(25)   underived lexical item $[\text{press}]_V$
        stratum 1 phonology: stress $[\text{préss}]_V$
        stratum 1 morphology: +*ure* $[[\text{préss}]_V \text{ ure}]_N$
        stratum 1 phonology   ———
        bracket erasure $[\text{préssure}]_N$
        stratum 2 morphology: #Ø $[[\text{préssure}]_N \text{ Ø}]_V$
        stratum 2 phonology $[\text{ʃ}]$
        bracket erasure $[[\text{préssure}]_N \text{ Ø}]_V$

At the time that Ø derivation applies on stratum 2, Bracket Erasure
ensures that the process has no access to the derivational affix assigned
on stratum 1, and so (22) does not block Ø derivation.

    The existence of various zero derivation processes predicts the existence
of triplets, such as those in (26).

(26)   protést$_V$ → prótèst$_N$ → prótèst$_V$ 'stage a protest'
        discóunt$_V$ → díscòunt$_N$ → díscòunt$_V$ 'sell at a discount'
        compóund$_V$ →cómpòund$_N$ →cómpòund$_V$ 'join or become joined in a
            compound'
        digést$_V$ → dígèst$_N$ → dígèst$_V$ 'make a digest'

Kiparsky's (1982) model predicts that, while V → N → V is possible, as in
(26), the reverse possibility, N → V → N, is not. Kiparsky suggests that
food$_N$ → feed$_V$ → feed$_N$ 'food for feeding livestock,' and brood$_N$ →
breed$_V$ → breed$_N$ 'genetic type produced by breeding' are potential
counterexamples. The derivation of *feed* (verb) from *food* must take place
at stratum 1, since the verb *feed* has stratum 1 inflection (i.e., *fed*). But this

change is not zero derivation of a noun to a verb, but rather umlaut, which can well be assigned to stratum 1.[10]

Other apparent counterexamples actually involve two distinct nominalizations from a verb on stratum 1, one being an act and the other either the effected object, as in (27a), the implement, as in (27b) or the agent, as in (27c) (Kiparsky 1982: 13).

(27)		*verb*	*'act'*	*'effected object'*	*'implement'*	*'agent'*
	a.	dischárge	díschàrge	díschàrge		
		spit	spit	spit		
		shit	shit	shit		
		sweat	sweat	sweat		
		splice	splice	splice		
	b.	paddle	paddle		paddle	
		brush	brush		brush	
	c.	scrub	scrub			scrub

Kiparsky gives several reasons for assuming the verb is basic in these cases and that more than one noun is zero derived from it. First, the various categories of noun in (27) are also expressed by overt affixes, for example, *shavings*, *spittle* (effected object), *router*, *mixer* (implement and agent). Second, some of these verbs have stratum 1 inflection, which is not possible for verbs that are zero-derived from nouns, which occurs only on stratum 2. Finally, verbs which are zero-derived from nouns do not form zero-derived nouns in the categories illustrated in (27), but require other suffixes to express these categories, as shown in (28).

(28)   a. rivet (N)   → rivet (V)   → riveting (act), riveter (implement, agent)
         b. condition (N) → condition (V) → conditioning, conditioner
         c. water (N)   → water (V)   → watering, waterer

When, in a noun–verb pair, the noun denotes the instrument with which the action of the verb is carried out, we have another source of information regarding which item is basic and the stratum on which the conversion is carried out. The verb is basic with stratum 1 derivation of the noun (or the pair is stem derived, both on stratum 1) if the noun is the typical, but not the only possible, implement for carrying out the activity of the verb. The examples in (29) show this for several such pairs.

---

[10] The model of Kiparsky (1983) would seem to predict N → V → N conversions and even quadruplets, which are not attested.

It is possible to hammer with a rock or a shoe, for instance, since *to hammer* means 'to strike with the flat side of a solid object,' rather than 'to strike with a hammer.' In addition, in pairs like *string* and *sting*, the verb has stratum 1 inflection *(strung, stung)* showing that the verb is basic.

(29)   He hammered the nail with a rock.
        He paddled the canoe with a copy of *The Globe and Mail.*
        He brushed his coat with his hand.
        String it up with a rope.
        They stung him with a needle.
        Can you whistle with a blade of grass?
        The prisoner sawed off the bars with her dentures.
        They anchored the ship with a rock.
        He combed his hair with his fingers.
        He wedged the window open with a screwdriver.

On the other hand, if the noun is necessarily involved as an instrument in the activity, the noun is basic and the verb is derived at stratum 2. Such pairs are illustrated by the ungrammaticality of the sentences in (30). *To tape* means 'to fasten with tape,' for example. Compound verbs also follow this pattern, since they are formed at stratum 2.

(30)   *She taped the picture to the wall with pushpins.
        *They chained the prisoner with a rope.
        *Jim buttoned up his pants with a zipper.
        *He pitchforked the manure with a shovel.
        *Let's bicycle across France on our tricycles.
        *Screw the fixture to the wall with nails.
        *He snowploughed the sidewalk with a shovel.
        *She charcoaled the drawing with ink.

Triplets such as *paddle* in (27b) must be of the stratum 1 type with a basic verb. When the noun is basic and indicates an implement, such as *bicycle*, it cannot be interpreted as an act, as shown in (31).

(31)   They went for a nice $\left\{ \begin{array}{l} \text{paddle} \\ \text{*bicycle} \end{array} \right\}$.

Furthermore, all verbs with stratum 1 inflection (e.g., *string*) are like *hammer*. Thus, you can string with a rope or sting with a needle. Most English verbs ending in *-ing, -ink* have ablaut inflection, which is on stratum 1. Apparent counterexamples are derived from nouns on stratum 2. Thus you have *ring* (a bell) with stratum 1 inflection (past *rang*), but *ring* 'supply with rings' with regular inflection (past *ringed*). The latter type is ungrammatical with other instruments, as in (32).[11]

(32)   *They ringed the pigeons with dye marks.
          *She inked the drawing with crayons.

Kiparsky (1983: 10) sums up these phenomena as follows: "We may conclude that the level-ordered framework discloses nontrivial regularities in the phonology, morphology, and semantics of English noun/verb pairs. It seems also that rather rich principles must be at work to permit the acquisition of this much structure that is not encoded by any overt affixes."

6.1.4   Properties of Phonological Strata

The phonological rules of the lexicon are necessarily word bounded, since they are integrated with the morphological derivations of the lexicon. In this model, only postlexical rules can apply to structures larger that the word, as we have seen in Chapter 5. Another commonly assumed property of lexical rules is that they are *structure preserving*. This means that lexical rules do not produce segments or segment types that are not also underlying. Postlexical rules commonly produce segment types that are not underlying. For example, in English, Aspiration results in aspirated voiceless stops, which do not occur in underlying representations. We will qualify this property slightly in two ways. One is that we allow lexical rules to create stress feet, while maintaining that no such feet occur in underlying representations.[12] The other is that we allow rules of stratum 2 phonology to produce the segment [ŋ] by assimilation to a following velar, even though there are no underlying velar nasals. While Aspiration produces completely new segment types, velar assimilation produces a segment that fits into the pattern of English underlying segments, in that there are velar stops and nasals at other points of articulation, and so the velar nasal is not a new *type* of segment. In other words, Aspiration involves the introduction of a noncontrastive feature [+spread glottis], while the velar nasal involves the recombination of features contrastive in other contexts, namely [+nasal, −anterior, −coronal].

---

[11] When *to ring* means 'to surround as in a ring' rather than 'to supply with rings,' it can have other instruments: *They ringed the town with artillery.*

[12] Some approaches to English stress (e.g., Hayes 1980) allow underlying feet (for example on the last syllable of *maniac*) in order to account for exceptions. In Section 4.3.1 of Chapter 4, we showed that such exceptions can be accounted for without this assumption.

Another property of lexical phonological rules is that they may have exceptions, while it is generally assumed in Lexical Phonology that post-lexical rules may not have exceptions. For example, the morphemes *nice* and *obese* are exceptions to Trisyllabic Laxing, as shown by the failure of this rule in the derivatives *nicety, obesity*. However, in contravention of the claim for postlexical rules, we noted in Footnote 15 of Chapter 5 that *Cyclops* may be a lexical exception to the postlexical rule of Diphthong Shortening. To summarize these observations, we give a table of the properties of various types of phonological rules in English in (33).[13]

(33)	stratum 1	stratum 2 (postcyclic)	postlexical
1. word bounded	yes	yes	no
2. structures accessed	word-internal structure at same stratum	word-internal structure at same stratum	phrase structure and segmental information only
3. cyclic	yes	no	no
4. Strict Cycle Condition	yes	no	no
5. structure preserving	strictly	less strictly	no
6. lexical exceptions	possible	possible	impossible or rare

6.2 Cyclicity

After this rather lengthy excursion into morphology, it is time to return to phonology. We noted in Chapter 4 that the stress rules of stratum 1 apply cyclically. The rules apply to underived lexical items, and then reapply after each layer of morphology on stratum 1, respecting some aspects of the previously assigned structure but changing other aspects. We will now show that all stratum 1 phonological rules are cyclic. We will further show that cyclic rules are subject to a constraint known as *strict cyclicity*, which has further consequences for the abstractness of underlying phonological representations.

SPE proposed Trisyllabic Laxing to account for a number of vowel alternations in English, already briefly introduced in Section 1.1.1 of

---

[13] Cyclicity of strata may vary in different languages. Mohanan and Mohanan (1984) claim that none of the four lexical strata they propose for Malayalam is cyclic. The number of strata may vary as well. Kiparsky (1983) proposed three lexical strata for English (all cyclic), while Halle and Mohanan (1985) proposed four lexical strata for English (only stratum 1 cyclic). However, there is no convincing evidence for more than two lexical strata in English, and, of these, only the first can be cyclic.

Chapter 1. *SPE* showed that a number of superficially different vowel alternations can be accounted for by one rule – Trisyllabic Laxing – supplemented by additional rules to produce the final phonetic vowel qualities. Trisyllabic Laxing is a stratum 1 rule in our terms, and will be discussed here along with other laxing rules; the additional rules belong to stratum 2 and will be discussed in detail in Chapter 7. A representative sample of the alternations involved in these rules is given in (34).

(34)		*Tense vowel* *(phonetic diphthong)*		*Lax vowel*		*underlying*
	a.	div*i*ne	[qɪ]	div*i*nity	[ɪ]	/i/
	b.	ser*e*ne	[iị]	ser*e*nity	[ɛ]	/e/
	c.	s*a*ne	[eị]	s*a*nity	[æ]	/æ/
	d.	verb*o*se	[ow]	verb*o*sity	[ɒ]	/ɒ/
	e.	prof*ou*nd	[æw]	prof*u*ndity	[ə]	/i/
	f.	red*u*ce	[juw]	red*u*ction	[ə]	/ʌ/
	g.	sh*oo*t	[uw]	sh*o*t	[ɒ]	/o/

The various pairs of vowels on each line (e.g., [qɪ] and [ɪ]) are phonetically rather different, and the various pairs are not so obviously related to each other. *SPE* proposes to relate all the pairs by factoring out the common element: each italicized vowel in the lax vowel column is derived from the underlying vowel by laxing.[14] Therefore the simplest underlying representations are ones that roughly have a *tense* version of the vowel that appears in the *lax vowel* column. It is then necessary to develop other rules to account for the phonetic diphthongs that result if laxing does not apply; we defer discussion of these until Chapter 7.

There are several laxing rules – the lax vowels in (34a, b, c, d) are the result of Trisyllabic Laxing, which we state in (35).[15]

(35)   *Trisyllabic Laxing*

$$[\ldots \ \sigma \quad \sigma_w \quad \sigma \ldots]_\omega$$
$$\text{V} \rightarrow [\text{-ATR}] / \underline{\qquad}$$

Trisyllabic Laxing laxes a vowel that is followed by two or more syllables in the same (minimal) prosodic word domain, as long as the syllable

---

[14] In the case of *shot* and *profundity*, the vowel is lowered as well. This results from additional rules discussed in Chapter 7.

[15] We assume that all laxing rules automatically remove a mora from the vowel. This could be explicitly stated in the rule if desired.

following the vowel in question is unstressed. We can establish stratum
I as the domain of Trisyllabic Laxing from the observation that laxing
takes place when its environment is created by the addition of stratum
I affixes (specifically +*ity* in the examples of 34a–e), but not when it is
created by the addition of stratum 2 suffixes, as in (36).

(36)   chíldlessness, heédlessness, légalism, stóicism, páganism

The requirement that the following vowel be unstressed is shown by
examples like those in (37), where the italicized vowel remains tense
despite the two following syllables brought about by stratum I suffixation.

(37)   a.   quòtátion, flòtátion, gỳrátion, cìtátion, mìgrátion
         b.   fìnálity, vìtálity, glòbálity, tònálity, tìtánic

This restriction on Trisyllabic Laxing has important consequences for the
interaction of this rule with the stress rules, as we will detail in Section 6.3.
Trisyllabic Laxing must apply in the first cycle of *hypocrisy* (i.e., it applies in
hypocrite prior to affixation of +*y*); otherwise it would be blocked in
hypocrisy by the restriction just noted. Compare *hypothesis*, which does
not involve a cyclic derivation, in which the first vowel remains tense due
to the same restriction, which blocks Trisyllabic Laxing here (Kiparsky
1982: 42).

A second laxing rule is Cluster Laxing, which laxes a vowel before a
sequence of two or more consonants. This is illustrated by (34f, g) (*shot* is
from underlying /ʃot+t/) and by the additional examples in (38). Voicing
Assimilation ((77) in Chapter 7) applies in *inscription*; Velar Softening
((41) in Chapter 7) applies in *deceive, deception*, and *deduce*, and allomorphy is required for *deceive* and *deception*.

(38)   a.   intervene   b.   intervention
            deceive   /de+kev/   deception   /de+kep+t+jən/
            inscribe   /ɪn+skɹib/   inscription /ɪn+skɹib+t+jən/
            deduce   /de+dʌk+ ɛ/   deduction   /de+dʌk+t+jən/
            sleep   slept   /slep + t/
            bite   bit   /bit + t/
            lose   /loz+ɛ/   lost   /loz+t/

The motivation for the underlying /k/ in the bound stem /kev/ is to
prevent this segment from undergoing the stratum I rule Fricative
Voicing (65) which would be the case if the initial segment of this stem
were the less abstract /s/, as discussed in Section 1.4.5 of Chapter 1. This
/k/ subsequently undergoes Velar Softening on stratum 2. The verb *lose* is

derived from the noun *loss* //lɔs// by addition of the suffix +ε, (see (61)). The resulting //lɔs+ε// is subject to ε-Tensing (63) and Fricative voicing (65). The past tense +*t* is attached to /loz/ substituting for the the suffix +ε; see Footnote 25. We formulate the rule for Cluster Laxing in (39).[16]

(39)   *Cluster Laxing*
        V → [–ATR] / ____ C [+cons]

We assume that the past tense forms *slept* and *bit* are derived by the stratum 1 past tense suffix /+t/. This is straightforward in the case of *slept*, where the addition of the suffix creates a cluster which is the context for laxing. We assume that the same occurs in *bit*. The underlying representation of the present tense is /bit/, which is realized phonetically as [bɑɪt][17] (compare *divine* in (34)). The addition of the suffix gives /bit+t/, which contains the cluster which is the context for laxing. After laxing, a rule of Degemination applies eliminating the geminate /tt/ and giving the phonetic form [bɪt]. We formulate Degemination in (40).

(40)   *Degemination*
        C_i → Ø / [... ____ C_i ...]_F

Degemination receives additional support from alternations involving the negative prefix *in*+, which is also located at stratum 1. This prefix has various realizations illustrated in (41).

(41)   inactive
        innocuous
        illegal
        irrational
        immoral
        impossible

Before a vowel, *in*+ undergoes no change and is simply realized as [ĩn] (*inactive*). Before a sonorant other than /n/, it undergoes complete assimilation to the sonorant and the resulting sequence of two sonorants degeminates (*illegal, irrational*). Before a labial it undergoes assimilation in place of articulation and is realized as [ĩm] (*impossible*).[18] Before /n/, there is Degemination (*innocuous*). For the complete assimilation of the

---

[16] The second of the two consonants must be [+consonantal], since we want to prevent laxing before the sequence *tj* in the suffix (combination) *-ation* (underlying /æt + jən/).
[17] Or as [bəɪt] by Diphthong Shortening ((49) of Chapter 5; see Section 5.3.4).
[18] In *impossible* the prefix is phonetically [ĩ] owing to Nasal Consonant Deletion ((31) of Chapter 5).

nasal to a following sonorant, we can use the autosegmental spreading format, as in (42a). For the assimilation in place of articulation to a following obstruent, we use the linear format with Greek letter variables, as in (42b).

(42)   n-*Assimilation*

a. $\begin{bmatrix} +\text{cons} \\ +\text{son} \end{bmatrix}$ [+son]

$$\underset{n}{\overset{}{\not{\vert}}} \qquad \underset{C}{\overset{}{\vert}}$$

b. $n \rightarrow \begin{bmatrix} \alpha\text{ant} \\ \beta\text{cor} \end{bmatrix} / \underline{\quad\quad} \begin{bmatrix} -\text{son} \\ \alpha\text{ant} \\ \beta\text{cor} \end{bmatrix}$

A third laxing rule operates before the suffix +*ic* (and possibly before the suffix +*ish*), as shown in (43).[19]

(43)   a. cone   b. conic
           satire   satiric
           cycle   cyclic
           metre   metric
           state   static
           Spain   Spanish

We formulate -*ic* Laxing in (44).

(44)   -ic *Laxing*

$$V \rightarrow [-\text{ATR}] / \underline{\quad\quad} C_1 \begin{Bmatrix} +\text{ic} \\ +\text{ish} \end{Bmatrix}$$

6.2.1   The Strict Cycle Condition

In (95) of Chapter 4 we gave a preliminary formulation of the Strict Cycle Condition, repeated here in (45).

---

[19] *SPE* includes a suffix +*id* in this list, as in *rapid, vapid*. A reader notes the tense vowel in *humid, stupid, lucid*, where, however, the phonetic [juw] is derived from lax /ɨ/ in our framework (cf. Section 7.1.2 in Chapter 7). However, if this truly is a suffix, it attaches only to bound stems, in which case we can assume that the stem has an underlying lax vowel anyway. Laxing berfore -*ish* may be limited to *Spanish*; in words like *greenish* the suffix is added at stratum 2.

(45)   *Strict Cycle Condition (preliminary formulation)*
         Cyclic rules may change structure only in derived environments.

There are several aspects to this condition. On the one hand, we want cyclic rules to be able to *add* structure in underived environments, for example to construct stress trees on underlying representations that lack metrical structure. On the other hand, we want metrical structure laid down on one cycle to be respected by the stress rules on the following cycle, while allowing for new metrical structure to be erected over new morphological material added on that cycle. Furthermore, we want similar results with cyclic segmental rules, such as the laxing rules just discussed. For example, Trisyllabic Laxing applies to *sanity*, because the addition of the suffix +*ity* to *sane* produces a derived environment. However, Trisyllabic Laxing should not apply to the vowel of the first syllable of *nightingale*, even though this vowel falls within the jurisdiction of the rule, because this form is underived.

SPE did not have anything like the Strict Cycle Condition, and had to find a way of exempting *nightingale* from Trisyllabic Laxing by manipulating its underlying representation. They assumed the underlying representation /nɪxtɪngæl/ (our symbols), with a lax vowel in the first syllable. Trisyllabic Laxing is therefore inapplicable; later rules convert the sequence /ɪx/ to /i/, from which phonetic [ɑɪ] is derived by Vowel Shift and other rules, as in *divine*. *SPE* uses underlying /x/ in other ways, for example, in the underlying representation of *right*, in order to block Spirantization (discussed in Section 7.4.4 of Chapter 7) from applying in the derivative *righteous*. This underlying /x/ is of course rather abstract, in that this segment does not appear phonetically in any words of (standard) English. With the Strict Cycle Condition regulating the application of cyclic rules, we can employ a more concrete underlying representation /nitɪngæl/. Trisyllabic Laxing is blocked by the Strict Cycle Condition, and other rules derive the correct phonetic form. Cases such as *vacancy*, *secrecy*, *potency*, and *piracy* can be exempted from Trisyllabic Laxing by assuming a final underlying glide /j/, which we motivated in other words in Chapter 4 on the basis of stress rules, especially derivatives in -*ary* and -*ory*. But for many words, including *stevedore*, *Averell*, and *Oberon*, no such tricks are available. However, the Strict Cycle Condition takes care of these as well as cases like *nightingale*, since they are all monomorphemic words; hence the first vowel is not in a derived environment. Of course, we still have to acknowledge certain lexical exceptions to Trisyllabic Laxing, such as *obese* and *nice*, as already mentioned in Section 6.1.4.

Kiparsky (1985) proposes to formalize the Strict Cycle Condition as in (46).

(46) *Strict Cycle Condition* (*SCC*, Kiparsky 1985: 89)
      If W is derived from a lexical entry W', where W' is nondistinct from
      XPAQY and distinct from XPBQY, then a rule A → B / XP____QY
      cannot apply to W until the word level.

Recall from Section 1.5.2 of Chapter 1 that we defined *distinctness* such that two items are distinct if they have contradictory feature values; i.e., one is marked + and the other is marked − for a particular feature in a particular position. We can expand this now to include metrical structure: two items are distinct if they contain contradictory metrical structure. Otherwise, the items are nondistinct. A string of segments with no metrical structure is nondistinct from the same string of segments with a specified metrical structure. Kiparsky defines the term *lexical item* as the output of one of the righthand boxes in Figure 6.1: this includes any item from the box labelled "underived lexical items" and also the output of each lexical stratum. If we apply this to *nightingale*, W is *nightingale* at the point in stratum 1 phonology just before the application of Trisyllabic Laxing, W' is the underived lexical item /nitɪngæl/, and the rule is Trisyllabic Laxing. W' is nondistinct from the input to Trisyllabic Laxing but distinct from the result of applying Trisyllabic laxing to W; i.e., /nɪtɪngæl. Therefore the conditions of (46) are met, and Trisyllabic Laxing cannot apply to W until the word level, defined as the last lexical stratum, i.e., stratum 2. But we have independently restricted Trisyllabic Laxing to stratum 1 − if it doesn't apply there, it doesn't apply anywhere. Hence, it does not apply at all to *nightingale*.

The Strict Cycle Condition defined by Kiparsky solves a complementary problem that arises with words such as *alibi, sycamore, camera, pelican, Amazon, Pamela, calendar*. Under the assumptions of *SPE*, these words could be derived at face value from underlying representations with a lax vowel in the first syllable. But they could also be derived from forms with a tense vowel in the first syllable, with Trisyllabic Laxing producing the phonetic lax vowel. Under the Strict Cycle Condition, however, Trisyllabic Laxing could not apply to these forms any more than in *nightingale*, so the face-value, less abstract, derivation is forced. Another possibility, which Kiparsky ultimately adopts, takes the vowel in the first syllable of words like *alibi* to be underspecified for tenseness. Under this interpretation, Trisyllabic Laxing can apply to these words in a feature-filling mode − here, the output of Trisyllabic Laxing is no longer distinct from the underlying representation of *alibi*.

In other cases, the Strict Cycle Condition (46) restricts rules to stratum 2, somewhat reducing the degree of arbitrary assignment of rules to strata. We will discuss two such cases in Chapter 7. One is *n*-Deletion (Section 7.4.5), which applies to underived items such as *hymn* and to this same item with stratum 2 derivatives, as in *hymns, hymning, hymn index*, but not with stratum 1 derivatives like *hymnal*.

Now, let us discuss the case where stress rules apply cyclically. Here we will have to add a codicil to the basic definition of the Strict Cycle Condition. In the derivation of *parental*, we start with the underived lexical item *parent* on stratum 1. The application of stress rules gives (47).

(47)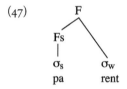

When we add the suffix +*al* on the second cycle, we ask whether the conditions of (46) are met. The structure resulting from affixation to (47) is W, which we show in (48).

(48)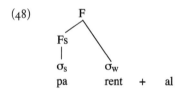

W' is the underived lexical entry *parent*, with no metrical structure. This is nondistinct from an input to stress assignment, but it is also not *distinct* from an output of stress assignment – distinctness of metrical structure requires contradictory metrical structure, but we have one item with no metrical structure, which does not count as distinct from the same item with metrical structure. Hence, the Strict Cycle Condition (46) does not prevent the English Stress Rule from applying and overriding the previously assigned metrical structure in (48). After Initial Destressing and Stray Syllable Adjunction we derive (49).

(49)

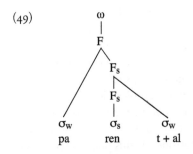

If we apply the same procedure to *legendary*, we get the wrong result. *Legend* will have the same structure as *parent* in (47) after the first cycle. The suffix +*ary* /ǽɹij/ contains a long vowel (from the underlying tense /ǽ/ lengthened by syllabification (step 2 of 70(2)) in Chapter 3) and is exempt from Syllable Extrametricality so that the English Stress Rule is applicable to it. This much is permitted by the Strict Cycle Condition (46). But the Strict Cycle Condition does not prevent further iterations of the English Stress Rule which, if allowed, would override the previously assigned metrical structure on *legend*, ultimately producing *legéndary, after Poststress Destressing, Initial Destressing, and Stray Syllable Adjunction. In other words, the Strict Cycle Condition as stated in (46) restricts rules only to applying or not; it does not restrict the number of iterations of an iterative rule such as the English Stress Rule. We need the additional restriction stated in (50).

(50)   *Restriction on iteration of metrical structure assignment*
        When a rule assigning metrical structure encounters previously assigned
        structure, it may destroy just as much structure as necessary to build new
        structure accommodating new morphological material.

In effect, (50) restricts the English Stress Rule to at most one iteration on each cycle after the first. We tacitly assumed such a restriction in Section 4.5 of Chapter 4, where we discussed the cyclic assignment of stress in English. In the case of *parental*, (50) allows the destruction of the weak branch of the foot in (47) to allow a new foot to be built to incorporate the added suffix +*al*. The original foot remains as a nonbranching foot, and the new foot is labelled strong because it is branching. The original foot is labelled weak and ultimately removed by Initial Destressing. Its syllable is adjoined to the new foot giving (49). With *legendary*, on the other hand, a new foot is constructed over the syllable containing the suffix, but no further iterations are required to accommodate this material, so the original foot remains.[20] This assumption is especially relevant for more complex cyclic cases, such as *proclamation* (to be examined in Section 6.4), which also involve cyclic segmental rules. In those cases, cyclic stress assignment produces left-branching word trees, contrary to the right-branching trees constructed over long monomorphemic words, such as *Appalachicola*.

Let us illustrate this further with a more complex derivation, that of *sensationality*, discussed in Kiparsky (1979). The first cycle is on *sense* (V), which assigns a monosyllabic foot. On the second cycle, the morphology adds *+ation*, which receives a foot marked strong. At this point we have (51).

(51)

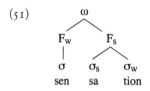

When we add the adjective suffix *+al* on the third cycle, the structure is minimally distorted to produce (52). In line with the Strict Cycle Condition (46) and the additional restriction in (50), we may assume that the last foot of (51) is redrawn with no change (vacuous application), since its second syllable (after resyllabification) is light, and the syllable over the suffix is adjoined to it, giving (52).[21]

(52)

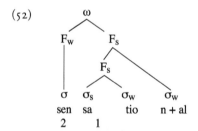

Finally, we add the suffix *+ity*. The minimal distortion of the structure in (52) needed to accommodate this suffix is to build a new foot on *-n+ality*,

---

[20] A few words are problematic in this regard, for example *elementary*. If derived from *element*, no stress would be assigned to the syllable *men* on the second cycle, and the incorrect stress pattern *élementàry* would be derived.

[21] The tense vowel in the second syllable of *sensational* is in the environment for Trisyllabic Laxing, but this rule does not apply. I assume that the morpheme *+ation* is marked as an exception to Trisyllabic Laxing. There is no laxing in this morpheme in other derivatives, like *realizational*. There is laxing, however, in similar words that do not contain the morpheme *+ation*, such as *national*.

removing the last syllable from the second foot. Certain adjustments to the foot structure and the final word-tree construction produce (53).

(53)

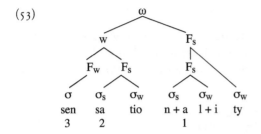

This results in the relative prominence of the secondary stresses in the first two syllables shown by the *SPE* stress numbers below the relevant syllables. The Rhythm Rule does not apply in (53) because of the restriction that it not produce a structure of the form (54) within ω (repeated from (85) of Chapter 4 and (68) of Chapter 5).

(54)   Not produced by Rhythm Rule, where the first s is nonbranching

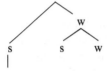

This shows that the relative prominence of the first two syllables of *sensationality* reflects the relative prominence of these same two syllables in *sensational*. Cyclically applying stress rules results in preserving aspects of the stress of embedded structures, in contrast to monomorphemic items like *Ticonderoga*, where the first syllable is more prominent than the second.[22]

The necessity of minimally destroying previously assigned cyclic structure only ever arises in English in the case of suffixes that do not support feet on their own, such as +*al* and +*ity*. The suffix +*ary* is assigned its own foot, as we saw with *legendary*. Stratum 1 prefixes are never phonetically stressed in English. Even when *in*+ is assigned stress, it gets destressed, in which case it is adjoined to a following foot.

---

[22] Kiparsky (1979) claims that both 231 and 321 contours are possible for *Ticonderoga*, but this is not clear: for me, only the 231 contour is possible for this word.

6.3   Additional Cyclic Rules

6.3.1   Tensing and Fricative Voicing

SPE (p. 181) proposed a rule to make vowels tense when followed by a sequence of a single consonant, a high front vowel or glide, and another vowel. This accounts for the alternations in (55), from Rubach (1984: 39).[23]

(55)   a. Canada   b.   Canadian
             Panama   Panamanian
             comedy   comedian
             colony   colonial
             Mongol   Mongolia, Mongolian
             Arab   Arabia, Arabian
             courage   courageous   /kəɹædʒ + jəs/
             Jordan   Jordanian
             college   collegian
             harmony   harmonious
             custody   custodian

It is clear that the words in (55a) have underlying lax vowels in the second syllable. If these vowels were tense, they would receive stress by our stress rules. Therefore, these alternations should be accounted for by a tensing rule rather than by a laxing rule. We give the formulation in (56), following Rubach (1984: 47).

(56)   *CiV Tensing* σ_w
                                            |

$$\begin{bmatrix} V \\ -\text{high} \end{bmatrix} \rightarrow [+\text{ATR}] / \underline{\hspace{1em}} C \begin{bmatrix} -\text{cons} \\ +\text{high} \\ -\text{back} \end{bmatrix} \begin{bmatrix} V \\ +\text{low} \end{bmatrix}$$

Some examples that show the restriction of the input vowel to ones that are [–high] are given in (57) (*SPE*: 182).

(57)   punctilious, Darwinian, reptilian, vicious

Rubach restricts the context vowel to those that are [+low] in order to exclude the suffix +*ion* from the context. This suffix has the underlying

---

[23] Rubach (1984: 46) lists *laborious* as an example of C*i*V Tensing, but this seems incorrect. Collins transcribes the second vowel of *laborious* as [ɔː], the same as the first vowel in *glorious* and also in *glory*, where it cannot be due to tensing. Other vowels do undergo tensing in this context (*hilarious*, cf. *hilarity*; *mysterious* (cf. *mystery*). The lack of tensing in words in ...*orious* seems a mystery.

representation /jən/, with a mid vowel.[24] This correctly prevents tensing in words such as those in (58).

(58)   companion, confession, battalion, procession, medallion, discussion

Since the last vowel of the suffixes +*ian*, +*ial*, and +*ous* is reduced to [ə] in (55b), we need to find contexts where the vowel is stressed in order to ascertain its underlying quality. The examples in (59) show that it is indeed [+low].

(59)   Canadiana, Christianity, artificiality, religiosity

Some simple exceptions are given in (60). *SPE* (p. 182 fn. 17) gives some of these a geminate before the suffix in order to exempt them from the rule.

(60)   Italian, Maxwellian, perennial, centennial, rebellious, special, gaseous, precious

Notice that the second segment in the environment can be either a vowel *i* (*Canadian*) or a glide *j* (*courageous*), although the *j* is often deleted by a later rule of *j*-Deletion, discussed in Chapter 7.

Another tensing rule tenses a vowel before a consonant followed by the verbalizing suffix +ε (*SPE*: 213, fn 46; 232; Hoard 1972: 138). This rule accounts for alternations such as those in (61).[25]

(61)   a.   *nouns*   b.   *verbs*
             breath   /bɹɛθ/   breathe   /bɹɛθ + ε/
             loss   /lɔs/   lose   /lɔs + ε/
             cloth   /klɒθ/   clothe   /klɒθ + ε/
             brass   /bɹæs/   braze   /bɹæs + ε/
             grass   /gɹæs/   graze   /gɹæs + ε/
             bath   /bæθ/   bathe   /bæθ + ε/
             glass   /glæs/   glaze   /glæs + ε/

We can see that the underlying vowel is lax in column (61a) and that it undergoes tensing to give (61b) rather than the other way round because

---

[24] Rubach gives it as /jon/, but there is no evidence that the vowel is [+round].
[25] The verbs in (61b) take stratum 2 inflection (*breathed*, etc.) except for *lose* (*lost*, *-t* suffixation on stratum 1). I assume that this inflectional suffix replaces the verbalizing suffix +ε rather than being after it, and a second cycle ensues on which Cluster Laxing operates. Since +ε is elided only on stratum 2, the correct form could not be derived if +ε were present at the time of inflectional affixation.
   A reader has noted that *halve* (from *half*) and *calve* (from *calf*) should be regarded as exceptions to (63).

there are similar pairs that have a tense vowel in both the noun and the verb, as in (62).

(62)   a. *nouns*   b.   *verbs*

mouth	/miθ/		mouth	/miθ + ɛ/
use	/ʌs/		use	/ʌs + ɛ/
house	/hɨs/		house	/hɨs + ɛ/
belief	bɪlef/		believe	/bɪlef + ɛ/

We give this tensing rule in (63).

(63)   ɛ-*Tensing*

$$V \rightarrow [+ATR] / \underline{\quad\quad} C + \begin{bmatrix} V \\ -high \\ -low \\ -back \\ -ATR \end{bmatrix}$$

As it happens, the +ɛ suffix is deleted by a stratum 2 rule, ɛ-Elision ((23) in Chapter 7). This rule also applies to *reduce* /ɹe+dʌk+ɛ/ after /ɛ/ triggers Velar Softening as compared to *reduction* /ɹe+dʌk+t-jən/, where we have Cluster Laxing.

In structures consisting of a latinate prefix plus stem, a stem-initial *s* is voiced after a vowel (64a) but not after a consonant (64b).

(64)   a. resign, design   b.   consign

                resume, presume   consume

                resist   consist

Rubach (1984: 38) proposes a rule of *s*-Voicing to account for these cases. His rule voices /s/ when it follows a tense vowel and precedes a vowel or glide. The noun–verb pairs in (61) and (62) also show voicing of a fricative in the verb and can be brought under the same generalization. Let us call the combined rule Fricative Voicing, given in (65).

(65)   *Fricative Voicing*

$$\begin{bmatrix} +cons \\ -son \\ +cont \\ +ant \end{bmatrix} \rightarrow [+voice] / \begin{bmatrix} V \\ +ATR \end{bmatrix} \underline{\quad\quad} [-cons]$$

Fricative Voicing applies only after tense vowels, as shown by examples like *fallacy, necessary, necessity, accessory, accessible.* We assume that the prefixes in (64a) have underlying tense vowels, but they are destressed by Initial

Destressing, and the vowels are shortened and laxed by Auxiliary Reduction ((69) in Chapter 4).

Fricative Voicing does not apply in a large number of monomorphemic words, such as *mason, bison, jacinth, mimosa, Isocrates, Medusa, ether, aphid*. By assigning this rule to stratum 1, the Strict Cycle Condition (46) blocks its application in such cases, while allowing it to apply in such cases as (61b), (62b), and (64a).

C*i*V Tensing is ordered before Fricative Voicing (feeding order) in order to account for alternations such as those in (66).

(66)   a.   Cauc*a*sus   b.   Cauc*a*sian
             Malth*us*   Malth*us*ian
             gymn*a*stics   gymn*a*sium

The stress pattern of *Caucasus* shows that it must have an underlying lax vowel in its second syllable. In (66a) we have a lax vowel and a voiceless fricative in the italicized position, while in (66b) we have a tense vowel and a voiced fricative in this position. This results from applying C*i*V Tensing and Fricative Voicing, in that order, to the forms in (66b).

Similarly, ε-Tensing is ordered before Fricative Voicing to account for (61b), also a feeding order.

6.3.2   i-*Laxing*

An alternation between tense and lax vowels is also found in examples like (67).

(67)   a.   revise   b.   revision
             excise   excision
             collide   collision
             precise   precision
             concise   concision

In *SPE* (p. 182) the laxing in (67b) was attributed to Trisyllabic Laxing, on the assumption that the suffix +*ion* had two syllables underlyingly. Observe, however, that Trisyllabic Laxing must be ordered before C*i*V Tensing; otherwise Trisyllabic Laxing would undo the effects of C*i*V Tensing in words like *Canadian*. We also showed that C*i*V Tensing must be ordered before Fricative Voicing to account for words like *Caucasian*. Now observe that *precision* has both a lax vowel in the second syllable and a voiced fricative before the suffix +*ion*. By the ordering relations just discussed, the lax vowel in *precision* cannot have resulted from Trisyllabic Laxing, because Fricative Voicing takes place only after a tense vowel, and the vowel preceding the fricative would be lax by the prior application of Trisyllabic Laxing. This shows that *i*-Laxing must be distinct from Trisyllabic Laxing, since Trisyllabic Laxing is ordered before C*i*V Tensing and *i*-Laxing is ordered after C*i*V Tensing. Therefore, Rubach (1984: 43) proposes a laxing rule, which we state in (68), that is restricted to applying to /i/ and ordered *after* Fricative Voicing.

(68)   i-*Laxing*
         i → [–ATR] / ____ C₀ j V

This accounts for the laxing that occurs in (67b), and allows Fricative Voicing to apply to the *s* in *precision* and *concision*, since the *i* in these words (before *s*) is still [+ATR] when Fricative Voicing is applicable (counterbleeding order). It also allows us to assume that the underlying representation of the suffix +*ion* is /jən/, a more concrete representation than the /iVn/ assumed in *SPE*, since this suffix never has phonetic [i]. It always has the vowel /ə/, and it may have an initial [j], as in *rebellion*, but the suffix-initial *j* is deleted in words like *revision* by *j*-Deletion, (48) in Chapter 7.

6.4   Interaction of Stress with Cyclic Segmental Rules

As we suggested in Section 4.4.5 of Chapter 4, Medial Destressing is ordered before Trisyllabic Laxing. We can show this by considering the derivation of *proclamation*. On the first cycle we have *proclaim*, with the structure in (69), where the right node is marked strong because it dominates a latinate stem in a verb. We give the underlying representation and stress numbers under each syllable.

(69)

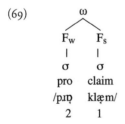

On the second cycle the suffix +*ation* is added and the cyclic rules are repeated. The English Stress Rule and Word-Tree Construction give (70), since, after the foot on +*ation* is constructed, no further disruption of the previously assigned structure is needed to produce a well-formed word tree.

(70)

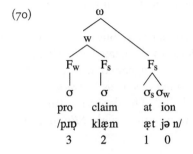

Medial Destressing cannot apply to (70), because the medial foot is marked strong. But the Rhythm Rule is ordered first and reverses the labelling of the first two feet, producing (71).

(71)

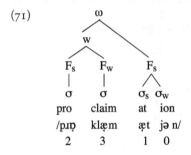

At this point Medial Destressing can remove the medial foot. The order of the Rhythm Rule before Medial Destressing is a feeding order in this derivation, because the Rhythm Rule creates the conditions for Medial Destressing to take place. This gives (72) after Stray Syllable Adjunction, which applies after each destressing rule.

(72)

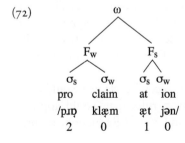

Trisyllabic Laxing can now apply to the first vowel, since the syllable containing this vowel is followed by two further syllables, the first of which is marked weak. Prior to Medial Destressing it was not marked weak, so this is another instance of a feeding interaction of two rules.

The word *resignation* is derived in a similar way, but with somewhat different rules. The morpheme *resign* is lexically designated as having Arab Destressing apply after the Rhythm Rule, as we suggested in Section 4.6 of Chapter 4. On the first cycle, stress is assigned exactly as in *proclaim* (69). The prefix has an underlying tense vowel: /ɹe/. The derivation runs as in (73), somewhat abbreviated in representing stress with *SPE* numbers rather than trees.

(73)   underlying   /ɹe + sɪɡn/
           stratum 1
              Cycle 1
                 Stress   2   1
                 Fricative Voicing   z
                 Cycle 2: morphology   /ɹe + zɪɡn + ǽtjən/

	F_w	F_s	
Stress	3	2	1

	F_s	F_w	
RR	2	3	1
Arab Destressing, SSA	2	0	1
Trisyllabic Laxing	ɛ		

           stratum 2 (rules to be   eɪʃən
              discussed in Chapter 7)
           phonetic   [ˌɹɛzɪɡˈneɪʃən]

We allow Arab Destressing to apply after Rhythm Rule in (73), since *resign* is lexically marked as allowing this order, as stated in Chapter 4, Section 4.6. Notice too that Fricative Voicing applies on the first cycle. The laxing of the prefix vowel is effected by Trisyllabic Laxing on the second cycle. This laxing would have the effect of preventing Fricative Voicing if it applied on the second cycle, since Trisyllabic Laxing is ordered before Fricative Voicing. The rules responsible for the phonetic form of the suffix *-ation* will be fully developed in Chapter 7.

If we did not add the suffix *-ation* on the second cycle, we would derive the word *resign*. In that case, the stratum 2 rules that would apply are Initial Destressing, Auxiliary Reduction, and Vowel Reduction, resulting in the vowel [ɪ] in the first syllable. Other stratum 2 rules are responsible for the conversion of /ɪgn/ in the second syllable to [ɑ̃ɪ̃n]. These rules are fully developed in Chapter 7. For now, it is interesting to note that the alternation between [ɛ] in *resignation* and [ɪ] in *resign* – both lax vowels – is derived from an underlying tense vowel /e/. This somewhat abstract underlying vowel is needed for Fricative Voicing, which only takes place after a tense vowel.

As a final example of the interaction of stress and segmental rules, consider *migratory*. On the first cycle, we derive *mígràte*. On the second cycle we add *-ory* /ɒɹij/, which receives stress, but the foot is marked weak because it is nonbranching at this stage. Medial Destressing cannot remove the second foot because the following foot is labelled weak, and this rule only applies when the following foot is labelled strong. Trisyllabic Laxing cannot apply to the vowel of the first syllable because the following syllable is stressed. On stratum 2, Sonorant Syllabification converts the final *j* to the vowel [ɪ]. Poststress Destressing is not able to destress the suffix *-ory*, despite the preceding stress, because the preceding stress is not stronger than the stress on *-ory*. The destressing of the second syllable cannot be done with the rules developed in Chapter 4. It cannot be Initial Destressing that does this because this rule is restricted to word-initial position. Furthermore, letting Initial Destressing destress *-ate* in *migratory* would allow other undesired medial applications; for example, it would incorrectly destress the second syllable of *àttèstátion*. Nanni (1977) has suggested that there is a special rule that destresses the suffix *-ate* in words that end in *-ative*, as in (74).

(74)   nominative
         imaginative
         iterative
         initiative
         cumulative
         generative

In these words, *-ate* is stressed because it has a long vowel. It is evidently destressed, but none of our destressing rules can remove this stress. In fact, there is no clash, since in each of the words of (74) there is a stress two syllables preceding *-ate*, but no stress on a syllable adjacent to *-ate*. She proposes the rule in (75), reformulated according to the metrical theory we have been assuming.

(75)   -ate *Destressing* (preliminary; after Nanni 1977)

$$F \rightarrow \emptyset \,/\, F \underline{\quad\quad}$$

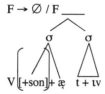

Since all destressing rules are restricted from removing a foot marked strong, we must assume that the foot over the suffixes *ate+ive* is labelled weak. Nanni assumes that marking the suffix *-ive* as extrametrical will suffice, but that is incorrect, at least in terms of our framework. The syllable dominating the suffix *-ive* is indeed marked extrametrical by Syllable Extrametricality, but it is adjoined to the preceding foot by Stray Syllable Adjunction prior to Word-Tree Construction. This is needed for the other cases we discussed in Chapter 4. For example, the sequence of suffixes *-ation* (/æt+jən/) is given main stress in words like *nomination*. It would seem that we need to mark the sequence *-at+ive* as an exception to clause (a) of Word-Tree Construction ((55) in Chapter 4), in addition to marking the final syllable extrametrical.

Extending this reasoning slightly, we suggest that *-ate* is destressed in *migratory* by a generalization of *-ate* Destressing. Here we actually have a stress clash – the syllable on *-ate* is preceded and followed by stresses. However, as already noted, none of the destressing rules developed so far removes that stress. To begin with, Nanni provides the segmental condition preceding *-ate* in (75) – that this suffix must be preceded by a vowel and optionally an intervening sonorant, since, according to her, *-ate* is not destressed if the preceding context is either an obstruent or a consonant cluster, as in (76).

(76)   innovative
        qualitative
        administrative
        legislative
        interpretative

However, this is subject to considerable dialectal and individual variation – for example, *-ate* in *administrative* seems particularly prone to destressing. If we drop the segmental condition on the material before *-ate*, and add *-ory* to the list of suffixes after *-ate* that can condition its destressing, we may approach the correct rule. We will still need a certain amount of lexical marking – for example, that destressing is obligatory in the context of (75) and prior to *-ory* regardless of the preceding segmental context, with variation in the case of (76). Other examples of destressing of *-ate* before *-ory* are given in (77).

(77) mandatory
rotatory
compensatory
hortatory
mutatory
obligatory
reverberatory

We give an approximation to the final form of this rule in (78).

(78) *-ate Destressing (final form)*

$F \rightarrow \emptyset$ / F____

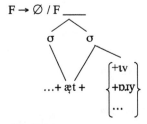

Conditions:
1. Obligatory if initial material is V([+son]) and suffix is *-ive*
2. Obligatory if suffix is *-ory*
3. Otherwise subject to dialectal, individual, and lexical variation

Now we come to establishing the position of this rule in the ordering. We observe that Trisyllabic Laxing does not apply to the vowel of the first syllable of *migratory*. This can be attributed to the stress on the second syllable of this word, assigned on the first cycle to *migrate*. Therefore, *-ate* Destressing must be ordered after Trisyllabic Laxing. As there is no evidence that it is cyclic, we can situate it on stratum 2. However, it must be ordered before Poststress Destressing, since *-ory* would otherwise be destressed in *migratory*. We will tentatively list it early in stratum 2, ordered before Poststress Destressing.

6.5 Summary of Stratum 1 Rules

In (79) we provide an ordered list of stratum 1 rules, as well as a list of stratum 2 rules introduced to this point.

(79)   a.   *Stratum 1 rules*

Consonant Extrametricality ((70) of Chapter 3)
(Re)Syllabification ((70) of Chapter 3)
Syllable Extrametricality ((42) of Chapter 4)
English Stress Rule (Parameters 1–4 of (31) of Chapter 4)
{ Arab Destressing ((77) of Chapter 4)
{ Sonorant Destressing ((73) of chapter 4)
Stray Syllable Adjunction ((75) of Chapter 4)
Word Tree Construction ((55) of Chapter 4)
Rhythm Rule ((83) of Chapter 4, with restriction (85) of Chapter 4)
Medial Destressing ((79) of Chapter 4)
Auxiliary Reduction ((69) of Chapter 4)
Trisyllabic Laxing (35)
Cluster Laxing (39)
ic-Laxing (44)
C*i*V Tensing (56)
ε-Tensing (63)
Fricative Voicing (65)
i-Laxing (68)
n-Assimilation (42)
Voicing Assimilation ((77) of Chapter 7)
Degemination (40)

b.   *Stratum 2 rules introduced to this point*

WTC for compounds and stratum 2 affixes (93 of chapter 4)
Minor relabelling (104 of chapter 4)
-ate Destressing (78)
Sonorant Syllabification (68 of chapter 4)
Poststress Destressing (64)
Initial Destressing (62)
-ary Rule (70 of chapter 4)
Special *j*-Vocalization (101 of chapter 4)
Vowel Shift (3 of chapter 7)
j-Deletion (48 of chapter 7)
ε-Elision (23 of chapter 7)

6.6   Exercises

6.1   Derivations

Discuss the derivation of the following words in terms of the morphological and phonological rules of this chapter in conjunction with the rules of previous chapters. Account for the ungrammaticality of the starred forms.

a. Hegelianism
b. to ábstràct 'to summarize, epitomize'
c. illegality
d. *misjudgeal
e. *speechlessify
f. sheathe 'to put into a sheath'
g. obligation (cf. *oblige* (/ɒblɪɡ+ɛ/ and obligate /ɒblɪɡ+æt/)

6.2 Conditions on Trisyllabic Laxing
Explain why the italicized vowel in each of the following words does not undergo Trisyllabic Laxing. There is a different explanation in each case.

a. n*i*ghtingale
b. f*ai*thlessness
c. ob*e*sity
d. m*i*gratory
e. v*a*cate
f. v*a*cancy
g. qu*o*tation

6.3 Rule Ordering
The derivation of each word on the left demonstrates the ordering of the two rules on the right. Give the underlying representation of the italicized portion of each word and show how the rules must be ordered to derive the correct output. Classify the order as feeding, bleeding, counterfeeding, counterbleeding, or mutually bleeding.

a. br*eathe*   ε-Tensing
                Fricative Voicing

b. Can*a*dian   Trisyllabic Laxing
                C*i*V Tensing

c. Cauc*a*sian   C*i*V Tensing
                Fricative Voicing

d. prec*i*sion   Fricative Voicing
                i-Laxing

e. *procla*mation Medial Destressing
                Trisyllabic Laxing

CHAPTER 7

Word-Level Phonology

In the theory of Lexical Phonology, the word level is defined as the last lexical stratum, or stratum 2 according to the model for English developed in Chapter 6. Like the first stratum, word-level phonology is word bounded, has access to word-internal structure assigned at the same stratum, and is structure preserving. Unlike the first stratum, however, word-level phonology is not cyclic (in English), and is not constrained by the Strict Cycle Condition. This difference allows rules like Vowel Shift and Velar Softening to apply freely in nonderived contexts.

7.1 Vowel Shift

In Chapter 6 we discussed a number of vowel alternations that involve the feature [ATR]. We follow *SPE* in factoring out the alternations in this feature from the rules that specify the phonetic realization of the tense ([+ATR]) vowels. There are alternations in both directions – in some cases underlying tense vowels are laxed in certain environments, and in others underlying lax vowels are tensed in other environments. Since the phonetic realizations of each tense–lax pair are rather complex, it is simpler to have the cyclic (i.e., stratum 1) rules change only the feature [ATR] and leave the phonetic realization of the tense vowels to word-level rules.

7.1.1 Front Vowels

Recall the basic tenseness alternations from Chapter 6 ((34) in Section 6.2), starting with the front vowels only, given in (1).

(1)		*Tense vowel* (*phonetic diphthong*)		*Lax vowel*		*underlying*
	a.	div*i*ne	[ɑɪ]	div*i*nity	[ɪ]	/i/
	b.	ser*e*ne	[iɪ]	ser*e*nity	[ɛ]	/e/
	c.	s*a*ne	[eɪ]	s*a*nity	[æ]	/æ/

As we stated in Chapter 6, we choose the underlying vowel as the tense version of the vowel that appears in the lax vowel column. Thus, when Trisyllabic Laxing (or some other laxing or tensing rule) applies, the only change is in the feature [ATR]. However, if the vowel remains (or becomes) tense, it shifts in height and becomes diphthongized. The height shift can be represented schematically as in (2). In the case of *serene* and *sane*, the phonetic height is one step above the underlying height; in the case of *divine*, the underlying vowel is high while the phonetic vowel is low.

(2)

$$
\begin{cases}
\nearrow \text{i} \searrow \\
\nearrow \text{e} \\
\text{æ} \swarrow
\end{cases}
$$

This shift can be expressed formally by the two rules in (3), applying in order. Like *SPE* but contrary to Halle and Mohanan (1985) we restrict Vowel Shift to stressed vowels, expressed by a dominating (optionally) strong syllable. This notation is intended to include a single syllable in a degenerate foot, which cannot be marked strong in the absence of a sister weak node. It also disregards the intervening moras.

(3)   *Vowel Shift*

a. $\sigma_{(s)}$
       |

$$
\begin{bmatrix}
V \\
+ATR \\
-low \\
\alpha high
\end{bmatrix} \rightarrow [-\alpha high]
$$

b. $\sigma_{(s)}$
       |

$$
\begin{bmatrix}
V \\
+ATR \\
-high \\
\beta low
\end{bmatrix} \rightarrow [-\beta low]
$$

In order to derive the phonetic diphthongs, we need a diphthongization rule, which we give as (4). This rule adds a front glide after front vowels and a back glide after back vowels, to be discussed in Section 7.1.2.

(4)   *Diphthongization*

$$\varnothing \rightarrow \begin{bmatrix} -\text{cons} \\ +\text{high} \\ \alpha\text{back} \\ \alpha\text{round} \end{bmatrix} / \begin{bmatrix} V \\ +\text{ATR} \\ \alpha\text{back} \end{bmatrix} \underline{\quad\quad}$$

An additional adjustment is needed for the phonetic low vowel, since the initial part of the diphthong [ɑɪ] in *divine* is back although it derives from the underlying front vowel /i/. We state Backness Adjustment in (5) so that it also affects back low vowels, to be discussed in Section 7.1.2. Backness Adjustment is necessarily ordered after Diphthongization, since the backness of the glide inserted by Diphthongization depends on the original backness of the vowel.

(5)   *Backness Adjustment*

$$\begin{bmatrix} V \\ +\text{low} \\ \alpha\text{back} \\ -\text{round} \\ +\text{ATR} \end{bmatrix} \rightarrow [-\alpha\text{back}] / \underline{\quad\quad} [-\text{cons}]$$

We give some derivations in (6) to illustrate the operation of these rules with tense front vowels.

(6)

underlying (or derived by tensing)	/i/	/e/	/æ/
Vowel Shift (3a)	e	i	—
Vowel Shift (3b)	æ	—	e
Diphthongization (4)	æɪ	iɪ	eɪ
Backness Adjusment (5)	ɑɪ	—	—

Notice that both parts of Vowel Shift apply to underlying /i/, giving a double shift from a high to a low vowel, while underlying /e/ undergoes only the first part, shifting from mid to high, and underlying /æ/ undergoes only the second part, shifting from low to mid. All three receive a front glide by Diphthongization, and only underlying /i/ undergoes Backness Adjustment.

7.1.2   Back Vowels

Extending the system of vowel-shift alternations developed so far to the back vowels involves a few complications, in the form of additional adjustment rules. However, the shift in height represented by diagram (2) also applies to back vowels, and this extension can be represented by the diagram in (7). Somewhat surprisingly, we do not need an underlying low back nonround tense vowel.

(7)

Let us consider the four back-vowel alternations in (8). We return to underlying /u/ in Section 7.1.3.

(8)

	Tense vowel		*Lax vowel*		*underlying*
	(phonetic diphthong)				
a.	verb*o*se	[ow]	verb*o*sity	[ɒ]	/ɒ/
b.	sh*oo*t	[uw]	sh*o*t	[ɒ]	/o/
	l*o*se[1]	[uw]	l*o*st	[ɒ]	/o/
c.	prof*ou*nd	[æw]	prof*u*ndity	[ə]	/ɨ/
d.	red*u*ce	[juw]	red*u*ction	[ə]	/ʌ/

Here the reasoning that the underlying vowel is a tense version of the vowel that appears in the lax-vowel column breaks down somewhat. It is true of (8a) and (8d). But, while (8b) has the same lax vowel as (8a) and (8c) has the same lax vowel as (8d), we clearly need distinct underlying representations because the tense vowels (phonetic diphthongs) have distinct realizations. If we consider (8a) first, it follows the pattern established for the front vowels exactly. Laxing (Trisyllabic Laxing or Cluster Laxing) simply produces a lax version of the underlying vowel in *verbosity*.[2] When tense, it is shifted from a low to a mid vowel exactly parallel to the corresponding front vowel in *sane*, is provided with a [w] glide by Diphthongization, and results in the phonetic diphthong [ow].

The derivation of the diphthong [uw] in *lose* (8b) from /o/ similarly follows the pattern of the front vowel /e/ – Vowel Shift raises it and Diphthongization provides the glide [w]. When laxed in *lost* – in this case by Cluster Laxing – it become a phonetic low vowel. We account for this with a rule of ɔ-Lowering, stated in (9). This and several other rules in this section are based on Halle and Mohanan (1985), with certain modifications.

---

[1] In Section 6.3.1 of Chapter 6 we showed that the vowel of the verb *lose* is derived from an underlying lax vowel (/ɔ/ as in *loss*) by ɛ-Tensing, parallel to a number of other noun-verb pairs. Thus /o/ is not strictly underlying here. Furthermore, the vowel of the past tense *lost* is lengthened and tensed in many American dialects (see Section 7.2.4).

[2] This holds for dialects that have a round vowel in *verbosity*. For speakers with an unround [ɑ] in these words, we assume a rule of ɒ-Unrounding, discussed in Section 7.2.4, given in (37).

(9)   ɔ-*Lowering* (Postlexical)

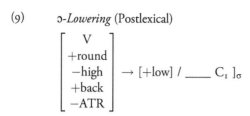

For *profound* (8c), we have a fairly close parallel to (1a) with an underlying high vowel. Vowel Shift changes this to low, and Diphthongization adds the glide [w]. The phonetic front quality of the vowel is derived by Backness Adjustment. Where the vowel becomes lax, as in *profundity*, it is phonetically mid rather than high – this is a consequence of the rule ɨ-Lowering, given in (10). We restrict this rule to stressed syllables since it does not apply to the suffix +*ure* /+ ɨɪ/.

(10)   ɨ-*Lowering*

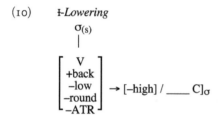

For *reduction* (8d), laxing the underlying /ʌ/ by Cluster Laxing gives phonetic [ə] directly. Two adjustments are required to account for the phonetic triphthong [juw] in *reduce*. Vowel Shift takes underlying /ʌ/ to tense /ɨ/. This needs to be rounded for most speakers – the rule is ɨ-Rounding, given in (11). For reasons to be detailed later in this section, we formulate this rule so that it applies to both tense and lax high back unrounded vowels.

(11)   ɨ-*Rounding*

$$\begin{bmatrix} V \\ +\text{high} \\ +\text{back} \end{bmatrix} \rightarrow [+\text{round}]$$

We must further account for the *j*-glide that appears before the sequence [uw] generated by these rules. As we noted in Section 3.4.1 of Chapter 3, onsets consisting of a consonant plus *j* are restricted in their distribution – they appear (almost exclusively) only before the vowels [u] and [ʊ]. In fact, we formulated a specific constraint, (44e) of Chapter 3, that excludes *j* from onset clusters at the initial syllabification. This enforces a syllable division between a consonant and *j* when such clusters appear between vowels where the second vowel is not [u] or [ʊ], as in *million*. Clusters of the form Cju and Cjʊ appear in the onset only as a result of *j*-Insertion, (12). This rule is necessarily ordered before *i*-Rounding (11) and so is formulated to apply to unrounded high back vowels, both tense and lax. Examples of its application to the lax vowel will be given shortly.

(12)   j-*Insertion*

$$\varnothing \rightarrow j \; / \; \underline{\hspace{1cm}} \begin{bmatrix} V \\ +\text{high} \\ +\text{back} \\ -\text{round} \end{bmatrix}$$

Although we transcribe *reduce* with [juw], we note that many North American speakers do not produce a *j* in this position. Halle and Mohanan (1985: 90) account for this with a different form of *j*-Insertion in these dialects, restricted so that, after coronals, *j* is inserted only if the following vowel is unstressed, as in *tenuous, venue, value*. This is incorrect, however. In the dialects in question, *j* may fail to appear even before stressless vowels, as in *òpportunístic*. Here the syllable *tu* would get a *j* inserted in all dialects under Halle and Mohanan's account, but there is no *j* here for those dialects that lack *j* in *reduce*. As we stated in Chapter 5, segmental rules that have traditionally been formulated with reference to stress are usually better stated in terms of the prosodic category foot. Rubach (1984: 49) proposes a rule of Dialectal *j*-Deletion; we follow this proposal, amending the rule to refer to the foot, a domain span rule, as in (13).[3]

(13)   *Dialectal* j-*Deletion*

$$j \rightarrow \varnothing / \; [_F \; (s) \; \begin{bmatrix} C \\ +\text{cor} \end{bmatrix} \underline{\hspace{1cm}} V \ldots]$$

By Stray Syllable Adjunction, as formulated in (75) of Chapter 4, the syllable *tu* in *opportunistic* is adjoined to the right, and hence is initial in its foot, even though stressless. This is the second example of a segmental rule whose operation is crucially dependent on adjunction operating as in Chapter 4. The first was Aspiration, formulated as (27) in Chapter 5.

---

[3] Dialectal *j*-Deletion also applies after coronals that are not absolutely foot initial, as in *stew*. For this reason we cannot appeal to the feature [+tense] assigned by Consonant Tensing, (26) in Chapter 5.

Some version of Dialectal *j*-Deletion applies even in dialects that retain *j* in *reduce, new, tune*, etc. Such speakers delete *j* after *r*, as in *rule*, and after *l* in clusters, as in *flute*. This puts it in the category of a variable rule (see C.-J. Bailey 1973).

A third is Palatalization, to be discussed in Section 7.4.2. These rules provide further justification for our adjunction procedure and for the use of prosodic categories as part of the context for segmental rules.

An example where *j*-Insertion applies before a lax /ɨ/ is the last syllable of *argue*. Since this syllable is unstressed, it cannot have an underlying tense vowel. Assuming the underlying representation /ɑɹgɨ/, the rules already given will produce [ɑɹgjʊ] (→ [ɑɹgju] by Stem-final Tensing (20)).

Halle and Mohanan also propose a rule to lengthen *ɨ* when it is stressed, as in *sulphuric* and *credulity*. We know that *sulphur* cannot have an underlying tense vowel in its final syllable, because otherwise it would be stressed there. Its underlying representation must be /səlfɨɹ/. However, the stressed vowel of *sulphuric* and *credulity* seems to be the same as that in *reduce*. We propose a rule that simultaneously tenses and lengthens stressed /ɨ/, given in (14).

(14)   *ɨ*-*Tensing*

$$\sigma_{(s)}$$

m   m

ɨ→ [+ATR]

An especially interesting aspect of this analysis is that phonetic [juw] can be derived from two distinct sources, /ʌ/ and /ɨ/ (Halle & Mohanan 1985: 104).

By way of summarizing this section, we present a table of derivations for some of the back vowels in (15).

(15)

	verbose	lose	profound	profundity	sulfuric	reduce	argue
input to stratum 2	/ɒ/	/o/	/ɨ/	/ɨ/	/ɨ/	/ʌ/	/ɨ/
Vowel (a)	—	u	ʌ	—	—	ɨ	—
Shift (b)	o	—	ɑ	—	—	—	—
ɨ-Lowering	—	—	—	ə	—	—	—
ɨ-Tensing	—	—	—	—	i	(vacuous)	—
Diphth.	ow	uw	ɑw	—	ɨw	ɨw	—
Back. Adj.	—	—	æw	—	—	—	—
j-Ins.	—	—	—	—	jɨw	jɨw	jɨ
i-Rounding	—	—	—	—	u	u	ʊ
Stem-final Tensing					[i]		u
output of stratum 2	[ow]	[uw]	[æw]	[ə]	[juw]	[juw]	[ju]

The fact that *j*-Insertion applies to both tense and lax *i* explains an otherwise curious fact: although the sequence [juw] of *reduce* alternates with stressed [ə] in *reduction*, as a consequence of Cluster Laxing, in other examples the sequence [juw] appears in an environment where you would expect it to undergo laxing. In *cubic*, the first vowel appears to violate -*ic* Laxing, while in *beautify* and *musical* the first vowel appears to violate Trisyllabic Laxing. These violations are only apparent, however. Where [juw] alternates with [ə], (both stressed) as in *reduce* and *reduction*, we propose underlying /ʌ/. Where [juw] does not alternate, as in *cube* and *cubic*, or alternates with an unstressed [ə], as in *sulfur* and *sulfuric*, the underlying vowel is lax /ɨ/. Because it is lax, it does not undergo Vowel Shift, but it does undergo *ɨ*-Tensing (when stressed), Diphthongization, *j*-Insertion, and *i*-Rounding so that the outcomes for /ʌ/ and /ɨ/ in stressed environments are both [juw].

Another result of this analysis involves the phrasal Rhythm Rule. Hammond (1984: 116) and Kager (1989: 172) regard *unique* (as in the phrase *unique story*) as an exception to the phrasal Rhythm Rule, which we discussed in Section 5.3.6 of Chapter 5. Both authors incorrectly assume that the first syllable of *unique* is heavy, and stressed. This problem is eliminated on the assumption that the first syllable of *unique* has the underlying lax vowel /ɨ/. It is then light and unstressed (destressed by Initial Destressing) – its derivation is like that of the final vowel in *argue* (last column of (15)). Since the Rhythm Rule reverses the relative prominence of two feet and the first syllable of *unique* is not a foot, there is no possibility of applying the Rhythm Rule to the phrase *unique story*.

7.1.3 [oɪ̯]

Thus far we have discussed the fate of all the underlying vowels in (7) except /u/. We have also not yet accounted for the phonetic diphthong [oɪ̯]. *SPE* constructed an ingenious argument for deriving the diphthong [oɪ̯] from an underlying tense low front round vowel that we can symbolize as /œ/.[4] The *SPE* version of Vowel Shift is restricted to vowels that agree in the features [round] and [back]; hence, /œ/ is not affected. Diphthongization supplies it with a [ɪ] because it is a front vowel, and

---

[4] *SPE* uses the symbol /œ̃/. They note that this segment does not undergo laxing in examples like *exploitative*, which they leave unexplained. In fact, laxing is blocked here on stratum 1 by the stress on -*ate*, as in *migratory*, discussed in Section 6.4 of Chapter 6. On stratum 2, -*ate* is destressed by -*ate* Destressing, (78) of Chapter 6.

Backness Adjustment turns the diphthong to [ɒɪ]. Therefore no new rules are needed for *SPE* to account for [oɪ] (in their treatment the first element of the diphthong is phonetically [+low]).

The flaw in this account is that English has no front round vowels phonetically and no other front round vowels underlyingly. The proposed underlying /œ/ is therefore quite abstract, although no absolute neutralization is involved. In terms of universal grammar, languages with front round vowels always include the high [y] before the mid [ø] or the low [œ]. It would be typologically very odd to have only the low front round vowel in the underlying inventory and then to have that vowel realized phonetically as the somewhat more common diphthong [oɪ].

Halle and Mohanan (1985: 102) consider two other possibilities for the vowel underlying [oɪ]. The most straightforward is /y/. Vowel Shift, applying to front rounded vowels, as in our analysis and Halle and Mohanan's, but contrary to *SPE*, converts /y/ to /œ/. Diphthongization and Backness Adjustment turn this to [ɒɪ], as in the *SPE* account. This adds an underlying /y/ to the system, which is in line with the universal distribution of front rounded vowels but still marked in that the system includes /y/ but not its back counterpart /u/.[5]

The remaining choice is /u/. Vowel Shift and Diphthongization convert this to [ɒw]. Backness Adjustment is inapplicable, since it affects only nonround vowels. A completely ad hoc rule is required, which we call *oɪ*-Adjustment, (16) (cf. Durand 1990: 125).

(16)   oɪ-*Adjustment*
        [ɒw] → [oɪ]

This solution, which we adopt, has the advantage of having a more natural underlying tense vowel system than either that of *SPE* or the solution with underlying /y/.

It can be noted that Fidelholtz and Browne (1971) made the quite radical suggestion that the underlying representation of [oɪ] should be /oɪ/ (cf. also Rubach 1984: 35, fn. 13). This is radical because, in the context of *SPE* theory and subsequent generative phonology, all English diphthongs are derived from underlying simple tense (or long) vowels. In Section 2.4.2 of Chapter 2 we mentioned three sources of evidence that simple vowels underlie diphthongs. These were syllabification, backwards speech, and the alternations of diphthongs with simple vowels discussed in this and the previous chapter. Just to recall the syllabification argument, when a

---

[5] A reader has observed that the analysis of [oɪ] as /y/ is even more abstract than *SPE*'s analysis because it has /œ/ as an intermediate step.

diphthong is followed by another vowel, the diphthong is syllabified together: the glide of the diphthong is not treated as an onset to the following vowel. That is, we have syllabifications *Toy.o.ta, voy.age, loy.al* rather than **To.yo.ta, *vo.yage, *lo.yal.* If the glide were present at the stage when syllabification is done, we would expect the latter syllabifications, in accordance with the Onset Principle, (2) of Chapter 3. This is especially striking in the case of a borrowed word like *Toyota*, which in Japanese, the source language, is indeed syllabified *To.yo.ta.* If the diphthongs are underlying simple vowels, there can be no onset to the second of two consecutive underlying vowels, and the observed syllabifications are predicted. Note further that the general lack of resyllabification on stratum 2, observed in Section 3.5 of Chapter 3, predicts that the diphthongal glide is not resyllabified as an onset after it is inserted by Diphthongization.

7.2 Additional Vowel Rules

7.2.1 Prevocalic Tensing

In addition to C*i*V Tensing and ε-Tensing, which apply on stratum 1, there are two rules of vowel tensing that apply on stratum 2. The first is Prevocalic Tensing, which, as its name suggests, tenses a vowel before another vowel. This rule is ordered before Vowel Shift, because its output undergoes Vowel Shift if it is stressed. The other is Stem-Final Tensing, which is ordered after Vowel Shift and whose output remains unshifted. Because of this ordering, the two rules cannot be collapsed.[6]

Prevocalic Tensing is motivated on the basis of alternations like those in (17).

(17)   a. var*i*ous, var*i*ation   b. var*ie*ty
             notor*i*ous   notor*ie*ty
             man*i*ac   man*i*acal
             simultan*e*ous   simultan*e*ity

      c. algebr*a*   d. algebr*ai*c
             formul*a*   formul*ai*c

In (17a), the italicized vowels are tensed because they precede another vowel but, as they are unstressed, they are not vowel shifted. In (17b), the

---

[6] Halle and Mohanan (1985: 83) collapse these two rules, but their formulation is quite complex. Furthermore, since their collapsed rule is ordered after Vowel Shift, they need an essentially allomorphic treatment of the quite regular alternations in (17). Part of the difficulty with their analysis stems from their treatment of Vowel Shift in terms of length rather than tenseness. As they observe, vowels are tensed, but not lengthened, in the prevocalic environment.

corresponding vowels are tensed and also vowel shifted (except for *simulta-neity*) and diphthongized because they are prevocalic and stressed. In (17c) the italicized vowels are underlyingly lax, since they are unstressed and reduced, but the corresponding vowels in (17d) have undergone tensing and Vowel Shift. We propose to formulate Prevocalic Tensing as in (18).

(18)   *Prevocalic Tensing*

$$\begin{bmatrix} V \\ -\text{back} \end{bmatrix} \rightarrow [+\text{ATR}] / \_\_\_ \ V$$

By ordering (18) before Vowel Shift, we obtain an account of the alternations in (17). We provide some partial derivations in (19) in order to clarify the point. As at the end of Chapter 6, we abbreviate the representations, using *SPE* stress numbers rather than full metrical structures; this is merely for expository convenience and does not affect the point at hand.[7]

(19)

	managerial	notoriety	algebra	algebraic
underlying	/mænədʒɛɪ+ɪæl/	/nɒtɒɹɪ + ɪtɪ/	/ældʒɪbɹæ/	/ældʒɪbræ + ɪk/
stratum 1				
stress	2 I	2 0 I	I	2 I
C*i*V Tens.	e	— — —	— — —	— — —
stratum 2				
PreV Tens	i	i	— — —	æ
Vowel Sh	i	o æ	— — —	e
Diphth	iɪ̯	ow æɪ̯	— — —	eɪ̯
BAdj	— — —	ɑɪ̯	— — —	— — —
StFinTens	— — —		i	— — —
VRed	ə	ə	I ə	I I
ə-Ins	iɪ̯ə	— — —	— — —	— — —
Postlexical				
Flapping	— — —	ɾ	— — —	— — —
Phonetic form	[ˌmænəˈdʒiɪ̯ɹɪəl]	[ˌnowtəˈɹɑɪ̯ɪɾi]	[ˈældʒɪbɹə]	[ˌældʒɪˈbɹeɪ̯k]

---

[7] In derivations, only relevant rules are listed. This should be interpreted as a shorthand for a display in which every rule at every stratum is tried for application on each form. Stem-final Tensing and Vowel Reduction are discussed in the next two subsections; ə-Insertion was given as (114) in Chapter 5, Section 5.3.8, and is given again as (38) in Section 7.2.4.

We can note that *vary, maniac* have a tense vowel in the first syllable of their underlying representations. The first syllable of *various* retains this tense vowel; it is not tensed by C*i*V Tensing. These words belong to the class that irregularly can undergo Initial Destressing (in the derived forms *variety, maniacal*) even though the vowel of the first syllable is tense (and bimoraic). See Section 4.4.1 of Chapter 4.

We can also note that the derivation of *notorious* involves complications that do not bear directly on Prevocalic Tensing; we therefore illustrate this rule with *managerial* instead. See Footnote 23 in Chapter 6.

We account for the irregular behaviour of *simultaneity* by stipulating that the morpheme *simultane-* is an exception to Vowel Shift.

7.2.2 *Stem-final Tensing*

As we saw in the derivation of *algebra* in (19), an underlying word-final low vowel becomes [ə] when unstressed. Nonlow vowels are not reduced in this position, but become tense by the rule Stem-final Tensing, which we give as (20).

(20)   ***Stem-final Tensing***

$$\begin{bmatrix} V \\ -\text{low} \\ \alpha\text{back} \\ \alpha\text{round} \end{bmatrix} \rightarrow [+\text{ATR}] / \underline{\qquad} \,]$$

This rule is ordered before Vowel Reduction. In Chapter 4 we saw that when a word ends in an underlying tense vowel, it is stressed on the last syllable, as in *obey, Manitou, veto, trustee*. Some words with a final tense vowel phonetically are nevertheless not stressed on the last syllable, such as those in (21).

(21)

	light penult	long vowel in penult	consonant-final penult
a.	broccoli	macaroni	Chianti
b.	kinkajou	kikuyu	jujitsu
c.	buffalo	albino	commando

The stress patterns in (21) are exactly parallel to the words in (34) of Chapter 4 (e.g., *lábyrinth, elítist, amálgam*). This is accounted for by assuming that the words in (21) have final lax vowels in their underlying representations, and that these vowels are tensed by Stem-final Tensing (20). This rule applies on stratum 2, after syllabification and stress on stratum 1, and so these vowels remain monomoraic and unstressed.

In RP, Stem-final Tensing is restricted to back vowels, so that final *ı* is not tensed in this dialect. In RP, the final vowel is lax in *broccoli, macaroni, Chianti, city*.

Stem-final Tensing (20) applies not only in word-final position, as in (21), but also before inflectional suffixes, stem finally in compounds, and before most stratum 2 suffixes. In the forms of (22) we find tense [i] at the end of the first stem in each case.

(22)   a. city
        b. cities
        c. city hall
        d. happiness

The formulation in (20) accounts for this with a morphological bracket as the context for tensing. Stem-final Tensing is a stratum 2 rule and all the morphological constructions in (22) are formed at stratum 2. In accordance with the theory of Lexical Phonology, morphological brackets are erased only at the end of a stratum; therefore, the bracket required for tensing is present following the stem-final vowel in all the examples in (22). There is, however, some variation in the application of the rule before stratum 2 suffixes. There is generally no tensing before *-ful* and *-ly*, as in *beautiful* and *happily*.

Stem-final Tensing could affect word-final ε as well. In Chapter 6 we observed that a number of verbs are derived from nouns by suffixation of +ε, such as *breathe* from *breath*. This suffix causes the tensing of the stem vowel and the voicing of the preceding fricative, but it is itself not phonetically realized. It is deleted by ε-Elision (23). This rule is ordered before Stem-final Tensing.

(23)   *ε-Elision*
        ε → Ø / _____]

7.2.3   Vowel Reduction

SPE assumed that all lax unstressed vowels were reduced to schwa [ə], that schwa was distinct from all other vowels of English, and that it was not present in underlying representations. Most subsequent authors have followed this tradition. We consider this an error on several counts, however. For one thing, in accordance with the naturalness criterion (15c of Chapter 1), there is no motivation for excluding nonalternating schwa from underlying representations, for example, as the final vowel in *sofa* or as the vowel of *but*, since this vowel patterns with other lax vowels in requiring a final consonant to make an acceptable stressed, monosyllabic English word. For another thing, there are three reduction vowels in many or most dialects of English, as pointed out in Section 2.4.3 of Chapter 2. It is not possible to attribute the phonetic realization of reduced vowels to mere matters of performance, as implied in *SPE* (pp. 110–111), in view of contrasting reduced vowels in *Lenin* [ɪ] versus *Lennon* [ə], at least in RP (Wells 1982: 167). In our discussion of systematic phonemics in Section

2.5 of Chapter 2, we transcribed the two unstressed vowels of *telegraphic* as [ɪ] rather than [ə], while the penultimate syllable of *telegraphy* has [ə], based on Collins Dictionary of the English Language (1979), which represents these reduced vowels systematically. Clearly, the quality of reduced vowels is a matter of competence, not just performance.

Certain instances of [ɪ] as a reduced vowel may be due to assimilation. We consider the alternations shown in an example from *SPE* (p. 235), given in (24).

(24)   a.   courage   [ˈkəɹɪʤ]
        b.   courageous   [kəˈɹeɪʤəs]
        c.   *underlying*   /kəɹæʤ/

Although *SPE* transcribes *courage* with [ə] in the last syllable, both *Collins* and the American Heritage Dictionary (1969) transcribe [ɪ] in this position (*American Heritage* writes *ĭ*, the same symbol they use for the vowel of *bit*). The underlying representation in (24c) is based on the alternations of the word shown in (24a, b) and differs in certain respects from *SPE*'s underlying representation /koɹægɛ/ (our symbols). Since the first vowel appears as [ə] in both stressed and unstressed position, there is no justification for *SPE*'s more abstract representation /o/ here. Also, there is no justification for any segments other than /ʤ/ at the end of the stem, since this is the phonetic realization in all phonetic alternants. The underlying /æ/ is justified on the basis of the alternation. It undergoes C*i*V Tensing in *courageous* (with the suffix /-jɒs/), Vowel Shift, Diphthongization and *j*-Deletion ((48) in Section 7.4.2). In *courage*, the second vowel undergoes Vowel Reduction and Assimilation, which we can express as (25).

(25)   *Vowel Reduction and Assimilation*

$$
\begin{array}{c}
\sigma_w \\
| \\
m \\
| \\
\begin{bmatrix} V \\ -ATR \end{bmatrix} \rightarrow \text{I} / \underline{\qquad} \begin{bmatrix} C \\ +cor \\ -ant \end{bmatrix}
\end{array}
$$

The reduced vowel appears as [ʊ] in the italicized positions in (26).

(26)   a.   m*u*sician   /ɨ/   cf. m*u*sic
        b.   *u*nique
        c.   form*u*la

It is obtained through the rule in (27), reducing a high back lax vowel.

(27)   *High Back Vowel Reduction*

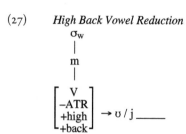

$$\sigma_w$$
$$|$$
$$m$$
$$|$$

$$\begin{bmatrix} V \\ -ATR \\ +high \\ +back \end{bmatrix} \rightarrow \upsilon \ / \ j \ \underline{\hspace{1.5cm}}$$

Besides cases like *courage*, where the reduced vowel [ɪ] appears by assimilation, front nonlow lax vowels are also reduced to [ɪ] when unstressed, as in the italicized positions of (28). The underlying form of this vowel is given in the second column, justified in the third column by a word where the corresponding vowel appears in stressed position.

(28)   a.   tel*e*graph   /ɛ/   cf. tel*e*graphy
             b.   med*i*cine   /ɪ/   cf. med*i*cinal
             c.   r*e*side   /e/   cf. r*e*sident (by TSL)
                 (in *reside*, /e/ → /ɛ/ by Aux Reduction (69) in Chapter 4)

A front nonlow lax vowel is reduced by the rule in (29).

(29)   *Nonlow Front Vowel Reduction*

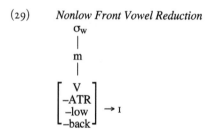

$$\sigma_w$$
$$|$$
$$m$$
$$|$$

$$\begin{bmatrix} V \\ -ATR \\ -low \\ -back \end{bmatrix} \rightarrow \textsc{i}$$

Any unstressed lax vowel that does not meet the specific conditions of rules (25), (27), or (29) undergoes reduction by (30).

(30)   *General Vowel Reduction*

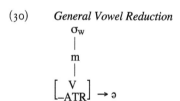

$$\sigma_w$$
$$|$$
$$m$$
$$|$$

$$\begin{bmatrix} V \\ -ATR \end{bmatrix} \rightarrow \textschwa$$

This General Vowel Reduction rule is responsible for reducing the unstressed lax vowels in the italicized positions in (31).[8]

(31)　a.　algeb*ra*　/æ/　cf. algeb*ra*ic　/æ l d ʒ ɪ b ɹ æ/
　　　b.　tab*le*　/ɨ/　cf. tab*u*lar　/tæ b ɨ l/
　　　c.　sulph*ur*　/ɨ/　cf. sulph*u*ric　/s ə l f ɨ ɹ/
　　　d.　curi*ous*　/ɒ/　cf. curi*o*sity　/k ʌ ɹ ɪ ɒ s/

We refer to the four rules (25), (27), (29), and (30) collectively as Vowel Reduction. The General Vowel Reduction rule (30) must be ordered after the others and (30) must not apply if any of the others have applied in a given derivation. Kiparsky (1973; 1982) has proposed a general grammatical principle, known as the Elsewhere Condition, that ensures this type of interaction. We give the formulation of this condition in (32), from Kiparsky (1982: 8).

(32)　*Elsewhere Condition*
　　　Rules A, B in the same component apply disjunctively to a form Φ if and only if
　　　(i)　The structural description of A (the special rule) properly includes the structural description of B (the general rule).
　　　(ii)　The result of applying A to Φ is distinct from the result of applying B to Φ.
　　　In that case, A is applied first, and if it takes effect, then B is not applied.

Two or more rules are said to apply *disjunctively* if only one of the rules can apply in any given derivation – the application of any one of the rules excludes the application of any of the others. We need to have the four vowel reduction rules apply disjunctively, since rule (30) would destroy the results of any of the other three rules if allowed to apply to vowels reduced by one of those rules. Condition (32i) is fulfilled because the structural description of each of (25), (27), and (30) properly includes the structural description of (30). Furthermore, the result of applying any of the vowel reduction rules is distinct from the result of applying any of the other vowel reduction rules – recall the definition of distinctness in Section 1.5.2 of Chapter 1: two segments are distinct if, for some feature [F], one segment is specified [+F] and the other is specified [–F]. Therefore, condition (32ii) is fulfilled. Thus, the Elsewhere Condition requires that

---

[8] *SPE* (p. 196) and Rubach (1984: 37) assume a rule that inserts *u* before the stem-final *l* in *tabular* (also *circular*, *titular*, etc.) Our analysis with an underlying *ɨ* makes these examples parallel to *sulphur*, but decisive evidence for preferring one analysis over the other is lacking.

rules (25), (27), and (29) apply disjunctively with respect to (30), with the result that only one of these rules can ever apply in any given derivation.

The reduced vowels [ə], [ɪ] that result from the rules of this subsection are also underlying vowels, as shown in (33). The vowel [ʊ] in unstressed position, as in *musician*, is not underlying, but seems always to be derived from underlying /ɨ/.

(33)   *stressed*   *unstressed*
      a.   [ɪ]   b*i*t   rabb*i*t
      b.   [ʊ]   b*oo*k   (m*u*sician)
      c.   [ə]   b*u*t   sof*a*

The structure preservation property of Lexical Phonology requires this, in fact. This is entirely contrary to the *SPE* position, where schwa is excluded from underlying representations. In *SPE* the final vowel of *sofa* would presumably be derived from /æ/, but there is no justification for a vowel other than /ə/ in the last syllable of this word, since there are no alternations. The failure to notice that there are three distinct reduced vowels in English, and the exclusion of [ə] from underlying representations, have been major impediments to progress in English phonology.[9]

7.2.4   Other Vowel Adjustments

We observed in Section 2.4.2 of Chapter 2 that the penultimate syllable of *Chicago* and *Catawba* are stressed but that the vowels of these syllables do not undergo Vowel Shift. We adopted Halle's (1977) suggestion that these vowels are underlyingly long (in our terms, provided with one mora in underlying representation) but lax, which accounts for these two facts. Phonetically, these vowels are tense, a feature supplied by the postlexical rule *a/o*-Tensing, which we state in (34).

(34)   a/o-*Tensing* (Postlexical)

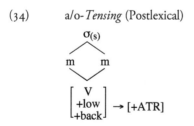

---

[9] Sainz (1988) permits [ə] in underlying representations, but stipulates that it cannot be stressed, and uses this idea to develop a noncyclic analysis of English stress.

Halle (1977: 620) notes that the vowel of the words *lost, long* is lengthened (and tensed) in the dialect of New York City.[10] He proposes a lengthening rule, which we give as (35). This is ordered before *a/o* Tensing, feeding it in appropriate cases.

(35)   *Low Back Lengthening* (Postlexical)

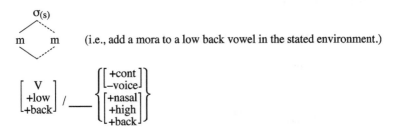

(i.e., add a mora to a low back vowel in the stated environment.)

We formulate *a/o*-Tensing (34) somewhat differently from Halle and Mohanan (1985). Their version applies to short [ɑ] and [ɔ], as in *balm* and *baud*. They do not accept Halle's (1977) suggestion for *Chicago* and *Catawba*, nor an underlying distinction in tenseness. In our treatment, there is no reason to have the underlying vowel in *balm* different from that in *Chicago* or that in *baud* different from that in *Catawba*, at least for North American dialects. For RP, where *baud* has a mid rather than a low vowel, we can assume an underlying mid vowel /ɔ/, which undergoes tensing. We observed in Section 2.4.1 of Chapter 2 that [ɔ] does not appear phonetically in English, except before [ɪ]. What happens if this vowel appears in an underlying representation in some other context? In word-final position it is tensed by Stem-final Tensing (20). There are other contexts where it is tensed also. We tacitly assumed that this is the underlying vowel in the first syllable of *obey* in Section 4.3.1 of Chapter 4 (cf. (33d) in Chapter 4). In some dialects this appears as (unstressed) [ə] (this is the transcription in *Collins*). This can result from General Vowel Reduction (30). In some North American dialects, it appears as [o], also unstressed. We can assume a rule of ɔ-Tensing for RP *baud* and North American *obey*, given in (36).

---

[10] The geographical range of this rule is undoubtedly much wider. This rule is also subject to a few lexical exceptions which vary according to dialects, for example, *song* in my own speech.

(36)   ɔ-*Tensing*

ɔ → [+ATR]

(Except before [ɹ]; in RP in closed syllables only)

The vowel we have transcribed throughout as [ɒ] is pronounced as such in RP but unrounded to [ɑ] in most North American dialects. The rule for this is ɒ-Unrounding, given in (37).

(37)   ɒ-*Unrounding* (Postlexical)

$$
\begin{array}{c}
\text{m} \\
| \\
\left[\begin{array}{c} \text{V} \\ \text{+low} \\ \text{+back} \end{array}\right] \rightarrow \text{[–round]}
\end{array}
$$

Before *r* and *l*, diphthongized tense vowels are followed by an intrusive [ə]. We discussed this in Chapter 5 in connection with the utterance-level postlexical rule of *r*-Insertion. We repeat the rule here as (38). Some examples are given in (113) of Chapter 5.

(38)   ə-*Insertion*

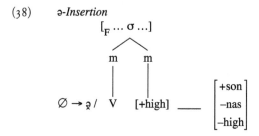

7.3   Summary

To summarize this discussion of the English vowel system, we give a chart of the underlying vowel system along with an example for each vowel in (39). Compare this with the charts of the phonetic vowels of English in Sections 2.4.1 and 2.4.2 in Chapter 2. The rules of this chapter apply to the underlying vowels to produce the phonetic vowels.

(39)   The English underlying vowel system

		$\begin{bmatrix} -\text{back} \\ -\text{round} \end{bmatrix}$			$\begin{bmatrix} +\text{back} \\ -\text{round} \end{bmatrix}$			$\begin{bmatrix} +\text{back} \\ +\text{round} \end{bmatrix}$	
	[+ATR]	[–ATR]		[+ATR]	[–ATR]		[+ATR]	[–ATR]		
$\begin{bmatrix} +\text{high} \\ -\text{low} \end{bmatrix}$	/i/ divine	/ɪ/ bit, city	/i/ profound	/ɨ/ cube, value	/u/ boy	/ʊ/ book
$\begin{bmatrix} -\text{high} \\ -\text{low} \end{bmatrix}$	/e/ serene	/ɛ/ bet	/ʌ/ reduce	/ə/ but, sofa	/o/ shoot, moon	/ɔ/ port, volcano, baud (RP)
$\begin{bmatrix} -\text{high} \\ +\text{low} \end{bmatrix}$	/æ/ sane	/æ/ bat, algebra		/ɑ:/ balm, Chicago, spa	/ɒ/ cone	/ɒ/ bomb /ɒ:/ Catawba

7.4 Consonant Rules

In this section we investigate a number of rules that are involved in the consonant system of English. These rules interact with each other and with the vowel rules in very interesting ways that support our view that a system of ordered rules provides the best description of the intricacies of the English sound system.

7.4.1 *Velar Softening*

Velar Softening is responsible for alternations such as those in (40).

(40)   *velar stop*   *coronal strident*
         critic, critical   criticize, criticism
         clinic, clinical   clinician
         medicate, medical   medicine, medicinal
         matrix   matrices
         intellect[11]   intelligent
         fungus, fungal   fungi
         analog, analogous   analogy, analogical
         legal, legality   legislate

Although Velar Softening is confined to the 'romance' vocabulary of English, mainly derived from Latin via French, it is highly productive in this area of the vocabulary. We can formulate the rule as in (41).

---

[11] Here underlying /g/ → [k] by voicing assimilation (77).

(41)   *Velar Softening*

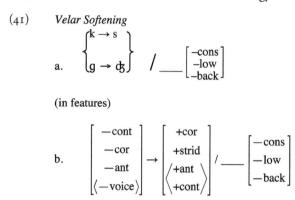

a. $\left\{\begin{matrix} k \rightarrow s \\ g \rightarrow \dʒ \end{matrix}\right\}$ / ___ $\begin{bmatrix} -cons \\ -low \\ -back \end{bmatrix}$

(in features)

b. $\begin{bmatrix} -cont \\ -cor \\ -ant \\ \langle -voice \rangle \end{bmatrix} \rightarrow \begin{bmatrix} +cor \\ +strid \\ \langle +ant \\ +cont \rangle \end{bmatrix}$ / ___ $\begin{bmatrix} -cons \\ -low \\ -back \end{bmatrix}$

This rather simple formulation, where the triggering context is a natural class, is achieved by ordering Velar Softening before Vowel Shift. If after Vowel Shift, Velar Softening would have to be triggered by a rather heterogeneous set of vowels, diphthongs, and glides, namely {ɑɪ, ɪ, iy, ɛ, j}.

7.4.2   Palatalization

Palatalization in English operates both lexically and postlexically. In phrases, a coronal obstruent becomes nonanterior before the high front glide [j] followed by a vowel (42a). Interestingly, it does not apply before high front vowels (42b) (cf. Halle & Mohanan 1985: 85).

(42)   a.   miss you   [mɪʃjə]
               got you   [gɒtʃjə]
               did you   [dɪdʒjə]

        b.   miss it   [mɪs ɪt]   *[mɪʃɪt]
               miss Eve   [mɪs iːv]   *[mɪʃ iːv]
               got it   [gɒɾ ɪt]   *[gɒtʃ ɪt]
               got even   [gɒɾ iːvən]   *[gɒtʃ iːvən]
               did it   [dɪɾ ɪt]   *[dɪdʒ ɪt]
               did eat   [dɪɾ iːt]   *[dɪdʒ iːt]

In its lexical application, Palatalization accounts for alternations such as those in (43). In the right-hand column the coronal obstruent is followed by [j] and a vowel at the point where Palatalization is applicable. The suffix +*ion* has the underlying representation /jən/ and the suffix -*ial* has the underlying representation /jæl/; in other cases a [j] has been inserted by *j*-Insertion (12).

(43) a. /s/ express   expression
            gas   gaseous
            space   spatial
            office   official
            artifice   artificial, artificiality
            presidency   presidential

     b. /z/ confuse   confusion
            supervise   supervision
            enclose   enclosure

     c. /t/ habit   habitual
            fact   factual
            depart   departure
            Christ   Christian
            digest   digestion

     d. /d/ grade   gradual
            proceed   procedure

Like the phrasal application, no lexical application of Palatalization is possible if the coronal obstruent is followed by a high front vowel, as in (44).

(44)   invidious   [ɪnˈvɪdiəs]   *[ɪnˈvɪdʒiəs]
        poinsettia   [ˌpɔɪnˈsɛtiə]   *[ˌpɔɪnˈsɛtʃiə]
        Kantian   [ˈkɑntiən]   *[ˈkɑntʃiən]
        accordion   [əˈkɔɹdiən]   *[əˈkɔɹdʒiən]
        Canadian   [kəˈneɪdiən]   *[kəˈneɪdʒiən]
        but [kəˈneɪdʒən] (from *Canada +ian* /jæn/; Orkin 1997)

Palatalization does not affect a consonant at the beginning of a stressed syllable. More generally, Palatalization does not affect a consonant at the beginning of a foot. For example, the italicized segment is not palatalized in (45), although it is followed by [j] plus a vowel. (The *j* is deleted in some dialects by Dialectal j-Deletion (13).)

(45)   a   en*d*ure   [ɪnˈdjuwəɹ]   *[ɪnˈdʒuwəɹ]
        b.   en*s*ue   [ɪnˈsjuw]   *[ɪnˈʃuw]
        c.   re*s*ume   [ɹɪˈzjuwm]   *[ɹɪˈʒuwm]
        d.   perpe*t*uity   [ˌpəɹpɪˈtjuwɪɾi]   *[ˌpəɹpɪˈtʃuwɪɾi]
        e.   *t*une   [ˈtjuwn]   *[ˈtʃuwn]
        f.   *t*uition   [tjuwˈɪʃən]   *[tʃuwˈɪʃən]
        g.   oppor*t*unistic [ˌɒpəɹtjʊˈnɪstɪk]   *[ˌɒpəɹtʃʊˈnɪstɪk]

Palatalization in *artificiality* seems to pose a problem for the claim that the rule is inapplicable before the high front vowel. However, we know from *artificial* that the suffix *-ial* is /jæl/ in underlying representation, so we can deduce that there is a /j/ present in *artificiality* to condition Palatalization at the time the rule applies. Let us assume, then, that this /j/ becomes a vowel [i] by a later rule. Then the contrast between Palatalization in *artificiality* and the lack of Palatalization in *perpetuity* seems a problem, since the segment in question is followed by a stress in both cases. The solution lies in the distinct syllabification of these words. At the time Palatalization is to apply, these two words have the prosodic structures partially represented in (46).

(46)   a. [F ɑɹtɪ] [F [σ fɪs]] [F [σ jæ] l + ɪtɪ]
        b. [F pəɹ [σ pɛ] [F [σ tjuw] + ɪtɪ]

Recall from Section 3.4.1 of Chapter 3 that we proposed a constraint against onsets consisting of one or two consonants followed by /j/ ((44e) of Chapter 3). This constraint was proposed to account for the peculiar distribution of syllable-initial C*j*V sequences in English: such onsets occur (almost exclusively) only when the vowel is [u] or [ʊ]. As shown in Section 7.1.2, the /j/ in such sequences is a result of *j*-Insertion and is not present in underlying representation. Such is the case with *perpetual*, where the underlying representation of the third syllable is /tɪ/. No constraint prevents this syllabification at stratum 1, and *j*-Insertion does not change this syllabification. However, in *artificiality*, constraint (44e) of Chapter 3 enforces a syllable boundary after /fɪs/. Consequently, the /s/ of *artificiality* is not foot initial, and can be palatalized. On the other hand, the /t/ in the third syllable of *perpetuity* is foot initial, like the italicized segments in the other examples of (45), and so Palatalization cannot apply to it. We can prevent Palatalization from affecting foot-initial consonants by restricting the input to consonants that are [−tense]. In Section 5.3.3 of Chapter 5, we introduced the feature [tense] for consonants as a way of accounting for Aspiration, since Aspiration affects only foot-initial voiceless stops. We suggested there that this feature is relevant to a number of other segmental rules, and Palatalization is one of them. The rule Consonant Tensing ((26) in Chapter 5) applies the feature [+tense] to foot-initial consonants; all other consonants are [−tense]. The consonant to be palatalized may be in the same syllable as the following *j*V, as in *enclosure*, or in the preceding syllable, as in *artificiality*. In both cases the *j*V must be in the same syllable – that is, the *j* must be (part of) the onset to the vowel, not a syllabic segment on its own. These considerations lead us to formulate Palatalization as in (47).[12]

(47)   *Palatalization*

$$
\begin{bmatrix} C \\ +cor \\ -son \\ \{-cont\} \\ \{+strid\} \\ -tense \end{bmatrix} \rightarrow \begin{bmatrix} -ant \\ +strid \end{bmatrix} / \underline{} \overset{\ldots m}{\overset{\wedge}{\begin{bmatrix} -cons \\ +high \\ -back \end{bmatrix} V}}
$$

The mora dominating the glide and the following vowel indicates that these two segments belong to the same mora (and the same syllable). The preceding ellipsis indicates that other material may precede in the same mora, which is the case when the segment undergoing Palatalization is syllable initial, as in *enclosure*. The feature [–tense] in the input prevents application to foot-initial consonants – this implies that Consonant Tensing is ordered before Palatalization. The fact that Palatalization is triggered by /j/ inserted by *j*-Insertion shows that *j*-Insertion is ordered before Palatalization also. It should be noted that Palatalization preserves continuancy – i.e., fricatives remain fricatives when palatalized and stops become affricates when palatalized. The distinctive feature system we proposed for English in Section 2.3 of Chapter 2 distinguishes affricates as [–continuant, +strident], so the feature [+strident] in the structural change has exactly this effect with stops; it is vacuous for fricatives (at least, for those fricatives that can undergo the rule), which are [+strident] to begin with. It can also be noted that Palatalization does not fit into any of the categories of prosodic rules developed by Nespor and Vogel (1986) and discussed in Chapter 5. That is, it is not a domain span rule, nor a domain limit rule, nor a domain juncture rule. In cases like *enclosure* it applies within a syllable but in cases like *expression* it applies at the juncture of two syllables within a foot and in cases like *artificiality* it applies at the juncture of two feet.

Although Palatalization is conditioned by a /j/ following the affected segment, no [j] is present phonetically when Palatalization applies word internally. We account for this with a rule of *j*-Deletion (48). Unlike Dialectal *j*-Deletion (13), this rule applies in all dialects.

---

[12] The features in curly braces ({}) exclude the segments θ, ð from the set of inputs to Palatalization, as in *enthusiasm*. The need for this exclusion has apparently gone unnoticed in previous treatments of Palatalization.

(48)   j-*Deletion*

$$j \rightarrow \emptyset \ / \ [\ \dots \ \begin{bmatrix} C \\ +\text{cor} \\ -\text{ant} \end{bmatrix} \_\_\_ \ \dots \ ]_F$$

Having j-Deletion as a foot-span rule prevents its application to foot-initial j. Halle and Mohanan (1985: 86) cite the example *fish university*, where j is retained, arguing that compounds are formed on a later lexical stratum (their stratum 3) where they escape stratum 2 phonological rules such as j-Deletion. However, their third and fourth lexical strata are highly suspect for two reasons. One is that very few phonological rules are proposed for these strata, and these rules turn out to be either unnecessary or analyzable in a better way using only two lexical strata. The second is that they require a loop from stratum 3 to stratum 2 in order to account for the fact that compounding and stratum 2 affixation apply freely to each other's output. The loop is obviously a serious weakening of the claims of Lexical Morphology and Phonology. In the case of j-Deletion, simply restricting it to apply within the foot has the desired effect without proliferating lexical strata.

In the derivation of words like *enclosure*, *pressure*, both j-Insertion and j-Deletion apply, with Palatalization applying between them. Some phonologists have objected to such derivations, in which the effect of one rule is undone by the operation of a later rule (see Section 8.3.4 of Chapter 8). However, we have not proposed this sequence of rules just to get the effects of Palatalization. J-Insertion is well motivated in many cases where the j remains, as in *pure*, and j-Deletion is well motivated for cases where it deletes underlying j, as in *expression*. Furthermore, Palatalization is conditioned both by underlying j, as in *expression*, and by inserted j, as in *pressure*. The simplest possible account of these facts is to allow both j-Insertion and j-Deletion to apply in derivations like that of *pressure*.

J-Deletion applies in *artificial* but not in *artificiality*. In the latter, j turns to a vowel by a rule of j-Vocalization. The suffixes /jæl/ and /ɪtɪ/ are both added on stratum 1, so this will be a cyclic derivation as far as stress is concerned. On the first cycle, *artifice* has the foot structure in (49a). The addition of the suffix /jæl/ and reapplication of syllabification and stress rules gives (49b). The structural description of Palatalization is met at this point, but this rule does not apply until stratum 2. On the third cycle we add the suffix /ɪtɪ/ and reapply syllabification and stress rules, including the Rhythm Rule, giving (49c). In this configuration the syllable and mora

structures are shown in greater detail to illustrate the operation of
j-Vocalization.

(49) a.

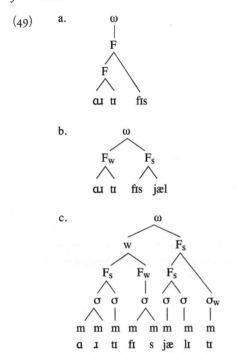

b.

c.

After Palatalization on stratum 2, the application of *j*-Vocalization creates a
new syllable without creating a new mora. The *j* at the beginning of the
fourth syllable moves from its original mora to the preceding mora, where
it becomes a syllable nucleus. The structure then looks like (50).

(50)

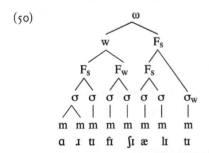

A somewhat cryptic formulation of *j*-Vocalization that has the right effect
is given in (51). The dotted line above the mora containing the [+cor]

segment indicates that it projects a syllable, i.e., creates a new syllable to dominate it. A somewhat less cryptic linear version of the rule is given also.

(51)   j-*Vocalization*

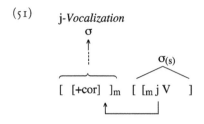

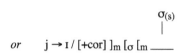

or   j → ɪ / [+cor]]ₘ [σ [ₘ ____

It is not actually necessary to order j-Vocalization before j-Deletion, since j-Deletion would not be applicable to (49c) (after Palatalization), since j-Deletion is restricted to apply within a foot and the j and the preceding s are in different feet in (49c). We will nevertheless assume the ordering in (52).

(52)   ⎧ j-Insertion (12)
        ⎪ Palatalization (47)
        ⎨ j-Vocalization (51)
        ⎩ j-Deletion (48)

These rules apply on stratum 2. *J*-Deletion cannot be cyclic, since it would apply to *artificial* on the second cycle (essentially (49b)) before the suffix *-ity* is added and j-Vocalization would not be able to apply on the third cycle after the addition of this suffix.

Palatalization is ordered after Velar Softening to account for alternations like those in (53).

(53)   electric   music   Greek
        electricity
        electrician   musician   Grecian

We derive *electrician* from /ɛlɛktɹɪk + jæn/. Velar Softening converts /k/ to /s/, feeding Palatalization, which turns /s/ to [ʃ].

7.4.3   Spirantization

There are alternations involving [t] and [s] in (54a). In addition, there appear to be instances of Palatalization where a stop [t] or [d] alternates with a fricative [ʃ] or [ʒ], respectively (54b, c), which seems contrary to the generalization that Palatalization does not affect the feature [continuant].

(54) a. [t]   [s]
           pirate   piracy
           secret   secrecy
           vacant   vacancy
           intricate intricacy
           delicate delicacy

      b. [t]   [ʃ]
           Egypt   Egyptian
           delete   deletion
           invent   invention
           part   partial
           exempt exemption

      c. [d]   [ʒ]
           decide   decision
           exclude exclusion
           invade   invasion
           explode explosion
           divide   division

The most straightforward approach is to propose a rule of Spirantization that converts /t/ to [s]. The examples in (54b) show that this change occurs before /j/, since the suffixes *-ian* and *-ion* have the underlying representations /jæn/ and /jən/, respectively. The phonetic [ʃ] then results from subsequent application of Palatalization. The examples in (54a) would seem to suggest that this change occurs before /i/ (or /ɪ/) as well. However, there are reasons to suppose that the change is conditioned by /j/ here also. One is that the change of /t/ to [s] or /d/ to [z] does not take place before suffixes whose underlying representations must begin with /ɪ/), such as *-ity* and *-ify*. That is, /t/ and /d/ are retained unchanged before these suffixes, as shown in (55).

(55)   sanctity, sanctify
         solidity, solidify

A second reason is that Trisyllabic Laxing does not take place in *piracy*, *secrecy*, *vacancy*. Trisyllabic Laxing would be expected to lax the vowel of the first syllable of these words if the final segment were a vowel in the underlying representation, which would then have two syllables following the first, just as do words like *sanity*, where Trisyllabic Laxing does take place. A third reason is the stress of *intricacy, delicacy,* which falls on the first syllable. Main stress on the fourth syllable from the end, followed by three unstressed syllables is an otherwise unattested stress pattern in English. It is not just a consequence of cyclic preservation of the stress of *intricate, delicate,* since the suffix +*y* cannot by itself support a foot. However, the stress of these words follows from the analysis of English stress in Chapter 4 without a hitch if the final orthographic <*y*> represents a glide /j/ in the underlying representation.[13] In fact, in Chapter 4 we saw instances of words with the suffixes -*ory*, -*ary*, where we assigned these suffixes an underlying final glide /j/ and a rule that vocalized this glide: Sonorant Syllabification, (68) in Chapter 4. Therefore, we assume that the suffix in *piracy* is a glide /j/ in underlying representation, and formulate Spirantization as in (56).

(56)   *Spirantization*

$$\begin{bmatrix} -\text{son} \\ +\text{cor} \end{bmatrix} \rightarrow \begin{bmatrix} +\text{cont} \\ +\text{strid} \end{bmatrix} / \left\{ \begin{matrix} [+\text{son}] \\ [-\text{cont}] \end{matrix} \right\} \underline{\quad\quad} j$$

The environment before the segment undergoing Spirantization requires either a [+son] or a [−cont] segment: this is to prevent Spirantization from occurring after a fricative. Therefore, there is no Spirantization in *digestion*, where /t/ is preceded by /s/, but there is Palatalization. In *piracy*, Spirantization takes place, since underlying /t/ is preceded by a sonorant (a vowel, in fact) and followed by /j/, after which *j* vocalizes. Here there is no Palatalization, because /j/ is not followed by a vowel. In *Egyptian*, there is Spirantization because /t/ is preceded by the [−cont] /p/ and followed by the /j/ of the suffix /jæn/. Palatalization also occurs because here *j* is followed by a vowel.

Spirantization does not apply in the context of *j* inserted by *j*-Insertion (12). This is shown in the examples of (57).

(57)   habit   habitual   [həˈbɪtʃuəl]   *[həˈbɪʃuəl]
        grade   gradual   [ˈɡɹædʒuəl]   *[ˈɡɹæʒuəl]

The most straightforward explanation is to order *j*-Insertion after Spirantization (counterfeeding). We summarize the orderings established in this subsection in (58).

---

[13] The stress of *democracy* and *hypocrisy* may be a problem for this analysis, if these are derived from *democrat, hypocrite.* We may assume that these words are exceptions to Syllable Extrametricality.

(58) ⎧ Spirantization
⎨ Sonorant Syllabification (68 of chapter 4)
⎪ *j*-Insertion
⎩ Palatalization

7.4.4   SPE *on* right *and* righteous

As stated in (56), Spirantization turns alveolar stops into the corresponding fricatives before *j* as long as the segment preceding the stop is not a fricative. This accounts for the contrast between *Egyptian*, where /t/ is spirantized and palatalized to [ʃ], and *digestion*, where /t/ is not spirantized because of the preceding fricative /s/, but palatalized to [ʧ]. In *righteous* we expect Spirantization to apply, given the underlying representation /ɹit + jɒs/, since /t/ is preceded by a sonorant (a vowel), but Spirantization does not apply; rather, we get Palatalization to [ʧ], as in *digestion*. How can we explain this?

SPE proposed an ingenious solution. Their underlying representation for *right* is /ɹɪxt/ rather than /ɹit/. For *righteous* they propose the underlying representation /ɹɪxt + ɪ + ɒs/,[14] with three syllables. They observe that the underlying representation /ɹit + ɪ + ɒs/ would be subject to Trisyllabic Laxing of the first vowel, just like the underlying representation /nitɪngæl/ for *nightingale* discussed in Section 6.2.1 of Chapter 6. Just as *nightingale* is derived from /nɪxtɪngæl/ in *SPE* by rules that convert the sequence /ɪx/ to /i/ ordered after Trisyllabic Laxing, *righteous* can be derived from /ɹɪxt + ɪ + ɒs/ by the same rules. These rules are also ordered after Spirantization, so that Spirantization is blocked by the fricative /x/ preceding /t/. Their proposed underlying representation therefore serves two functions: it blocks both Trisyllabic Laxing and Spirantization.

In Section 6.2.1 of Chapter 6 we argued against *SPE*'s solution for *nightingale* in light of Kiparsky's Strict Cycle Condition, which blocks the application of Trisyllabic Laxing to the more concrete underlying representation /nitɪngæl/, since it is an underived environment and Trisyllabic Laxing is a cyclic rule. We cannot take the same approach to *righteous*, however, since, under our analysis, Spirantization is not cyclic and the environment for the rule is derived in this case. However, if we adopt Rubach's underlying form /jɒs/ for the suffix, there is no longer an environment for Trisyllabic Laxing. However, there is still a context for

---

[14] We make certain symbol substitutions based on the transcription system used throughout the book. This does not affect the point under discussion.

Spirantization. The explanation for *nightingale* in terms of the Strict Cycle
Condition undermines support for an underlying /x/, a segment that does
not appear phonetically in English (at least in the principal dialects under
discussion) and for the rules that convert /ɪx/ to /i/.

Borowsky (1986: 53ff) suggests a solution in terms of underspecification (discussed in Chapter 1, Section 1.5.2). Segments that show an
alternation between *t* and *s* are unspecified underlyingly for the feature
[continuant]. She states Spirantization as a feature-filling rule that specifies
a segment [+continuant] in the environment of (56); otherwise it is
specified [–continuant] by a default rule. She explains the restriction that
the rule does not apply after a fricative in terms of the Obligatory Contour
Principle (OCP; Section 1.5.1 of Chapter 1). Specifying the segment
[+continuant] after another segment marked [+continuant] would violate
this principle. For *righteous*, she proposes that the final segment of *right* is
marked [–continuant]. Ordinarily, [continuant] would be left unspecified
for /t/ and filled in as [–cont] by default unless specified as [+continuant]
by a rule like Spirantization. But if it is specified [–cont], this cannot be
changed by Spirantization, interpreted as a feature-filling rule only. It is
possible that her analysis involves marking three distinct values for [con-
tinuant] in underlying representations in the same environment, namely
+, –, and o, violating general principles of underspecification theory (see
Section 1.5.2 of Chapter 1). Furthermore, Borowsky's analysis depends on
her assumption that Spirantization is cyclic. More generally, she suggests
that underspecification may provide a reanalysis of many effects attributed
to strict cyclicity. However, since we regard Spirantization as noncyclic,
such a reanalysis does not seem to be possible in our terms. We may simply
have to mark the morpheme *right* as an exception to Spirantization.

7.4.5 n-*Deletion*

Some morphemes in English end in the underlying sequence /mn/. This
sequence remains before vowel-initial stratum 1 suffixes but is simplified
by deletion of the final /n/ in other contexts. Thus we have alternations
such as (59).

(59) a. n *retained before*   b. n *deleted elsewhere*
          stratum 1 suffix   *(word-final, with stratum 2 affixes,*
                                         and in compounds)

          damn + ation   damn # ing
          damn + able   damn # s
                                         damn

hymn + al	hymn
hymn + ody	hymn # s
hymn + ology	hymn ## index
condemn + ation	condemn
	condemn # ing
solemn + ity	solemn, solemn#ly
autumn + al	autumn, autumn#like
column + ar	column, column#inch

We give the rule of *n*-Deletion in (60).

(60)   n-*Deletion*

$$n \rightarrow \emptyset \ / \ \begin{bmatrix} +\text{nasal} \\ -\text{cont} \end{bmatrix} \underline{\hspace{1cm}}]\!]$$

This rule deletes *n* when it follows a nasal and precedes a morphological bracket. This condition is met in underived words like *hymn* and in stratum 2 derivations like *hymn index*. As long as (60) is restricted to apply on stratum 2, it will not affect stratum 1 derivations like *hymnal* because Bracket Erasure ((24) in Chapter 6) removes the morphological bracket assigned on stratum 1 when the form moves into stratum 2.

Kiparsky (1985) argues that the Strict Cycle Condition (SCC), in the version he proposes in that paper and which we gave in (46) of Chapter 6, restricts *n*-Deletion to stratum 2, so that it is not necessary to state this stratum assignment in the grammar. We repeat this version of the SCC in (61).

(61)   *Strict Cycle Condition* (*SCC*; Kiparsky 1985: 89)
        If W is derived from a lexical entry W', where W' is nondistinct from
        XPAQY and distinct from XPBQY, then a rule A → B / XP____QY
        cannot apply to W until the word level.

For *damnation*, the lexical entry W' is ⟦damn⟧. On the first cycle on stratum 1, W is also ⟦damn⟧. W' is nondistinct from the structural description of (60), i.e., it contains the sequence [+nasal] n]], and is distinct from the structural change of (60), which specifies that there be only one nasal, so the SCC is applicable and (60) cannot apply on cycle 1. On the second cycle of stratum 1 we add *+ation*. W is now ⟦ ⟦damn⟧ ation⟧; W' is still ⟦damn⟧, and so still nondistinct from the structural description of (60) and distinct from its structural change, so (60) cannot apply on cycle 2. Once we move into stratum 2, Bracket Erasure has eliminated the brackets, giving ⟦damnation⟧, and (60) is no longer applicable. However, *damn*, *damning*, and the other examples in (59b) still have a bracket at stratum 2, so (60) can apply to these forms.

Another possible explanation for this distribution is syllabification. We could propose that morpheme-final *n* is realized only when it can be syllabified. The English Coda Condition, (63) in Chapter 3, does not allow *mn* as a coda. Morpheme-final *n* can be resyllabified as an onset at stratum 1 in words like *damnation*. Given our assumption that there is no resyllabification on stratum 2, the Coda Condition will prevent syllabifying *n* as an onset in *damning*. There are two flaws in this idea. One is that we have to permit a number of exceptions to the Coda Condition to allow words like *Arctic* and the suffix *+ation* (underlying representation /æt + jən/). The other is that a word-final coda *mn* may be permitted by the Maximal word-final syllable condition in (68) of Chapter 3; i.e. coda *m* plus coronal appendix *n*. So this explanation may not be available.

7.4.6   Prenasal g-Deletion

An alternation similar to that discussed in the previous subsection is shown in (62).

(62)   a. sign, signing   b. signature
            malign, maligning   malignant
            resign, resigning   resignation
            paradigm, paradigms   paradigmatic
            phlegm   phlegmatic
            diaphragm, diaphragms   diaphragmatic

In (62a) there is a (generally long) vowel followed by a morpheme-final nasal; in (62b) the same vowel appears short followed by /g/ and a nasal. We assume the underlying representation /sɪgn/ for *sign*. This sequence of segments remains in the derivative *signature* but is modified in *sign* itself by the rule of Prenasal *g*-Deletion, (63).

(63)   *Prenasal g-Deletion*
        g→ Ø / V ____ [+nasal]]

In addition to deleting the /g/, we need to create a long, tense vowel in all of (62a) except *phlegm* and *diaphragm*. In Halle and Mohanan's (1985: 96) analysis this lengthening is built into the statement of the rule. This lengthening of a vowel when a consonant is lost from a syllable coda is known as *compensatory lengthening*, and is quite common in the languages of the world. Ingria (1980) has proposed that, when an element is deleted from a syllable coda, its metrical structure is retained, to be reassociated

with the preceding syllabic nucleus, producing a long segment. We reformulate this in moraic terms in (64), part of what Ingria calls the Empty
Node Convention.

(64)

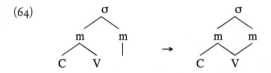

If this is accepted, we can leave Prenasal *g*-Deletion in its relatively simple
form (63). We assume that, along with lengthening, the vowel is specified
[+ATR]. This rule must precede Vowel Shift, since the lengthened vowel
in *sign* gets shifted. We must also somehow exempt *phlegm* and *diaphragm*
from lengthening. Since all the examples of lengthening involve /i/, *SPE*
(p. 234) suggests that (in our terms) compensatory lengthening accom-
panies (63) only with [+high] vowels.

Prenasal *g*-Deletion deletes the *g* in ⟦sign⟧ and ⟦ ⟦sign⟧ing ⟧, since in
both these forms the sequence *gn* appears before a boundary at stratum 2.
This is because the suffix *#ing* is added at stratum 2. In *signature*, the suffix
+ature is added at stratum 1, and Bracket Erasure erases the internal
brackets at the end of stratum 1. There is thus no boundary in *signature*
to condition Prenasal *g*-Deletion, which applies only on stratum 2. In fact,
this follows from Kiparsky's version of the Strict Cycle Condition (61) just
as in the case of *n*-Deletion.

As with *n*-Deletion, it may be possible to account for Prenasal
g-Deletion as a consequence of syllabification, with, however, the same
potential flaw.

7.4.7 Nasal Assimilation and Noncoronal Deletion

As we mentioned in Chapter 2, Section 2.2, the velar nasal [ŋ] is
somewhat marginal in English. While [m] and [n] can be clearly
motivated as underlying segments, this is not the case with [ŋ].
Accordingly, *SPE* derives all instances of velar nasals from underlying
sequences of [n] plus a velar obstruent. The voiceless stop [k] is
retained after assimilation, while the voiced [g] is deleted under certain
conditions. First, we need a rule of nasal assimilation. We formulate it
as in (65) on stratum 2. In accordance with underspecification theory
(Section 1.5.2 of Chapter 1), we can assume that some nasals are
unspecified for point of articulation in underlying representations. In

such cases, (65) operates in feature-filling mode; otherwise it acts to change feature specifications (cf. (42) in Chapter 6).[15]

(65)   *Nasal Assimilation*

$$[+\text{nasal}] \rightarrow \begin{bmatrix} \alpha\text{cor} \\ \beta\text{ant} \end{bmatrix} / [\ldots \underline{\quad} \begin{bmatrix} -\text{son} \\ \alpha\text{cor} \\ \beta\text{ant} \end{bmatrix} \ldots]_F \quad (\text{F is minimal})$$

Now we need a rule to delete the final *g* of *sing*. Halle and Mohanan (1985) propose a slightly more general rule, Noncoronal Deletion, that also deletes the final *b* of *bomb*, *iamb*. We give this rule in (66).

(66)   *Noncoronal Deletion* (Halle & Mohanan 1985: 96)

$$\begin{bmatrix} -\text{son} \\ -\text{cor} \\ +\text{voice} \end{bmatrix} \rightarrow \varnothing \;/\; [+\text{nasal}] \underline{\quad}]$$

Borowsky (1986) suggests that Noncoronal Deletion should be formulated as a syllable domain limit rule (in our terms). We give the syllable version of the rule in (67).

(67)   *Noncoronal Deletion* (Borowsky 1986)

$$\begin{bmatrix} -\text{son} \\ -\text{cor} \\ +\text{voice} \end{bmatrix} \rightarrow \varnothing \;/\; [+\text{nasal}] \underline{\quad}]_\sigma$$

In this formulation, the rule also accounts for the loss of /g/ in examples like (68).[16]

(68)   angma, anxiety, angstrom, gangway, orangutan

The only possible syllabification of *ang.ma* is as shown, since *gm* is not a possible onset. The /g/, being syllable final after a nasal, will then delete by (67). There is no justification for a morphological boundary here. Rule

---

[15] Nasal Assimilation on stratum 2 is a foot-domain rule. It applies only within the minimal foot. Observe that assimilation is obligatory in *cóngress* but optional in *congréssional*. For the latter, we assume that Nasal Assimilation can optionally apply postlexically ((63) in Chapter 5), where it is not confined to the foot domain. Postlexical assimilation is also not structure preserving: observe that *in France* can be pronounced [ɪɱ fɹæns]: the labiodental nasal [ɱ] is quite impossible in the Lexical Phonology.

[16] In *gangway* and *orangutan* we need to assume compound structures, whereas the others can be considered monomorphemic. *Gangway* is a compound of *gang* in the obsolete sense of 'passage.' *Orangutan* is derived from a compound in Malay; it is not clear that it retains this status in English.

(67) also accounts for deletion of /g/ in *singer* (69c), where *#er* is a stratum 2 affix, on our assumption that there is no resyllabification in conjunction with stratum 2 affixation,[17] thus the syllabification *sing.er*. Thus we prefer the syllable version of the rule on empirical grounds.

These rules account for only a few alternations, such as in (69a). In the case of *g*, the main motivation for the rules is the limited distribution of [ŋ]. Alternations involving *b* are shown in (69b). Some nonalternating forms that nevertheless undergo Nasal Assimilation and Noncoronal Deletion are given in (69c).

(69)   a. long   longer, longest, prolongation
           strong stronger, strongest

      b. bomb   bombard
          iamb   iambic

      c. sing   singer, singing
          bang   banger, banging
          song   songs

The reason that /g/ is deleted in *singer, singing* is that the suffixes *#er* and *#ing* are attached at stratum 2, and so /g/ appears before a syllable boundary (both *g*s in *singing*). Halle and Mohanan (1985: 63) suggest that the retention of stem-final *g* in *longer, longest, stronger, strongest*, is the result of irregularly attaching the suffixes *er, est* at stratum 1 in these forms. Bracket Erasure then prevents Noncoronal Deletion from affecting these words on stratum 2. This explanation is available with the syllable version of the rule (67) also – there is resyllabification on stratum 1, so with syllabifications like *lon.ger*, *g* will not be deleted.

7.4.8 h-Deletion

Another segment with restricted distribution is [h]. It has frequently been noted that [h] and [ŋ] are in complementary distribution – in our terms, [h] appears only at the beginning of a foot, while [ŋ] never occurs there.[18] In taxonomic phonology, the two segments were not considered to be members of the same phoneme due to their lack of phonetic similarity. In

[17] Resyllabification is necessary in conjunction with rules like *j*-Vocalization and ɛ-Elision that change the number of syllables in a word, but not simply as the result of affixation.
[18] Minkova (2014: 101) notes that /h/ can be retained in some borrowings where it is not (in our terms) foot initial, such as *maharaja, aloha*.

generative phonology, too, this complementarity appears to be accidental. We state the rule of *h*-Deletion in (70).

(70)   h-*Deletion*

$$\begin{bmatrix} h \\ -\text{tense} \end{bmatrix} \rightarrow \emptyset$$

There are very few alternations involving *h*; we list some in (71).

(71)   no [h]   [h]
        véhicle   vehícular
        pròhibítion   prohíbit
        níhilism   nihílity

SPE (p. 234) observed that [ŋ] occurs in a number of words where there is no overt velar obstruent and also where /g/ cannot have been deleted by (66) or (67). We list these in (72).

(72)   dinghy, hangar, gingham, Birmingham (West Midlands)

For these *SPE* suggests underlying representations with /x/, e.g., /dɪnxɪ/. Borowsky (1986: 69) suggests that these are derived from underlying representations containing the sequence /nh/, e.g., /dɪnhɪ/. Because /h/ is [–son, –ant, –cor], it, along with velar obstruents, causes a preceding nasal to become velar by the operation of (65). Subsequently, *h* is deleted by (70) because it is not foot-initial in these words.

7.4.9   Epenthesis and Voicing Assimilation

The regular plural suffix of English, a stratum 2 affix, has three phonologically predictable alternants (see exercise 2.4b in Chapter 2). We give a representative sample of forms in (73).

(73)   a.   [z]   b.   [ɪz]   c.   [s]
              cows   horses   cats
              hens   wishes   ducks
              dogs   hedges   cuffs

While there has been some dispute as to the underlying representation of this suffix, the most economical solution is to take it as /z/, with an epenthesis rule to derive the alternant in (73b) and a voicing assimilation rule to derive the alternant in (73c). Before we state the rules, we should note that the regular past tense suffix for verbs, another stratum 2 suffix, shows similar alternations, as shown in (74).

(74) a. [d]   b. [ɪd]   c. [t]
        banned   mended   walked
        buzzed   fitted   seeped
        cried   rusted   mashed

Epenthesis inserts the vowel [ɪ] between two coronal obstruents at a morphological boundary, where the second is voiced and the two segments agree in stridency – that is both are strident or both are nonstrident. We state the rule in (75).

(75) *Epenthesis*

$$\emptyset \rightarrow \text{ɪ} \; / \; \begin{bmatrix} -\text{son} \\ +\text{cor} \\ \alpha\text{strid} \end{bmatrix}] \; \_\_\_\_ \; \begin{bmatrix} -\text{son} \\ +\text{cor} \\ +\text{voice} \\ \alpha\text{strid} \end{bmatrix}]$$

The voicing assimilation seen in (73c) and (74c) is *progressive*: an underlyingly voiced segment is devoiced in assimilation to a preceding voiceless obstruent. There is also *regressive* voicing assimilation in certain verbs that undergo suffixation of /t/ at stratum 1 (see Section 6.2 of Chapter 6). Some examples are given in (76).

(76) leave   left   /lev+t/
        cleave cleft /klev+t/
        lose   lost   /lɔz+t/ (after Cluster Laxing on stratum 1;
                                  cf. Chapter 6; Footnote 25)
        bend   bent   /bɛnd+t/

In both the regular forms (73c, 74c) and the irregular forms (76), the voiced segment assimilates to the voiceless one. Halle and Mohanan (1985: 105) suggest a mirror image voicing assimilation rule, which we give in (77). A mirror image rule operates in both directions, and is indicated by using the percent sign (%) instead of the environment slash (/) of standard phonological rules. This rule is a domain span rule, where the domain is the foot.[19]

(77) *Voicing Assimilation*
        [–son] → [–voice] % [... ____ [–voice] ...]_F

This rule applies on both stratum 1 and stratum 2. On stratum 1 it is ordered before Degemination ((40) in Chapter 6) to account for forms like

---

[19] Halle and Mohanan (1985: 105) claim that the domain of this rule is the syllable, but it must be the foot, because obstruents of opposite voicing can appear at syllable boundaries across foot boundaries (e.g., *Áztèc*) but not between syllables belonging to the same foot (e.g., *áster*).

bent in (76) (feeding order). On stratum 2 the order Epenthesis before Voicing Assimilation is bleeding in examples like *fitted.*

7.5   Types of Rule Ordering

In Section 5.4 of Chapter 5 we defined a *feeding* order of rules as one in which one rule creates the condition for a subsequent rule to apply. There we noted that the ordering of Nasal Consonant Deletion before Flapping was a feeding order in the derivation of *winter.* In Section 6.4 of Chapter 6 we noted that the order of the Rhythm Rule before Medial Destressing is another feeding order in the derivation of *proclamation.* In Section 7.4.2 of this chapter we observed that the ordering of Velar Softening before Palatalization is a feeding order in derivations like *Grecian.* In each of these cases the application of the first rule creates the conditions for the application of the second rule, conditions which were not present before the first rule applied. Had Palatalization been ordered before Velar Softening, the former would not have been able to apply, and we would obtain the incorrect form *[gɹiɪsjən]. Therefore the rules must be applied in the order Velar Softening, then Palatalization.

In Section 5.4 of Chapter 5 we observed that the ordering of Flapping before Glottalization is a *bleeding* order in derivations like *great idea.* In a bleeding order, the first of two rules destroys the conditions for the operation of the second. An example in Section 7.4.9 is that Epenthesis bleeds Voicing Assimilation in derivations like *horses* and *fitted.*

An ordering relation is called *counterfeeding* if the second rule creates the conditions for the first to apply but the first is unable to apply because its turn has already come and gone. An example occurs in the derivation of *habitual,* in the order we established in (58).

(78)   start of stratum 2   /hæ'bɪt + ɨ + æl/
       Spirantization   — — —
       j-Insertion   j
       Palatalization   ʧ
       j-Deletion   Ø
       other rules (*i*-rounding, Vowel Reduction)   [hə'bɪʧʊəl]

Spirantization is not applicable to the initial form, because it affects *t* only when *j* follows. The next rule, *j*-Insertion, inserts *j* in the correct position to trigger Spirantization of the preceding *t*; however, Spirantization has been passed in the ordering, and so does not take place. Had *j*-Insertion been ordered before Spirantization, the latter rule could have applied. This would have been a feeding order and would have produced the incorrect result *[həˈbɪʃʊəl]. Therefore, we must apply the rules in the counterfeeding order given in (78). A counterfeeding order is therefore one where the reverse order would be feeding.

A *counterbleeding* order is defined analogously as one in which the reverse order would be bleeding. Consider Nasal Assimilation and Noncoronal Deletion, which must apply in that order in derivations of words like *sing*. In the reverse order, Noncoronal Deletion would bleed Nasal Assimilation, producing an incorrect *[sɪn] for *sing*. This would be a bleeding order. But the actual order is counterbleeding, since the reverse order would be bleeding.

Two rules in a particular order may exhibit both bleeding and counterbleeding properties, a situation known as *mutually bleeding*. Such a situation obtains with Poststress Destressing and Initial Destressing in derivations like *abracadabra*. Both rules are potentially applicable as the form enters stratum 2. Poststress Destressing is ordered first, and applies, bleeding Initial Destressing. But Initial Destressing, if it were ordered first, would apply, bleeding Poststress Destressing. This is therefore an example of mutual bleeding.

It is important to see that the same order of rules can have different feeding or bleeding relations in different derivations. A simple example is Velar Softening and Vowel Shift, which we have argued must apply in that order. Consider the derivations of *medicate* and *criticize* in (79). In *medicate*, Velar Softening isn't applicable, because the velar *k* is followed by a low vowel and Velar Softening affects velars only when they are followed by nonlow front vowels or glides. Vowel Shift subsequently changes the vowel to nonlow *e*; however, Velar Softening is no longer applicable. This is therefore a counterfeeding order – in the reverse order, Vowel Shift would feed Velar Softening.

(79)	start of stratum 2	/ˈmɛdɪˌk + æt/	/ˈkɹɪtɪˌk + iz/
	Velar Softening	— — —	s
	Vowel Shift	e	æ
	other rules	[ˈmɛdɪˌkeɪt]	[ˈkɹɪɾɪˌsɑɪz]

However, in *criticize*, Velar Softening is applicable to the initial form, changing *k* to *s*. Then Vowel Shift applies, changing the original high vowel *i* to a low vowel *æ*. This low vowel would block Velar Softening; however, Velar Softening has been passed (and has applied), and hence can no longer be blocked. Therefore, this is a counterbleeding order. In the theory of phonology we have been using, there is a single order of rules as part of the grammar.[20] The rules are applicable in this order to all

---

[20] However, we allowed for the possibility of lexically marked variation in ordering, such as we observed with Arab Destressing, Sonorant Destressing, and the Rhythm Rule in Section 4.6 of Chapter 4.

underlying representations. However, feeding and bleeding relations may differ from one derivation to another owing to the varied nature of the underlying representations.

7.6   Summary of Stratum 2 Rules

In (80) we give the ordered list of all the stratum 2 rules that have been discussed in this and previous chapters, with curved lines showing the crucial orderings.

(80)   Word Tree Construction for stratum 2 morphology (93 in chapter 4)

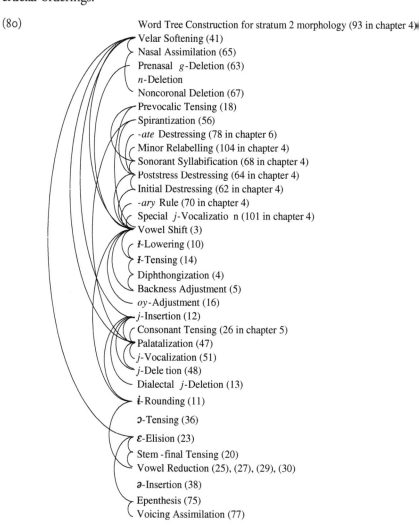

Velar Softening (41)
Nasal Assimilation (65)
Prenasal ɡ-Deletion (63)
n-Deletion
Noncoronal Deletion (67)
Prevocalic Tensing (18)
Spirantization (56)
-ate Destressing (78 in chapter 6)
Minor Relabelling (104 in chapter 4)
Sonorant Syllabification (68 in chapter 4)
Poststress Destressing (64 in chapter 4)
Initial Destressing (62 in chapter 4)
-ary Rule (70 in chapter 4)
Special j-Vocalizatio n (101 in chapter 4)
Vowel Shift (3)
ɪ-Lowering (10)
ɪ-Tensing (14)
Diphthongization (4)
Backness Adjustment (5)
oy-Adjustment (16)
j-Insertion (12)
Consonant Tensing (26 in chapter 5)
Palatalization (47)
j-Vocalization (51)
j-Dele tion (48)
Dialectal j-Deletion (13)
ɪ-Rounding (11)
ɔ-Tensing (36)
ɛ-Elision (23)
Stem -final Tensing (20)
Vowel Reduction (25), (27), (29), (30)
ə-Insertion (38)
Epenthesis (75)
Voicing Assimilation (77)

7.7 Exercises

7.1 Rule Application
Explain why the italicized portion of the word on the right does *not* undergo the corresponding rule on the left. If the form does not meet the structural description of the rule, state precisely why.

a.	Spirantization	diges*t*ion
b.	Prenasal *g*-Deletion	si*g*nature
c.	Palatalization	en*d*ure
d.	Spirantization	habi*t*ual
e.	*n*-Deletion	autum*n*al
f.	Velar Softening	dupli*c*ate

7.2 Derivations
Fill in the table showing how each form is affected by the rules listed in the left-hand column (segmental rules only).

UR of stem	/gɹæd/	/ɪnvit/	/mædʒɪk/
Input to stratum 2	/ˈgɹæd + ɨ + æl/	/ˌɪnvɪˈt + æt + jən/	/mæˈdʒɪk + jən/
Velar Softening			
Spirantization			
Vowel Shift			
Diphthongization			
j-Insertion			
Palatalization			
j-Deletion			
i-Rounding			
Vowel Reduction			
Output of stratum 2	[ ]	[ ]	[ ]

7.3 Alternations
Determine the underlying representations of the italicized vowels in the following words. State the rules (including stress rules) in the correct order to derive the phonetic forms of these vowels.

a. l*i*ne   l*i*near
b. ab*ou*nd   ab*u*ndant
c. f*u*me   f*u*migate
d. res*u*me   res*u*mption
e. harm*o*nious   harm*o*nic   (cf. *harmony*)
f. m*a*n*i*ac   m*a*n*i*acal

7.4 Types of Rule Interaction

The derivation of each word on the left demonstrates the ordering of the two rules on the right. Give the underlying representation of the italicized portion of each word and show how the rules must be ordered to derive the correct output. Classify the order as feeding, bleeding, counterfeeding, counterbleeding, or mutually bleeding.

a. ri*ng*   Nasal Assimilation (65)
                 Noncoronal Deletion (67)

b. classi*ci*ze Velar Softening (41)
                 Vowel Shift (3)

c. opti*ci*an   Velar Softening (41)
                 Palatalization (47)

d. ambig*uo*us *j*-Insertion (12)
                 i-Rounding (11)

e. wind*ow*   Stem-final Tensing (20)
                 Vowel Reduction (30)

f. even*tu*al   Spirantization (56)
                 j-Insertion (12)

g. deduc*e*   ɛ-Elision (23)
                 Vowel Reduction (29)

CHAPTER 8

Further Issues in Phonological Theory

8.1 Umlaut and Ablaut

In Chapter 6 we observed that irregular inflections were located on stratum 1, and that these included umlaut and ablaut. However, we concentrated our attention there on derivational morphology. It is now appropriate to return to inflections and the role of umlaut and ablaut in English, which are actually involved in derivations as well. In previous treatments of these phenomena in terms of Lexical Phonology (Kiparsky 1982; Halle & Mohanan 1985), umlaut and ablaut have been considered as phonological rules in modern English. This is inconsistent with the logic of the theory, according to which, inflectional forms are determined in the lexicon prior to their insertion in the syntax, as shown in the diagram of the model in Figure 1.1 of Chapter 1, so that umlaut and ablaut cannot be regarded as the phonological spelling out of syntactically determined categories. In fact, umlaut was originally phonological but became morphological with the loss of the phonological conditioning environment. Ablaut, however, has been morphological since Indo-European times. The distinction between phonological rules and morphological rules is entirely straightforward. A phonological rule effects a change in one or more phonological features in a phonological context without regard to meaning and without having any effect on the meaning.[1] A morphological rule is analogous to an affix in having a specific effect on both the phonological form and the meaning of an item.

Umlaut is a very old phenomenon in the Germanic languages, being attested as an historical change in all Germanic languages except Gothic. Originally it was a purely phonologically conditioned fronting of the vowel in a stem syllable under the influence of a front vowel or glide in a

---

[1] There may be some morphological conditioning, as in stress rules that depend on syntactic category, but there is no specific dependence on or effect on the meaning.

suffix. However, as attested in Old High German (OHG) and Old English (OE), the oldest Germanic languages where it is found, the phonological motivation for umlaut was lost, and the rule appears to have become a morphological one. A morphological rule is one that simultaneously changes the form of a morpheme and adds some element of meaning to it. Morphological rules are somewhat controversial, since there are few constraints on what changes of form can take place under the application of such rules. Bermúdez-Otero (2012: 44) in fact develops a theory in which "all morphology must be concatenative" while Anderson (1992) proposes that even the straightforward addition of a prefix or suffix is the result of a process. The intermediate position (e.g., Jensen 1990) reserves the term 'processes' for operations like infixation, reduplication, umlaut, and ablaut, which are difficult to characterize as simple affixation. For the purpose of the discussion in this chapter, we will assume a process formulation for such operations, retaining morpheme concatenation for cases where this can be done straightforwardly.

Umlaut is responsible for forming the plurals of seven irregular nouns in English, given in (1).

(1)	singular		plural		*underlying*
	man	['mæ̃n]	men	['mẽn]	/mæn/
	woman	['wʊ̃mə̃n]	women	['wɪmɪ̃n]	/wʊmæn/
	foot	['fʊt]	feet	['fiɪt]	/fʊt/ (/fot/)
	tooth	['tuwθ]	teeth	['tiɪθ]	/toθ/
	goose	['guws]	geese	['giɪs]	/gos/
	mouse	['mæws] ~ ['məws]	mice	['mɑɪs] ~ ['məɪs]	/mɪs/
	louse	['læws] ~ ['ləws]	lice	['lɑɪs] ~ ['ləɪs]	/lɪs/

The plurals in (1) can be derived from the singulars by the application of the morphological rule in (2), given in transformational format.

(2)   *Umlaut plural*
$$\llbracket_{N} \quad C \quad V \quad X \rrbracket$$
$$1 \quad 2 \quad 3 \quad 4 \quad \rightarrow \quad 1 \quad 2 \quad 3 \quad 4$$

$$\text{opt [+plural]} \quad \begin{bmatrix} -\text{back} \\ -\text{low} \\ -\text{round} \end{bmatrix}$$

This rule states that a noun undergoes a simultaneous change of syntactic category (to plural) and of the vowel following the initial conso-nant, which becomes nonback, nonlow, and nonround. The rule is optional, as indicated by 'opt' under the arrow: if it applies we get the plural, if not we get the singular. Only nouns specially marked for this morphological rule can undergo it (namely, the nouns in (1)). Two of the nouns in (1) have additional irregularities. In *foot*, the vowel also becomes [+ATR] in the plural (alternatively, we might assume that its vowel is underlyingly tense (/fot/) and that it undergoes laxing in the singular). In *woman*, both vowels appear to undergo umlaut. Since rule (2) is a rule of stratum 1 morphology, it necessarily applies before Vowel Shift, a phonological rule of stratum 2. Vowel Shift is responsible for the phonetic vowels in *tooth*, *teeth*, *goose*, *geese*, *mouse*, *mice*, *louse*, and *lice*, with Diphthong Shortening ((49) in Chapter 5) also having an effect (depending on dialect) in *mice*, *lice*, and, for some, in *mouse* [ˈmǝws] and *louse* [ˈlǝws].

Umlaut has a limited role in derivation also. Umlaut converts *food* to *feed* 'give food to' and perhaps *brood* to *breed*. Both *feed* and *breed* can undergo zero derivation to nouns on stratum 1, giving *feed* 'food for feeding livestock' and *breed* 'genetic type produced by breeding.' The verbs *feed* and *breed* both have their past tense formed at stratum 1: *fed*, *bred*. Hence they must be formed on stratum 1 themselves. Kiparsky (1982) mistakenly takes this for a counterexample to his claim that N→V→N formations are incompatible with his view of zero derivation, namely, that V→N zero derivation takes place on stratum 1 and N→V zero derivation takes place on stratum 2. However, the conversion of *food* to *feed* is not zero derivation, but umlaut, as we have just seen, and so is completely compatible with Kiparsky's claims about zero derivation.

Ablaut is an even older morphological phenomenon that appears in the oldest Indo-European languages. The system is clearest in Classical Greek. It involves the interchange of the vowels [ɛ] and [ɔ] with zero in certain verb tenses in Greek, of which we give an example in (3).

(3)   *present*   *perfect*   *aorist*   *gloss*
       ˈlɛɪpoː   ˈlɛlɔɪpa   ˈɛlɪpɔn   'leave' (first person singular)

In the present tense of the verb 'leave,' there appears the diphthong [ɛɪ]. In the perfect we have the diphthong [ɔɪ]. In the aorist we have the vowel [ɪ]. The constant in all these forms is the vowel [ɪ], which appears as a glide [ɪ̯] in the diphthongs. The variable is the Indo-European ablaut variation [ɛ] [ɔ], and zero. The various tenses also have prefixes and suffixes which are not part of our immediate concern.

As a consequence of a series of sound changes, this system changed in the Germanic languages. The chart in (4) summarizes these changes from Indo-European to modern English using the Indo-European root for 'ride.'[2]

(4)

	present	preterite singular	past participle
Proto-Indo-European	*reidh-	*roidh-	*ridh-
Proto-Germanic	*riːd-	*raid-	*rid-
Old English	riːdan	raːd	riden
Middle English	riːden	rɔːd	riden
Modern English	[ɹɑɪd]	[ɹowd]	[ɹɪdən]
	'ride'	'rode'	'ridden'

The modern English phonetic forms are derived from underlying representations that resemble the Middle English forms. It is evident that the historical forms have been reconstructed and that the Indo-European ablaut system is no longer synchronically operative in modern English. However, it is probable that there is some residue of the historical ablaut system in modern English irregular verb inflection, and the question is just what form this takes.

Halle and Mohanan (1985) propose a series of ablaut rules, and some additional rules, to account for the past tense and past participles of those verbs in modern English that are subject to ablaut. Their system suffers from a misconception, however. They claim that these ablaut (and other) rules are phonological rules that apply to verbs whose tense or participial status has already been determined by the syntax, following the conception in *SPE* phonology. But this is contrary to the logic of Lexical Phonology, the framework in which their article is cast, and also the framework of this book. In Lexical Phonology the phonological form of inflected forms is determined in the lexicon, *before* lexical items are arranged by the syntax. Accordingly, we will need to introduce certain modifications to their proposal. Chief among these is that the ablaut rules are *morphological* rules (like Umlaut, as in (2)), not phonological rules, and that the ablaut rules have stratum 1 as their domain, not stratum 2 as claimed by Halle and Mohanan. They argue that, as *phonological* rules, the Strict Cycle Condition ((46) in Chapter 6) could block the application of the ablaut rules to the apparently underived verb forms for which they are required. On our view that the ablaut rules are *morphological*, it is reasonable to assume that the Strict Cycle

[2] The Indo-European and Germanic forms are cited as roots only, in the form regularly used for reconstructed forms (i.e., not strictly phonetic transcriptions). The Old and Middle English forms have the infinitive suffix in the present column. The *-en* is a suffix in the past participle column for Old, Middle, and modern English. The modern English forms are given phonetically and orthographically.

Condition does not restrict the operation of morphological rules, and so it is possible to assign the ablaut rules to stratum 1 of the morphology, along with the other irregular inflections of English.

Let us start with perhaps the simplest example, the present and past tenses of the verbs in (5).

(5)

	present	past		present	past
a.	sit	sat	b.	eat	ate [eɪt]
	spit	spat		lie	lay
	bid	bade [bæd]	c.	choose	chose
	drink	drank			
	begin	began			
	ring	rang			
	shrink	shrank			
	sing	sang			
	sink	sank			
	spring	sprang			
	stink	stank			
	swim	swam			

In (5a) it is evident that the past tense is formed by replacing the (stressed) vowel of the present tense by a low vowel. The same is true of (5b, c) as long as ablaut is followed by Vowel Shift, as it must be according to the organization of the Lexical Phonology we assumed in Chapter 6. Ablaut is a morphological rule of stratum 1, while Vowel Shift is a phonological rule of stratum 2. We can formulate the required ablaut rule as in (6), retaining Halle and Mohanan's characterization of the rule as Lowering Ablaut, but formulating it as a morphological rule.

(6)   *Lowering Ablaut*
$$[_V \quad X \quad V \quad C_0]$$
$$1 \quad 2 \quad 3 \quad 4 \quad \rightarrow \quad 1 \quad 2 \quad 3 \quad 4$$
$$\text{opt} \quad [+\text{past}] \qquad [+\text{low}]$$

As a morphological process, Lowering Ablaut simultaneously changes the syntactic category of the verb to include the feature [+past] and converts its last vowel to [+low]. For (5b, c) we assume derivations such as those in (7), where the underlying representations for the present are those required in any event, given our arguments in Chapters 6 and 7 for the synchronic rule of Vowel Shift.[3]

---

[3] The British pronunciation [ɛt] for 'ate' is not the result of ablaut, but of stratum 1 affixation of *-t* followed by Cluster Laxing and Degemination, analogous to *bit* (from *bite*); cf. (38) in Chapter 6.

(7)

	'eat'	'lie'	'choose'
underlying	/et/	/li/	/ʧoz/
Lowering Ablaut	/æt/	/læ/	/ʧɒz/
Vowel Shift, etc.	[eɪt]	[leɪ]	[ʧowz]
	'ate'	'lay'	'chose'

A second ablaut rule is required for the verbs of (8).

(8)

		present	past		present	past
	a.	cling	clung	c.	get	got
		dig	dug		tread	trod
		fling	flung	d.	break	broke
		sling	slung		wake	woke
		slink	slunk	e.	wear	wore
		spin	spun		swear	swore
		spring	sprung		bear	bore
		stick	stuck		tear	tore
		sting	stung			
		win	won			
		wring	wrung			
	b.	bind	bound			
		find	found			
		grind	ground			
		wind	wound			

The verbs in (8) need a rule of Backing Ablaut. For (8a) the ablaut rule needs only to make the vowel [+back]. Underlying lax /ɪ/ is turned to /ɨ/, which undergoes ɨ-Lowering ((10) in Chapter 7) to become [ə], the correct phonetic vowel. In (8b) Backing Ablaut converts the underlying tense vowel /i/ to the corresponding back vowel /ɨ/ in the past. In both the present and the past, Vowel Shift and associated rules operate to produce the phonetic diphthongs [qɪ] in the present and [æw] in the past. In (8c, d, e) the underlying vowel is nonhigh, and the ablauted vowel is round (unlike the nonround vowels that result from ablaut in 8a, b). In (8c) it is simply a matter of adding the features [+back, +round] to the underlying vowel /ɛ/. This produces /ɔ/, which undergoes ɔ-Lowering ((9) in Chapter 7) to give the phonetic [ɒ] of British dialects, which is unrounded to [ɑ] in North American dialects by ɒ-Unrounding ((37) in Chapter 7). In (8d, e) underlying tense /æ/ is backed and rounded to /ɒ/. As with (8b), both present and past undergo Vowel Shift and associated rules to give the phonetic diphthongs [eɪ] and [ow], where the vowel quality is somewhat affected by the following [ɹ] in (8e).

Backing Ablaut is formulated as in (9) to give the past tense forms for all of (8). It makes the vowel back for all cases, and also makes the vowel round if the underlying vowel is nonhigh.

(9)   *Backing Ablaut*

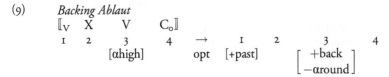

Lowering Ablaut (6) and Backing Ablaut (9) also are implicated in the derivation of past participles of some of these verbs. The situation is rather complicated. For example, *sit* has Lowering Ablaut for both the past tense and the past participle *sat*, while *drink* has Lowering Ablaut for the past *drank* and Backing Ablaut for the participle *drunk*. Under Halle and Mohanan's interpretation of these rules as phonological, it is simply necessary to mark certain past tenses and certain participles as undergoing the appropriate ablaut rules. Under our interpretation of these rules as morphological, it is necessary to have separate ablaut rules for the past tense and the participle. This would appear to be an unnecessary duplication but is unavoidable under the basic assumptions of Lexical Phonology and Morphology.

We next consider the past tense of the verbs in (10).

(10)

	present	past
a.	ride	rode
	drive	drove
	rise	rose
	smite	smote
	strive	strove
	thrive	throve
	write	wrote
	bide	bode
	dive	dove
	stride	strode
	shine	shone[4] [ʃown]
b.	cleave	clove
	freeze	froze
	heave	hove
	speak	spoke
	steal	stole
	weave	wove

---

[4] The pronunciation indicated is US. The British and Canadian pronunciation [ʃɒn] requires an additional laxing rule.

Halle and Mohanan propose that these verbs are subject to both Lowering Ablaut and Backing Ablaut, in that order, as shown in the sample derivations in (11). It should be noted that the synchronic derivation of *rode* is quite different from the historical derivation shown in (4).

(11) | underlying | /ɹid/ | /fɹez/ |
|---|---|---|
| Lowering Ablaut | ɹæd | fɹæz |
| Backing Ablaut | ɹɒd | fɹɒz |
| Vowel Shift, etc. | [ɹowd] | [fɹowz] |

There are two potential objections to this analysis. One is the need to order morphological processes according to this approach. While phonological rules are normally ordered, morphological processes are normally unordered, except for assignment to one of the two strata of the lexicon. The second objection, under our conception of ablaut as a morphological rather than phonological rule, is that two processes with the same meaning are applied to the same form. While double markings are not excluded in principle, they are rather rare in English. The doubly marked plural *feets* is one case that appears dialectically or in children's speech. The form *children* is historically doubly marked for plural (cf. Old English *cilderu* and the *-en* plural of *oxen*). Nevertheless, for the present, we waive these objections and consider this analysis to be basically correct.

Double marking of the past tense is also evident in the verbs of (12).

(12) | | *present* | *past* |
|---|---|---|
| a. | sell | sold |
| | tell | told |
| b. | shoot | shot |
| | lose | lost |
| c. | flee | fled |
| d. | shoe | shod |
| e. | see | saw |

In (12a) the past tense is formed by suffixing *-d* at stratum 1 and by Backing Ablaut. In order to account for the tense, diphthongized vowel in the past tense of these verbs, Halle and Mohanan postulate a special rule of ɔ-Lengthening, ordered after Vowel Shift but before Diphthongization. In our terms this would be a rule of ɔ-Tensing; we actually proposed such a rule in (36) of Chapter 7 to account for the failure of [ɔ] to appear phonetically in English except before [ɹ]. Halle and Mohanan (1985: 111) propose a much more specific rule (lengthening, for them), which we give in (13). This is a purely phonological rule, not morphological. We did not commit to a specific ordering for ɔ-Tensing in Chapter 7, but tentatively listed it after Diphthongization, since the *o* of *obey* is not diphthongized. For now we leave the questions open as to whether this is the same rule and what the ordering relations of the rules are.[5]

(13)   *ɔ-Tensing (Halle & Mohanan)*
        ɔ → [+ATR] / ____ lC

The form *shot* [ʃɒt] in (12b) is derived similarly to *lost*, except that the vowel of *shot* is lax, while that in *lost* is tense [ɒ:] in some US dialects. Halle and Mohanan claim that *shot* undergoes Lowering Ablaut, but this is clearly unnecessary, given that the vowel is laxed by Cluster Laxing ((39) in Chapter 6) and lowered by ɔ-Lowering ((9) in Chapter 7). We attributed the tenseness of the vowel in *lost* in US dialects to its having been lengthened Low Back Lengthening ((35) of Chapter 7), followed by *a/o*-Tensing ((34)of Chapter 7). We repeat Low Back Lengthening here as (14).

(14)   Low Back Lengthening

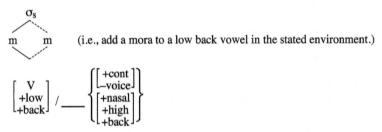

(i.e., add a mora to a low back vowel in the stated environment.)

Since the lengthening rule does not apply in *shot*, its vowel remains short and lax; it may, however, be unrounded by ɒ-Unrounding ((37) in Chapter 7) in those dialects that are subject to this rule.

The laxing of the vowel in the past tenses *fled* and *shod* is a consequence of a minor laxing rule which we give as (15). Halle and Mohanan attribute this laxing (shortening, for them) to a rule they call Shortening Ablaut. However, this cannot be an ablaut rule in our terms, since it is never solely responsible for the morphological categories in which it appears (i.e., there

[5] Halle and Mohanan (1985: 111) mistakenly assume that this rule is postlexical, but this is not possible even in their framework, since it is ordered before Diphthongization, which is on stratum 2. Given our reanalysis of the vowel system, we take it to be a tensing rule rather than a lengthening rule, as it is in Halle and Mohanan's treatment. In order for either version of ɔ-Tensing to apply in closed syllables, the forms involved would have to be marked as exceptions to ɔ-Lowering ((9) in Chapter 7) or else the required rule would have to be ordered before ɔ-Lowering.

is also the suffix +*d*). It is a strictly phonological rule, but a minor one, in that it applies only in specially marked lexical items. Clearly, laxing cannot be effected here by Cluster Laxing, as it is in *shot, lost, slept*, etc., because the addition of the suffix -*d* after a vowel in *fled, shod*, does not produce a cluster. Minor Laxing must be ordered before Vowel Shift; we will assume that it applies on stratum 1.

(15)   *Minor Laxing*
$$V \rightarrow [-ATR] / \underline{\quad} C_1 \begin{Bmatrix} \text{past tense} \\ \text{past participle} \end{Bmatrix}$$

Minor Laxing is also responsible for the lax vowel in the past participle of the verbs in (16).

(16)

present	past participle
write	written
drive	driven
ride	ridden
rise	risen
shrive	shriven
smite	smitten
strike	stricken
stride	stridden
strive	striven
thrive	thriven

The verbs in (17) lose their stem-final nonanterior consonant in the past tense, which is formed by affixation of -*t* at stratum 1 plus Backing Ablaut.

(17)

present	past
seek	sought
wreak	wrought
beseech	besought
teach	taught

Halle and Mohanan (1985: 106) propose a rule of *x*-Formation, which converts the stem-final consonant to the velar fricative /x/, which is later deleted, building on the *SPE* analysis with underlying /x/ in certain words, which is converted to [h] in syllable onsets and deleted elsewhere. In Section 6.2.1 of Chapter 6 and in Section 7.4.4 of Chapter 7 we argued against the underlying /x/ in *SPE*'s analysis of *nightingale* and *right*. We could, however, retain the essence of Halle and Mohanan's analysis of (17) by changing the nonanterior consonant to /h/ rather than to /x/, since we also have a rule that deletes *h* (*h*-Deletion, (70) in Chapter 7). We give our version of this rule in (18).

(18)   h-*Formation*

$$\begin{bmatrix} -\text{son} \\ -\text{ant} \end{bmatrix} \rightarrow h \; / \; \underline{\hspace{1cm}} \;] \; t \;]$$

H-Formation is assigned to stratum 1, where it precedes Cluster Laxing. By way of illustration, we give the derivation of *sought* in (19).

(19)   underlying   /sek/
       stratum 1
         Morphology
           /+t/ affixation and Backing Ablaut   /sok+t/
         Phonology
           h-formation   /soh+t/
           Cluster Laxing   /sɔh+t/
       Postlexical Phonology
           ɔ-Lowering   /sɒht/
           Low Back Lengthening   /sɒ:ht/
           a/o-Tensing   /sɒ̞:ht/
           h-Deletion   [sɒ̞:t]

In (20) we have some additional verbs that illustrate these rules, although one additional rule is needed for *thought*.

(20)   *present*   *past*   *underlying*
       a.   see   saw   /se/
       b.   buy   bought   /bi/
       c.   think   thought   /θɪnk/
       d.   fight   fought   /fit/

The present tense *see* [siɪ] is derived straightforwardly from underlying /se/ by Vowel Shift and Diphthongization. The past is derived by Lowering Ablaut, Backing Ablaut, Minor Laxing, and *a/o*-Tensing. The past *bought* requires +*t* affixation, Lowering Ablaut, Backing Ablaut, and Minor Laxing.[6] For *fought*, Cluster Laxing applies instead of Minor Laxing. For *thought*, we adopt Halle and Mohanan's suggestion of a rule of Nasal Deletion, (21). This rule is also assigned to stratum 1.

(21)   *Nasal Deletion* (Halle & Mohanan 1985: 109)

$$[+\text{nasal}] \rightarrow \varnothing \; / \; \underline{\hspace{1cm}} \begin{bmatrix} +\text{cons} \\ -\text{ant} \end{bmatrix}] \; t \;]$$

---

[6] A possible alternative for *bought* is to propose the underlying representations /bih/, with an underlying final /h/. The laxing in the past tense is then brought about by Cluster Laxing, as in *sought*. This is in fact Halle and Mohanan's proposal (with /x/ in place of our /h/). They also propose an underlying /x/ in *fight*,, which, however, is not necessary in our analysis.

Thought also requires a triple marking for past tense, with the suffix +*t*, Lowering Ablaut, and Backing Ablaut.

The two verbs in (22) require no new rules, although superficially they look rather different from those considered so far. In fact, they simply require the application of rules motivated for other alternations.

(22)   *present*   *past*   *underlying*
    a.   fly   flew   /fli/
    b.   strike   struck   /strik/

In both verbs of (22), we assume that Backing Ablaut derives the past tense and that Minor Laxing is applicable. This derives the vowel /ɨ/ in both cases. In *flew*, this vowel is in an open syllable, and so subject to *ɨ*-Tensing, Diphthongization, and *i*-Rounding, emerging as [uw]. In *struck*, this same vowel is in a closed syllable, and so subject to *ɨ*-Lowering, producing [ə].

Halle and Mohanan continue their discussion with a group of verbs which we list in (23).

(23)   *present*   *past*
    a.   fall   fell
    b.   hold   held
    c.   shake   shook
           take   took
           forsake   forsook
    d.   run   ran
           come   came
           give   gave
           slay   slew
           catch   caught
    e.   say   said
    f.   blow   blew
           crow   crew
           grow   grew
           know   knew
           throw   threw
    g.   draw   drew

In Halle and Mohanan's discussion, the verbs in (23) all have the characteristic of being subject to an ablaut rule in the present tense. For example, *run* is given the underlying representation /ɹɨn/, and is subject to Backing Ablaut in the present tense (giving /ɹʌn/), which then becomes [ɹən] by *ɨ*-Lowering. In the past tense it is subject to Lowering Ablaut, giving [ɹæn] directly. While extremely ingenious, this solution suffers from a fatal flaw in terms of the theory of Lexical Phonology, which is that ablaut rules should properly speaking be morphological rules, and therefore associated with a change in category. We cannot, therefore, allow present-tense forms to be generated by a rule such as Backing Ablaut (9), which specifically entails the change in syntactic category to [+past] or participle. We therefore suggest that the correct approach to (23), that is consistent with the theory of Lexical Phonology, is allomorphy: i.e., the present- and past-tense forms simply have different underlying representations.[7]

8.2   Affix Order and Bracketing Paradoxes

A major claim of Lexical Morphology and Phonology, as presented in Chapter 6, is that the morphological operations of a given stratum are unordered with respect to each other, governed only by subcategorization requirements, while the lexical operations of stratum 1 are strictly ordered before those of stratum 2. For English, this means that stratum 1 morphology can never follow stratum 2 morphology. This view has been challenged in two ways. On the one hand, there seem to be a limited number of cases of stratum 2 morphology preceding stratum 1 morphology. On the other hand, Fabb (1988) claims that subcategorization alone predicts most of the relevant morphological operations, and that stratum ordering actually has relatively little effect on the morphology, although it is needed for phonology. We will look at each of these questions in turn.

8.2.1   Apparent Violations of Stratum-Ordered Affixation

Since there are two lexical strata in English, and both prefixes and suffixes, there are four possible ways in which there could be violations of the predictions of stratum ordering. Kiparsky (1983) considers each of these, which we list in (24).

(24)   a.   [[stem # suffix$_2$] + suffix$_1$]   *national#ism+ous
        b.   [prefix$_1$ + [prefix$_2$ # stem]]   *in+anti#religious
        c.   [prefix$_1$ + [stem # suffix$_2$]]   *in+success#ful
        d.   [[prefix$_2$ # stem] + suffix$_1$]   *un#equal+ize

---

[7] It may be possible to motivate a solution in terms of umlaut for *fell*, from underlying /ɔ/. In view of the small number of forms involved, it is not clear that this would be better than the allomorphy solution.

For the most part, the predictions of stratum-ordered morphology are correct, as shown by the ungrammaticality of the words in the rightmost column of (24). In two cases, (24b, c), the predictions of stratum ordering have no exceptions whatever. That is, there are no examples of a stratum 1 prefix preceding a stratum 2 prefix before a stem, as in *inantireligious. There are also no examples of a stratum 1 prefix added to a word previously derived with a stratum 2 suffix, as in *insuccessful. The cases with a prefix and a suffix need to be considered with especial care, since the stratum 1 affix might be added before the stratum 2 affix. In the case at hand, we might have the prefix in- added to the stem success prior to the addition of the suffix #ful, which would be in accord with stratum ordering. However, subcategorization requires that in+ is added to adjectives, not to nouns, and so it cannot have been added to the noun success. Therefore, the only possible derivation of *insuccessful is one where #ful is added prior to adding in+, but this order of affixation is excluded by stratum ordering.

There appear to be a few counterexamples to the type in (24a), where a stratum 2 suffix appears before a stratum 1 suffix. We list these in (25). In each case Kiparsky suggests a reanalysis that is compatible with stratum ordering.

(25)   a.   govern#ment+al
          b.   national#ist+ic
              relativ#ist+ic
              ideal#ist+ic
              cannibal#ist+ic
              character#ist+ic
          c.   analyz#abil+ity
          d.   bapt#ism+al
              exorc#ism+al
              catech#ism+al

For governmental, Aronoff (1976: 54) notes that the word government is ambiguous. It can mean either '(act of) governing' or 'ruling authority.' The derivative governmental can refer only to the latter meaning. Kiparsky suggests that +ment in such cases is attached at stratum 1, and so there is no violation of stratum ordering.[8]

[8] This proposal may entail a problem with stress assignment, since government would undergo a second cycle of stress on stratum 1, producing *govérnment.

For *nationalistic,* Aronoff (1976: 118) notes that many words in (25b) do not have a base in *-ist,* e.g., **cannibalist.* Kiparsky suggests analyzing *+istic* as a unitary suffix in these cases.⁹

For *analyzability,* Kiparsky suggests that *-able* is added on stratum 1 in such cases. In fact, Aronoff (1976: 121–129) shows that there are two suffixes of this phonological shape, one on stratum 1 and the other on stratum 2. We will summarize his discussion in Section 8.2.3.

For *baptismal,* Kiparsky argues that these do not contain stratum 2 #ism at all. Aronoff (1976: 57) notes that +al does not attach to #ism when the latter is truly the stratum 2 suffix, as in (26).

(26)   *dogmat#ism+al
        *fatal#ism+al

In *baptism,* *bapt-* is a bound stem, suggesting that *baptism* must be formed on stratum 1, given that stratum 2 affixes do not normally attach to bound stems.¹⁰ Kiparsky suggests that *baptism* is derived from *bapt+ize* by a suffix *+m,* both suffixes being from stratum 1. This *+m* appears in *poe+m, spas+m, plas+m.* Cluster Laxing will apply in *bapt+ize+m.*

The final type of violation, (24d), is perhaps the most interesting; it has certainly created a lot of controversy. Like (24c), identifying examples in this category requires reference to constituent structure and the semantics of the affixes involved. However, there are no examples of the type in (24c). Examples of the type in (24d) are fairly abundant, although there are also many examples such as **unequalize* that do not exist. Kiparsky notes that there are examples of this type involving every stratum 2 prefix in combination with many stratum 1 suffixes, and that there are many additional examples with compounds and with lexicalized phrases. We give his examples in (27).

---

⁹ Kiparsky suggests that the suffix is added on stratum 1. It may have to be on stratum 2 because of *characteristic.* The stress of *cháracter* shows that the underlying representation has final /1/, with no vowel between the final two consonants. But the appearance of the vowel in *characteristic* shows that the stratum 2 rule of Sonorant Syllabification ((67) in Chapter 4) has applied, which it could not have done if the bracket after *character* had been erased in *characteristic,* as would necessarily occur if it were derived on stratum 1.

¹⁰ It could be objected that *dogmat-* in *dogmatism* is also a bound stem; however, it is more likely simply the allomorph of *dogma* that appears before certain suffixes (cf. *dogmatic*).

(27)   a.   *stratum 2 prefixes*
            ungrammaticality   bilaterality
            untruth   extraterritoriality
            prefabrication   hydroelectricity
            renegotiable   archducal
            reburial[11]   microparasitic
            polysyllabicity   vice consulate
            extrametricality   vice presidential
            nondenumerability   self consistency

       b.   *compounds*
            set theoretical   wind instrumental
            root parasitic   cross sectional
            twenty fifth   lord mayoral
            folk etymological   lieutenant colonelcy

       c.   *lexicalized phrases*
            three dimensional   double helical

In some sense, such words represent a blend of two existing words. That is, *ungrammaticality* is a blend of the words *ungrammatical* and *grammaticality*. However, not all such blends are well formed; there are no words such as those in (28).

(28)   *unequalize   *symphony orchestrate
       *nonfictionalize   *music departmental
       *anti-Americanize   *outboard motorize
       *chair personify   *freak accidental
       *sheet metallic   *white elephantine
       *witch doctoral

Kiparsky discusses a number of possible solutions to this question, all of which involve weakening the lexical theory of morphology. For example, Selkirk (1982a: 101) proposes that prefixes like *un-* can belong to both stratum 1 and stratum 2. This is unfortunate because there are no instances, apart from figuring in the formation of words like *ungrammaticality*, in which *un-* behaves as a stratum 1 prefix. The absence of words like (24b) indicates that stratum 2 prefixes cannot follow stratum 1 prefixes. Stratum 2 prefixes can appear in both mutual orders (*reoutwit,*

---

[11] In our analysis, noun-forming *#al* is on stratum 2 (Section 6.1.2 of Chapter 6), so this example may not be appropriate.

outreanalyze) and cannot occur with bound roots *(*anticeive, *misgest)*.[12] Stratum 2 prefixes do not undergo *n*-Assimilation *(*ullimited, *norrenewable)* or destressing and Vowel Reduction, nor do they condition Fricative Voicing: compare *re#sign* [ˌɹiˈsaɪn] 'sign again' with *re+sign* [ɹɪˈzaɪn] 'quit.' Only stratum 2 prefixes allow *gapping*, that is factoring out a common stem in conjunction in examples like *pre- and post-war, over- and underestimate*. This is true even in cases where Selkirk would analyze them as stratum 1 in order to allow cases like (27), as in *mono- and polysyllabicity, bi- and multilaterality, over- and underestimation*. Dual membership of such prefixes would ignore these generalizations.

More generally, the proposal that these prefixes have dual membership leaves a number of generalizations unexplained. One is that the stem +suffix combination is always an actual word (e.g., *grammaticality*). This might not be the case under Selkirk's proposal, since stratum 1 prefixes can attach to bound stems. Second, recall Kiparsky's claim that all stratum 2 prefixes can combine with many stratum 1 suffixes. Selkirk (1982a: 102–103) in fact claims that three stratum 2 prefixes, *ex-, step-,* and *non-,* do not have this property, on the basis of examples like **ex#patriot+ic, *non#exempl+ify,* but Kiparsky suggests that these too are included, citing *exterritoriality, step-parental, noncompositionality*. Finally, the fact that compounds and lexicalized phrases behave the same way causes difficulties. Either they have to be treated in an entirely different manner, or else compounding and phrases have to have stratum 1 status also, greatly weakening the claims of the theory.

Kiparsky proposes an ingenious solution that retains the basic premises of Lexical Morphology and rejects dual membership. His proposal is first to allow certain forms to be exceptions to Bracket Erasure ((24) in Chapter 6). The second part is to allow reanalysis, subject to the requirement that subcategorization requirements be met at every stratum. For example, *ungrammaticality* is derived as in (29), starting from a point after the attachment of +*ic* and +*al*.

(29)   stratum 1   [[grammatical]]ₐ + ity]ₙ   suffix +*ity*
        stratum 2   [un#[[grammatical]]ₐ + ity]ₙ]ₙ   brackets retained; prefix *un#*
                    [[un#[grammatical]]ₐ]ₐ + ity]ₙ   reanalyzed

The reanalysis is permitted since +*ity* is still attached to an adjective and moreover is forced by the requirement that *un#* be attached to an adjective

---

[12] As discussed in Section 6.1.1 of Chapter 6, there are a few exceptions such as *unkempt, ruthless, grateful, gruesome*. Cf. Giegerich (1999: 50).

(not a noun). No reanalysis is possible if there are two prefixes (24b *inantireligious*) or two suffixes (24a *nationalismous*). Hence, these types cannot be generated by the mechanism illustrated in (29). Other apparent examples of blends (*denatural, *deforestry, *degaseous*) are also underivable. This is shown in (30). Reanalysis is excluded because +*al* would thereby be attached to a verb after reanalysis, whereas its subcategorization requires it to be attached to a noun.

(30)   stratum 1 $[[\text{nature}]_N+\text{al}]_A$ suffix +al
        stratum 2 $[\text{de\#}[[\text{nature}]_N+\text{al}]_A]_V$ brackets retained; prefix de#
                     $*[[\text{de\#}[\text{nature}]_N]_V +\text{al}]_A$ no reanalysis possible

Examples like (24c) are excluded because the stratum 1 prefix *in*+ can only be added to adjectives, not nouns, so the output of stratum 1 (**insuccess*) is not a possible lexical item.[13] Cases like this might be derived that were the exact mirror image of *ungrammaticality*, that is, with a category-changing prefix and a non–category-changing suffix. The only prefixes that could work are *be*+ and *en*+, which change nouns into verbs, as in (31a).

(31)   a   becloud, behead
             empower, enthrone
        b.   *besanity, *empressure
        c.   *emMarxist, *enkingdom

However, Kiparsky suggests that the prefixes *be*+ and *en*+ attach only to underived nouns, as shown by the ungrammaticality of the examples in (31b), formed with stratum 1 suffixes, and of (31c), with stratum 2 suffixes, since reanalysis would result in these prefixes being attached to derived nouns on stratum 2. Examples like (24d) are relatively common because nearly all stratum 2 prefixes are non–category changing, and so permit reanalysis.

The proposal to derive a limited set of violations of type (24d) as in (29) localizes the idiosyncrasy of these forms. That *ungrammaticality* is possible is a fact about *grammaticality*, or about the suffix +*ity*, rather than a fact about *un#*. In other words, *grammaticality* can occur reanalyzed with other stratum 2 prefixes, as in *semigrammaticality*, but *ungrammatical* cannot necessarily occur with other stratum 1 suffixes, so we do not have **ungrammaticalize*. Kiparsky suggests that such reanalysis is possible with +*ity*, +*ic* (*al*), +*ation*, but rare or impossible with +*ize*, +*ify*, +*ous*, +*atory*.

---

[13] Kiparsky claims that these cases also show the need for subcategorization requirements to be met before reanalysis. However, this is not the case with (29) when *un#* is first added: it is initially added to a noun.

8.2.2 Subcategorization and Stratum Ordering

Fabb (1988) claims that stratum ordering is not actually necessary to account for the ordering of suffixes in English. He does not consider all suffixes, and he doesn't discuss prefixes at all. Nevertheless, he makes some interesting observations. A major finding is that many English suffixes can only be attached to underived stems, similar to the prefixes *be+* and *en+* discussed in the previous subsection. We give his list of suffixes with this property in (32), reorganized into strata.

(32)   Suffixes that attach only to underived items (Fabb 1988)
Stratum 1

noun-forming +*an*	librarian
adjective-forming +*(i)an*	reptilian
noun-forming +*ant*	defendant
adjective-forming +*ant*	defiant
+*ance*	annoyance
+*ate*	originate
denominal +*ify*	classify
deadjectival +*ify*	intensify
+*ive*	restrictive
denominal +*ize*	symbolize[14]
+*ory*	advisory
+*ous*	spacious

Stratum 2

deverbal #*age*	steerage
denominal #*age*	orphanage
denominal #*ed*	moneyed
denominal #*ful*	peaceful
deverbal #*ful*	forgetful
#*hood*	nationhood
#*ish*	boyish
denominal #*ism*	despotism
denominal #*ist*	methodist
deadjectival #*ly*	deadly
#*ment*	containment
adjective-forming #*y*	hearty

Thus, Fabb would exclude *national#ism+ous* (24a) not by virtue of stratum ordering, which disallows a stratum 1 affix being added outside a stratum 2 affix, but by restricting +*ous* so that it does not attach to any already suffixed form, whether at stratum 1 or stratum 2. This claim seems

---

[14] Fabb mistakenly regards +*ize* as a stratum 2 suffix.

to be borne out in the lists in Walker (1936), with the single exception (which Fabb notes) of *differ-ent-iate*, where -*ate* is added to an adjective derived with the suffix -*ent*. There are a few anomalies in this list, however. One is that certain suffixes are split into two. For example, Fabb considers #*ism* as two suffixes, one of which is added to adjectives, as in *modernism*, and the other of which is added to nouns, as in *despotism*. The same division is made for #*ist*. The denominal versions of these suffixes appear to attach only to unsuffixed nouns, but the deadjectival ones attach fairly freely to derived nouns, as in *commercialism, classicism, classicist*. Similarly with +*ize*: when denominal, it adds only to unsuffixed nouns *(symbolize)*, but when deadjectival it adds freely to derived adjectives, as in *classicize, naturalize*. Nevertheless, this restriction is also a problem for stratum-ordered morphology, especially with respect to the stratum 2 suffixes. While there is no problem, in principle, for subcategorization to require that the base of affixation be nonderived, a stratum 2 suffix with this restriction should nevertheless be able to add to a form derived on stratum 1, because of bracket erasure ((24) in Chapter 6). Recall that Kiparsky made crucial use of this concept in zero derivation, discussed in Section 6.1.3 of Chapter 6. That is, it is possible to add a zero suffix to the noun *pressure* (derived by adding the stratum 1 suffix +*ure*) to obtain the verb *to pressure* on stratum 2, because the internal bracket has been eliminated. With a stratum 2 suffix, such as #*er*, we cannot add a zero suffix to form a derived verb (*to singer). Only in the latter case is the internal bracket visible to the process of zero derivation. Fabb notes this problem but offers no solution for it. As he acknowledges, the phonological effects we attributed to affixes of the two strata are valid in any case. At most, Fabb's discussion requires us to state additional restrictions on certain affixes; it does not entail wholesale abandonment of stratum ordering in morphology and phonology.

8.2.3   Two Suffixes -able

Aronoff (1976: 121–129) makes a convincing case for the suffix -*able* as (in our terms) being located on both stratum 1 and stratum 2, or, equivalently, as being two separate suffixes. There is a considerable convergence of phonological, morphological, and semantic evidence for this division. Thus, these suffixes nicely illustrate the principles of Lexical Phonology and Morphology.

One type of evidence is the existence of minimal pairs; that is, where both suffixes can be attached to the same stem. Aronoff cites the pairs in (33).

The stress may shift with the stratum 1 version of the suffix, but not with the stratum 2 version.[15]

(33)

+*able*	#*able*	*stem*
cómpar+able	compár#able	compáre
répar+able	repaír#able	repaír
préfer+able	prefér#able	prefér
dísput+able	dispút#able	dispúte

The stratum 1 +*able* may attach to an allomorph of the stem, as shown in (34). The stratum 2 #*able* always attaches to the free form of the stem.

(34)

+*able*	#*able*	*stem*
circumscript+able	circumscrib#able	circumscribe
extens+ible	extend#able	extend
defens+ible	defend#able	defend
percept+ible	perceiv#able	perceive
divis+ible	divid#able	divide
deris+ible	derid#able	deride

A related property is that stratum 1 +*able* attaches to bound stems, which is not possible for stratum 2 #*able*. Stratum 2 #able can be attached to a full word derived from a bound stem plus another suffix, shown in (35) with the suffix +*ate*.

(35)

+*able*	#*able*	*stem*
deline+able		deline+ate
toler+able	tolerat#able	toler+ate
negoti+able		negoti+ate
vindic+able		vindic+ate
demonstr+able		demonstr+ate
exculp+able		exculp+ate
cultiv+able	cultivat#able	cultiv+ate
communic+able	communicat#able	communic+ate
poss+ible		
vulner+able		
horr+ible		

The stratum 2 negative prefix *un#* tends to go with words derived by stratum 2 #*able*, while the stratum 1 negative prefix *in+* tends to go with words derived by stratum 1 +*able*. Stratum ordering actually only predicts the impossibility of *in+* prefixed to words derived on stratum 2.

---

[15] With the underlying representation /əbɪl/, the stress of the +*able* column is derived by assuming that these forms are subject to Minor Relabelling, (104) in Chapter 4.

Nevertheless, the tendency for both prefix and suffix to be of the same stratum is fairly strong, as shown in (36).

(36) | *in+...+able* | *un#...#able* | *un#...+able* |
|---|---|---|
| impossible | | *unpossible |
| impalpable | | *unpalpable |
| irregulable | | *unregulable |
| | unregulatable | *irregulatable |
| inviolable | unviolatable | *inviolatable, *unviolable |

Similarly, the negative prefix *in+* is attached to words showing stem allomorphy, while *un#* is attached to words derived from the basic stem as in (37).

(37) imperceptible (*unperceptible)   unperceivable (*imperceivable)
      indivisible (*undivisible)   undividable (*individable)

The negative prefix *in+* likewise goes with words whose stress shifts with *+able* suffixation, while *un#* goes with words whose stress is unshifted with *#able* suffixation.

(38) irréparable (*unréparable)   unrepaírable (*irrepaírable)
      irrévocable (*unrévocable)   unrevókable (*irrevókable)

There are a couple of counterexamples to the claim that allomorphs, where available, appear with stratum 1 derivation. These are shown in (39).

(39) in+conceiv+able (*inconceptible)
      in+describ+able (*indescriptable)

Semantically, the stratum 2 suffix *#able* is more compositional, in that the meaning of words derived with this suffix is more predictable. Words derived with stratum 1 *+able* often have an idiosyncratic, unpredictable meaning, either in addition to or to the exclusion of the compositional meaning, as shown in (40).

(40)   *+able*   *#able*
   a. cómpar+able   compár#able
       'capable of being compared'   'capable of being compared'
       also 'roughly equivalent'

       The two models are simply not $\left\{ \begin{array}{l} \text{compárable} \\ \text{cómparable} \end{array} \right\}$.

       This is the $\left\{ \begin{array}{l} \text{*compárable} \\ \text{cómparable} \end{array} \right\}$ model in our line.

b. tóler+able   tolerat#able
   'capable of being tolerated'   'capable of being tolerated'
   also 'moderately good, fair'

   We had a $\left\{ \begin{array}{c} \text{tólerable} \\ *\text{toleratable} \end{array} \right\}$ lunch today.

   How are you feeling today? $\left\{ \begin{array}{c} \text{tólerable} \\ *\text{toleratable} \end{array} \right\}$.

c. appreciable   appreciat#able
   'capable of being appreciated'   'capable of being appreciated'
   also 'substantial'

   An $\left\{ \begin{array}{c} \text{appreciable} \\ *\text{appreciatable} \end{array} \right\}$ majority favoured the plan.

d. percept+ible   perceiv#able
   'capable of being perceived'   'capable of being perceived'
   also 'large enough to matter'
   There is a perceptible difference in quality.

e. imperceptible   unperceivable
   'incapable of being perceived'   'incapable of being perceived'
   also 'insignificant'

   There is a flaw in the gem but it's $\left\{ \begin{array}{c} \text{imperceptible} \\ *\text{unperceivable} \end{array} \right\}$.

Thus, there is a fair amount of evidence for both a stratum 1 *+able* and a stratum 2 *#able*. The existence of such affixes is clearly consistent with the theory of Lexical Phonology and Morphology, but the theory would be seriously weakened if many affixes showed similar behaviour. There have been a number of claims to this effect in the literature, of which Giegerich (1999) is representative. We do not have space to do justice to all the complex issues involved, but it is necessary to base any judgements on an in-depth phonological analysis, rather than on possibly misleading appearances. To give just one example where I think Giegerich is on the wrong track, he discusses the suffix *-ant/-ent* (largely following Szpyra 1989) in words such as (41).

(41) | *stress shifting and laxing* | | *stress neutral, no laxing* | |
      |---|---|---|---|
      | presíde | président | defý | defíant |
      | resíde | résident | relý | relíant |
      | confíde | cónfident | cohére | cohérent |

Szpyra and Giegerich conclude from this pattern that this suffix is on stratum 1 in the stress shifting and laxing cases, and on stratum 2 in the other cases. Actually, as we showed in Chapter 4 , there is no reason to expect stress shift in the regular stratum 1 affixation of this suffix, as in *defiant*. Under our analysis the suffixes *-ant/-ent* are added on stratum 1 in all cases. It is actually the stress-shifting and laxing cases that require special phonological treatment, but one that is also situated on stratum 1. That is, we attributed stress shifting and laxing in the left column of (41) to a rule of Minor Relabelling, (104) in Chapter 4. It is not possible to conclude from these patterns that the suffix *-ant/-ent* is also located on stratum 2. The conclusion is that Szpyra's and Giegerich's discussion has not seriously weakened support for stratum ordered morphology, since they rely on rather superficial discussion of the facts of stress, and not on the in-depth analysis that is required.

8.3   Optimality Theory

In Section 1.5.3 of Chapter 1 we gave a brief sketch of Optimality Theory (OT) as one of the several post-*SPE* phonological developments. In this section we show that a number of central phonological processes of English cause severe difficulties for this theory. OT is either unable to account for the phenomena at all, or can do so only clumsily and not in an insightful way. We conclude that the ordered rule theory, in conjunction with metrical, prosodic, and lexical theory, provides a superior analysis.

8.3.1   Stress

Stress is accounted for in OT by constraints such as those listed in (42) (Pater 1994; 2000).

(42)   Foot Binary (Ft-Bin): A foot contains two syllables (or two moras).
Trochaic (Troch): Stress feet are left headed.
Nonfinality (Nonfin): The main stress foot must not be final in the prosodic word.
Align Head: Align the main stress foot with the right (or left) edge of the prosodic word.
Parse-syllable: A syllable must belong to a foot.
Weight-to-Stress: A heavy syllable is stressed.
*Clash: stressed syllables may not be adjacent.

As is usual in OT, these constraints (along with some others we will discuss later) are assumed to be universal, with languages differing only in the relative ranking of the constraints. It will be seen that these constraints bear considerable resemblance to the parameters of stress that we discussed in

Chapter 4. Weight-to-Stress, for example, encodes quantity sensitivity. The difference is that OT constraints are violable, but constraint violation is minimal and can only arise through satisfaction of higher-ranked constraints. For example, in Chapter 4 we required syllables to belong to feet and enforced this (when syllables are left stray by destressing or extrametricality) by a procedure of Stray Syllable Adjunction. In contrast, an analysis using OT allows syllables to remain stray, if some other constraint outranks Parse-Syllable in a particular language. As a simple example, consider Warao again, whose stress system we analyzed parametrically in Chapter 4. We repeat the relevant data in (43).

(43) a. yàpurùkitànehása   'verily to climb'
      b. nàhoròahàkutái   'the one who ate'
      c. yiwàrabáe   'he finished it'
      d. enàhoròahàkutái   'the one who caused him to eat'

Here, Ft-Binary (a foot contains two syllables), Trochaic, Align-Head (right), and *Clash are met in all forms. In OT terms, this means that these constraints are undominated, hence never violated. However, Parse-Syllable is violated in forms such as (43c, d), where the first syllable is left unparsed. Assigning this syllable to a foot would mean putting it alone in a foot, which would violate the higher-ranked constraint Ft-Bin (and also *Clash).

English stress is considerably more complex, of course. The main source for an OT analysis of English stress is two papers by Pater (1994; 2000). There are a number of significant drawbacks to his analysis, compared to the rule-based analysis we developed in Chapter 4. Pater (2000) acknowledges some of these problems in an appendix. We will mention two of them.

The first problem is that Ft-Bin (a foot contains two moras) must be undominated in Pater's analysis, yet there are violations, such as *sátìre*, *ràccóon*. The first syllable of each of these words is light, yet supports a foot on its own, representing primary stress in *satire* and secondary stress in *raccoon*.[16] Pater discusses a number of possible solutions, but each causes additional problems of its own. This problem highlights an interesting difference between the notion of constraints and the procedures inherent in rules. In OT, a constraint such as Ft-Bin must be satisfied in output forms, unless a violation is forced by a higher ranked constraint. In a

---

[16] In *raccoon* the first syllable is unstressed and reduced in some dialects, such as RP. In such dialects it is not an exception to Initial Destressing.

rule-based analysis, the English Stress Rule says to build maximally binary feet. The output of the rule will be binary feet *where possible*, but a foot of a single syllable or a single mora will be built if there is not enough material available for a binary foot, as happens at the left edge of *satire* and *raccoon*. Building a nonbinary foot on these syllables in no way violates the *rule* of English stress. *Satire* is in fact entirely regular in our analysis. The first syllable of *raccoon* would ordinarily be destressed by Initial Destressing; we had to mark this word as an exception to this rule. Lexical exceptions to individual rules are quite common in rule-based frameworks. A framework without rules, like OT, obviously cannot have exceptions to rules, and so examples of this type cause serious difficulties for such frameworks.

The second problem also involves exceptions. In Chapter 4 we discussed a number of examples like those in (44).

(44)   a.   chìmpànzée   b.   Àrgentína
              Ìstànbúl   àmpersánd
              òdòntólogy   sìmultáneous
              òstèntátious   dìssertátion

In each of the words in (44b), Sonorant Destressing has applied, removing the stress on the second syllable. We analyzed the words in (44a) as exceptions to Sonorant Destressing, which is an entirely straightforward solution. Pater proposes a far more roundabout analysis. Since it is not possible to have exceptions to rules in OT, he claims that words like (44a) have a lexical stress on the second syllable. But this alone is not enough. In OT, lexical specifications do not appear in output forms if there are constraints with high enough ranking to disallow such specifications. Consequently, Pater requires an additional, lexically specific constraint, Ident-Stress-S_I, where S_I refers to the class of items for which this constraint is required. This constraint requires that output forms maintain the stress of the corresponding input forms in specifically marked forms. This analysis is doubly redundant. The first redundancy resides in placing a lexical stress on the second syllable of *chimpanzee*, a heavy syllable which would be expected to be assigned stress in any event, because of Weight-to-Stress. The second redundancy is that two lexical marks are required to account for this type of exception: the lexical stress and a lexical marker indicating membership in the class S_I and so subject to the constraint requiring maintenance of this lexical stress. These redundancies are absent from the rule-based analysis, which simply requires a single exception marking, stating that *chimpanzee* (and other words like 44a) are exceptions to Sonorant Destressing. Furthermore, the analysis involving exceptions to rules is more constrained than Pater's approach to the treatment of exceptions. Pater's approach could easily describe unattested (and impossible) forms like *chìmp[ə]zée*, with a medial stressed light syllable between two stressed syllables, simply by having a lexical stress on this syllable and a high-ranking constraint requiring faithfulness to that stress. The rule-based approach correctly excludes such unattested patterns.

This question of the treatment of exceptions will arise in some of the other cases we will discuss. We conclude that, even if English stress can literally be analyzed in OT with a range of coverage at least as great as that of our rule-based analysis, OT offers no new insights into English stress and in fact seems rather clumsy in comparison to an analysis using rules.

8.3.2   Vowel Shift

Vowel Shift is a chain shift, as illustrated graphically in (7) of Chapter 7. In a chain shift, segments change without merging, since an item that potentially merges with another is itself shifted. Kirchner (1996) discusses a chain shift in Nzɛbi, illustrated in (45).

(45)   i → i
        e → i
        ɛ → e
        ɑ → ɛ

The problem that chain shifts pose for OT is that the shifted output cannot be considered less marked (in OT terms, more 'harmonic') than its corresponding input, since each such input is itself the output of some other shift (in Nzɛbi, except *a*). Kirchner proposes a constraint Raising that requires vowel height to be maximized. Undominated, this constraint would turn all input vowels into high vowels in the output. It is evaluated gradiently; that is, a single violation mark is assigned to a mid vowel (since it is one step from a high vowel) and two violation marks are assigned to a low vowel (two steps from a high vowel). To ensure stepwise raising, Kirchner invokes constraints requiring maintenance of the input features [±high] and [±low]. In addition, he employs a particular type of constraint that is violated only if the output differs from the input in *both* of these features. This is called *local conjunction* of constraints: two individual constraints are combined into a conjoined constraint, which is counted as violated only if both the conjoined constraints are individually violated. The results can be set out in the form of a tableau, as in (46), where Parse (low) & Parse (high) is the local conjunction of two constraints Parse (low) and Parse (high). Here we use the English front vowels to illustrate, to see how this would fare as an account of English Vowel Shift.

(46)

	Parse (low) & Parse (high)	Raising
æ → æ		**!
☞ æ → e	(only Parse (low))	*
æ → i	*!	
e → e		*!
☞ e → i	(only Parse (high))	
e → æ	(only Parse (low))	*!*
☞ i → i		
i → e	(only Parse (high))	*!
i → æ	*!	**

In a tableau, the constraints are listed across the top row, in order of ranking, with the leftmost constraint being the highest ranked, and candidate forms (here input–output relations) are listed down the left. An asterisk (*) marks a violation of a constraint for a particular candidate. An exclamation mark (!) marks a fatal violation, that is, one which eliminates a particular candidate. The winning candidate is indicated by the pointing hand (☞). A similar tableau is correct for Nzɛbi. However, it is not correct for input /i/ in English, which should emerge as a low vowel.

The device of local conjunction increases the number of possible constraints by a very large factor, since, in principle, any two constraints can be conjoined.[17] But even this powerful addition to the theory does not account for English Vowel Shift, where high vowels become low, rather than staying put, as they do in Nzɛbi. For the English case, a purely arbitrary correspondence constraint, relating input high vowels to output low vowels, is required. So even if English Vowel Shift can literally be interpreted in OT terms, it requires enormous additional power and offers no insight into the process. It is certainly no improvement over the rule-based approach.

---

[17] The single constraints that are conjoined are still available individually in this extension of OT, though they are necessarily ranked below the conjoined constraint in order for the latter to have any effect.

8.3.3 Laxing

In Chapter 6, we proposed three separate laxing rules: Trisyllabic Laxing, Cluster Laxing, and -*ic* Laxing. There have been a number of attempts to unite these into a single generalization. Myers (1987) claims that all three rules are instances of laxing (for him, shortening) of vowels in closed syllables. With final consonants extrametrical, *sleep* has an open syllable in which a long (tense) vowel is permitted. In *slept*, however, the final *t* is extrametrical but the syllable is closed by *p*, causing the vowel to shorten. In *sane* and *cone* the syllable is open, again assuming final consonant extrametricality. For *sanity* and *conic*, Myers proposes a rule of resyllabification that shifts a consonant from the onset of an unstressed syllable so that it becomes the coda of a preceding stressed syllable. That is, the *n* of *sanity* and *conic* becomes a coda, closing the first syllable of each of these words, again causing vowel shortening. This proposed rule of resyllabification is problematic from the point of view of stop allophones discussed in Chapter 5. For example, resyllabifying the *t* of *metric* would remove it from the domain of Alveopalatalization and put it in the domain of Glottalization, predicting the wrong outcome.

Resyllabification can be avoided by regarding laxing (shortening) as having the foot as its domain, rather than the syllable. Here, the idea is that an optimal foot is maximally (as well as minimally) bimoraic, disregarding the effects of extrametricality. For example, we might represent the words in the previous paragraph as in (47), where parentheses enclose feet and angled brackets enclose extrametrical consonants (an extrametrical syllable in *sanity*). Starred items are too long, containing either a long vowel followed by a nonextrametrical consonant in one syllable or a long vowel followed by another syllable within the foot.[18]

(47) a. (slee)<p>
      b. (slep)<t>
          *(sleep)<t>
      c. (să)<ne>
          (cō)<ne>
      d. (săni)<ty>
          (cŏni)<c>

---

[18] These might be two separate constraints. The first is essentially our Coda Condition, (63) in Chapter 3, which disallows a branching second mora within a syllable. We allowed a fair number of exceptions to this principle – it could be considered a violable constraint in OT if the exact conditions under which it can be violated were worked out and given as constraints that dominate it.

e.   *(sāni)<ty>
      *(cōni)<c>

An analysis of these patterns in OT would have to be integrated with an analysis of stress, which itself is problematic, as we saw in Section 8.3.1. Assuming these difficulties can be overcome, there are additional challenges. One is that the starred foot types in (47b, e) are possible in underived forms, as in (48a, b), and in some derived forms, as in (48c, d).

(48)   a.   (fin)<d>
              (poīn)<t>
        b.   (nīghtin)(ga<le>)
              (cȳa)(ni<de>)
        c.   o(bēsi)<ty>
              (nīce)<ty>
        d.   (heāp)<ed>
        e.   Ca(nādi)<an>

The rule-based analysis of these forms relies on the Strict Cycle Condition to permit (48a, b), since the laxing rule is not permitted to change structure in a nonderived environment. For (48c) we simply claimed that the roots *obese* and *nice* are lexical exceptions to laxing. In (48d) the derivation of the past tense on stratum 2 bypasses the laxing rule on stratum 1. And in (48e) the foot *(nādi)* is a consequence of a rule: C*i*V Tensing. In none of these cases is there an obvious candidate for a dominating constraint that would override the constraint demanding laxing (shortening) in these cases. OT has no direct analogue of the Strict Cycle Condition because, without rules, there cannot be cyclic ordering of rules, and thus no constraints that refer to such ordering.[19] In particular, it is not possible within OT to account for the difference between cases like *nightingale* and cases like *obesity*. Kiparsky (1982) gave an elegant account of this difference in terms of Lexical Phonology and underspecification, as we described in Section 6.2.1 of Chapter 6. For *nightingale*, the vowel of the first syllable is tense in the underlying representation, the form is underived, and the Strict Cycle Condition prohibits changing a tense vowel to a lax vowel in an underived representation. The retention of a tense (long) vowel in the second syllable of *obesity* is attributed to the morpheme *obese* being listed as an exception to

---

[19] Some OT analyses (e.g., Łubowicz (2002) seek to achieve the effects of the (strict) cycle in terms of constraint conjunction.

Trisyllabic Laxing. In a regular derived form like *sanity*, Trisyllabic Laxing applies regularly in a derived form, while words like *alibi* can have an underlying vowel in the first syllable unspecified for [ATR], with the value [–ATR] filled in by Trisyllabic Laxing, which in this case counts as adding – not changing – structure in a nonderived environment. An explanation along these lines is impossible in OT, for various reasons. Most versions of OT reject underspecification, as part of a general programme of rejecting constraints on inputs – in this theory all generalizations are stated on outputs, not inputs. Probably the best approach in this theory is to have a lexically specific constraint requiring faithfulness to underlying vowel length in both *nightingale* and *obesity*. This lexically specific constraint necessarily dominates the constraints that enforce laxing (shortening) in these contexts. This is similar to the lexically specified constraints that Pater uses to account for exceptional stress patterns in English (Section 8.3.1). Such an approach would not make any distinction between cases like *nightingale*, which are simply lexically specified for length in a shortening context, and ones like *obesity*, which are outright exceptions. Even if the theory can be adjusted to produce the correct forms, it does not make the important distinction between these two types of cases.

8.3.4 Opacity

Opacity is acknowledged as a major problem for OT by proponents and opponents alike. The rule-based analysis of English phonology developed in this book is opaque in a number of ways. Kiparsky (1973) defines opacity as in (49).

(49)   . . .a process P of the form A → B/C____D is opaque to the extent that there are phonetic forms in the language having either (i) or (ii).
(i)   A in the environment C____D
(iia)   B derived by the process P in an environment other than C____D
(iib)   B not derived by the process P (i.e., either underlying or derived by another process) in the environment C____D

The rule of Velar Softening in English offers an example of the first two types of opacity. We give some relevant examples in (50).

(50)   *Velar Softening*
a.   Opaque by case (49i)
      medicate
      obligation

    b.   Opaque by case (49iia)
        criticize
        oblige
    c.   Transparent (rule applies, context appears in output)
        medicine
        medicinal
        analogy
        legislate
    d.   Transparent (rule does not apply, its context does not appear in output)
        medical
        medic
        analogous
        analogue
        legal

Opacity by case (49i) frequently arises as a result of counterfeeding rule order. As discussed in Chapter 7, Velar Softening is ordered before Vowel Shift. In a case like *medicate* (50a), Vowel Shift converts the underlying vowel to one which could trigger Velar Softening, but too late for this rule to apply. McCarthy (1999) refers to this type of opacity with the term *not surface apparent*. Opacity by case (49iia) frequently arises as a result of counterbleeding order. In *criticize* (50b), Velar Softening applies before Vowel Shift has a chance to convert the vowel into one which would not trigger Velar Softening. McCarthy (1999) refers to this type of opacity as *not surface true*. Velar Softening has transparent cases as well (50c, d), where it applies and the triggering vowel remains in the output (50c), or where it does not apply and the following vowel is not a trigger, either in the input or output (*medical*) or where it is not followed by any vowel (*medic*). In these cases there is no interaction with Vowel Shift. In what follows we will disregard type (49iib), which is simply contextual neutralization of the type in German *Rat* 'advice,' with an underlying final /t/, as opposed to *Rad* 'wheel,' with a phonetic [t] derived from underlying /d/.

    To see why the interaction of Velar Softening and Vowel Shift (or indeed any pair of rules that interact in counterfeeding or counterbleeding fashion) is a problem for OT, we will consider a possible (and rather sketchy) analysis. Ignoring the difficulties that Vowel Shift alone causes for OT, let us just say that there is a constraint enforcing the correspondence between the input tense vowels and the output diphthongs discussed in Chapter 7. In standard OT fashion, we will take Velar Softening to be a pair of constraints. One, which we will simply refer to as Velar Softening, disallows the occurrence of a velar stop followed by a vowel (or glide) which is [–low, –back]. The other is a faithfulness constraint requiring that an underlying velar stop remain as such in the output. We can construct the relevant tableaux in (51).[20]

(51)

a.	medicate /kæ/	Vowel Shift	Velar Softening	Faith Velar
	[kæ]	*		
☹	[keɪ]		*	
💣	[seɪ]			*

b.	criticize /ki/			
	[ki]	*	*	
💣	[kɑɪ]			
☹	[sɑɪ]			*

c.	medicine /kɪ/			
	[kɪ]		*	
☞	[sɪ]			*

In these tableaux we use the frowning face (☹) for the desired (but not successful) candidate and the bomb symbol (💣) for the (incorrect) candidate actually selected by the ranking, in addition to the usual pointing hand (☞) for a correct candidate selected by the ranking. Only where Vowel Shift is not involved can we select the correct output. It is clear that no change in the ranking can improve on this result. Velar Softening must dominate Faith Velar, since otherwise no velars would ever be softened. The ranking of Vowel Shift is immaterial. In particular, the bomb

---

[20] There is still a problem in stating what the velar stop turns into when it gets softened. We will disregard this in the interests of giving a reasonably straightforward (if oversimplified) view of the opacity problem in OT.

candidate meets all three constraints in (51b), while the desired candidate fails Faith Velar.

A number of proposals have been made to deal with such situations, all of which involve major extensions of the basic model of OT. McCarthy (1994) allows constraints to refer to inputs as well as to outputs. He proposes a Canonical Constraint Schema, whose general form is (52).

(52)   Canonical Constraint Schema (McCarthy 1994)

*	Condition	Level
α		
β		
Linear Order		
Adjacency		

In this schema, the large star indicates a constraint disallowing any configuration meeting the conditions stated. Conditions on α and β are features, linear order specifies the order in which these two elements appear, and adjacency refers to what elements, if any, may intervene between them. The level column can specify input, output, or indifferent for each of the elements in the schema. McCarthy uses this framework to describe a process of spirantization in Tiberian Hebrew, by which a stop becomes a fricative after a vowel, including vowels which are deleted, as in [malxē] 'kings of' from /malakē/. Stated in terms of such a schema, English Velar Softening could have the form in (53).

(53)

*	Condition	Level
α	[–cont, –cor, –ant]	output
β	[–cons, –low, –back]	input
Linear Order	α > β	indifferent
Adjacency	strict	indifferent

Stated in this way, Velar Softening would actually derive the ⊗ candidates in (51a, b). Hale and Reiss (2000: 166–167) point out a number of problems with this proposal. In place of the standard OT claim that there is a universal, innate constraint set that is literally present in all grammars, with only their ranking stipulated on a language-specific basis, this proposal allows language-specific parametrized constraints which have to be learned. More important, such constraints are no longer phonetically grounded. In fact, the structures that violate such a constraint not only need not be output strings but may not be strings at any level of representation.

An extension of this idea appears in Archangeli and Suzuki (1997), who account for Yokuts (Yawelmani) vowel harmony in terms of a constraint that can refer to inputs (if possible) or to outputs (if a relevant input is not available, for example, under epenthesis). This is a classic case where a rule (in an ordered rule framework) is ordered after an epenthesis rule but before other rules that crucially modify the vowel, whether underlying or epenthesized, and it further dilutes the OT claim that well-formedness is determined on outputs.

The proponents of various extensions of OT take some pains to show that the theory crucially does not allow some interactions that are possible in serial derivations. For example, another type of opacity that can arise in the rule-based framework involves crucial reference to intermediate representations that are not present either in the input or in the output. Kager (1999: 58) considers the hypothetical derivation in (54).

(54) Lexical form: /XAY/
      Rule 1 A → B /X____   XBY
      Rule 2 Y → Z / B____   XBZ
      Rule 3 B → C / X____Z   XCZ
      Surface form: [XCZ]

McCarthy (1999: 377) presents a hypothetical derivation of essentially the same sort, and claims that "if real languages like this do not in fact exist – and I claim that they don't – then we have here a situation where rule-based serialism significantly overgenerates.... I will show that sympathy theory does not share this liability." And Kager (1999: 58) remarks that "it seems fair to conclude that the radical abstractness of the type (11) [our (54)] that rule-based theory predicts to be possible in natural languages is rarely – if ever – attested. Overwhelmingly, phonological generalizations refer to the *output*, possibly in relation to the input."

As a matter of fact, we have derivations of exactly the form of (54) in English. In our discussion of Palatalization in Section 7.4.2 of Chapter 7, we noted that Palatalization applies before /j/, including /j/ that is inserted by *j*-Insertion. The *j* in some cases is subsequently deleted. Consider the derivation of *pressure* in (55).

(55)   Input   /prɛs + ɨɪ/
            j-Insertion   prɛs + jɨɪ
            Palatalization   prɛʃ + jɨɪ
            j-Deletion   prɛʃ + ɨɪ
            ɨ-Rounding   prɛʃ + ʊɪ
            Vowel Reduction   prɛʃ + ʊɪ
            Phonetic form   [ˈprɛʃʊɪ]

As we observed in Section 7.4.2 of Chapter 7, we did not propose the rules involved in the derivation in (55) simply to get that particular result. The rules in question apply in numerous other derivations where they do not interact with the other rules in the derivation of (55) and where they are often quite transparent. *J*-Insertion applies transparently in *pure*, where it remains in the output. Palatalization applies in the context of underlying *j* in words like *expression*, *official*, although here it is opaque because *j* is deleted, showing, in fact, that underlying *j* is also deleted just like inserted *j*. If McCarthy is correct in stating that derivations like (54) and (55) cannot be modelled in OT, even extended by sympathy theory, then OT cannot describe the phonology of English.[21]

It seems that such Duke of York derivations are not particularly uncommon. An example similar to the English derivation in (55) occurs in Modern Greek (Newton 1972), where "in at least some dialects the palatalization of /s/ to /š/ is triggered by [y] but not [i]" (his symbols: [y] = IPA [j] and [š] = IPA [ʃ]). In these dialects we find derivations like /nisía/ 'islands' → nisyá (Glide Formation) → nišyá (Palatalization) → [nišá] (Postpalatal yod deletion). That is, a glide is created which then conditions palatalization and is then deleted.

Green (2004) seeks to reanalyze opaque relationships as morphological, denying that there is any genuine case of phonological opacity. He analyzes three cases in Tiberian Hebrew, including the one that inspired McCarthy's sympathy analysis, in terms of an overriding morphological constraint. However, he also presents two cases that seem to be opacity of a purely phonological nature. One is velar palatalization in Bulgarian, which is conditioned by a following front vowel, including the front *yer* which is

---

[21] Pullum (1976) introduced the term "Duke of York gambit" to describe this type of rule interaction, on the basis of a traditional rhyme:

> *The Grand Old Duke of York*
> *He had ten thousand men*
> *He marched them up a great high hill*
> *And he marched them down again.*

later deleted (counterbleeding, with apparent overapplication of palatalization). The other is dorsal assimilation in German, which converts /ç/ to /x/ after a back vocoid, which is followed by a rule vocalizing [ʀ] to [ɐ̯] in codas. In the word *durch* [dʊɐ̯ç] 'through' the front dorsal [ç] appears after the back vocoid [ɐ̯], the result of a counterfeeding interaction with apparent underapplication of dorsal assimilation. In neither of these cases does morphology play any obvious role.

Another approach to opacity within OT is McCarthy's (1999) Sympathy Theory, which allows faithfulness constraints to refer to failed candidates. In all the cases McCarthy discusses, the failed candidate in question is identical, in the relevant aspects, to an intermediate form in a serial derivation. Sympathy Theory seems to admit such intermediate forms by the back door, thus even further diluting the output orientation of OT.

Yet a further approach is Stratal OT (Kiparsky 2000), which uses stratum ordering. On each stratum there is a ranking of constraints. The ranking on one stratum may not correspond to the ranking of another stratum; thus, opaque interactions can arise between strata but not within a stratum.

Rydzewski (2018) illustrates this approach by considering Diphthong Shortening and Flapping in English as discussed in Section 1.1 of Chapter 1. Consider the derivation of *writer* in (13) of Chapter 1, repeated here as (56).

(56)   Lexical   /ˈɹɑɪt + əɹ/
        Diphthong Shortening   əɪ
        Flapping   ɾ
        Phonetic   [ˈɹəɪɾəɹ]

Rydzewski considers four constraints: Raise-Diphthong, which favours a raised diphthong before voiceless consonants; Ident-Low, which favours retention of the input value of [low] in the output; Flap, which bars low sonority elements intervocalically, and Ident-Manner, which favours retention of the input manner of articulation of a segment in the output. Diphthong Shortening occurs on stratum 1, where Raise-Diphthong » Ident-Low, where '»' indicates 'is ranked over'. Assigning this ranking to stratum 1 accounts for Diphthong Shortening in *write* and the lack of Diphthong Shortening with stratum 2 suffixes (*eyeful*) or compounds (*eye slip*). The successful candidate from stratum 1 forms the input to stratum 2, where these two constraints are reranked as Ident-Low » Raise-Diphthong. Now with the attachment of the stratum 2 suffix #*er*, *writer*

retains the raised diphthong of *write*. On the first two strata Ident-Manner
» Flap, so no flapping occurs on these strata. On stratum 3 (postlexical),
these two constraints are reranked as Flap » Ident-Manner so that now
flapping occurs in *writer* (with its raised diphthong) and also in phrases
(great idea). In a sense, this approach uses strata to account for phenomena
that we have attributed to prosodic categories.

Stratal OT is another illustration of the development away from the
original claim of OT that phonological generalizations are determined by
outputs and that evaluation applies all at once (in parallel) rather than in
stages (serially). That is, OT increasingly adopts derivational procedures,
though expressed in terms of constraints rather than rules.

Referring to Bloomfield (1939) *SPE* (p. 18, fn. 4) develops the concept
of depth of ordering, where from any sequence of ordered rules it is
possible to extract a subsequence of *n* rules such that "the grammar
becomes more complex if any two successive rules of this subsequence
are interchanged in the ordering." The depth of ordering in Bloomfield's
description of Menomini is at least eleven, and in Chomsky's (1951)
description of Modern Hebrew the depth of ordering is at least 25 (cf.
SPE: 18, fn. 4).

One effect of Stratal OT is to severely limit the depth of ordering in the
grammar. The constraints responsible for transparent interactions can be
appropriately ranked on a single stratum, while the constraints responsible
for opaque interactions must have distinct rankings on at least two strata.
In rule-ordering terms this amounts to counting only those rules that
interact opaquely as contributing to depth of ordering.

Kiparsky (2000) points out additional problems with Sympathy Theory,
and with other fully parallel OT systems for modelling opacity, including
transderivational constraints that relate distinct outputs (Benua 1995).
Both systems are unable to capture certain generalizations. In the interaction of stress and epenthesis in Palestinian Arabic, discussed in rule-based
terms by Brame (1974), epenthetic vowels are invisible to stress. Kager
(1999: 290) proposes a constraint requiring that vowels not present in the
input not be stressed in the output, but this is unable to account for cases
where stress appears on some syllable other than the one with an epenthetic vowel, but where the epenthetic vowel is not counted in placing the
stress. In fact, the epenthetic vowel is invisible to all processes of word
phonology, such as shortening of vowels in closed syllables. Of course, this
is easily accounted for in a rule-based account by ordering the stress rule
and other rules of word phonology before Epenthesis, and in a Lexical
Phonology account, by situating Epenthesis on the postlexical level, after

all processes of word phonology on a lexical level. A sympathy account would require additional sympathy constraints for each word-level process that is invisible to epenthesis, resulting in a serious loss of generalization. Kiparsky's Stratal OT avoids these problems by incorporating strata into OT, each stratum having its own constraint ranking. These strata correspond roughly to the strata of standard Lexical Phonology and morphology. Since each stratum is independently motivated in terms of morphology, this is a considerable improvement over standard OT and sympathy theory, and "imposes a small upper limit on the depth of opaque interactions" (Kiparsky 2000: 362).

Stratal OT (also called Derivational OT) has been invoked to account for several instances of Duke of York derivations. Rubach (2003) analyzes two examples from Polish in terms of three levels, and Odden (2008) discusses several examples from the tonal phonology of several African languages.

The logical consequence of Stratal OT is that any two processes in an opaque relation must necessarily belong to separate strata. This may not always be possible in English, if the strata are limited to the three that appear to be motivated in our discussion, namely two lexical strata and one post-lexical stratum. For example, the opaque relation between Velar Softening and Vowel Shift would seem to require splitting stratum 2 into two strata, yet there is no morphological or other motivation for such a split. Similarly, stratum 2 would have to be split into two or three strata to account for derivations such as (55). We have observed several opaque interactions in the postlexical stratum as well, for example, the interaction of Diphthong Shortening and Flapping. Indeed, Rydzewski's account of this interaction shifts Diphthong Shortening from the postlexical stratum to stratum 1. Similarly, it might be possible to account for the interaction of Vowel Nasalization and Nasal Consonant Deletion in a similar way by shifting Vowel Nasalization to stratum 1. Investigation is needed to determine if it is possible to account for all the opaque interactions in English by such manoeuvres within the number of strata that are morphologically motivated.

It should be noted that both Diphthong Shortening and Vowel Nasalization are not structure preserving, which in standard Lexical Phonology should exclude them from lexical strata. In addition, Diphthong Shortening violates the Strict Cycle Condition (Section 6.2.1 of Chapter 6) in that it changes structure in a nonderived environment in examples like *write*. Principles of Lexical Morphology and Phonology like structure preservation and the strict cycle condition need to be reevaluated for the further development of Stratal OT.

Benua (1995) proposes constraints that relate distinct outputs, as might appear for example in a morphological paradigm. As McCarthy (1999: 385ff.) points out, this device cannot account for all cases of opacity. An example in English is the interaction of Diphthong Shortening and Flapping in (56). Hayes (2004: 189) argues that this opaque (counter-bleeding) interaction could be accounted for in terms of such Output–Output constraints. That is, *writer* can have a raised diphthong because *write* has one, and the raised diphthong appears transparently in *write*. This Output–Output constraint must arbitrarily stipulate that it is the shortened diphthong that [ɹəɪɾəɹ] inherits from [ɹəɪt'], and not the glottalization of [t]. It should be noted that Output–Output constraints are necessarily language specific, so this extension of OT cannot maintain the claim that all constraints are universal.

There are, however, cases where the sequence [əɪɾ] appears in this dialect in words that have no morphological correspondent where the raised diphthong appears transparently. Some examples are in (57).[22]

(57) nightingale
item
vitamin
Titus
clitoris
title

The existence of such words is evidence that Diphthong Shortening is purely phonological in English and that its interaction with Flapping is a case of purely phonological opacity, with no necessary connection to morphology. As such, it constitutes a challenge to Green's attempt to treat opacity in terms of morphology within OT.

It may still be necessary to investigate why opacity is not more extensive than it is in a theory that allows unlimited recourse to rule ordering. These questions deserve more study than I am able to give them here, but the fact remains that the phonological system of English, as described in these chapters with over eighty rules in many complex interactions, presents a serious challenge to any purely constraint-based account, including Stratal OT.[23]

---

[22] *Vitamin* and *clitoris* have alternate pronunciations with [ɪ] in the first syllable, at least in RP. When pronounced with a diphthong, Diphthong Shortening operates in these words in the dialect in question.

[23] It is interesting to note that much work on OT and Stratal OT still speaks in terms of 'processes' rather than sticking to purely constraint terminology. While perhaps informal, this may indicate that processes have some reality even in a theory that tries to enforce all such operations strictly by constraints.

It is not necessarily the case that opacity is a particularly difficult challenge for language acquisition. The idea is that even opaque rules have transparent cases and that these facilitate the learning process. In Velar Softening, for example, the existence of transparent cases like *medic*, *medical, medicine*, allows one to observe the basic generalization. Vowel Shift is usually transparent, although it has exceptions (like *oblique*, cf. *obliquity*) and it does not apply to some tense vowels that are tensed by rules ordered after Vowel Shift (e.g., Stem-final Tensing). So, once Vowel Shift is learned, it is necessary to determine the interaction between it and Velar Softening, and it should be relatively straightforward to determine that Velar Softening is ordered before Vowel Shift. The same can be said about the other opaque processes in English.

In effect, OT claims that opacity is highly marked in natural languages and that it needs complex and baroque devices like Sympathy Theory to be modelled. Even then OT excludes certain types of opacity, such as (55). Rule ordered theory may concede that opacity is marked – this was what Kiparsky had in mind in the definition cited in (49) – but should be allowed in principle. Probably all languages – and English in particular – are characterized by opaque as well as transparent processes, and the theory has to be able to model all the processes and their interactions as they occur in natural languages.

Another revised version of OT that attempts to address the issue of opacity is OT with candidate chains (OT-CC; McCarthy 2007). At the risk of oversimplifying, in this approach the candidates are chains of forms, in effect whole derivations. Chains are restricted to make a single change at a time and must be harmonically improving with respect to the constraint hierarchy of the language.

The initial member of a chain is a fully faithful parse of the input that can differ from the input only in such particulars as are not governed by faithfulness constraints, such as syllabification. Each subsequent member of the chain differs from its predecessor in one localized unfaithful mapping (LUM), retaining all the LUMs of all the previous steps. This is called the gradualness requirement. Among other things, gradualness disallows a chain of the hypothetical form <pap, pa.pə, pa.bə, pab> "because it adds and then withdraws a DEP-violating LUM" (McCarthy 2007: 78). Each step must be more harmonic than the previous step. Two (or more) chains may converge if they produce the same final output and differ only in the order in which the LUMs occur (McCarthy 2007: 96). This is analogous to the situation in rule-based phonology where two (or more) rules are not crucially ordered.

A new type of constraint is required, *precedence constraints*, which require that some particular change (LUM) occur earlier in the chain than another. A precedence constraint of the form Prec(A, B), where A and B are faithfulness constraints, is violated if either a violation of B occurs earlier in the chain than a violation of A or if a violation of B is not preceded by a violation of A. If both conditions are present, the chain receives two violation marks (McCarthy 2007: 98). A ranking metaconstraint requires that B be ranked over Prec(A, B) (McCarthy 2007: 98–99). This is to ensure that the precedence constraint must not affect whether B is violated, although it depends on whether B is violated.

McCarthy illustrates counterbleeding opacity with an example from Bedouin Arabic. In this language, velar stops are palatalized when preceding a front vowel. Another process deletes short high vowels in nonfinal open syllables. In a rule-based framework these rules apply in this order, producing derivations like (58) (McCarthy's transcriptions).

(58)   /ħaːkim-iːn/ → ħaːk^{y}im-iːn → ħaːk^{y}m-iːn 'ruling (masculine plural)'

McCarthy analyzes this in terms of the constraint hierarchy (59), where *iCV disfavours [i] in medial open syllables, *ki disfavours back velars followed by front vowels, Max disfavours deletion, and Id(back) requires identity in the feature [back]. These constraints are not sufficient to ensure the correct outcome, since *ki could as well be satisfied by changing /k/ to t or something else, or deleting it, or changing the vowel. A more complete analysis would require additional constraints, but we leave this problem aside. The precedence constraint Prec(Id(back), Max) requires that a change violating Id (back) must occur earlier in the winning chain than a change violating Max.

(59)   *iCV, *ki » Max » Prec(Id(back), Max) » Id(back)

The successful chain is thus (60). This is harmonically improving in that the first step removes a violation of *ki and the next step removes a violation of *iCV.

(60)   </ħaːkim-iːn/, ħaːk^{y}im-iːn, ħaːk^{y}m-iːn>

McCarthy demonstrates the need for harmonic improvement with the input form /t-ħakum-in/ 'they (fem.) rule,' which should yield *t-ħakm-in*, as indeed is the result in the rule-based analysis. In the OT-CC analysis there are two rival chains in (61).

(61)   a.   <t-ħakum-in, t-ħak^{y}um-in, t-ħak^{y}m-in >
         b.   < t-ħakum-in, t-ħakm-in>

Chain (61a) is not harmonically improving since the first step shows palatalization in a nonpalatalizing context, but does meet the precedence constraint in having a violation of Id(back) that precedes a violation of Max, and so would be judged superior to (61b), which does not meet the precedence constraint. The requirement that chains be harmonically improving eliminates (61a), allowing (61b) to be victorious. We can see that this requirement is an artefact of the attempt to do rule ordering with constraints rather than rules. This requirement is entirely superfluous in the rule theory, since a rule palatalizing velars before front vowels could never produce a palatalized velar in some other context.

McCarthy illustrates counterfeeding opacity with another pair of processes in Bedouin Arabic, one which raises low vowels in open syllables and one that epenthesizes a vowel between two word-final consonants, which in a rule framework would give derivations like (62). Raising does not apply to low vowels that come to be in open syllables by virtue of epenthesis.

(62)   /gabr/ → gabr (raising inapplicable) → gabur (epenthesis) *gibur

McCarthy invokes the constraints in (63), where Prec(Id(low), Dep) ensures that a violation of Id(low) occurs earlier in a successful chain than a violation of Dep.

(63)   *Comp-Coda » Dep » Prec(Id(low), Dep) » *aCV » Id(low)

Again we leave aside the problem of how to ensure the correct outcomes.

Let us now return to our example of the opaque interaction of Velar Softening and Vowel Shift in (51), which illustrates both counterfeeding and counterbleeding. We add a precedence constraint to ensure that the change entailed by Velar Softening precedes a change by Vowel Shift. We add a faithfulness constraint, Faith Vowel Height, which requires that vowel height be preserved. For the purpose of illustration we assume that Vowel Shift can be considered a correspondence constraint that specifies the relation between a given input and a particular output, as before. Velar Softening is represented by the constraint schema in (53) and is violated just in case there is an input /k/ followed by an input nonlow front vowel that does not correspond to an output [s]. The revised tableau in (64) shows that the correct outputs are now selected. The harmonic improvement requirement is presumably met in the case of Velar Softening, but not with Vowel Shift, since this is a circular shift involving three vowel heights and none of the three is more 'harmonic' than the others.

(64)

		Velar Softening	Vowel Shift	Faith Vowel Height	Prec (Faith Velar, Faith Vowel Height)	Faith Velar
a.	medicate /kæ/					
	</kæ/>		*!			
☞	</kæ/, keɪ>			*	*	
	</kæ/, keɪ, seɪ>			*	**!	*

b.	criticize /ki/					
	</ki/>	*!				
	</ki/, kaɪ>	*!		*	*	
☞	</ki/, si, sɑɪ>			*		*

c.	medicine /kɪ/					
	</kɪ/>	*!				
☞	</kɪ/, sɪ>					*

In *medicate*, the chain terminating in [seɪ] violates the precedence constraint twice, since a change in vowel height precedes a change in the velar and the change in vowel height is not preceded by a change in the velar.

Clearly, the precedence constraint functions as a rule ordering statement. In the account that we have presented in Chapter 7, the rules and their ordering generate the correct forms without the need for the additional devices of a constraint hierarchy, harmonic improvement, and the other mechanisms that McCarthy requires in OT-CC.

Although OT-CC is able to account for some cases of opacity, it excludes well-motivated analyses. In particular, the gradualness requirement would disallow the analysis of *pressure* in (55) since the successful chain would include a sequence <...sɨ, sjɨ, ʃjɨ, ʃɨ...>, which, like McCarthy's hypothetical example cited above, "adds and then withdraws a DEP-violating LUM," and similarly the analysis of *r*-Insertion in Section 5.3.8 of Chapter 5 and the next section.

McCarthy (2007: 4) criticizes rule-based phonology for its "dearth of explanation and absence of typological predictions," yet there is no more explanation in a system as complex and cumbersome as OT-CC.

8.3.5 *r-Insertion*

In (109) of Chapter 5, we introduced the rule *r*-Insertion as an example of a rule that is sensitive to the prosodic category Utterance. This rule inserts [ɹ] at the end of a vowel-final prosodic word after a lax, nonhigh back vowel before another vowel within the utterance in nonrhotic dialects of English, such as RP and Eastern Massachusetts. We repeat some of the relevant data in (65).

(65) clear
      clea[ɹ]est
      gnaw
      gnaw[ɹ]ing
      Wanda
      Wanda[ɹ] arrived
      that spider is dangerous   ...spide[ɹ] is...
      the panda eats bamboo   ...panda[ɹ] eats...

This rule poses considerable problems for OT, in that the phenomenon does not seem to be describable without rules, that is, with constraints alone. McCarthy (1993) proposes to account for the phenomenon in terms of the constraints in (66).[24]

(66)   Coda(r) Condition: /ɹ/ is licensed only in syllable onset position.
        Final C: A prosodic word cannot end in a short vowel.

With Coda(r) Condition ranked above Final C, /ɹ/ will appear in final position of words like *Homer*, *Wanda*, only when a vowel-initial word follows, with the /ɹ/ parsed as an onset. This analysis requires the assumption that such consonants are ambisyllabic, a concept which we argued in Chapter 5 to be neither necessary nor desirable (see Jensen 2000). A deeper problem with McCarthy's analysis concerns where the /ɹ/ comes from. In OT work, an epenthetic segment is generally a default segment, and, as

---

[24] McCarthy's term is simply Coda Condition. I use Coda(r) Condition to avoid confusion with the Coda Condition of Section 3.4.3 of Chapter 3.

McCarthy is at pains to point out, /ɹ/ is not the default consonant in English. *R*-Insertion is essentially an arbitrary rule of English, whose effects cannot be obtained by ranking universal constraints. To deal with this problem, McCarthy proposes a rule of *r*-Insertion. But what can be the meaning of a rule in an OT analysis? According to McCarthy (1993: 190), "By a 'rule' here I mean a phonologically arbitrary stipulation, one that is outside the system of Optimality. This rule is interpreted as defining a candidate set {Wanda, Wandar̲}, and this candidate set is submitted to the constraint hierarchy." Halle and Idsardi (1997: 337–338) comment:

> This move...is unsatisfactory both on conceptual and on empirical grounds. Conceptually, reliance on an arbitrary stipulation that is outside the system of Optimality is equivalent to giving up the enterprise. Data that cannot be dealt with by OT without recourse to rules are fatal counterexamples to the OT research programme...From an empirical point of view the proposed extension encounters a number of serious problems overlooked by McCarthy....the use of standard generative rules is sufficient to solve the problem, without OT constraints, candidates, and evaluation.

However, as Blevins (1997: 234) points out, "Gen, in its current incarnation will already generate candidates including {*Wanda, Wanda?, Wandar*} among others," so the problem lies not in obtaining candidates with a final /ɹ/. The problem lies in arranging the constraints to pick that candidate without some arbitrary stipulation, since /ɹ/ is not the default consonant of English. The rules outlined in Chapter 5 are adequate to the task, while no pure constraint system accounts for all the facts. Blevins's solution within OT also requires a rule of *r*-Insertion linked to the constraint Final C.

Halle and Idsardi opt for a solution with rules alone but note a potential problem in the fact that /ɹ/ will sometimes be deleted only to be inserted again later in the derivation (another Duke of York situation). For example, *Homer* has an underlying final /ɹ/, as shown by its stratum 1 derivative *Homeric*, with /ɹ/ pronounced. In isolation, *Homer* is pronounced ['howmə], with /ɹ/ deleted by our *r*-Deletion rule. In the phrase *Homer is*, /ɹ/ is first deleted by *r*-Deletion, but then /ɹ/ is inserted by *r*-Insertion. Halle and Idsardi (1997: 344) object to this sort of rule interaction "on the grounds that the gambit subverts the essential difference between rules, which reflect idiosyncratic facts of a language, and repairs, which are consequences of general structural principles obeyed by the language." This objection is not clear, since it has been established that *r*-Insertion is an arbitrary rule of English. Even if it "repairs" the effect of *r*-Deletion in cases like *Homer is*, it is not a general structural principle. Given the rules we developed in Section 5.3.8 of Chapter 5, we get derivations such as those in (67).

(67)   output of lexicon   /'howməɹ ɪz/   /'ældʒɪbɹə ɪz/
         r-Deletion   ∅   — — —
         r-Insertion   ɹ   ɹ

Halle and Idsardi seek to prevent *r*-Deletion from applying in such cases by an extension of the Elsewhere Condition (see discussion in Section 7.2.3 of Chapter 7). However, as they note, the Elsewhere Condition (quoted in (32) of Chapter 7) is not relevant, since in neither of the two rules in question (*r*-Insertion and *r*-Deletion) does the structural description of one properly include the structural description of the other.

8.3.6 Conclusion

A major motivation for the development of OT was the desire to explain conspiracies. A conspiracy occurs when two or more independent rules appear to lead to a common goal, as discussed by Kisseberth (1970) in Yawelmani. Here there are rules of vowel epenthesis and vowel deletion that seem to lead to a common output – a particular syllable structure. We now ask whether conspiracies are evident in English. We have certainly seen no overwhelming evidence of any. One place to look would be stress. English stress shows certain clear tendencies: there tends to be alternating stress, heavy syllables tend to be stressed, and adjacent stresses seem to be avoided. Our rules do seem to have such goals in mind: the English Stress Rule produces maximally binary feet, giving alternating stress in words like *hamamelidanthemum*, and also stressing heavy syllables. Destressing rules remove stresses, generally when they clash with an adjacent stress. On the other hand, we find sequences of stressed syllables (*èxpèctátion*), heavy syllables that are unstressed (the second syllable of *Àrgentína*), sequences of unstressed syllables (*génerative*), and stressed light syllables adjacent to another stress (*sátìre, ràccoón*). This doesn't point to a conspiracy. It is simply the way the rules apply, without reference to the final output. Kiparsky (1982: 73) says the following about conspiracies:

> Recent developments in phonology have done little to support the idea that "conspiracies" are a unitary category of phenomena requiring some basic theory of their own. On the contrary, the various puzzles that have been consigned to that category have proved to be of a rather heterogeneous sort. Some "conspiracies" have found a principled explanation in autosegmental theory (see e.g. Goldsmith 1976 on "tone stability" in reference to a

"conspiracy" in Lomongo). Others such as the Yawelmani case analyzed in Kisseberth (1970) and cited—together with a similar Tonkawa case—in the present context by Kenstowicz and Kisseberth (1977, 142–144) yield to the theory of syllabic phonology in now obvious ways. The real unity in these phenomena seems to be that they involve prosodic organization of the type that earlier generative phonology was ill equipped to handle and which therefore appeared particularly problematic.

On the one hand, conspiracies are not thick on the ground in English, if they exist at all. On the other hand, certain individual processes of English (Sections 8.3.1–8.3.3) present considerable difficulty for an OT analysis, while the interactions of these processes and others, especially when they involve opacity, present even greater challenges. English can hardly be unique in this respect. While OT may appear to be explanatory in analyzing isolated phenomena in certain languages, it is necessary to test the theory on a substantial body of phenomena from a single language. We have tried to do this with English in terms of the theory of Lexical Phonology. As Halle and Mohanan (1985: 57) put it, "[i]t has been our experience that one of the best ways of coming to grips with such theoretical issues is by confronting the theory with a rich body of empirical data." Our analysis, also based on Lexical Phonology, has extended that of Halle and Mohanan considerably, with extensive use of metrical and prosodic approaches. To be sure, there are still a number of loose ends, unsolved puzzles, and further issues to be discussed.

It is also said (e.g., Kager 1999: 20) that OT solves the duplication problem, where in *SPE* a morpheme structure rule (or condition) expressing regularities within morphemes is duplicated by a derivational phonological rule in the active phonology. OT solves this problem by simply rejecting any constraints on underlying representations through richness of the base (Section 1.5.3 of Chapter 1). However, as we noted in Section 1.4.3 of Chapter 1, Lexical Phonology solved the duplication problem long before the arrival of OT. Lexical Phonology solves this problem by allowing lexical rules, in conjunction with underspecification (Section 1.5.2 of Chapter 1), to function both as rules of the active phonology and to express regularities within lexical items.

OT began by restricting the analysis rather severely, in response to an apparent belief that standard generative theory provides too rich an apparatus – one that can describe interactions beyond what actually occurs in natural language. Our discussion of opacity in the previous subsection raises some doubts about this claim, since a considerable number of opaque interactions are attested in various languages. The further development of OT has backtracked from this strong claim in many ways. Much of this development has resulted in the introduction of new types of constraints, mainly 'faithfulness' constraints, many of which can hardly be claimed to be universal. Correspondence relations have been extended to reduplicants (McCarthy & Prince 1986), unsuccessful candidates (Sympathy Theory), and the outputs of other inputs (e.g., Benua 1995). For an excellent overview of the issues, see Vaux (2008), who discusses the reasons for adopting rule-based phonology in considerable detail. These extensions increasingly belie the claim that Optimality Theory is more restrictive than earlier versions of generative grammar. As Kiparsky (2000: 355) puts it, we need to "look at entire phonological systems, not just toy examples of a few interacting constraints" in order to capture the appropriate generalizations. Our brief excursus into OT in this section suggests that this theory, even with these extensions, is unlikely to provide better insights into English phonology than the lexical, metrical, and prosodic theories in which we have given our analysis. Only time and future research will tell.

References

American Heritage Dictionary of the English Language (1969). Boston: Houghton-Mifflin.

Anderson, Stephen R. (1992). *A-Morphous Morphology*. Cambridge: Cambridge University Press.

Andronov, A. V. (2002). *Materiali dlja Latyšsko-Russkogo Slovarja*. Sankt-Peterburg.

Archangeli, Diana (1984). *Underspecification in Yawelmani Phonology and Morphology*. PhD dissertation, MIT.

Archangeli, Diana & Keiichiro Suzuki (1997). The Yokuts Challenge. In *Derivations and Constraints in Phonology*, ed. Iggy Roca, 197–226. Oxford: Oxford University Press.

Aronoff, Mark (1976). *Word Formation in Generative Grammar*. Cambridge, MA: MIT Press.

Bailey, Charles-James N. (1973). The patterning of language variation. In *Varieties of Present-Day English*, ed. Richard W. Bailey & Jay L. Robinson. New York: Macmillan.

Bailey, Don C. (1962). *Glossary of Japanese Neologisms*. Tucson: University of Arizona Press.

Benua, Laura (1995). Identity effects in morphological truncation. In *University of Massachusetts Occasional Papers in Linguistics 18: Papers in Optimality Theory*, ed. Jill N. Beckman, Laura Walsh Dickey, & Suzanne Urbanczyk, 77–136. Amherst, MA: GLSA.

Bermúdez-Otero, Ricardo. (2012). The architecture of grammar and the division of labor in exponence. In *The Morphology and Phonology of Exponence*, ed. Jochen Trommer, 8–83. Oxford: Oxford University Press.

Bing, Janet (1979). *Aspects of English Prosody*. PhD dissertation, University of Massachusetts, Amherst (Indiana University Linguistics Club, 1980).

Blevins, Juliette (1995). The syllable in phonological theory. In *The Handbook of Phonological Theory*, ed. John A. Goldsmith, 206–244. Oxford: Blackwell.

(1997). Rules in optimality theory: two case studies. In *Derivations and Constraints in Phonology*, ed. Iggy Roca, 227–260. Oxford: Oxford University Press.

Bloomfield, Leonard (1933). *Language*. New York: Holt, Rinehart, & Winston.

(1939). Menomini morphophonemics. *Travaux du cercle linguistique de Prague* 8, 105–115. Reprinted in Makkai (1972), 58–64.

Borowsky, Toni Jean (1986). *Topics in the Lexical Phonology of English*. PhD dissertation, University of Massachusetts, Amherst.

(1989). Structure preservation and the syllable coda in English. *Natural Language and Linguistic Theory* 7: 145–166.

Brame, Michael (1974). The cycle in phonology: Stress in Palestinian, Maltese, and Spanish. *Linguistic Inquiry* 5: 39–60.

Brooks, Marie Zagorska (1965). On Polish affricates. *Word* 29: 207–210.

Burzio, Luigi (1994). *Principles of English Stress*. Cambridge: Cambridge University Press.

Chambers, Jack (1973). Canadian raising. *Canadian Journal of Linguistics* 18: 113–135.

Chao, Yuan Ren (1920). A system of tone letters. *Le Maître Phonétique* 45: 24–47.

Chomsky, Noam (1951). *Morphophonemics of Modern Hebrew*. Unpublished master's thesis, University of Pennsylvania.

(1964). *Current Issues in Linguistic Theory*. The Hague: Mouton.

(1965). *Aspects of the Theory of Syntax*. Cambridge, MA: MIT Press.

Chomsky, Noam & Morris Halle (1968). *The Sound Pattern of English*. New York: Harper & Row.

Clements, George N. (1985). The geometry of phonological features. *Phonology Yearbook* 2: 225–252.

Clements, George N. & Elizabeth V. Hume (1995). The internal organization of speech sounds. In *The Handbook of Phonological Theory*, ed. John A. Goldsmith, 245–306. Oxford: Blackwell.

Clements, George N. & Samuel Jay Keyser (1983). *CV Phonology: a Generative Theory of the Syllable*. Cambridge, MA: MIT Press.

Collins Dictionary of the English Langue (1979). London: Collins.

Cowan, Nelson, Martin D. S. Braine, & Lewis A. Leavitt (1985). The phonological and metaphonological representation of speech: evidence from fluent backward talkers. *Journal of Memory and Language* 24: 679–698.

Downing, Bruce Theodore (1970). *Syntactic and Phonological Phrasing in English*. PhD dissertation, University of Texas, Austin.

Dresher, B. Elan (2016). Covert representations, contrast, and the acquisition of lexical accent. In *Dimensions of Phonological Stress*, ed. Jeffrey Heinz, Rob Goedemans, & Harry van der Hulst, 231–262. Cambridge: Cambridge University Press.

Durand, Jacques (1990). *Generative and Nonlinear Phonology*. London: Longman.

Emonds, Joseph E. (1976). *A Transformational Approach to English Syntax: Root, Structure Preserving, and Local Transformations*. New York: Academic Press.

Fabb, Nigel (1988). English suffixation is constrained only by selectional restrictions. *Natural Language and Linguistic Theory* 6: 527–539.

Fidelholtz, James L. (1967). English vowel reduction. Ms., MIT, Cambridge, MA.

Fidelholtz, James L. & E. Wayles Browne (1971). Oy, oy, oy. In *Towards Tomorrow's Linguistics*, ed. Roger W. Shuy & Charles-James N. Bailey 159–184. Washington, DC: Georgetown University Press.

Fudge, Eric C. (1967). The nature of phonological primes. *Journal of Linguistics* 3: 1–36. Reprinted in Makkai (1972), 500–521.

Furby, Christine E. (1974). *Garawa Phonology*. Pacific Linguistics, series A, No. 37, 1–11, Canberra: Australian National University.

Giegerich, Heinz J. (1992). *English Phonology: An Introduction*. Cambridge: Cambridge University Press.

(1999). *Lexical Strata in English: Morphological Causes, Phonological Effects*. Cambridge: Cambridge University Press.

Goad, Heather (2012). *s*C clusters are (almost always) coda-initial. *The Linguistic Review* 29: 335–373.

Goldsmith, John A. (1976). *Autosegmental Phonology*. PhD dissertation, MIT.

(1990). *Autosegmental and Metrical Phonology*. Oxford: Blackwell.

Green, Anthony D. (2004). Opacity in Tiberian Hebrew: Morphology not phonology. In *Papers in Phonetics and Phonology, ZAS Papers in Linguistics* 37, ed. S. Fuchs & S. Hamann, 37–70. ROA 703-0105.

Gussenhoven, Carlos & Heike Jacobs (1998). *Understanding Phonology*. London: Arnold.

Hale, Mark & Charles Reiss (2000). Phonology as cognition. In *Phonological Knowledge: Conceptual and Empirical Issues*, ed. Noel Burton-Roberts, Philip Carr, & Gerard Docherty 161–184. Oxford: Oxford University Press.

Halle, Morris (1959). *The Sound Pattern of Russian*. The Hague: Mouton.

(1977). Tenseness, vowel shift, and the phonology of the back vowels in modern English. *Linguistic Inquiry* 8: 611–625.

(1997). On stress and accent in Indo-European. *Language* 73: 275–313.

Halle, Morris & William J. Idsardi (1997). R, hypercorrection, and the Elsewhere Condition. In *Derivations and Constraints in Phonology*, ed. Iggy Roca, 331–348.

Halle, Morris & Karuvannur Puthanveetti Mohanan (1985). Segmental phonology of modern English. *Linguistic Inquiry* 16: 57–116.

Halle, Morris & Kenneth N. Stevens (1971). A note on laryngeal features. *Quarterly Progress Reports* 101: 198–213. Research Laboratory of Electronics, MIT.

Halle, Morris & Jean-Roger Vergnaud (1987). *An Essay on Stress*. Cambridge, MA: MIT Press.

Hammond, Michael (1984). *Constraining Metrical Theory: A Modular Theory of Rhythm and Destressing*. PhD dissertation, UCLA. Indiana University Linguistics Club.

(1999). *The Phonology of English: A Prosodic Optimality-Theoretic Approach*. Oxford: Oxford University Press.

Harris, James W. (1969). *Spanish Phonology*. Cambridge, MA: MIT Press.

(1983). *Syllable Structure and Stress in Spanish: A Nonlinear Analysis*. Cambridge, MA: MIT Press.

Harris, John (1994). *English Sound Structure*. Oxford: Blackwell.

Haugen, Einar (1956). The syllable in linguistic description. In *For Roman Jakobson*, ed. Morris Halle, Horace G. Lunt, Hugh McLean, & Cornelius H. van Schooneveld, 213–221. The Hague: Mouton.

Hayes, Bruce (1980). *A Metrical Theory of Stress Rules.* PhD dissertation, MIT. (Indiana University Linguistics Club, 1981).

(1982). Extrametricality and English stress. *Linguistic Inquiry* 13: 227–276.

(1986). Inalterability in CV phonology. *Language* 62: 321–351.

(1989a). Compensatory lengthening in moraic phonology. *Linguistic Inquiry* 20: 253–306.

(1989b). The prosodic hierarchy in meter. In *Phonetics and Phonology*, Volume 1, *Rhythm and Meter*, ed. Paul Kiparsky & Gilbert Youmans, 201–260. New York: Academic Press.

(1995). *Metrical Stress Theory: Principles and Case Studies.* Chicago: University of Chicago Press.

(2004). Phonological acquisition in optimality theory: the early stages. In *Constraints in Phonological Acquisition*, ed. René Kager, Joe Pater, & Wim Zonneveld, 158–203. Cambridge: Cambridge University Press.

Hoard, James E. (1971). Aspiration, tenseness, and syllabication in English. *Language* 47: 133–140.

(1972). Naturalness conditions in phonology, with particular reference to English vowels. In *Contributions to Generative Phonology*, ed. Michael K. Brame, 123–154. Austin: University of Texas Press.

Hockett, Charles F. (1942). A system of descriptive phonology. *Language* 18: 3–21. Reprinted in Makkai (1972), 99–112.

Hooper, Joan B. (1972). The syllable in phonological theory. *Language* 48: 525–540.

Hyman, Larry (1985). *A Theory of Phonological Weight.* Dordrecht: Foris.

Idsardi, William James (1992). *The Computation of Prosody.* PhD dissertation, MIT.

(2009). Calculating metrical structure. In *Contemporary Views on Architecture and Representations in Phonology*, ed. Eric Raimy & Charles E. Cairns, 191–211. Cambridge, MA: MIT Press.

Ingria, Robert (1980). Compensatory lengthening as a metrical phenomenon. *Linguistic Inquiry* 11: 465–495.

Itô, Junko (1986). *Syllable Theory in Prosodic Phonology.* PhD dissertation, University of Massachusetts, Amherst.

(1989). A prosodic theory of epenthesis. *Natural Language and Linguistic Theory* 7: 217–259.

Jackendoff, Ray (1972). *Semantic Interpretation in Generative Grammar.* Cambridge, MA: MIT Press.

Jakobson, Roman & Morris Halle (1956). *Fundamentals of Language.* The Hague: Mouton.

Jensen, John T. (1990). *Morphology: Word Structure in Generative Grammar.* Amsterdam: Benjamins.

(1993). *English Phonology.* Amsterdam: Benjamins.

(2000). Against ambisyllabicity. *Phonology* 17: 187–235.

Jones, Daniel (1966). *The Pronunciation of English* (fourth edition). Cambridge: Cambridge University Press.

370 *References*

Kager, René (1989). *A Metrical Theory of Stress and Destressing in English and Dutch*. Dordrecht: Foris.
(1999). *Optimality Theory*. Cambridge: Cambrige University Press.
Kahn, Daniel (1976). *Syllable-based Generalizations in English Phonology*. PhD dissertation, MIT. Indiana University Linguistics Club.
(1980). Syllable-structure specifications in phonological rules. In *Juncture*, ed. Mark Aronoff & Mary-Louise Kean. Saratoga, CA: Anma Libri.
Kenstowicz, Michael (1994). Evidence for metrical constitency. In *The View from Building 20: Essays in Linguistics in Honor of Sylvain Bromberger*, ed. Kenneth Hale & Samuel Jay Keyser, 257–273. Cambridge, MA: The MIT Press.
Kenstowicz, Michael & Charles W. Kisseberth (1977). *Topics in Phonological Theory*. New York: Academic Press.
(1979). *Generative Phonology: Description and Theory*. New York: Academic Press.
Kiparsky, Paul (1966). Über den deutschen Akzent. *Studia Grammatica* 7: 69–98.
(1968). How abstract is phonology? In *Explanation in Phonology*, ed. Paul Kiparsky (1971), 119–163. Dordrecht: Foris.
(1973). Abstractness, opacity, and global rules. In *Three Dimensions of Linguistic Theory*, ed. O. Fujimura, 57–86. Tokyo: TEC. Also in *The Application and Ordering of Grammatical Rules*, ed. Andreas Koutsoudas, 160–186. The Hague: Mouton,
(1979). Metrical structure assignment is cyclic. *Linguistic Inquiry* 10: 421–441.
(1982). Lexical morphology and phonology. In *Linguistics in the Morning Calm*, ed. I. S. Yang, 3–91. Seoul: Hanshin.
(1983). Word formation and the lexicon. In *Proceedings of the 1982 Mid-America Linguistics Conference*, ed. Frances A. Ingeman. University of Kansas, Lawrence, Kansas.
(1985). Some consequences of lexical phonology. *Phonology Yearbook* 2, 85–138.
(1988). Phonological change. In *Linguistics: The Cambridge Survey*, Volume 1, *Linguistic Theory: Foundations*, ed. Fritz Newmeyer, 363–415. Cambridge: Cambridge University Press.
(1993). Blocking in nonderived environments. In *Phonetics and Phonology*, Volume 4, *Studies in Lexical Phonology*, ed. Sharon Hargus and Ellen Kaisse, 217–313. New York: Academic Press.
(1995). The phonological basis of sound change. In *Handbook of Phonological Theory*, ed. John A. Goldsmith, 640–670. Oxford: Blackwell.
(2000). Opacity and cyclicity. *The Linguistic Review* 17: 351–365.
Kirchner, Robert (1996). Synchronic chain shifts in optimality theory. *Linguistic Inquiry* 27: 341–350.
Kisseberth, Charles W. (1970). On the functional unity of phonological rules. *Linguistic Inquiry* 1: 291–306.
Klavans, Judith L. (1982). *Some Problems in a Theory of Clitics*. PhD dissertation, University College, London. IULC.

(1985). The independence of syntax and phonology in cliticization. *Language* 61: 95–120.

Lazdiņa, Terēza Budiņa (1966). *Teach Yourself Latvian*. London: English Universities Press.

Leben, William (1973). *Suprasegmental Phonology*. PhD dissertation, MIT.

Levin, Juliette (1985). *A Metrical Theory of syllabicity*. PhD dissertation, MIT.

Liberman, Mark & Alan S. Prince (1977). On stress and linguistic rhythm. *Linguistic Inquiry* 8: 249–336.

Łubowicz, Anna (2002). Derived environment effects in Optimality Theory. *Lingua* 112: 243–280.

Makkai, Valerie Becker (ed.) (1972). *Phonological Theory: Evolution and Current Practice*. New York: Holt, Rinehart, & Winston.

Malécot, André (1960). Vowel nasality as a distinctive feature in American English. *Language* 36: 222–229.

Marchand, Hans (1969). *The Categories and Types of Present-Day English Word-Formation: A Synchronic-Diachronic Approach* (second edition). München: C.H. Bech'sche Verlagsbuchhandlung.

Mascaró, Joan (1967). *Catalan Phonology and the Phonological Cycle*. PhD dissertation, MIT. Indiana University Linguistics Club.

McCarthy, John J. (1981). A prosodic theory of nonconcatenative morphology. *Linguistic Inquiry* 12: 373–418.

(1991). Synchronic rule inversion. *Proceedings of the 17th Annual Meeting of the Berkeley Linguistics Society*, ed. Laurel A. Sutton, Christopher Johnson & Ruth Shields, 192–207. Berkleley, California: Berkeley Linguistics Society.

(1993). A case of surface constraint violation. *Canadian Journal of Linguistics* 38: 169–195.

(1994). Remarks on phonological opacity in optimality theory. In *Proceedings of the Second Colloquium on Afro-Asiatic Linguistics* (1996), ed. Jacqueline Lecarme, Jean Lowenstamm, & Ur Shlonsky 215–243. The Hague: Academic Graphics. ROA-79.

(1999). Sympathy and phonological opacity. *Phonology* 16: 331–399.

(2007). *Hidden Generalizations: Phonological opacity in Optimality Theory*. London: Equinox.

McCarthy, John J. & Alan S. Prince (1986). *Prosodic Morphology*. MS, University of Massachusetts, Amherst & Brandeis University. Published as *Prosodic Morphology 1986*, Technical Report #32, Rutgers Center for Cognitive Science, 1996.

(1990). Foot and word in prosodic morphology: the Arabic broken plural. *Natural Language and Linguistic Theory* 8: 208–283.

(1993). *Prosodic Morphology I: Constraint Interaction and Satisfaction*. RuCCS-TR-3.

(1995). Faithfulness and reduplicative identity. In *University of Massachusetts Occasional Papers in Linguistics 18: Papers in Optimality Theory*, ed. Jill N. Beckman, Laura Walsh Dickey, & Suzanne Urbanczyk, 249–384. Amherst, MA: GLSA. ROA 60.

McCawley, James D. (1968). *The Phonological Component of a Grammar of Japanese*. The Hague: Mouton.

McMahon, April (2000). *Lexical Phonology and the History of English*. Cambridge: Cambridge University Press.

Mielke, Jeff (2005). Ambivalence and ambiguity in laterals and nasals. *Phonology* 22: 169–203.

Minkova, Donka (2014). *A Historical Phonology of English*. Edinburgh: Edinburgh University Press.

Miyamori, Asatarō (1932). *An Anthology of Haiku, Ancient and Modern*. Tokyo: Maruzen. Reprinted (1970), Westport, CT: Greenwood.

Mohanan, Karuvannur Puthanveetti (1986). *The Theory of Lexical Phonology*. Dordrecht: Reidel.

Mohanan, Karuvannur Puthanveetti & Tara Mohanan (1984). Lexical phonology of the consonant system in Malayalam. *Linguistic Inquiry* 15: 575–602.

Myers, Scott (1987). Vowel shortening in English. *Natural Language and Linguistic Theory* 5: 485–518.

Nanni, Debbie L. (1977). Stressing words in *-Ative*. *Linguistic Inquiry* 8: 752–763.

Nespor, Marina & Irene Vogel (1986). *Prosodic Phonology*. Dordrecht: Foris.

Newton, Brian (1972). *The Generative Interpretation of Dialect: A Study of Modern Greek Phonology*. Cambridge: Cambridge University Press.

Odden, David (2008). Ordering. In *Rules, Constraints, and Phonological Phenomena*, ed. Bert Vaux & Andrew Nevins, 61–120. Oxford: Oxford University Press.

Orkin, Mark M. (1997). *Canajan, Eh?* Toronto: Stoddart.

Osborn, Henry A. Jr (1966). Warao I: phonology and morphophonemics. *International Journal of American Linguistics* 32: 108–23.

Pater, Joe (1994). Against the underlying specification of an 'exceptional' English stress pattern. *Toronto Woking Papers in Linguistics* 13(1): 95–121.

(2000). Nonuniformity in English secondary stress: the role of ranked and lexically specific constraints. *Phonology* 17: 237–274.

Pike, Kenneth L. (1947). Grammatical prerequisites to phonemic analysis. *Word* 3: 155–172. Reprinted in Makkai (1972), 153–165.

Postal, Paul M. (1968). *Aspects of Phonological Theory*. New York: Harper & Row.

Prince, Alan S. (1980). A metrical theory for Estonian quantity. *Linguistic Inquiry* 11: 511–562.

(1983). Relating to the grid. *Linguistic Inquiry* 14: 19–100.

Prince, Alan S. & Paul Smolensky (1993). *Optimality Theory: Constraint Interaction in Generative Grammar*. Technical Report 2. Rutgers Center for Cognitive Science.

Pulgram, Ernst (1970). *Syllable, Word, Nexus, Cursus*. The Hague: Mouton.

Pulleyblank, Douglas (1986). *Tone in Lexical Phonology*. Dordrecht: Reidel.

Pullum, Geoffrey K. (1976). The Duke of York gambit. *Journal of Linguistics* 12: 83–102.

Rialland, Annie & Mamadon Badjimé (1989). Réanalyse des tons du Bambara: Des tons du nom à l'organisation générale du système. *Studies in African Linguistics* 20: 1–28.

Ross, John Robert (1972). A reanalysis of English word stress (part I). In *Contributions to Generative Phonology*, ed. Michael Brame, 229–323. Austin: University of Texas Press.

Rubach, Jerzy (1984). Segmental rules of English and cyclic phonology. *Language* 60: 21–54.

(1996). Shortening and ambisyllabicity in English. *Phonology* 13: 197–237.

(2003). Duke-of-York derivations in Polish. *Linguistic Inquiry* 34: 601–629.

Rydzewski, Paweł (2018). Canadian Raising and Flapping in Derivational Optimality Theory. In *Phonology, Fieldwork and Generalisations*, ed. Bartłomiej Czaplicki, Beata Łukaszewicz, & Monika Opalińska, 47–64. Berlin: Peter Lang.

Sagey, Elizabeth Caroline (1986). *The Representation of Features and Relations in Non-linear Phonology*. PhD dissertation, MIT.

Sainz, Susana (1988). A noncyclic analysis of English word stress. *Working Papers of the Cornell Phonetics Laboratory* 3: 1–82.

Selkirk, Elisabeth O. (1978). On prosodic structure and its relation to syntactic structure. In *Nordic Prosody II*, ed. T. Fretheim, 111–140 (1981). Trondheim: TAPIR.

(1980a). Prosodic domains in phonology: Sanskrit revisited. In *Juncture*, ed. Mark Aronoff & Mary-Louise Kean, 107–129. Saratoga, CA: Anma Libri.

(1980b). The role of prosodic categories in English word stress. *Linguistic Inquiry* 11: 563–605.

(1982a). *The Syntax of Words*. Cambridge, MA: MIT Press.

(1982b). The syllable. In *The Structure of Phonological Representations (Part II)*, ed. Harry van der Hulst & Norval Smith, 337–383. Dordrecht: Foris.

(1984a). *Phonology and Syntax: The Relation between Sound and Structure*. Cambridge, MA: MIT Press.

(1984b). On the major class features and syllable theory. In *Language Sound Structure*, ed. Mark Aronoff & Richard T. Oehrle, 107–136. Cambridge, MA: MIT Press.

Siegel, Dorothy C. (1974). *Topics in English Morphology*. PhD dissertation, MIT.

Stanley, Richard (1967). Redundancy rules in phonology. *Language* 43: 393–436.

Szpyra, Jolanta (1989). *The Morphology-Phonology Interface: Cycles, Levels, and Words*. London: Routledge.

Tauber, Abraham (1963). *George Bernard Shaw on Language*. New York: Philosophical Library.

Trager, George L. & Henry Lee Smith, Jr (1951). *An Outline of English Structure*. American Council of Learned Societies, Washington, DC. Reprinted by Johnson Reprint Corporation, New York.

Tryon, Darrell T. (1970). *An Introduction to Maranungku, Northern Australia* (Pacific Linguistics Monographs, Series B, No. 15), Canberra: Australian National University.

Vaux, Bert (2008). Why the phonological component must be serial and rule-based. In *Rules, Constraints, and Phonological Phenomena*, ed. Bert Vaux & Andrew Nevins, 20–60. Oxford: Oxford University Press.

Walker, John (1936). *The Rhyming Dictionary*, revised and enlarged by Lawrence H. Dawson. New York: R.P. Dutton.

Wang, William S.-Y. (1967). Phonological features of tone. *International Journal of American Linguistics* 33: 93–105.

Wells, J.C. (1982). *Accents of English*. Cambridge: Cambridge University Press.

Withgott, Mary Margaret (1982). *Segmental Evidence for Phonological Constituents*. PhD dissertation, University of Texas, Austin.

Zec, Draga (1988). *Sonority Constraints on Prosodic Structure*. PhD dissertation, MIT.

Index

The designation n following a page number indicates a reference to a note on that page. The designation ff following a page number indicates the start of a longer discussion on that page.

For EU product safety concerns, contact us at Calle de José Abascal, 56–1°, 28003 Madrid, Spain or eugpsr@cambridge.org.

www.ingramcontent.com/pod-product-compliance
Ingram Content Group UK Ltd.
Pitfield, Milton Keynes, MK11 3LW, UK
UKHW020402140625
459647UK00020B/2612